RURAL DEVELOPMENT

About the Author

Dr. Sujit Kumar Paul is a Social Scientist, obtained Master's and Ph.D. degree in Rural Development from Visva-Bharati (A Central University). He is also a development practitioner, researcher and resource person in the field of rural development. He has conducted several research projects funded by National and International agencies. As prolific writer, he has published 60 research papers on various developmental issues in the national and international journal of repute. He authored two books—"*Tribal Agriculture and Modernization: The Change and Continuity*" by Daya Publishers, New Delhi and "*Poverty, Health and Development*" by Commonwealth Publishers, New Delhi. He also edited three issues of the *International Journal of World Education*, published by the Association for World Education, Denmark. Presently, Dr. Paul is working as Associate Professor in the Department of Lifelong Learning and Extension, Visva-Bharati (A Central University). He also served as Deputy Dean in the Institute of Rural Reconstruction of the same University. Dr. Paul visited different countries for academic, research and extension activities. He is closely associated with various government and non-governmental organizations, societies and associations in different capacities. He is the Chairman (India Chapter) and Vice President (International) of the Association for World Education—An NGO with consultative status in the United Nations. *Email*: skpaulrd@gmail.com

RURAL DEVELOPMENT
Concept and Recent Approaches

Sujit Kumar Paul

CONCEPT PUBLISHING COMPANY PVT. LTD.
NEW DELHI-110059

ISBN-13: 978-93-5125-162-0

First Published 2015

Published and Printed by

Concept Since 1974

Concept Publishing Company Pvt. Ltd.
A/15-16, Commercial Block, Mohan Garden
New Delhi-110059 (India)
T: 25351460, 25351794, *F*: 091-11-25357109
E: publishing@conceptpub.com, W: www.conceptpub.com
Editorial Office: H-13, Bali Nagar, New Delhi-110 015, India.

Cataloging in Publication Data--Courtesy: D.K. Agencies (P) Ltd. <docinfo@dkagencies.com>

Paul, Sujit Kumar, 1970- **author.**
Rural development : concept and recent approaches / Sujit Kumar Paul.
pages cm
Includes bibliographical references (pages) and index.
ISBN 9789351251620

1. Rural development--India. I. Title.

DDC 307.14120954 23

Foreword

In a rapidly urbanizing world, a new book on rural development may appear to be unnecessary. The received wisdom on development suggests that all societies become modernized and developed when a large proportion of their population shifts to non-rural occupations and habitations. This has been the trend in Europe, North and South America and parts of North Africa.

But this may well not be the case in many parts of Asia, and indeed in India. China, India and Indonesia are three large Asian societies where a substantial proportion of population still lives in rural areas. Is it conceivable that such Asian societies can be labelled as modern and developed while a large percentage of their population continues to live in rural areas? The case of India may begin to challenge some of those prevailing notions about development.

India is the largest democracy in the world; despite its socio-economic backwardness, higher percentage of rural voters, as compared to urban, continue to exercise their franchise in every election in the country. It has the second largest population in the world; its median age is 24, implying that nearly 620 million Indians are below the age of 24 years; implying they were all born after the advent of market-oriented economic reforms of 1991. India is the third largest economy (on purchasing power parity basis) in the world; agriculture and allied sectors contribute only 18 per cent to its present GDP. Can 67 per cent of Indian population living in rural areas be adequately supported by such a small share of Indian GDP? Is it likely that large-scale migration from rural to urban areas may significantly transform this situation in a decade?

It is within the above set of critical questions that any discussion on rural development has to be situated. This book focuses on three ingredients which may provide some answers to the above puzzle.

First is the question of livelihood. For a large number of rural households in India, agriculture provides a partial answer to livelihood. With small and fragmented land-holdings and inadequate irrigation facilities, most households in rural areas have to complement their livelihood needs with some form of non-agricultural activity; much of it is wage labour, in both rural and urban areas. New forms of livelihood opportunities related to agriculture have arisen both at input and output ends of farming.

It is here that Self-Help Groups (SHGs) have become quite a significant driver of non-farm, off-farm and of-&-on-farm livelihood options. Promoted as social collectives of mutual trust and mutual support in the 1980s by a handful of NGOs, SHGs have now become an integral part of government's development strategy. Though massification of SHGs has taken place, their social character has been neglected in the rush to make them vehicles for microfinance. As a consequence, innovative models of cooperative nature around agriculture and related operations have not flourished to scale much.

The third dimension to understanding this puzzle is decentralized governance and Panchayati Raj System. Introduced through constitutional amendments in 1992, PRIs have become a statutory reality nationwide. However, institutional capacity of these local governance bodies has not been adequately built in most states of the country. Kerala's exceptional experience in this regard owes much to its socio-geography—large settlements make panchayats covering several thousand households, and an almost seamless urban-rural transition across the state. It, therefore, begs the question whether panchayats can continue to be vehicles for socio-economic development of rural India in the manner that was envisaged nearly two decades ago?

Dr. Sujit Kumar Paul brings his considerable academic expertise and practical experiences in the field to begin to present in this volume a coherent set of arguments about rural development in India. In so doing, may I suggest that certain emerging trends may need to be paid further attention to as students and practitioners of rural development understand their profession.

The nexus of meaningful devolution is moving towards the block; as an administrative unit, it is more cohesive, has certain minimum critical mass of panchayats and households, and is the first stage of rural-urban linkage (all block headquarters are urban local bodies with elected representatives as well). Viewed in this lens, the future studies of development may acquire more 'rurban' character, than a traditional rural/urban divide.

As migration is likely to gain pace, larger numbers of young people will be 'in transition' for livelihood. Some will be 'in transition' for employment, some for self-employment, and some in search of a livelihood. At the moment, a larger number of these are 'running away' from rural areas, merely in search of 'good life' (whatever that means). Is it possible to develop a theory of development for those 'in transition'? Since a large number of Indians from rural areas do not get themselves totally disconnected from their 'motherland', it may be a plausible alternative to the traditional modernization/development models. It may well support a less consumptive life-style, and hence more sustainable in the long run.

I invite readers of this book to ask many such questions as they interface emerging theories of rural development with rapidly shifting realities of India.

Dr. Rajesh Tandon
Founder-President,
Participatory Research in Asia (PRIA), New Delhi
&
UNESCO Chair on Community-based Research and Social Responsibility in Higher Education

Preface

Since time immemorial India is a land of village. About 70 per cent of Indian people live in rural areas. Undoubtedly, in earlier days Indian villages were the backbone of Indian economy, which are in a very dilapidated condition at present. Economic growth, technological upgradation has altered the entire image of India in the world but the quality of life of the rural people remains unaltered to a huge extent. The country cannot be called developed unless and until the fruits of development reaches villages, that is, to the 70 per cent of rural population. Hunger, poverty, disease, illiteracy, lack of minimum infrastructure on education, medical facilities, and transport is the very common incidence for rural India. The essential requirements of the people are far away from their doorsteps in spite of the presence of plentiful natural resources and labour force. Despite the considerable and sustained economic growth, and the reduction of the poverty, the progress of India is significantly less as demanded earlier.

After Independence, rural India is witnessing exciting changes in terms of peoples' articulation of new demands, gender assertiveness, environment consciousness, grass root movements and decentralization. Simultaneously, dimensions of rural development and its problems are assuming greater complexities due to the emerging socio-political scenario in India. Keeping parity with the emerging situation, Government has adopted various approaches and strategies for the development of rural people. One of the abiding tasks before the Government of India since independence was integrated development of rural areas. Following Mahatma Gandhi's dictum that 'India lives in villages', Indian policy-makers have time and again stressed on the cardinal importance of villages to the overall development of the country and commits to work towards development of rural areas. In conformity of this commitment, our policy-makers have accorded foremost priority to development in rural areas and eradication of poverty, unemployment, illiteracy and hunger from the face of rural India. A number of initiatives have been taken since Independence for providing employment, reducing poverty, creation of social and economic infrastructure in rural areas as well as to provide food security and fulfil other basic needs of the rural populace.

Rural development aims at improving rural people's livelihoods in an equitable and sustainable manner, both socially and environmentally, through better access to assets (natural, physical, human, technological and social capital), and services, and control over productive capital (in its financial or economic and political forms) that enable them to improve their livelihoods on a sustainable and equitable basis. This book has made an attempt to highlight the most important aspects of rural development in India.

The book consists of seven chapters. The history, concept, importance, problems, strategies and other various aspects of rural development in India are discussed in the first chapter. Livelihood development is defined as adequate and sustainable access to income and resources to meet basic needs. The livelihood pattern of the population throws a searching light on the economic and social life of the area. Livelihood approaches are a way of thinking about the objectives, scope and priorities for development. The Rural Livelihood issues have been discussed in second chapter. Decentralised governance has been conceived as a mechanism of local self-government for promoting healthy and sustainable development. Decentralised governance is assumed to provide more effective and competitive delivery of services at the grass root level. In India, decentralisation and effective implementation is possible through Panchayati Raj Institutions. The third chapter deals with the Decentralisation and Panchayati Raj Institutions. Self-Help Group (SHG) has emerged as the most successful strategy in the process of participatory development and empowerment of the majority of the rural population in India. Significant changes in the living standards of SHG members have taken place in terms of increase in income levels, assets, savings, borrowing capacity and income generating activities. Self-Help Group has been discussed in fourth chapter. After Independence, rural India was suffering from unemployment and poverty. To reduce the poverty and generate employment opportunities in rural areas, Government of India was taking one after other policies and programmes to solve both the problems but the success is not up to the level. The National Rural Employment Guarantee Act [Now Mahatma Gandhi National Rural Employment Guarantee Act (MGNREGA)] 2005 is landmark legislation in Indian history of social security legislation after Independence. MGNREGA and Rural Development have been discussed in fifth chapter. Tribal are the integral part of the Indian civilization. Various involvements of Indian civilization were contributed by the tribal. Tribal population constitutes a considerable percentage in our country. Since Independence, considering the general socio-economic backwardness of the tribal communities, Government of India has been planning and launching programmes to develop and integrate them with the mainstream of Indian national life. The sixth chapter discusses about tribal development. The Millennium Development Goals (MDGs) constitute the first ever set of shared development goals at international level, on which there is an unprecedented level of consensus. India has an important role to play in the achievement of the Millennium Development Goals. As a largest democracy, India has the obligation to ensure national development and historic contributions that have been made to the ideals of modern global society. The Millennium Development Goals (MDGs) play an important role in development policies today. MDGs and Rural Development in India have been discussed in seventh chapter.

On the whole, the book gives a holistic picture of rural development in India. This book will be useful to the students, researchers, teachers, academicians, development workers, planners, policy-makers and various development organizations interested in rural development. The book will be extremely useful for the students of Rural Development, Social Work, Sociology, Economics, Geography, Political Science, Public Administration, Journalism and Mass Communication and the like.

I would like to express my gratitude to those who have been kind enough to encourage and support me in the preparation of this book. I also would like to acknowledge the support and help extended by my research scholars, specially, Sri Anindya Mitra and Smt. Anindita Gupta to complete this volume. I am thankful to my wife Dr. Kakali Paul for her constant encouragement, support and cooperation and for the rounds of discussions that we had on the subject towards completion of this book. I am also grateful to my daughter Nilormi for kindly sparing the time for completing the volume. I have no words to express my gratitude to my parents, who inspired and encouraged me in every moment to complete this work. I am extremely grateful to Dr. Rajesh Tandon, President of PRIA (Society for Participatory Research in Asia) and Co-Chair of the prestigious UNESCO Chair on Community Based Research and Social Responsibility in Higher Education for writing the Foreword for this book. It will be my pleasure to have suggestions, comments and remarks from the users of this publication for bringing about improvements in future publications.

1st January, 2015

Sujit Kumar Paul
Department of Lifelong Learning and Extension
Institute of Rural Reconstruction
Visva-Bharati (A Central University)
Sriniketan–731236
Birbhum, West Bengal
Email: skpaulrd@gmail.com
sujit_kakali@rediffmail.com

Contents

1 Concept and Importance of Rural Development

Introduction

Rural development has always been a significant concern in all debate pertaining to sustainable development, especially of developing countries, throughout the world. India, as a developing country is not an exception. Rural development has great importance for a country like India, where majority of the population, around 68.64 per cent (as per 2011 Census) of the people, live in rural areas. The present strategy of rural development in India mainly focuses on poverty alleviation, better livelihood opportunities, financial inclusion, provision of basic amenities like health, education, communication, etc., infrastructure facilities and technological advancement through innovative programmes resulting to inclusive growth of India's economy.

Since, early 90's India has been experiencing high economic growth while a large majority of rural people continue to suffer from persistent poverty. The socio-economic inconsistency between rural and urban areas are widening and creating tremendous pressure on the social and economic structure of Indian economy. Despite significant advancement in industrial development, Indian economy is still predominantly rural in nature and depends on agro-based activities. The rural areas have been suffering from poor infrastructure, lack of resources, poor communication, and technological deficits. These factors, among many others, tend to highlight the importance of rural development in India. The India's Policy-makers recognize the importance of rural development and have been implementing a host of programmes and measures to achieve rural development objectives throughout the country. While some of these programmes have achieved impressive results, others have failed to make a significant impression on the problem of persistent rural underdevelopment.

The concept of rural development has gained extensive demand in recent past. Rural development became a planning concern as it was understood that the problem of poverty and inequality in rural areas of developing countries especially in India cannot be solved by technocratic strategies. It needs the multi-dimensional and multi-disciplinary approach to address the various problems related to development of rural areas. Consequently, it also was understood that apart from efforts to improve the agriculture and industrial sectors, it is also necessary to provide education, health, basic service, employment and to eradicate poverty in rural areas. The increasing scope and interest in rural development in India is an outcome of the insight that a systematic and organized effort is essential to create better living environment in the rural areas where the vast majority of populations of the country reside.

Concept of Development

Development is a process of growth in the direction of modernity, especially towards nation-building and socio-economic progress. The aim of development should be to enrich the quality of all (Goel and Kumar, 2004). It basically means growth, evolution, stage of inducement or progress. This progress or growth is gradual and had sequential phases with increasing differentiation. It also refers to the overall movement towards greater efficiency and complex situations. In other word 'Development' is a subjective and value-loaded concept and, hence, there cannot be a consensus as to its meaning. The term is used differently in diverse contexts. It basically means 'unfolding', 'revealing' or 'opening up something which is latent. When applied to human beings, it therefore, means unfolding or opening up their potential powers (Singh, 1986).

In economics term some author has treated development as economic growth in terms of Gross National Product. However, within the term economics, development has also been taken not only as economic growth but also incorporating the fundamental changes in consumer behaviour. Researchers also accepted the distinction between growth and development. Growth basically refers to quantitative change while development indicates both qualitative and quantitative changes.

The term development has been used in many ways and has become a catchword and is creating more confusion because of various definitions given by different authors. Despite the fact that there is no consensus on the meaning of development, at least in one way there is agreement that development does not merely refer to the material growth of people but, in fact, it supposes to include transformation of people in economic, social, political and cultural terms (Sharma, 1983). The concept is applicable at all levels ranging from individual to community, and nations and the world as a whole. Development is cherished by all individuals, communities and nations, irrespective of culture, religion and spatial location.

These days, development has become a diversified and multi-dimensional concept which evolves various new dimensions of development such sustainable development, participatory development, gender-sensitive development, resource development and so on. In present context, sustainable development has become a buzzword. It basically means 'balanced and continued development'. In other words the concept of sustainable development designates continuous improvements in the present standard of life at a lower intensity of resource utilization, thus leaving behind for future generations an undiminished or even improved stock of natural resources and other assets. Various researchers have opined that human actions are components of an open dynamic socio-economic subsystem which is rooted in the global ecosphere. The rapid growth of socio-economic subsystem in present times has started to overload some of the capabilities of the ecosystem (locally, regionally and globally) and disturb the ecological balance. As a result the socio-economic growth (especially material-intensive) would not be sustainable in long run, as the ecosphere is finite.

According to the World Commission on Environment and Development, 'Sustainable development is development that meets the needs of the present without compromising the ability of future generations to meet their own needs'. This definition emphasize the need for society to ensure inter-generational equity in the sense that the present generation does not consume so much as to exclude the option of the future generations to enjoy at least the present level of consumption, security and comfort. The concept has shifted the development paradigm towards equitable growth, where social (distributional objectives are being recognized as distinct form and as significant as economic efficiency. It has some basic elements like:

- Sustainability is to live within the regenerative levels of the system.
- It is to bequeath to the future the inheritance received and, therefore, to live in the present, without using up the resources of the future.
- Sustainability means the sustainability of the empowerment

process and livelihood system of the vulnerable and marginalized.

- It is the ability of the people to manage their own affairs and prolong the same, till necessary, with their own resources.
- The dynamic growth, in harmony with nature.
- It is opposed to homogenization.
- It is against the marginalization, or disempowerment of women.
- Integrated with nature, not to control it.

Policy-makers have recognized three distinct approaches of sustainable development which meet the desired features of development mentioned above, i.e., economic or financial, ecological or environmental and socio-cultural sustainability. The economic approach of sustainability is based on the Hicks-Lindahl concept of the maximum flow of income that could be generated while at least maintaining the stock of assets which yield these benefits. The ecological or environmental concept of sustainable development focuses on the stability of biological and physical systems. Protection of biological diversity and environmental balance is the key to this concept. Socio-cultural approach of sustainable development focuses on stability of socio-cultural structure, including reduction of destructive conflicts. Both intra-generational equity (especially eradication of poverty and hunger), and inter-generational equity (includes the rights of future generation) are important components of this approach.

The Conceptual Framework of Rural Development

Like the term 'development', 'rural development' has also different definitions and it is because of absence of any clear-cut view. Often, it creates confusion due to identical characteristic of economic or agricultural development. Rural development simply means a strategy designated to improve the social and economic life of people in rural setting and in particular it focuses on the rural poor who are the most marginalized and vulnerable section of the society. Rural development in a complete sense, is a process of social action in which people of a community organize themselves for planning and action, define their common and individual needs, make group and individual plans to meet their needs, and execute these plans with maximum reliance upon community resources, when necessary, with services and material from governmental and non-governmental agencies.

The term rural development is now visualized in a larger consequence than it was understood previously. The concept of rural development is not just a rubric or code word used by various people for solving some purpose. It is actually a process, through collective efforts, aimed at improving the well-being and self-realization of people living in the rural areas. According to James Coop, a famous sociologist "it is not an infrastructure, it is not factories, it is not better education or housing or even communities. These are only means; if they leave the spirit of man untouched, they are but sound fury…ultimately how we view ourselves and our relationship to other, the environment, and the cosmos is what is important. I believe rural development is about people, their well-being, and what they can become".

The Rural Development Sector Policy Paper of the World Bank (1975) observed that "Rural Development is a strategy designed to improve the economic and social life of a specific group of people'—the rural poor. It involves extending benefits of development to the poorest among those who seek a livelihood in the rural area. The group includes small and marginal farmers, tenants and landless. The paper also stated that rural development recognizes, however, that improved food supplies and nutrition, together with basic services such as health and education, cannot only directly improve the physical well-being and quality of life of the rural poor, but can also indirectly enhance their productivity and ability to contribute to the national economy. It is concerned with the modernization and monetization of rural society and with its transition from traditional isolation to integration with the national economy. Again, a World Bank publication defined rural development as improving the living standard of the means of the low income population residing in rural areas and making the process of rural development self-sustaining.

The term rural development connotes overall development of rural areas to improve the quality of life of rural people. In this sense, it is a comprehensive and multi-dimensional concept, and encompasses the development of agriculture and allied activities, village and cottage industries and crafts, socio-economic infrastructure, community services and facilities and, above all, human resources in rural areas. As a phenomenon, rural development is the end-result of interactions between various physical, technological, economic, social, cultural and institutional factors. As a strategy, it is designed to improve the economic and social well-being of a specific group of people—the rural poor. As a discipline, it is multi-disciplinary in nature, representing an intersection of agriculture, social, behavioural, engineering and management sciences (Singh, Katar, 1999).

In other words Rural Development (RD) is a process, which aims at improving the well-being and self-realization of people living outside the urbanized areas through collective process. Rural development designates the utilization of approaches and techniques under one single programme, which rally upon local communities as units of action. It provides a large umbrella under which all the people engaged in the work of community organizations, community progress and community relation.

According to Robert Chambers (1983), Rural Development is a strategy to enable a specific group of people, poor rural women and men, to gain for themselves and their children more of what they want and need. It involves helping the poorest among those who seek a livelihood in the rural areas to demand and control more of the benefits of rural development.

The United Nations defines Rural Development as: Rural Development is a process of change, by which the efforts of the people themselves are united, those of government authorities to improve their economic, social and cultural conditions of communities into the life of the nation and to enable them to contribute fully to national programme. Rural Development is a process of bringing change among rural community from the traditional way of living to progressive way of living. It is also expressed as a movement for progress.

Globally Rural Development has been seen as a process which leads to a continuous rise in the capacity of the rural people to control their environment accompanied by a wider distribution of benefits resulting from such control. This concept of rural development includes three basic components:

1. Rural development should be viewed as a process of raising the capacity (knowledge, skill and attitude) of the rural people to control their environment. Environment does not mean only agriculture or economic development. It includes all aspects of rural life—social, economic, cultural and political.
2. Rural development as a process should continuously raise the capacity of the rural people to influence their total environment, enabling them to become initiators and controllers of change in their environment rather than being merely the passive objects of external manipulation and control.
3. Rural development must result in a wider distribution of benefits accruing from technical developments and the participation of weaker sections of the rural population in the process of development.

The aim of rural development can be defined as the improvement of sustainable livelihoods (especially impoverished groups), with careful attention paid to local characteristics. Frequently, the concept of rural development is used confusedly with "agricultural development" or "regional development", however, these concepts differ from each others. "Agricultural development" mostly focuses at increasing agricultural products such as crops, livestock, fish, etc. Human-beings, land and capital are simply regarded as production goods and means. On the other hand, "Rural Development" mainly targets on people and institutions. It includes agricultural development activities, however, it is one of the means of economic revitalization for active farmers and targeted rural villages. Again, Regional has a wide meaning to describe "area" (i.e. a certain area in country) or "region" (i.e., continent of countries). It implies to a broader area includes both rural and urban development.

Many international organizations emphasize poverty reduction as an important international goal for development. A number of organizations has grown with the realization that most impoverished groups live in rural areas and taken rural development as a strategy to reduce poverty. The World Summit for Social Development held in Copenhagen in 1995 declared the goal to reduce absolute poverty in the world by half through people-centred social development. As a result of this conference, the goal of reducing the ratio of the poor by half (in between 1990 to 2015) was adopted at the DAC High Level Meeting of OECD in 1996. In addition, the UN General Assembly (Millennium Summit) in 2000 promoted this effort as one of its Millennium Development Goals (MDGs). As a result of these international trends towards poverty reduction, the number of organizations engaging in rural development has increased.

Rural development in the final analysis involves the provision of opportunities for the optimum utilization of human resources in rural areas. It is, therefore, essential to support rural development programmes with the principal objective of providing chance for the human population to accomplish optimum expression of their physical and mental potential.

Importance of Rural Development

Mahatma Gandhi wrote in *Harijan* "India is to be found not in its few cities but in its 7,00,000 villages. But we town dwellers have believed that India is to be found in its towns and the villagers were created to minister to our needs. We have hardly paused to enquire if those poor folk get sufficient to eat and clothe themselves with and whether they have a roof to shelter themselves from sun and rain". The predominantly rural character of India's national economy is reflected in the very high proportion of its population living in rural areas. It was 89 per cent in 1901, 83 per cent in 1951, 80 per cent in 1971, 74 per cent in 1991, 72 per cent in 2001 and 68 per cent in 2011. Over 70 per cent of the population living in rural areas is dependent on agriculture for livelihood. A majority of these families spend over 90 per cent of their earnings on basic needs such as food, fuel and health care. Over 50 per cent of the rural families who are not able to meet even these essential needs fall under the category of the poor. Thus, in an agrarian country like India, for improving the economic status of the population it is not enough to enhance the per capita GNP, but it is also necessary to ensure prosperity among the poor. Industrial development and adoption of modern technologies are likely to generate additional employment in urban areas and pay rich dividend to elite and rich investors. Thus in turn might widen the gap between the urban and rural as well as the rich and the poor, with respect to wealth accumulation, resulting in further hardship to the poor. Rural development is, therefore, an absolute and urgent necessity in India now and will continue to be so in future. It is the *sin qua non* of development of India.

Rural development has been a national necessity and has considerable importance in India because of the following reasons:

1. About 68.64 per cent of India's population live in rural areas, thus rural development is needed to develop nation as whole.
2. Majority of the people in rural areas are poor and lacking employment in a regular basis. Rural development can tackle the incidence of poverty, hunger and unemployment in the rural areas.
3. The rural India develops the production base of the whole country.
4. Agriculture is the prime occupation of the rural India. Nearly 70 per cent people in rural areas are engaged in agricultural activities. It contributes 13.75 per cent to India's GDP at the present price rate.
5. Bulks of raw materials for industries come from agriculture and rural sector.

6. Increase in industrial population can be justified only in rural population's motivation and increasing the purchasing power to buy industrial goods.
7. The recent trends of market economy has a great focus on the rural masses to improve their purchasing power.
8. Growing disparity between the urban elite and the rural poor can lead to political instability.
9. Rural areas have huge potential to develop human resources which can change the balance of Indian economy and provide huge economic growth.
10. Extensive use of natural resources needs more attention. Rural development can ensure conservation and sustainable use of natural resources.

Components of Rural Development

Rural development can also be seen in terms of achieving combination among ordinate and inordinate entities. This development of Man as entity has to be acquired in such a way that it does not excessively affects fellow human beings, other beings, environment and all these over time. In this context, rural development can be divided in three components: (1) People's development, (2) Area development, and (3) Institutional development and also the union between these development concepts. The protective measure need to be taken in such a way that development of a component should complement development of other component and *vice versa*. The people's development includes, knowledge development, skill development, attitudinal change, behavioural change, development of good practices, intra-group development, inter-group development, capacity to access and control resources. On the other hand area development encompasses with infrastructural development, betterment of existing public facilities, employment generation, technological improvement, ensuring equitable distribution and utilization of facilities, ensuring eco-balance and sustainable use of available resources. Institutional development deals with development of institutions, people's participation, leadership development, improving governance system, developing institutional value system, policy improvement. They all together bring pace in the rural development process and bring long-term sustainable change in lives of rural people.

All the tasks mentioned above are of two types—

1. Short-term task or soft tasks which are tangible, time-bound, less effort to be delivered and have short term affects on the rural life.
2. Long-term task or hard tasks which need more time and efforts to be delivered and having medium term effects on the development process.

These two tasks together bring long-term effects on the peoples of rural areas.

Activities or Tasks	*People's Development*	*Area Development*	*Institutional Development*
Short-term or soft-tasks	• Knowledge development • Skill development	• Infrastructural development • Betterment of existing public facilities	• Development of institutions
Long-term or hard tasks	• Attitudinal change • Behavioural change, • Development of good practices, • Intra-group development, • Inter-group development, • Capacity to access and control resources	• Employment generation, • Technological improvement, • Ensuring equitable distribution and utilization of facilities, • Ensuring eco-balance and sustainable use of available resources	• People's participation, • Leadership development, • Improving governance system, • Developing institutional value system, • Policy improvement

Fig 1.1: Components of Rural Development

In development process both the short-term and long-term tasks under three distinct rural development components have equal importance. If only short-term or soft tasks are achieved and nothing made towards implementing long-term or hard task, the changes resulted through achieving short-term tasks remain diluted and failed to bring desired result. In the same way all the components should be taken into the grant for the development of rural area. So, there is need to simultaneous initiatives towards achieving all the components and tasks for bringing proper impact and achieving sustainable rural development.

Nature and Scope of Rural Development

Rural development aims at improving rural people's livelihoods in an equitable and sustainable manner, both socially and environmentally, through better access to assets (natural, physical, human, technological and social capital), and services, and control over productive capital (in its financial or economic and political forms) that enable them to improve their livelihoods on a sustainable and equitable basis.

The basic objectives of Rural Development Programmes have been, alleviation of poverty and unemployment through creation of basic social and economic infrastructure, provision of training to rural unemployed youth and providing employment to marginal farmers/labourers in order to discourage seasonal and permanent migration to urban areas. In order to understand the importance of rural development, one needs to ask oneself about the existence of mankind without giving importance to land, forests and the water bodies. For this is precisely the pivot on which the societies turn and grow. Development of the rural is in a way development of the urban. The rural areas, especially the villages serve as the satellites of the cities and towns. Much of the cultivation of crops takes place here on a large scale. It feeds the rest of the population who are unaware of the efforts of the rural masses that take time and make efforts to feed the nation. Understanding the importance of rural development needs a heart. Let us now have a glance at the key points which explain why rural development is important:

- First and foremost, we have the basic need of agriculture. It is a known fact that everyone needs food for survival. One can pay a price for food and easily buy but it takes pain to cultivate and monitor the growth of food. This is the work of rural farmers and cultivators and they deserve importance for that. Developing their conditions and helping them out with their day to day problems is a direct assistance to the nation itself. Especially in a country like India, where wealth is concentrated in a few hands, it becomes very essential to help the rural masses.
- The government should not be ignorant of the fact that rural masses are poor, illiterate and unskilled people. Their development is the true development of the nation. Lots of people who can be turned into a massive labour force are turned down just because they lack education and the necessary skills and knowledge. Around 68 per cent of people in India live in villages

and majority of them are illiterate. If one can modulate their growth by way of education, the country would be developing at a faster rate. Today's industries need a literate and skilled labour force. Therefore, rural development is needed to increase the education level of the majority of the rural population.

- Migration of rural masses to urban towns is very common. Half the year, these rural masses are engaged in cultivation of crops and when the seasons are not favourable they migrate to urban places in search of jobs. They basically are forced to do all odd jobs since they are master of none! This causes a huge rural urban influx. The current rate of rural to urban migration in India is unattainable. It is much more than the rate at which industrial jobs and urban infrastructure are growing. Therefore, rural development is a must to slow down migration.
- Rural development is also important if we focus on the quality of life of rural people. It suffices the basic needs of the people, administers and caters to necessary medical emergencies as well. It also lays emphasis on women empowerment, education, employment and rightful ownership of land issues. Rural people can be misled by others due to lack of education, therefore, rural development is a must.
- Rural development implies both the economic betterment of people as well as greater social transformation. The basic objective of all rural development programmes has been the welfare of the millions. In order to achieve this, planned attempts have been made to eliminate poverty, ignorance and inequality of opportunities. A wide spectrum of programmes has been undertaken so far, to alleviate rural poverty and ensure improved quality of life for the rural population especially those below the poverty line. In the initial phase of planned rural development, the concentration was on sectors of agriculture, industry, communication, education and health.

Objectives of Rural Development

Objectives are expressions of the ends towards which our efforts through various programmes are to be directed. In other words, the term 'objective' indicates the direction of movements. Rural development, the world over, has emerged as one of the critical issues on the International arena of development during the 1990s. All International Development Agencies have expressed their concern and further proclaimed their strong commitment towards rural development. Programmes for Rural Development have been included under important objectives of India's Planned Development from the beginning of the plan era. It is reported that ever since the inception of planning, the objectives and programmes being designed and redesigned, keeping these cardinal principle in mind.

The objectives of rural development include sustained increase in the per capita output and incomes, expansion of productive employment and greater equality in the distribution of the benefits of growth. This implies reducing poverty and the human misery by increasing profitability of the rural poor and providing them greater access to goods and services and also enabling them to take advantage of the safety nets to be provided by the government. Rural development aimed at target groups must constitute a major part of a developmental strategy, if large segment of the poor in greater need are to benefit (Jalihal and Shivamurthy, 2003).

Development refers to growth or evolution, stage of advancement. In the context of rural background it means developing better physical, social and economic conditions of the populations living in the rural area. The broad objective of the rural development programme is to raise the economic and social level of the rural people. However, the specific objectives of rural development are:

1. To develop farm, home, public service and village community.
2. To bring improvement in producing of crops and animals living condition.
3. To improve the condition of health and education of the rural people.
4. To improve the condition of the villagers through their own efforts.
5. To improve village communication

The definition and objectives of the rural development as laid down by the authors vary according to their area of emphasis. All the same, the objectives have been better reflected in the views of Michael Todaro that rural development encompasses: (i) improvement in level of living, including employment, education, health and nutrition, housing and a variety of social services; (ii) decreasing inequality in the distribution of rural incomes and in rural-urban balances in income and economic opportunities; (iii) increasing the capacity of rural sector to sustain and accelerate the pace of these improvements. The foregoing views are inclusive of all aspects that have bearing on rural development in true sense.

Principles of Rural Development Programmes

Rural development strategies usually take the form of programmes which implement projects in a specific rural area. Such programmes form the basis of most government and non-government efforts to assist rural areas, and they include both agricultural and non-agricultural projects programmes. The following principles are suggested to implement rural development programmes:

***Access for all*:** First principle is to ensure that the programme and its benefits should reach to those in needs, and beware of the consequences if some beneficiaries have access to the programme while others do not.
***Independent in action*:** Secondly, it drives a programme which helps and supports the rural beneficiaries but does not make him or her dependent upon the programme.
***Sustainability*:** Thirdly, it ensures that the programme's plans and solutions are relevant to the local economic, social and administrative circumstances. Short-term solutions may yield quick results, but long-term programme that are suitable to the local environment have greater success.
***Technological Innovation*:** Technological aspects of rural development programmes help the communities to take the next step in his development. It is better to secure a modest advance which can be sustained than to suggest a substantial advance which is beyond the ability of most.
***People's Participation*:** It is one of the major factors responsible for successful implementation of programmes. It seeks out people's ideas and involvement in the process.
***Effectiveness*:** A programme should be based on the effective use of local resources and not necessarily on their most efficient use. While efficiency is important, its requirements are often unrealistic.
***Integration*:** It has been realized that development programme should be integrated one. This is possible when sectoral development programmes, human resource development programmes, social welfare programmes, infrastructure development programmes are brought within the framework of a prospective plan for implementation, where each programme reinforce the other through their linkages.

History of Rural Development in India

Literally and from the social, economic and political perspectives the statement is valid even today, that around 65 per cent of the total population of India is living in rural areas. People in rural areas should have the same quality of life as is enjoyed by people living in sub-urban and urban areas. Further, there are cascading effects of poverty, unemployment, poor and inadequate infrastructure in rural areas on urban centres causing slums and consequential social and economic tensions manifesting in economic deprivation and urban poverty. Hence, Rural development which is concerned with economic growth and social justice, improvement in the living standard of the rural people by providing adequate and quality social services and minimum basic needs becomes essential. The present strategy of rural development mainly focuses on poverty alleviation, better livelihood opportunities, provision of basic amenities and infrastructure facilities through innovative programmes of wage and self-employment. The above goals will be achieved by various programme supports being implemented creating partnership with communities, non-governmental organizations, community based organizations, institutions, Panchayati Raj Institutions (PRIs) and industrial establishments, while the Department of Rural Development will provide logistic support both on technical and administrative side for programme implementation. Other aspects that will ultimately lead to transformation of rural life are also being emphasized simultaneously.

The rural way of life in a country like India demands special introspection. Therefore, a study into the history of Rural Development needs to be done. It dates back into time because India as a self-sufficient nation was basically a labour intensive economy right from the start. Even today, India is more agricultural in nature, even with advent of technologies. Farming and crop cultivation is an occupation that has been carried on from generation to generation. Since, crops and cultivation products cannot grow in the urban areas on large scale, it explains why mankind has a special place for rural people, land and its various problems. If we take the whole world into account, then it must be noted that continents which are on the northern hemisphere started development at an earlier phase due to technological advancements at a higher rate. The rest of the world was still under the clutches of widespread turbulences which hindered their growth. Speaking of India, we are still developing, therefore, rural as a word, finds much applicability here ! We were not modernized until we were freed from slavery. Then the green revolution came in 1960, creating a landmark in the history of rural development and growth. However, with the advancement here and there we also unemployed millions of people, thus explaining the origin of migration in the rural masses. The government has a key role to play in the history of rural development and the implementation of strategies can be seen in the first three Five Year Plan. Down the sands of time, things changed a lot. Now there is a shift in Government's approach towards development. Instead of relying only on increase in general affluence to enhance the living standards of citizens, the approach is to consider acquisition of minimum levels of education, health, employment and nutrition as basic entities and recognize the key role of the state in providing them to every needy citizen in the country, the shift is towards universalization and entitlements.

There is also increased emphasis on promoting balanced development in which all regions in country have the opportunity to develop evenly. This equity-promoting role demands that resources be allocated to the backward regions to remove gaps in the provision of basic services for human development.

As a result, large investments will flow to those districts of the country which are classified as backward. Admittedly, these are the most difficult districts to implement developmental programmes because of poor governance structures, low organizational capacity, weak infrastructure and unequal power structures.

There is also a fundamental change in how government programmes are funded and executive increasingly key programmes are being funded by the Union Government and executed by State Governments. This ensures that on one hand, no entitlement programme is made to suffer due to resource constraint and on the other, funds are available with greater regularity to implement the programmes of districts, blocks and Panchayati Raj Institutions (PRIs) so that programme outcomes can be achieved with local participation, ownership, initiative and supervision.

Since these flagship programmes are bound by the common objective of delivering entitlement on a universal scale, it is necessary that they converge at the grass roots and their individual plan systems are integrated harmoniously. Such integration would ensure common implement at framework for all the schemes.

Above all, adequate and appropriate administrative and institutional arrangements are essential for the success of these programmes. In their design, these programmes provide for a multi-structure of administrative and institutional arrangements for implementation and monitoring of specified roles and responsibilities. The agencies involved are the respective ministries of the Union Government, Departments of the State Governments and the local governments.

The concept of rural development, from the perspective of recent history, is based on the sustainable development. Rural development approach can be made from several perspectives. Rural development involving equitable and balanced economic development, with high levels of social cohesion and inclusion and accountability for the use of natural resources and environmental protection, is sustainable rural development.

Rural Development during the British Rule

Since time immemorial, India has been predominantly a rural country. Thus rural development has always been in the priority concern of national development. In those days, our villages were self-sufficient and self-sustained and any effort for the betterment in their conditions was made by the respective rulers. But during the British rule, they were not concerned with the socio-economic development of India and thus our rural economy was severely damaged resulting in the miserable conditions of the rural people. It was the famine of 1899 which forced the British Government to think about the people of India who were dying of hunger.

The recurrent famines forced the State Administrators to seize the foodgrains and make arrangements for the distribution among the famine-affected people. All this was done without any apparent legal sanction, motivated as the action purely was by determination to control profiteering and alleviate rural suffering. As B.B. Mishra further says, "Rural development thus began as a humanitarian act, and the practice was not backed by any executive or legal sanction in the beginning. Legality and legitimacy were provided later".

Later, with the recommendations of Famine Commissions of 1866 and 1880 and with the initiative of Lord Curzon, Provincial Department of Agriculture with Agricultural College and Provincial Research Institute were established. In 1906 the Indian Agricultural Service was constituted. A number of British officers according to their interest and inclination tried out a few experiments in rural reconstruction. The spread of such programmes was thin and only small financial outlays could be made for them. They were not pursued with any noticeable sense of urgency.

Rural Development during Pre-Independence Period

In the pre-independence period, a number of rural development programmes were started by the Nationalists and Social reformers. Some of these programmes gradually disappeared or some were merged with Government-sponsored schemes later. This is because of various reasons like lack of encouragement from the Government, lack of financial support, inadequate, inexperienced and untrained staff. The other reasons are lop-sided approach to different aspects of development, absence of needed supplies and services, inadequate co-ordination and co-operation from other departments and agencies.

The most important rural development efforts during the pre- independence era were:

1. Rural Reconstruction programme by Mahatma Gandhi,
2. The Sriniketan Experiment by Rabindranath Tagore,
3. The Martandam Experiment,
4. The Gurgaon Experiment,
5. Rural Reconstruction Programmes in Baroda, and
6. The Firka Development scheme.

Rural Reconstruction Programme by Mahatma Gandhi

Gandhiji's dream of nation development was exclusively rural. He observed India's greatness in intelligent, independent, contented and hard working peoples in its villages not in highly industrialized, developed and sophisticated cities. He was appalled by the ignorance, disease and poverty of rural people and visualized village reconstruction programme that would fire the imagination of rural poor and lend them through self-help to ensure ample food for all, adequate health protection and medical services, free education, local self-government and self-employment through cottage industries (Varma, R., 1967).

Mahatma Gandhi started the programmes for rural reconstruction at Sevagram in Wardha. The main components of his programme were: (1) communal harmony, (2) removal of untouchability, (3) prohibition, (4) use of Khadi, (5) promotion of village industries, (6) uplift of youth, (7) full development and utilization of local resources, (8) promotion of economic equity, (9) self-sufficient village economy, (10) self-reliant village community. In this programme he had given attention on the importance of developing rural people and rural areas.

The Gandhian Constructive Programme is essentially a programme of human activity in various fields that is beneficial for the economic growth of rural India. Gandhiji wished to evolve a philosophy of life which would achieve the welfare of all (*Sarvodaya*).

Gandhiji was greatly disturbed by the decline of rural industries. He believed that the extinction of village industry would complete the ruin of 7,00,000 villages. He gave special attention to revive rural crafts especially spinning and weaving, traditional oil press, grain processing and leather work.

According to Gandhiji, the return to traditional village industry could ensure full employment and well-being to the overwhelming population of the country. This philosophy inspired and informed the activities of Gandhiji to the constructive workers who dedicated their lives to village development programmes.

Gandhian rural reconstruction activities were based on the principles of truth and non-violence. His ideas of rural reconstruction were accepted officially and resulted in the adoption of Khadi and Village Industries Programme, the principle of Village Self-sufficiency and the faith in the Panchayati Raj and Sahakari Samaj Movement by the Government are some of the examples of the impact of Gandhian tradition.

Sriniketan Experiment by Rabindranath Tagore

In 1920, Rabindranath Tagore laid the foundation of the Sriniketan Institute for Rural Reconstruction and formulated a programme for the all-round improvement in the village of his *zamindari* with the objective of studying rural problems and of helping the villagers to develop agriculture, improving the livestock, formation of co-operatives and improving village sanitation.

Tagore believed in self-help and mutual help and wanted the village workers to be involved in the life of rural people and work for their welfare. He started this programme in the cluster of eight villages but was not very successful and can only be described as rural welfare works. The absence of market facilities, professional guidance, lack of co-ordination between the implementing authority and improper incentives for workers made the task more difficult and desired results could not be achieved.

Sriniketan experiment was meant for bringing back life in its completeness into the villages, making rural folks self-reliant and engraving self respectful. Acquainted with the cultural traditions of their own country and competent to make an efficient use of modem resources for the improvement of their physical, intellectual and economic conditions. Though this experiment was not successful, it attained certain physical and notable results.

Rabindranath Tagore, the greatest figure of the Indian Renaissance has, conferred through his poems, dramas, short stories, essays, songs, paintings, etc., which expressed his spiritual ideologies. He is not only the greatest of Indian poets, but also a patriot, a philosopher, an artist, an educationist, a humanist and so many other things. For a long time he has been at the centre of India's life. He is a phenomenon. He is a poet for all readers and for all ages. He has such a wide range of creativity that anyone can begin with Tagore and end with Tagore. In the field of rural reconstruction, he was a pioneer in our country.

Tagore viewed rural reconstruction not only as a means for economic self-sufficiency but also for cultural reawakening. He observed that people were passing through a period of intense social and emotional disorganization, narrow-mindedness and superstitious belief, which pervaded the entire sense of being humane. He also felt that people were facing an all-round cultural crisis and were steeped in poverty, ignorance and disease. Tagore, therefore, addressed the task of fighting these systems of decay and stagnation and started to create a society in rural India through his multifarious designs of social activities to fill life with vigour and joy, aesthetic beauty and sublime happiness. He recognized that the living standard of the rural folks cannot be raised without solving the problems of reconstructing the social and economic fabric. He had a clear perception of problems and conceptualized rural development in its totality, consistent with the Indian situation.

Dream about Education and Rural Reconstruction

Tagore studied literature, philosophy, art and religion of the East and the West with an open mind. Some of these have influenced his mind consciously or unconsciously though his thinking and views are his own. In Tagore's view, only one way of protecting the weak is to give them strength. The most effective way of giving strength, according to him is, to impart proper education. Education, according to Tagore, is the all-round growth and development of the individual in harmony with the universal, the Supreme person who has in himself the various levels or planes of consciousness and experience corresponding to man's physical self, life, mind and soul. Tagore had founded a unique institution that aimed at connecting hearts to each other, whether between the teacher and the taught or among the learners themselves. Tagore started his own movement for self-reliance through his Visva-Bharati. His understanding of nature and dissemination of the knowledge process through the elements that control the body, mind and soul of human beings has made Visva-Bharati a unique global village. Visva-Bharati located in the twin campus of Santiniketan and Sriniketan, has as its motto—"Where the world makes its home in a single nest". Establishing a link with the world was one aspect of the Santiniketan, Visva-Bharati ideal of totality from its very inception. On the other hand was its ideal of total activity, the attempt to make education relate to life in all its aspects. Sriniketan was deliberately made into a laboratory for this endeavour although the spirit of it was always there in the Santiniketan education. Visiting the villages and getting acquainted with them had, for instance, been part of the curriculum for the students and teachers of Santiniketan.

Tagore was convinced that education cannot be imparted fruitfully and meaningfully unless the teachers are close to the students and hence chose the ancient *tapovan* (hermitage) model of education. In this system, teachers and pupils lived together and education was imparted in the freedom of nature without unhealthy competition and routine examination. It was obligatory for the teachers and students of the school to visit the neighbouring villages to probe and understand the problems of the villagers. He explains the significance of Visva-Bharati—"If schools in a true sense are established in India, then its sciences of economics, agriculture, hygiene and in fact all its operative sciences, should be spread out to the surrounding rural areas, centering around the original institution. This institution will then occupy the central place of Indian life style. This institution will arrange tilling the best way, look after the cattle and weaving in ideal manner and by adopting cooperative method will achieve financial self-sufficiency. They will have to associate with neighbouring residents intimately; I have proposed to name this kind of institution as Visva-Bharati".

The aim of education for Tagore is to realize the 'complete man', the 'eternal man', and the 'universal man' in one's being. Tagore was unsatisfied with the popular method of education which according to him is not useful for practical purposes and which cannot properly educate man to be a 'universal man'. Tagore emphasized that man is essentially a social being and hence his ideal of education should be—to help him to be a useful member of the society, to be a good citizen of the country. He believed that man is at the same time social, political, and spiritual, and hence his education aims at development of all aspects of man's personality. For proper education he gives much stress on the surrounding atmosphere.

He said that education should not only be informative, but it should make our life in harmony with all existence. According to him that ideal can best be realized—in the model of *tapovans* of ancient India. In Santiniketan, he founded his school in natural surroundings, a modern form of ancient *ashramas* of India. The education which students acquire from only books cannot help them in their social life, but when they come in contact with living persons and nature, they can get the best education. He says, "Where mind is developed, there should be open space around it. In nature one's mind can get that open air variously and beautifully." According to Tagore the aim of education is to strengthen our sense of values as well as to provide us training to apply them.

Sriniketan Experiment and Development

Tagore believed that the soul of India lies in her villages and only when the villages are awakened and rose to its full potential, will India be truly independent and usher in a new era of social and economic order with justice, which is the main idea of decentralization. It has been widely recognized that the education shapes the life of a person and exposes the lifestyle and occupation depending upon the level of education. Values are the outcome of education one receives from the family, social environment and educational institutions. Tagore believed that the education of the people would help to change their attitudes and behaviours to a great extent, which will empower them to think positively and contribute meaningfully to self and the society at large. He felt that the care of semi-starved, malaria-stricken people, who live in poverty and despair, had to be included in the scheme of education. In order to help them to enjoy health and physical well-being villages had to be reconstructed, and the old civilization had to be reviewed in the light of the new.

Rabindranath Tagore, the greatest poet of the modern India and visionary, was basically a humanist and his heart ached in deeply at the distressing conditions of the villagers who were reeling under acute poverty and suffering from malnutrition, ill-health, various ailments and illiteracy. For improving the conditions of these deprived villages, Tagore initiated the "Sriniketan Experiment" in 1922 in Visva-Bharati and which was later on acknowledged and acclaimed even by the outside world as an eminent institution. In the words of Tagore, the object of his programme was "to bring back life in its completeness into the villages making them self-reliant and self-respectful, acquainted with the cultural tradition of their own country and competent to make an efficient use of modern resources for the improvement of their physical, intellectual and economic conditions". Tagore's mission of rural reconstruction was based on four principles—self-interest, self-respect, self-reliance and joy in work. Tagore wanted to construct the villages in such a way that the villagers would be self-sufficient in all their needs. He wanted to make a 'complete man' of each person and make the people aware of the larger society through appropriate education, and inspire them to cultivate a spirit of cooperation and self-reliance.

A thorough reconstruction of the socio-economic life of the villages and an integrated programme for the solution of the problems of agriculture, industry, health, education and recreation worked out by the effort of the villagers themselves, were to Tagore, the mainstay of his rural reconstruction programme. Thus, Sriniketan was concerned with the improvement of the methods of traditional cultivation by helping farmers to adopt new farming technologies, hybrid variety of seeds, better fertilizer and pesticide; combine Indian traditional arts to foreign arts and develop artifacts into our culture; improve health conditions with due preventive and curative care; improve the village sanitation; train rural artisans with modern equipment and organize credit and consumer cooperatives of different kinds to ensure self-help. In other words, the idea was to develop human resources, make use of the available resources and develop sustainable rural organizations on cooperative principles.

For the improvement of the living condition of village India in a synthetic way Tagore thus felt it essential to reconstruct the degenerating social and human dimension of the villages by inculcating the spirit of self-reliance among the people. Instead of trying to improve the economic, health, social, or civic dimensions separately in terms of development inputs from outside, Tagore emphasized the reconstruction of the constructive as well as the creative spirit of man, reinforcing the ambience of pleasure and collective conscience.

The rural reconstruction programme as envisaged by Rabindranath took its full form when Leonard Elmhirst came from England and joined it at the end of 1921. Kalimohan Ghosh and Gourgopal Ghosh, two teachers from Santiniketan along with ten students started the work with Elmhirst. The area centred on Sriniketan and the Institute of Rural Reconstruction was formally established in 1922 within his broad educational philosophy at Visva-Bharati. The *Surul Samity,* which came into existence in 1922 had already started the Sriniketan work under the Surul Department of Agriculture. At the beginning, Elmhirst took up the task for agricultural improvement in the villages. But Rabindranath wanted a total improvement in the village taking in agriculture, education, health and social living together. Elmhirst soon appreciated the importance of this approach. Sriniketan's contribution to village reconstruction work is this concept of a total approach.

Initially the activities of Sriniketan were three fold. These were: (a) Research and Experiments; (b) Training, and (c) Extension and Development. For research and experiment in agriculture the Surul farm was started in 1922. Chemical manure was used here for the first time in 1926. Villagers from the surrounding areas watched the results keenly. Needless to add, increase in the productivity of land was the primary object of the Sriniketan work. At the same time, organizing a health programme for general medical care and the eradication of malaria were equally important. The Sriniketan dispensary was established in 1923 and the cooperative health societies in 1932. Sanitation work in the villages, the clearing of jungles, the spraying of kerosene oil into *dobas* and pits were also being implemented. All these works were not confined to the territorial boundary of Sriniketan. These measures were taken to the surrounding villages, and Sriniketan was the centre for research, experiment, training and extension for reconstruction. At the centre, economists, agriculturists, social workers, doctors, midwives and specialists in various fields of rural industry and education experimented and worked together to solve different aspects of rural problems. Villagers came with their problems and tried out some of the results of the experiments in their fields. In addition to all these activities the scout movement was initiated and a *Brati-Balak Samgathana* (children scouts) was formed in village Mahidapur as early as in 1922. The aim was to make the village self-reliant. It was hoped that the mobilizing of the children would draw in the elders. As more villages joined the Sriniketan experiment, an approach had to be devised to involve the boys in each village and the *Brati-Balak* method was found to be simplest and least expensive. The objective was to awaken in the minds of the village elders, torn by dispute among themselves, the need for cooperation as well as the spirit of self reliance and confidence.

Education in itself became a major part of the Sriniketan organization in the first decade of its existence. There were different levels at which education was imparted. The *Brati Balak* method was one. There was also Sriniketan's extension service. In addition, the Sriniketan authorities invited apprentices from villages on stipends of rupees twenty to be attached for a year or more to the different departments of village organization, agriculture and industries, health and sanitation.

At Sriniketan there were four different educational institutions: the *Siksha-Satra* (1924) for village boys, the *Loka-Siksha Samsad* (1936) for those who wanted to study without going to school and college, the *Siksha-Charcha Bhavana* for village school teachers and the *Diploma in Rural Reconstruction* (1922) for college students. A fundamental premise of the Sriniketan education was in its teaching of handicrafts which included leather work, weaving, book-binding, needle-work, pottery, wood carving and block printing handicrafts, taught at *Silpa Bhavana*.

One of the major efforts of Sriniketan was in setting up cooperative societies. The Visva-Bharati Central Cooperative Bank was established in 1927. The Cooperative Society was established in this area for agricultural credits, irrigation, granaries, etc. This kind of work could be done on the basis of village surveys. Sriniketan took up such surveys from the beginning. Specialists depended on these surveys for their total approach to the village. The Sriniketan programme underwent a change in the late thirties. The comprehensive development of selected villages, however, also continued to shape the idea of making villages self-reliant.

The Martandam Experiment

Dr. Spencer Hatch of the Young Men's Christian Association (YMCA) set up a Project in 1921 at Martandam, 25 miles south of Thiruvananthapuram. The purpose of this experiment was to bring about a complete upward development towards a more complete and meaningful life for rural people, spiritually, mentally, physically, socially and economically.

The main stress in his programme was on the principle that people should not depend on Government for support because when concessions and help in any field are not given, the people develop in them a feeling of self-help and self-reliance.

The objective of this programme was the YMCA should work in the villages to eliminate poverty. For this, the Rural Demonstration Centre at Martandam had a demonstration farm, prized animals, equipment for the honey industry and other cottage vocations in its campus. Some industries like weaving, poultry and bee-keeping were started on a co-operative basis. Dr. Hatch could demonstrate the lucrative possibilities of these enterprises. The project had following objectives:

- Developing the rural communities using locally available resources.
- Eliciting people's participation and enable them to make their own decisions and plan of action.
- Promote self-help and giving priority to the poorest of the poor.
- Covering the entire community irrespective of religion, caste.
- Developing a spiritual basis for rural development.

The Marthandam Project had taken some strategic interventions for achieving desired goals. They were:

- Demonstrate improved system of farming, animal husbandry, bee-keeping, poultry and cattle rearing and entrepreneurship development.
- Promoting village cottage industries to generate livelihood and income.
- Establishment of egg marketing societies and bee-keeping cooperatives.
- Provide primary education and health education.
- Organizing leadership training courses for the rural mass.
- Raising funds from the local community.

The major achievements of the programme were the change in the attitudes of the rural people, formation of a desire to improve the spirit of cooperation and self-respect. This experiment was followed by other states and its workers helped the states of Baroda, Mysore, Cochin and Hyderabad to set up centres of Transfer for Rural Reconstruction.

The Gurgaon Experiment

In 1927, the Gurgaon experiment was started by F.L. Bryne, who was the Deputy Commissioner of Gurgaon District in Punjab. The programme aimed at improving agriculture, education, health and sanitation facilities, co-operation and social development with greater vigour. The Gurgaon Project had the specific objectives as follows:

- Incorporating the virtue of hard work, self-respect, self-help and mutual support.
- Convincing the rural mass that improvement is possible by demonstrating the methods to fight successfully against climatic challenges, diseases and pests.

Through these comprehensive efforts, he intended to remove poverty through a mass movement. He stressed on the dignity of labour, self-help and conducted propaganda through films, songs, skits and plays with a view to increase farm yields and improving health standards under this programme. For the first time, a 'Village guide' was posted in each village who was to work as a link to pass on new innovations to the villagers. Brayne believed that these objectives could be achieved if they were based on four fundamental principles of village organization, mass education, leadership and spirit of service and duty towards fellow men. The programme was carried out with the help of several institutions established by Bryne. The School of Rural Economy, the School of Domestic Economy and Health Associations were introduced to deal with various issues related rural development. The project created awareness among the local people that their participation is essential for the upliftment of their standard of living and also provided opportunities to the rural people to know about modern technologies.

The main reason for the failure of this programme was that the reforms were imposed on the people, rather than initiated by themselves. This widened the gap between the 'haves and have-nots'.

Rural Reconstruction Programme in Baroda

The Maharaja of Baroda was a progressive and enlightened man and he started the Baroda experiment in 1932. This programme aimed at developing "will to live better" and a capacity for self-help and self-reliance. The Baroda project was focused mainly on:

- Alter the attitude of the agriculturists and develop a aspiration for premier standard of living.
- Capacity building and Rural leadership development.
- Conduct adult education.

In primary phase the programme covered 10 villages and later it was extended to 35 villages. The programme included the following items:

1. Improvement of communication,
2. Digging of drinking water wells,
3. Anti-malarial measures,
4. Pasture development,
5. Distribution of improved seeds,

6. Training in Cottage crafts.
7. Establishment of Panchayats and Co-operatives covering every village,
8. Development of village schools as Centres for teaching agriculture and for improving the will to live better.

The experiment gave special importance to educational development. It also gave special focus on human development and organizational development. The programme had full legislative and financial support.

The FIRKA Development Scheme

The Firka Development Scheme of Madras was a Government sponsored scheme in 1946. This programme aimed at organising the villagers for a happier, more prosperous and fuller life in which the individual villagers had the opportunity to develop both as an individual and as a unit of a well integrated society.

The short-term objectives of the scheme was to develop basic amenities and an institutional framework for carrying out communication, water supply, sanitation, formation of local self-governments (i.e. panchayats) and cooperatives. 'The long-term objectives were to attain self-sufficiency in food, clothing, shelter, development of agriculture, animal husbandry, khadi and village industries.

The administrative machinery consisted of Director of Rural Welfare at the State level, the Collector at District level, the Rural Welfare Offcer at Firka level and 5 to 10 Grama Sevaks under him. Besides these, staffs for Agriculture and Public Works were also provided for every Firka.

Later in 1953-54, when the Community Development Programme and National Extension Service Programme were adopted by Madras State, the Firka Development Scheme was merged with it.

Rural Development since Independence

Immediately after the attainment of independence and before the commencement of planned economic development through Five Year Plans, three important programmes of rural reconstruction were introduced in India.

They were:

1. The Etawah Pilot Project.

2. The Nilokheri Experiment.
3. The Bhoodan Movement.

The Etawah Pilot Project

In 1948, Albert Mayor started the Etawah Pilot Project for the development of the rural areas of Etawah District in Uttar Pradesh. The main objective of the project was "to see what degree of productive and social improvement as well as initiative, self-confidence and co-operation can be developed. The problem was to ascertain how quickly these results may be attained and remain permanently a part of the people's mental, spiritual, technical equipment and outlook after the special pressure is lifted."

The other important features were: production intensity, people's cooperation, and development of appropriate attitudes, careful selection of personnel, self-reliance, local resources and supply and development of village leadership. The effort was made to introduce the concept of decentralised economy leading to Agro-Industrial Economy which in turn led to the development of agriculture, horticulture, poultry, piggery, fishery and other forms of animal husbandry.

For intensive operation of the programme, 97 Villages of Mahadeva Block in Etawah District were selected. Various activities like agricultural demonstrations, soil conservation, improvement in animal husbandry, village sanitation and the co-operation of various departments and non-official agencies were carried out. In order to secure people's participation, a programme of social education was also started. The Project was successful in achieving its aim and within 3 years, it was extended to 300 villages of the Etawah District in UP.

The Nilokheri Experiment

S.K. Dey, the former Minister for Community Development and Cooperation was the founder of the Nilokheri Experiment in 1948, when nearly 7,000 displaced persons were rehabilitated in Nilokheri town after independence. The scheme was also known as "Mazdoor Manzil" because of its principle 'he who will not work, neither shall he eat'. The main objectives of this programme were:

- To rehabilitate displaced persons;
- To attain self-sufficiency by utilizing the labour and talents of the refugees; and

- To meet the basic needs of the populations.

Under this programme, the main activities were a Vocational Training Centre run on co-operative lines and the Colony had its own dairy, poultry, piggery, printing press, engineering workshops, tannery and bone-meal factory. People were given vocational training of their choice to run these Co-operative Enterprises. Rights for education and medical care for the sick were also guaranteed.

The Nilokheri project, in spite of its limitations, left an imprint on the Community Development Programme in the country. It gave the idea of agro-Industrial Township as the nerve-centre of rural development. The programme found place in the First Five Year Plan and in the lay-out of the Financial Plan of the first 52 Community Projects.

Nilokheri was seen as a symbol of progress, but the Colony developed its own hierarchial structure and the industries started facing troubles due to lack of competitive advantages. Nilokheri is still an important centre for the training of Panchayati Raj and Rural Development Functionaries.

The Bhoodan Movement

Acharya Vinoba Bhave, one of the earlier social reformers of India is the propounder of Bhoodan movement. In the words of Vinoba Bhave, *Bhoodan Yagna* is an all-comprehensive movement directed to the reform in all walks of life. Today everyone thinks of himself alone and feels for himself only. But Bhoodan makes the people think and do just the opposite of what they do now. It makes the people first think of their neighbours, and if he has no land, it must be their duty to provide him with it. In *Bhoodan,* distribution of land is not the only question. It aims at the moral regeneration of the whole nation. Through it we hope to solve the economic difficulties, encourage Village Industries and remove the difference between the educated and the uneducated by making them both to join in common work.

The inspiration for *Bhoodan* came to Vinobaji in 1951 when he was touring the Telangana District of Hyderabad. The basic objective of Bhoodan campaign was to prevent the emergence of bloody revolution by solving the land problems in a peaceful way.

At one stage, it was thought that Vinoba had succeeded in converting the minds of large numbers of big landholders. Acres upon acres and later villages upon villages were shown as being given away to the landless or the tenants. But later, it was found that, in most such cases, the Bhoodan proved to be a failure; in one manner or another, the land was retained by the large landholders.

Problems of Rural India

Rural India faces series of problems which affect their survival and quality of life. There are various factors which have created problems and come in the way of effective rural development. These problems are very serious and need immediate attention by the Government and other development agencies. The problems of the rural poor throughout the country are same. However, the intensity of these problems varies widely and a few of them need to be addressed on priority basis. The factors responsible of these problems also vary, like, due to the family size, employment status, ownership of various resources, socio-economic background, religious beliefs, etc. These restrictions need to be taken into consideration, while proposing suitable solutions for tackling the problems of rural development. Some of the basic problems of rural areas are discussed below:

Increasing Size of Population in Rural Areas

Increasing size of population over the last six decades after independence has become an alarming situation for India. The country is already feeling the challenges of huge population and tried to cope up with the situation. The growth rate of population for India in last decades was 17.64 per cent. The growth rate of population in rural and urban areas was 12.18 per cent and 31.80 per cent respectively. India's population in 1901 was about 238.4 million and in 1951 it was 361 million which has exceeded to 1,210 million in 2011. India is representing the world's second highest populated country after China and having 17 per cent of world population. The rural and urban population size in 2011 were 833 million (68.84%) and 377 million (31.16%) respectively. The increase in population would result in a very serious problem in country's planned development effort to alleviate rural poverty and unemployment.

Large Area of Marginal Land which cannot be used for Achieving Economy of Scale

The marginal land in India accounts almost one-third of the total landholding. These marginal lands have less economic prosperity and can only contribute substantially to the national income. However, technological advancement in India tried to solve this problem but still a lot is to be done for economically use marginal lands. Due to population explosion, there has been a alarming rate of increase in the number of small and marginal farms and their proportion in the total ownership holdings. These small and marginal farmers, most of whom are small and marginal landholding along with agricultural labourers, constitute such a big proportion of agricultural labour force and it will be very difficult to provide livelihood security to this huge population.

Low Agricultural Production in Rural India

Rural population in India largely depends on agriculture and allied activities. Majorities of the farmers are either small or marginal in India. Small size of landholding, technological backwardness and lack of proper marketing structure force the farmer to go for subsistent farming. The commercialization of agriculture is far in most of the States of India. This is one of the major causes for increasing rural poverty and unemployment as well as disparity between rural and urban economy. However, improved agricultural production is essential factor for poverty eradication.

According to UNCTAD "in most Less Developed Countries (LDCs) the area in which reforms are lacking to have their greatest impact is agriculture. Agriculture is the single most independent sector in LDCs economies in terms of its contribution to adequate employment and income. Increased production in agriculture is essential if living standards of a majority of poor, who live in the rural areas, are to be raised and food security is to be enhanced".

The reasons behind low agricultural productivity in rural areas are:

- Increase in number of nuclear family in rural areas causes fragmentation of land which creates large number of small and marginal holding. Without proper technological improvement and irrigation facility these lands become economically unviable.
- Improved production in agriculture and allied sector needs use of additional inputs like improved seeds, fertilizer, manure, cattle feed, machineries, etc., which increase the cost of production. However, there are always risks and uncertainty in benefits for agriculture due to disease, pest attack, price fluctuation, lack of

market. So, lack of security and safety nets from the Government restrict the farmers to use additional inputs to improve the agricultural production.

- Rural poor have also lack of knowledge and access to products and services provided by the Government and Non-government agencies.
- Agriculture highly depends on climate factor. In recent past the changes in climatic condition make agriculture and allied sector vulnerable.
- Due to high diversity among the States it is very difficult to develop proper policy. Generally Government makes uniform policy for entire nation, which is not suitable to meet the needs of States.
- Most of modern technologies are not sustainable around the States of India.

Poor Management of Small and Marginal Farms

Poor attention to small and marginal farm management has increased production cost and risk. In spite of the fact, that 75 per cent of cultivators in India are unirrigated, the Government's effort has been focused on irrigated agriculture leaving the majority of the farming community. Therefore, it becomes a prime responsibility of the Government to develop and induce some suitable technology with low input cost and easy accessibility to minimize the production fluctuation and risks.

Lack of Employment Opportunities in Rural Areas

In country like India where 70 per cent of the rural population depends on agriculture, it is expected that employment are to be provided in the agriculture and allied sector. However, in reality agriculture and allied sector have failed to absorb unemployed and under-employed rural population. This is one of the major factors causing rural poverty. Another factor is the inadequate progress of the non-foodgrain agriculture which is also responsible for low absorption of labour.

The village small scale and cottage industries could not run in a profitable venture due to tough competition from mechanized industries. This caused the decline of employment opportunity in village small scale and cottage industries. Earlier, the Seventh Plan had recognized some of the challenges faced by the cottage industries in India which are:

- Technological Obsolescence;
- Inadequate and irregular supply of raw materials;
- Lack of organized market channels;
- Imperfect knowledge of market conditions;
- Unorganized nature of operation;
- Inadequate ability of credit;
- Constrains of infrastructure facilities; and
- Deficient management and technical skills.

Source: Eighth Plan Document, 1992.

Due to poor growth of cottage industries, maximum pressure of employment in rural areas falls upon the agriculture sector. Since, employment opportunity in agriculture is limited and seasonal; the rate of unemployment in rural areas is rising day by day.

Poor Resource and its Mobilization in Rural Areas

Inadequate resources and its poor distribution is one of the major problems in rural areas. The rural poor are lack of resources; the only resource they own is the land resource. While landless people are more vulnerable as they do not own any land. The landless people have to depend on other's land as share cropper or tenant or as self-employment through establishing subsidiary micro enterprises.

Another problem in this regard is the poor distribution of surplus land to rural poor. One of the important objectives of the Land Reform was to fix ceiling on agricultural land and take over the excessive land from the owner, so that the surplus land could be distributed to the landless people. But most of the States were failed to follow the land reform norms.

In India, area of cultivable waste land which can be transformed into cultivable land is very high. These cultivable waste lands have potential to be converted into the cultivable land. But poor distribution of cultivable waste land is one of the major factors responsible for poor resource status among the rural poor.

Reduced Labour Productivity and Poor Level of Farm Mechanization

The rural social structure and relationship is undergoing through a rapid transformation in both economic and social outlook. The coordination, cooperation and harmony in rural areas have drastically reduced over time and this has also affected the bond of relationship between employer and worker. This has resulted in reduced labour productivity in rural areas. Another fact is that technological advancement and farm mechanization in agricultural operation have substantially improved the productivity but it could not be possible in a large scale due to steady decrease in land holding pattern over a period of time.

Extensive Use of Natural Resources causes Environmental Degradation

The rural areas are rich in natural resources and highly diversified. But in recent past these resources have been used extensively which hampers the balance of the environment. The unsustainable use of natural resources cause natural disasters which have high effects on the rural life.

Infrastructural Backwardness

According to Amartya Sen, if a country had globalization at highest possible speed and pays no attention to lack of social opportunities, illiteracy, and lack of health care it will be creating problem for itself. Following the same infrastructural backwardness have been major challenges for rural areas in India. The road communication, health centres, hospital, school, colleges, safe drinking water, market places have been the basic infrastructural need of rural areas. But unfortunately rural areas are lacking of these basic infrastructural requirements. Lack of proper road hampers the marketing of rural agricultural goods on time. Education and health facilities are also very important aspects of rural development. In spite of 67 years of independence, India has not been able to provide better educational and health facilities in its villages. The problem of poor sources of drinking water and inadequate sanitation facilities are also part of rural areas.

However, a plenty of programme and schemes on infrastructural development in rural areas have been implemented by both the Government and Non-government agencies but the progress is unsatisfactory. So at present context, top priority is needed for rural infrastructural development.

Inadequate Access to Basic Services

Majority of villages are lacking basic services like elementary education, safe drinking water, health services, sanitation, etc. In spite of having a school, class rooms are not adequate in number. The services from

Anganwadi centres are also poor. Sometimes villagers have to fetch water from distance sources. Access to primary health care is so difficult in rural areas. It is very usual case in rural areas that sick persons cannot be taken to nearest Primary Health Centres because of distance and lack of communication. Poor sanitation facility is also a problem in rural areas. Open defecation, inadequate drainage system and lack of toilets are very common pictures of rural areas.

Beneficiaries are Not Aware of their Entitlement

The rural beneficiaries of Government programmes are not aware of their entitlements like subsidies, concession rate of interest, loan, agricultural inputs, etc., under various schemes. The middle man and broker have pocketed the benefits by taking the unawareness of the ignorant. This also creates lack of transparency and accountability in the development process.

Poor People's Participation in Development Process

One of the essential factors for success of rural development programmes is the effective participation of rural poor in both the planning, implementation and monitoring of the programmes. But rural people keep them out of this endeavour. Lack of people's participation hampers the proper implementation and results in poor impact on the rural poverty. After 73rd and 74th Constitutional amendments, people's participation was made mandatory at the grass roots governance and Gram Sabhas have been provided with power to plan for the local development. However, the entire process has highly politicized in recent past and diluted the objective of decentralized governance. Lack of commitment from Gram Panchayats is also a factor which is hindering the people's participation.

Poor Participation of Poor Rural Women

Although rural development had been started long after independence but less attention has been given to the empowerment of rural women. However, the role of women in developing rural India is very crucial and should be taken into the grant. Women's empowerment through basic education, primary health care, family planning services and access for means of production is a pre-condition of breaking the poverty cycle

(Haq, 1995). Women's social and economic upliftment is a critical issue to the poor rural households. In recent past the Self-help Group movement had contributed a lot to social, economic and political empowerment of women.

Poor Economy of Scale lead to Subsistent Type of Living in Rural Areas

The production level of rural poor is small and subsistent in nature, which is hampering the achievement of economy of scale. The rural poor have utilized the entire production for consumption purpose. So unless, organized efforts are made to improve the rural production and also pool the production of rural poor to get advantage of the economy of scale, the rural poor remain in low income category. In recent past the cooperative activities and group work have helped rural poor to get the advantage of economy of scale.

Lack of Proper Planning and Implementation of Development Programmes

Decentralized planning and implementation is very crucial for the success of rural development programmes for eradicating rural poverty and improve the quality of life. The 73rd and 74th Constitutional Amendment, mandated the role and responsibilities of rural grass root institutions. It gave special focus on decentralized planning at all PRI levels. The District Planning Commission has also made a part of the grass roots planning. But lack of coordination and organization hampers the entire planning process. Hence, a top-down approach comes into account rather than the bottom-up approach and that fails to meet the desired development of local areas.

Lack of Coordination among the Development Agencies

Rural development efforts are implemented by various departments at local level. There are so many Government departments which are responsible for implementation of rural development programmes. However, lack of proper distribution of work and understanding of responsibilities among the respective line departments causes difficulties in coordination at operational level. This poor coordination hinders the progress of rural development a lot.

Lack of Accountability and Transparency in the Delivery Mechanism

The lack of accountability and transparency at operational level is another factor hampering the success of rural development programmes. It has been found that a huge amount of money was being fritted away and the actual target population, i.e., rural poor had not been benefited. In several cases unsatisfactory and unfair dealing of accounts and transparency have been pointed out which are also responsible for high level of corruption. In the recent past social audit, a grass root monitoring and evaluation mechanism had been introduced in most of the development programmes for ensuring accountability and transparency. However, lack of commitment from PRIs, political interference and the poor people's participation have diluted the objective of the social audit.

Political Interference hampers the Development Process

Political interference in the development process has increased in recent times. The Gram Panchayats have made the grass root institution for managing finance and executing majority of rural development programmes, hence, it became the major institution of rural local power centre. This influences the political parties to take command of the PRIs. The excessive politicization of PRIs hampers the development process as because the PRIs now run through respective political will and agenda.

India's Approaches for Rural Development

Of late, rural development has assumed global attention especially among the developing nations. It has great significance for a country like India where majority of the population, around 65 per cent of the people, live in rural areas. The present strategy of rural development in India mainly focuses on poverty alleviation, better livelihood opportunities, provision of basic amenities and infrastructure facilities through innovative programmes of wage and self-employment.

India has vast experience in the implementation of rural development programmes. The approaches of rural development in India have changed over a period of time. In the light of the experience gained by following a specific approach, a new approach has been evolved. Sometimes urgent requirements of the country also encourage adopting a new approach for rural development. The transformation of approaches is not only accelerating the motion of growth in rural areas but also ensure social justice among the rural poor.

Equity Oriented Approach

The central idea of this approach is equity generation. The multiple objectives of this approach are sought to be achieved by the capacity building of communities to involve itself in the development process. The community development programme is a classic example of equity oriented approach which aimed at nation building and equity development. The critical assumption of this approach is that the government can restructure the societal power relationships, and centralized bureaucrats can learn to share power with community groups. Successful implementation of this strategy requires complex decentralized matrix structure, with permanent mechanism for vertical and lateral integration, a combination of specialist and generalist skills, institutional leadership, social intervention capability and system management (Ickis, 1983). But due to lack of good governance structure and other prerequisite for successful implementation, this approach was failed to achieve the desired goal.

Growth Centre Approach

The growth centre approach has been an important strategy in rural development. It has been applied predominantly to agriculture sectors. The growth centre is based on the central place. The central place provides the functions and services to its tributary area that is located at the centre of minimum aggregate travel, providing minimum cost to the customer and maximum benefit to the seller. Under growth centre approach, the peripheries to the centre stand to benefit from the growth centre in direct proportion to their capacity. If the peripheries have developed, it can generate more benefits from the growth centre.

Area Specific Approach

The central idea of this approach is that if a specific area can be developed, people of that area will automatically get developed. The inputs provided for the development under such an approach are more related to requirements of an area. The merit of this approach is that a specific area is being recognized and selected on the basis of its backwardness and focus has been given to solve the problems of that area. The demerit of this approach is the assumption that the development of an area leads to develop its people also. But in actual situation only a few section of the society have able to get benefits from the development initiatives while majority of the people could not avail the benefits. Another fact is that all areas are not the same and different areas demand different types and different levels of development and similarly the following trend is found in case of the people also. Thus, area approach could not ensure the development of different sections of population residing in a particular area at different levels of backwardness.

Decentralized Approach

In a vast country like India, rural development cannot be achieved unless attention is paid to decentralize planning. Development programmes ought to be related to local resources and requirement. This alone can make both quantitative and qualitative difference to the planning process. India has been experimenting with the decentralized planning process for quite some time. Further, with the passing of 73rd Constitutional Amendment Act in 1992, a new system of decentralized governance was brought into being. This institutional arrangement promised an alternative to the hitherto followed bureaucratic mechanism. However, empirical evidences from various Indian States have shown that the decentralization exercises have succeeded, to some extent, in a few States such as West Bengal, Karnataka, Kerala, Maharashtra and Madhya Pradesh. If one has to understand the dilemma of decentralised governance, has to understand the nature of political process, political institutions, local organizations and their temperament towards the development.

Technocratic Approach

The technocratic approaches give emphasis on using improved technologies to bring about modernization in the farm management. However, India having an agronomic system there is some drawbacks while adopting this approach. The improved technologies can only be availed by the large farmers. It cannot provide benefit to the landless, small and marginal farmers. It is the fact that, the technocratic approach not only helped to maintain present disparity, but also actively contributed to substantial increase in the disparity.

Basic Need and Basic Service Approach

The central idea behind this approach is to make the basic services available and accessible to all areas and communities, especially the most deprived and vulnerable sections of the society. This is an effective policy measures to ensure provision of basic needs to the rural poor. Although, effective community participation is a must needed element of this approach. Another fact is that provision of basic need only can solve the few areas of rural problem but cannot bring rural development as a whole.

Target Group Approach

The socially backward and economically vulnerable sections of society could not avail themselves of the development benefits due to their inability, ignorance and existing social structure. So, there is an urgent need to identify the vulnerable sections and promote development so that they can avail a better standard of living. Such approaches are termed as target group approach. High income for target group as well as minimum needs of education, shelter, health facilities are provided under this approach. The central idea of this approach is expansion of goods and services available to the rural poor that will enable them to take benefits from entire range of economic and social activities. However, target group approach is good to identify and take some development measures but it cannot ensure rural development.

Participatory Rural Development

Participatory rural development is an approach of development, planned to enhance sustainability and self-reliance and to achieve social justice through improvements in the quality and quantity of people's participation. The principle objective of participatory development is the qualitative enhancement of people's participation in local self-governance. The central focus of participatory development is not essentially to enhance production of material goods and services; instead, it should promote and enhance people's capability and attitude to have an active role in their society's development. At the end, people should be willing to involve in a wide range of development activities, as agents and beneficiaries of development process. It is the people's participation that is important in the development process. Participatory development is required both as a goal and as a tool of development.

Participatory development is not an attempt to substitute the top-down development approach with a local-community-led-bottom-up approach rather it attempts to introduce a decentralized approach of development in order to remedy the government-led approach's shortcomings and bottlenecks, specifically by focusing on qualitative improvements in grass root participation.

The past experiences of rural development in India have revealed the fact that the top-down government approaches were in one hand concentrated investment of scarce resources into industry while in other hand ignored the rural people and placed them in a passive position because of their insufficient participatory capabilities. This emerged the need of a participatory developmental approach focusing on the decentralized governance system in rural areas. The participatory approach of development ensures sustainable upgrading of participation quality. To achieve this, there is a need of long-term participatory approach with comprehensive developmental initiatives which includes raising the awareness of rural people, forming community groups, upgrading their requisite resource management abilities, and creating norms or internalizing their mechanisms, and improving capabilities for external negotiations. The objectives of participatory rural development are:

- To enhance betterment in the standard of living or well-being of the rural masses by ensuring the provision of basic needs of rural people.
- To establish every sectors of rural areas that is more productive and less vulnerable to climatic shocks, hazards, poverty and any kind of exploitation.
- To ensure self-sustainability of any development initiatives and people's participation in the development process.
- To strengthening decentralized governance system and ensure more local autonomy in the grass root governance.
- To ensure economic growth with equitable distribution of wealth and social justice.
- To ensure sustainable use of rural resources of the country and environmental conservation.
- To enhance the coordination among Government, Non-government and Corporate agencies at national and international levels.
- To ensure good governance through enhancing the level of transparency and accountability.

People's Participation and Rural Development

People's participation is a central feature of present thinking for accelerating rural development. There appears to be a rising consensus that people's participation is indispensable for effective development. The effective people's participation created potentially commanding tool, together with communication and education. Present concerns with people's participation have been a constant theme since the beginning of rural development in all over the globe. Before going to the various aspects of people's participation in rural development, there is a need for defining what constitutes rural development, which would indicate the nature of scope, the limitations and the manner in which people could participate in their development process. Again, the fundamentals of the rural development process are the stimulation of grass root initiatives, development of local leadership, and optimal utilization of local resources. In addition to these, self-help and self-reliance, sustainable interest and co-operation are other important aspects in the concept of rural development. The trust in rural development is people's participation in the total process and in the entire gamut of development, and simultaneously development of people, their conditions and quality of life.

The specific objective of providing for people's participation in the process is imparting the community with knowledge, skills, attitude, strategies, opportunities and support to improve its own performance towards self-sufficiency, self-development and self-sustainability. In concrete terms, the goal of people's participation in rural development could be encouraging and helping rural people to build their own organization and institutions equipped with and capable of accelerating their own development. This indicates that the rural community which is continuously being provided with opportunities for participation in the rural development process will one day take on itself the role which has been played by the development agency. Further, it follows that all development agencies and their programmes have a time-bound engagement in their interventions for the development of the vulnerable sections and thus, the rural people themselves, who have to come forward and take the opportunity to carry forward the development process in a right direction.

In present days, rural development is conceptualized decentralized, people centred and participatory in nature, which give emphasis on the betterment in the quality of life as well as on human resource through people's participation at all stages of development process. People's participation actually means people's involvement with development agencies in planning of activities, fixing up priorities, taking initiatives to implement the projects by giving their knowledge, idea, material, labour and time. The scope of people's participation depends on the nature of involvement, time engaged, the technical specificities, location, the amount of fund, and above all the scope provided by the development agency for community participation at various levels and magnitude of participation expected from the community.

People's participation in rural development is a comprehensive concept which includes all the phases of development, started with community initiation and ended with the sustainability. In the context of rural development, people's participation encompasses with the following facts:

- Reorganization and responding to the development initiation, involve in the process and adapting technologies and innovation;
- Extending ethical support to the process;
- Coordinate with the development agencies;
- Participate in the decision-making process and implementation of the programme;
- Make contribution in terms of fund, time, labour and material;
- Mobilize all types of existing resources in the rural areas;
- Showing leadership and ownership of the programme; and
- Sensitize others to participate in the process.

People's participation in broader view, is beyond the rural or urban development. It is a concept which organize the community and build them more responsive, active and democratic in nature. It is a type of non-formal education and education through active involvement. It is actually a process of learning which transfers the knowledge, skills and attitude to the people while they participate in the development process. Participation is democratic process and it gives equal opportunities to all and also strengthen the democratic structure of the country.

Strategies to Accelerate Rural Development

Rural development is a long run phenomenon and to accelerate the process, it needs effective and flexible strategies both in Central and State levels. In order to accelerate rural development in India it is also essential to make plans and policies keeping in mind the specific objectives and goals that the country wishes to achieve. We have already seen various strategies and approaches of rural development in Indian and realized that there is no single path towards rural development. Experiences of promoting rural development in India and also in other developing counties have suggested some important strategies to accelerate the rural development are discussed below:

Effective Strategy Formulation for Rural Development through Decentralization

In the present context, rural development needs an effective decentralized strategy. The formulation of rural development strategy should be based on a complex decentralized matrix structure with effective mechanism of vertical and horizontal integration, proper development of skill, knowledge and attitude of rural community, institutional leadership, people's participation and effective grass root governance mechanism. It needs a combination of complementary power structure of Central, State and Local governments. All of these three governments possess their own resources and capabilities that should be integrated to complement each other's work. The main challenges in this process is to develop linkages between these development agencies in such a manner that their weaknesses are counter balanced and their comparative strengths are being used for rapid development of rural areas.

Focus on Local Planning through Grass Roots Governance

In a country like India, rural development cannot be achieved unless attention is paid to local level planning. This can be achieved by strengthening the grass root governance which emphasized the problem areas in the sense that they require systems of governance and also ensure that public resources are being delivered efficiently and effectively. Hence, any development initiative has to be related to local resources and requirements. This can add both quantitative and qualitative improvement to the planning processes. The quantum of outcome can be increased by better utilization of resources, both natural, physical and human resources. It can also develop social capital in the rural areas.

The World Bank (1975) also argued that "Ideally, the planning and implementation of rural development programmes involve adequate regional planning, strong central coordination, effective local level organization, and the participation of rural people in the planning and implementation processes. Few countries have been able to come close to this ideal. Regional planning is desirable both because rural development cuts across all sectors and because rural programmes need to be framed to meet regional conditions".

The experiences gathered during the period of experimentation revealed the fact that centralized planning strategy had failed to provide rural employment and ameliorating the conditions of the rural poor in India. It has also been realized that unless planning was made from the lower level the desired result might not have been achieved and there should have been decentralized planning process in grass root level and participation of people through democratic institutions for promoting the rural development.

Promotion of Participatory Approach

A vital fact about rural development is that it can not be delivered to a passive group. Whatever, the programmes are in the field of agriculture, employment generation, health, education, sanitation, environment, infrastructural development or any other, the active participation and cooperation of rural people is must, if the desired results are to be effective, widespread and sustainable. Participatory development is a process where the participants come forward to recognize their requirements, prioritize them, formulate small projects, implement the selected ones, monitor, evaluate and also execute necessary follow up action. Over time it has been realized that it is not the lack of resources and funds that inhibited poverty reduction but it is the lack of interest and poor participation of rural people responsible for rural poverty and inequality. The experiences from precious rural development programmes in India have highlighted the empowerment of people as a strategy. Participatory approach tries to empower local people and emphasized on finding solutions to poverty and other problems that are locally based and involve both economic and social development.

Development of Agriculture and Allied Sectors

Inadequate policies and neglect of agriculture and allied sector is one of the important problems in attacking rural poverty and promote rural development in India. In spite of high economic growth rate and industrial development, India has been very slow in its agricultural development.

The past experiences of rural development has revealed the fact that the fastest, surest and the most effective strategy to alleviate poverty, unemployment and disparity in India is to tap vast unutilized potentials of agriculture and allied sector of India.

Agriculture is a vital development tool for achieving rural development. Majority of India's population depend directly or indirectly on agriculture for their livelihoods. Agriculture is a strong option for spurring growth, overcoming poverty, and enhancing food security in India. Agricultural productivity growth is vital for stimulating growth in other parts of the economy. But accelerated growth requires a sharp productivity increase in small holder farming combined with more effective support to the millions coping as subsistence farmers, many of them in remote areas. Hence, emphasis should be given to generate rural jobs by diversifying into labour-intensive, high-value agriculture linked to a dynamic rural, non-farm sector. Today, rapidly expanding domestic and global markets; institutional innovations in markets, finance, and collective action; and revolutions in biotechnology and information technology all offer exciting opportunities to use agriculture to promote development. But seizing these opportunities will require the political will to move forward with reforms that improve the governance of agriculture.

Balanced Approach for Rural Development

In spite of high economic growth rate India is still suffering from the high incidence of rural poverty, unemployment and inequality which raises the need of a new balanced strategy of development. The balance strategy includes development of modern sector economy, i.e., the industrial development as well as development of traditional rural economy, i.e., the agriculture sector and village industries along with the rural infrastructure and basic needs. This strategy tries to reduce the disparity between the rural-urban economic structures and ensures environmental sustainability.

According to the World Bank (1975) "This requires emphasizing growth of modern sector economy as well as uplift of the traditional sector consisting of the rural poor". It also argues that "a strategy for rural development aimed at raising growth rates and distributing the fruits of growth more fairly implies greater interaction between the modern and traditional sectors, especially in the form of increased trade in farm produce and in technical inputs and services".

Another fact is that the urban and rural areas are interdependent economically, socially and environmentally. At present time, a substantial proportion of the country's population continues to live in rural settlements, particularly in developing countries. In order to achieve a more sustainable future for the country, these rural areas need to be valued and supported. Insufficient infrastructure and services, lack of environmentally sound technology, and pollution resulting from the adverse impacts of unsustainable industrialization and urbanization contribute significantly to the degradation of the rural environment. In addition, lack of employment opportunities in rural areas increases rural-to-urban migration and results in a loss of human capacity in rural communities. Hence, strategies for the sustainable development of rural areas that integrate rural regions into the national economy require strong local and national collaboration for the planning and management of rural areas that place emphasis on rural-urban linkages and treat villages and cities as two ends of a human development continuum.

In coming years we could see a fourfold increase in the size of the global economy and major reductions in poverty, provided that governments act now to avert a growing risk of severe damage to the environment and profound social unrest. Lack of proper policies and poor governance in past decades have contributed to environmental disasters, income inequality, and social imbalance in some areas, often resulting in deep deprivation, riots, refugees fleeing famine and civil wars. Today, many poor people depend on fragile natural resources for livelihood. Similarly, trust between individuals, which can be destroyed by civic unrest, is a social asset with important economic benefits, since it enables people to make agreements and undertake transactions that would otherwise not be possible. So, development policies need to be more sharply focused on protecting these natural and social assets. On the basis of above discussion the World Development Report 2003 suggests "new alliances are needed at the local, national and global levels to better address these problems. The burden for development must be shared more widely. Rich countries must further open their markets and cut agricultural subsidies that depress incomes of third world farmers, and they must increase the flow of aid, medicines, and new technologies to developing countries. Governments in the developing world, in turn, must become more accountable and transparent, and ensure that poor people are able to obtain secure land tenure, as well as access to education, health care, and other basic services".

Focus on Sustainable Development

At present context, sustainable development is a most concern phenomena in India. Globally every country especially the developing countries think very much about it because they realize that their future generation will have to be suffered due to scarcity of resources which is obviously the basic need for survival. The meaning of needs is something that is necessary for the individual to live a healthy life. It is necessary for the sustainable development that the policies and technologies should be green so that environmental ability meets present and future generation in equal manner. Sustainable development ensures the well-being of individual by integrating every spare of life, i.e., socio-economic development, and environmental conservation and protection. The challenges for sustainable development in India are clearly visible which includes high growth rate of population, inequity, scarcity of natural resources and environmental degradation. Thus, there is a need of a clear vision and way of thinking and acting for sustainable development in India. It cannot be brought about through policy and programmes only; it should be brought about by the community at large as a principle guideline of the society.

Sustainable development can be achieved through optimizing gains from several variables, rather than maximizing those from a single one. This requires government departments, by convention sectorally organized, to work together, or in some cases as a single multi-disciplinary authority. For this joint planning, transparency and coordination in implementation are required.

Ensure Equity in Growth among the Rural Poor

It is very obvious that the results of development initiatives must be focused on sustainable development and ensure equitable distribution in the rural areas. This needs specific strategy for development and implementation of programmes in rural areas. It is very unfortunate that, it is not happening at present in India. The past experiences of development initiatives in India indicates that the poverty eradication programmes have successfully provided a certain amount of employment to the rural poor and also generated some durable assets in rural areas but the achievements and impact of these programmes have not been adequate with the resources utilized for them. The income generated through various poverty alleviation programmes has helped the rural poor to either survive or to cross the poverty line only; it could not be used for any asset purchase or entrepreneurial activity. The assets were neither generated in huge amount nor utilized by the rural mass at a large. So, it is necessary to introduce some strategic interventions to help the rural mass to attain sustainable development by increasing their income adequately.

Development of Rural Growth Centres

Growth centre as a concept is a powerful model for promoting rural development in an effective manner. The community development initiative in India has a history of about six decades by now in which rural growth centres have played a significant role in organizing the rural areas. For a developing country like India where majority of the population live in the rural areas, it is necessary that efforts are made to modernize the rural areas and enhance the tempo of economic activity. So it is a very crucial factor for the development planner of rural areas, to identify and locate the growth centres or focal points of growth through which growth impulses could be transmitted to the surrounding areas which would bring some pace in the process of economic development of the entire space.

Strengthen PRIs for Implementation of Rural Development Programmes

The 73rd and 74th Constitutional Amendments have established Panchayati Raj Institutions (PRIs) as the prime organizations for promoting development in rural areas. PRIs have provided with administrative and financial power to run various developmental programmes. However, poor grass root governance and poor people's participation have caused low impact of various developmental initiatives. In present days PRIs have become a political entity rather a development agency. So, it needs to rejuvenate and reorient the PRIs and clear their ultimate objectives. PRIs should be strengthened through capacity building and infrastructure development so that they can handle both administrative and financial issues and implement development programmes with high efficiency.

Provide Safety Nets to the Rural Poor

Nobel Laureate Amartya Sen highly emphasized on provision of safety nets to the rural poor in terms of "economic development without providing safety nets to the rural poor is meaningless". Vulnerability, climate shocks and other risk factors existing in rural areas are the major reasons for rural poverty in India. The rural development cannot be attained until some risk mitigation strategies have been adopted. Thus government strategies to provide safety nets to the rural poor to reduce uncertainty and to increase risk mitigation capabilities of rural people, is very important for effective rural development. Another point is to be noted that infrastructure development, technological improvement, capacity building and access to credit are not sufficient conditions for people's participation as well as effective rural development. So, development strategy should carefully examine various issues and factors related to risk and provide safety nets to the rural poor in terms of insurance, introduction of low cost and improved technology, providing easy access to credit services, improved marketing and processing facilities, providing market intelligence, necessary capacity building and entrepreneurial skill development.

Focus on Region Based Development

The Government of India possesses informality in its policy resolution. However, India is a country of high diversity in its geographic, topographic, social, economic, ethnic, cultural, human and other aspects. Past experiences have shown that government has taken almost similar strategies for every region of the country, i.e., coastal or mountain or plane land or dry area, etc. But it is very obvious that these regions have their own specificities and competitive advantages from each other which needs a variety of policy to development these areas. It is also experienced in India that regional backwardness and political willingness have caused unequal development lead to disparities in some areas. The North East part of India, the Himalayan hills and Tribal based regions are deprived of various developmental issues which results into the regional unrest. In the past although Government has taken some area specific approaches for rural development but it failed to create sustainable impact. So, in the present context it is very necessary to adopt region based development policy framework to speed up the development process.

Ensuring the Access to Basic Services among the Rural Poor

The Government of India has developed various kinds of institutions to provide all kinds of basic services to the rural poor with the expectation that these institutions can improve the rural conditions through acting as a service providers. But situations have not been changed very much in rural areas. The rural poor are still not getting access to various services.

However, it has been realized that the provision of basic services not only causes human development but also an important parameter of economic development and development of physical and financial resources in rural areas. The Eleventh Five Year Plan of the country advocates an inclusive growth which aims at making the benefits of growth reach to all individuals in all sections of the society. The Planning Commission of India in its Approach Paper for the Eleventh Plan (Planning Commission, 2006) explicitly states, "Large parts of our population are still to experience a decisive improvement in their standard of living. The percentage of the population below the poverty line is declining, but only at a modest pace. Far too many people still lack access to basic services such as health, education, clean drinking water and sanitation facilities without which they cannot be empowered to claim their shares in the benefits of growth". Another fact is that the poorer outcomes among the economically weak population could be a result of poor provisioning of the primary services to them. The provisioning of primary access to services thus needs to be checked among the poor and the poorest of the poor population especially in the rural areas. It becomes essential to verify directly such a hypothesis regarding the provisioning of these services to the poor.

Empowerment of Women and Engaging them in the Development Process

A woman is the nucleus of the family, particularly, in rural India. Unfortunately, in spite of their laudable and vulnerable roles, which cannot be substituted by machine or men, women have been neglected since generations. Active participation of any community in the development process is recognized as a tool for its empowerment. In Indian social set-up, the participation of women in the development process has to be ensured through tangible measures taken at various levels for their overall development. The government has taken a conscious view to make adequate provisions in its policies and programmes, through which it is to be ensured that the women of the country are not only empowered but also become active participants in the development process in the country. In present context some gender sensitive women empowerment strategies are to be taken which includes:

- Drudgery reduction to facilitate participation in economic development.

- Involvement in decision-making process, identification of strategic gender needs and addressing them.
- Capacity building in technical skills, information sharing and leadership development.
- Formation of Self-Help Groups for solidarity, awareness and motivation, addressing common problems and micro-financing.
- Economic development: Enhance abilities to contribute to family income, access to credit and assets and reduce economic dependence.
- Staff orientation: To adopt suitable approaches to address the problems and encourage participatory development.
- Gender vigilance to ensure women's participation in all fronts and access to benefits in training, entrepreneurship and activities of Panchayati Raj Institutions (PRIs).

Enhancement of Accountability and Transparency in Governance

In recent years, Government of India has realized that the 'transparent and accountable governance' is a major issue for the country. In spite of substantial enhancement of public sector outlays for basic social sector development, it failed to provide desired outcomes of education, health, water and sanitation. Poor governance and lack of transparency and accountability is responsible for this paradox. The Eleventh Five Year Plan explicitly focused on the urgent requirement of improving governance for inclusive growth (Planning Commission, 2008).

According to Levy (2007), "Public sector governance refers to the way that the state acquires and exercises the authority to provide and manage public goods and services, including both public capacities and public accountabilities". Governance is distinct from government, and is the process through which various stakeholders articulate their interests, exercise their rights, and mediate their differences (Debroy, 2004). Transparency means, the criteria, process and systems of decision-making are openly known to all in a public manner while accountability means being answerable for the performance of tasks assigned to a person. Accountability requires the clear specification of tasks to be performed, the time frame and budget available for performing those tasks. It is clear that the Government of India is following a set of standards for reforming governance in the country, which are essentially citizen-centric-transparency, accountability and efficiency of all institutions, agencies and actors of the government, with particular attention to those citizens who have been largely excluded so far. However, India is still experiencing misappropriation of government funds and corruption in the various government programmes. Thus strategy is required to stop corruption practices and enhance accountability and transparency in governance system.

Civil Societies and Rural Development

The role of civil societies became crucial after Independence, especially after 1970s. Development practitioners, government officials and foreign donors consider that civil societies by virtue of being small scale, flexible, innovative and participatory, are more effective and successful in reaching the poor and in poverty alleviation. Civil societies like NGOs, Trusts and Volunteer Organisations (VOs) involved in initiating and implementing rural development programme.

Civil societies like NGOs, Trusts and Volunteer Organizations are a legally constituted organizations created by legal persons that operate independently from any government and a term usually used by governments to refer to entities that have no government status. These organizations are funded totally or partially by governments and foreign agencies. The civil societies are of different types based on their functional attributes. Some of them work directly with the oppressed sections of society at grass roots level while some provide services that would strengthen the capacities of grass roots NGOs, Panchayati Raj Institutions, co-operatives and others to function more effectively. Some organizations act as a forum or network to share experiences, carry out joint development endeavours as well as engage in lobbying, advocacy and policy making.

Conclusion

The process of development has been considered as a guaranteed mechanism of progressive transformation. The term of rural development includes a wide range of development initiatives that focus at developing rural areas through the creation of all types of assets to ameliorate the condition of the rural people. Rural development in India is essentially an aspect of planned development launched by the Government of India in terms of succession of programmes and strategies formulated in the Five Year Plans of national development and viewed as an integral part of national development.

Rural development is the prime focus of the recent time and hence a matter of global concern. It is because rural people make the largest pool of human capital. The rural areas provide livelihood to a large section of India's population through agriculture and allied activities. The urban sectors also depend on rural areas for its survival. However, the present condition of rural people is desperate. Majority of the rural population are victim of vicious of poverty, illiteracy, malnutrition, and deprived condition and considered as the bottom of the pyramid. Hence, the development of the poorest of the poor in the rural areas is of course a prime aspect and also vital for survival of the nation as a whole.

In Indian point of view rural development may be defined as optimization of production in agriculture and allied sectors in rural areas including rejuvenation of rural industries with emphasis on village and cottage industries, promoting maximum possible livelihood opportunities in rural areas especially for the most vulnerable section of the society so as to help them to improve their living standard and providing certain basic necessities like drinking water, electricity, communication facilities, health care, education, credit and marketing facilities and other important infrastructure in the rural areas.

In the concluding remarks rural development would thus mean improving the quality of life or what is now termed as increasing the human happiness. To separate the rural fabric of society and economy from the total society seems to be artificial and false. The basic hypothesis which is advanced is that we cannot develop the rural sector as a separate entity which is allowing the non-rural sector as constant. There can be no rural development that does not have any effort on the total economy and on the total society. Thus process of rural development ensures the overall development both for rural and urban settlement.

References

Arora, R.C.; (1979), *Integrated Rural Development*, S. Chand & Company, New Delhi.

Biju, M.R. (ed); (2012), *Rural Development Under Decentralised Governance,* Concept Publishing Company Pvt. Ltd., New Delhi.

Census Report; (2001) Government of India, New Delhi.

Chamber, Robert; (1983), *Rural Development: Putting the Last First*, Longman, London.

Copp, James, H.; (1972), Rural Sociology and Rural Development, *Rural Sociology*, Volume 37, December 1972.

Dar, S.U.; (1992), *Impact of Integrated Rural Development Programme*, Anmol Publications, New Delhi.

Debroy, B.; (2004), *Agenda for Improving Governance*. Academic Foundation, New Delhi.

Deogaonkar, S.G.; (1980), *Administration for Rural Development*, Concept Publishing Company, New Delhi.

Deogaonkar, S.G.; (1994), *Tribal Administration and Development*, Concept Publishing Company, New Delhi.

Desai, A.R.; (1969), *Rural Sociology in India*, Popular Prakashan, Bombay.

Desai, Vasant; (1991), *Rural Development,* Himalaya Publishing House, New Delhi.

Dutta, S.K.; (1991), *Cooperative Societies and Rural Development*, Mittal Publications, New Delhi.

Dutta, Sujit K; Ghosh, Dilip K.; (1994), "Peoples Participation in Rural Development: Need and Scope", *Participation and Governance,* Vol. 1, No. 2, November 1994.

Dwivedi, Rishi Muni; (2005), *Poverty and Development Programmes in India*, New Century Publications, New Delhi.

Goel, S.L. and Kumar, R.; (2004), *Administration and Management of NGOs,* Deep & Deep, New Delhi.

Haq, Khalija; (1995), Poverty has a woman's face, published in *Our Planet,* 15-17.

Haragopal, G.; (1980), *Administrative Leadership and Rural Development in India,* Light and Life Publishers, New Delhi.

Ickis, John, C.; (1983) Structural Response to New Rural Development Strategies, Ed. by David, C., Korten and Falip, B., *Bureaucracy and the Poor: Closing the Gap*, Kumarian Press, West Hartford.

Jafri, S.S.A. and Bajpai, B.K. (eds); (2012), *Rural-Urban Fringe: Problems and Management*, Concept Publishing Company Pvt. Ltd., New Delhi.

Jalihal, K.A. and Shivamurthy, M.; (2003), *Pragmatic Rural Development for Poverty Alleviation: A Pioneering Paradigm*, Concept Publishing Company, New Delhi.

Joshi, R.P.; Narwani, G.S.; (2002), *Panchayat Raj in India—Emerging Trends across the States,* Rawat Publications, Jaipur and New Delhi.

Karalay, G.N.; (2005), *Integrated Approach to Rural Development—Policies, Programmes and Strategies*, Concept Publishing Company, New Delhi.

Kothari, Shanti, and Roy, Ramashray; (1981), *Relation between Politicians and Administrators at the District Level*, Indian Institute of Public Administration, New Delhi.

Levy, Brian; (2007), *Governance Reform: Bridging Monitoring and Action*. Washington DC. The World Bank.

Maheshwari, Shriram; (1995), *Rural Development in India—A Public Policy Approach,* Sage Publication, New Delhi.

Mehta. Shiv R.; (1984), *Rural Development Policies and Programmes*, Sage Publications, New Delhi.

Pachauri, S.K.; (1984), *Dynamics of Rural Development in Tribal Areas,* Concept Publishing Company, New Delhi.

Pannikar, K.K.; (1974), *Community Development in Kerala*, S. Chand & Co. Pvt. Ltd., New Delhi.

Paul, Sujit Kumar; (2008), "Self-Help Group: The Association for Rural Indian Women", in Suzanne Arcand *et al.* (eds). *Violences faits aux Femmes,* Presses de l'Universite du Quebec, Canada.

Paul, Sujit Kumar; (2011), Women Participation for Building of Model Villages: Ability and Participation of the Gram Panchayat Members, *Man and Life, A Journal of the Institute of Social Research and Applied Anthropology,* Vol. 37, No. 3 and 4.

Planning Commission (Government of India); (2008), *Eleventh Five Year Plan 2007-2012, Vol. I, Inclusive Growth.* New Delhi, Oxford University Press.

Rao, Raghab; (1980), *Panchayats and Rural Development,* Asish Publishing Housing, New Delhi,

Roy, Upendranath and Singh Saini, Jasmer (eds); (2009), *People's Empowerment and Sustainable Rural Development—A Technological Approach*, Rawat Publications, New Delhi.

Sen, Amartya; (1998), Address at the first press conference on 15th October, 1998 after getting the Nobel Prize, published in *Economic Times,* on 16th October, 1998.

Sharma, Om Prakash; (1987), *Rural Reconstruction in India,* Anmol Publications, Delhi,

Sharma, Soumitra; (1983), *Development Strategy and Development Countries,* South Asian Publishers Pvt. Ltd., New Delhi.

Singh, B.D.; (1992), *Planning for Rural Development and Poverty Alleviation,* Mittal Publication, New Delhi.

Singh, Katar; (2009), *Rural Development: Principles, Policies and Management,* Sage Publication India Pvt. Ltd., New Delhi.

Singh, Prabhakar; (1982), Community Development Programme in India, Deep & Deep Publications, New Delhi.

Srinivas, M.N.; (1982), Social Structure, Hindustan Publishing Corporation, Delhi.

Thomas William, A. and Shristopher, A.J.; (2011), *Rural Development—Concept and Recent Approaches*, Rawat Publications, New Delhi.

UNCTAD; (1997), UNCTAD Report, published in *Deccan Herald*, September 27, 1997.

Varma, R.B.S.; (1995), "Development Administration and Integrated Rural Development Programme", *Contemporary Social Work,* Vol. XII, April 1995.

Varma, Ravi; (1967), Ramrajya and Community Development, *Kurukshetra,* A symposium Publication Division, Government of India.

World Bank; (1975), *Rural Development—Sector Policy Paper,* Washington D.C., U.S.A.

World Bank; (2003), *World Development Report 2003—Sustainable Development with a Dynamic Economy,* Washington D.C., U.S.A.

World Bank; (2008), *World Development Report 2008—Agriculture for Development*, Washington D.C., U.S.A.

2

Sustainable Rural Livelihood

Introduction

Livelihood development is defined as adequate and sustainable access to income and resources to meet basic needs. The livelihood pattern of the population throws a searching light on the economic and social life of the area. Livelihood approaches are a way of thinking about the objectives, scope and priorities for development. They place people and their priorities at the centre of development. They focus poverty reduction interventions on empowering the poor to build on their own opportunities, supporting their access to assets, and developing an enabling policy and institutional environment. The Sustainable Livelihood approach defines livelihoods as the capabilities, assets (including both material and social resources) and activities required for a means of living. Livelihood strategies are the combination of activities that people choose to undertake in order to achieve their livelihood goals. They include productive activities, investment strategies and reproductive choices. Livelihood approaches try to understand the strategies pursued and the factors behind people's decisions to reinforce the positive aspects of these strategies and mitigate against constraints. The choice of strategies is a dynamic process in which people combine activities to meet their changing needs.

The central aim of enhancing economic productivity of India is to improve the overall welfare of majority of Indian households who are living below poverty line. As we are observing since six decades after independence, the existence of people in a state of social, economic, political and knowledge disempowerment is considered to be a major hindrance to overall development. The global economy, even at the dawn of twenty-first century can be encapsulated in one sharp contrast: the widening inequalities and disparity between the rich and the poor. On the one hand the affluent sections enjoy comfortable life style; on the other hand the poorest of the poor live in severe deprivation characterized by illiteracy, malnutrition, lack of shelter, vulnerability to diseases, lack of educational opportunities and employment opportunities.

After 66 years of freedom, India has not been able to provide the expected physical, mental, social and political development to its citizens. Years ago, poverty had been a social curse for the country. Today, though the ratio has declined a little, yet it is still an issue of concern. There have been several changes in both the Central as well as State Governments in terms of leadership but none have been able to make any dent in the developmental process. Over the years, there have been constitutional commitments, amendments, long-term and short-term planning, processes and various other minor beneficial schemes, plans and projects by the successive Governments for poverty alleviation with major issue of reaching the un-reached, yet the plight of poverty remained same.

Mass poverty is one of the major critical problems confronting planners in India. Poverty can be defined as a social phenomenon in which a section of the society is unable to fulfil even its basic necessities of life. In India, poverty is mainly a rural problem. More than 68 per cent of the country's population lives in rural areas and about 193 million rural people are poor. For more than 15 per cent of rural poor people, poverty is a chronic condition. Agriculture wage earners, small and marginal farmers and casual workers engaged in non-agricultural activities, constitute the bulk of the rural poor. Such a high incidence of poverty is a matter of concern in view of the fact that poverty eradication has been one of the major objectives of the development planning process. Initially, India adopted a development strategy which was based on the trickle down concept. Then the government realized the need for direct intervention in favour of the poor, since that development strategy failed to meet the basic needs of millions of the rural poor. Consequently, the government embarked on the preparation and implementation of comprehensive and coherent antipoverty programmes.

Livelihood development lies at the very root of a society. It is the watchword especially in the context of poverty alleviation and rural development because rural poor are too unorganized and powerless to be individually able to better their lot in societies. The benefits of growth failed to trickle down to the poor who are often marginalized if not excluded from the mainstream of development process. Developing rural poor enhances the self-confidence, dignity and self-determination capacity of rural and poor people to eliminate the implicit and explicit socio-economic disadvantages and thereby provides a means to improve the effectiveness of development policy initiatives and programmes.

India is one of the oldest civilization and biggest democracy in the world. It possesses rich and highly diversified socio-cultural heritage. The economic structure is predominantly rural in nature with 68.84 per cent rural population (as per Census data 2011) and about 52 per cent of its population is engaged in agriculture and allied activities. Agriculture and allied activities support more than one billion people and contributes about 13.7 per cent of India's Gross Domestic Product (as per Central Statistics Office data 2012-13) of current price. Over the last six decades of Independence, India has achieved impressive progress in the field of science and technology, and is now self-sufficient in foodgrain and milk production. On other side, India has not yet been able to develop and harness its human and natural resources for the benefit of its people and it has yet to solve its problems of illiteracy, poverty, unemployment and vulnerability to natural calamities. In a predominantly rural country like India, rural development is *sine qua non* of overall development and rural livelihood development especially the agriculture and non-farm sector is a prerequisite for rural development.

India's commitment to planned economic development reflects government's determination to improve the economic condition of its people and an affirmation of the role of the government in bringing about this outcome through a variety of social, economic, and institutional means. India's First Five Year Plan (1951-56) was aimed at equity development and economic stabilization. This Plan supported community development aimed at transforming the social and economic conditions of the villages. It was holistically designed to simultaneously achieve the goals of growth, welfare, equity development and community participation. The Second Five Year Plan initiated structural transformation with an emphasis on rapid increase in agricultural production, heavy industrialization and economic growth. The first two plans laid the foundation for development planning in India. In the present day context of a changing economic scenario, increasing population pressure on resources and hence, the livelihoods of the people, especially the poor, has emerged as an important challenge for the nation. Over the years, many institutions, government and non-government have made several attempts to address this issue. Some of these efforts have been in terms of actions or interventions, while others have tried to change the context within which the livelihoods are embedded. In all, there have been many efforts and, therefore, there has been a growing need for stocktaking, something that has been voiced at many forums.

A critical element in India's Twelfth Five Year Plan (2012-2017) is the generation of productive and gainful employment on a sufficient scale. The aim of such planning is to systematically absorb the growing working population in the unorganized sector of an expanding economy. This sector contributes about sixty per cent of the country's GDP. In fact it employs workers in micro enterprises, unpaid family work, casual labour and home based work on a mammoth scale. In addition, it also absorbs migrant labourers, farmers, artisans and more importantly out of school rural youth. Having discussed the different views about livelihoods and different frameworks to understand it, researchers argues that though Article 39 of the Constitution of India recognizes the right to livelihood, efforts in this direction are wanting. It highlights the fact that labour shortages in India coexist with massive unemployment. Employment growth in recent years accelerated to 2.62 per cent per annum from 1.25 per cent in the last decade. But the labour force grew at a faster rate of 2.84 per cent with an increase in unemployment rate. Though GDP growth rates have touched new heights, employment has not caught up in this period of 'Jobless Growth'. While the tertiary sector offered the best potential for supporting large number of livelihoods, both in terms of their contribution to GDP and their employment growth, these sectors were dependent on the agricultural and manufacturing sectors, which offered no or little potential to support more livelihoods.

Livelihood—Definition and Concept

While defining livelihood, there may be many definition for the term. "Generating Income", "Making a living", or "Supporting a family" all designate a livelihood. Livelihood is the activities, the assets and the access that jointly determine the living gained by an individual or household (Ellis, 2000). Livelihood is always more than just a matter of findings or making shelter, transacting money and preparing food to put on the table or exchange in the market place. It is equally a matter of the ownership and circulation of information, the management of social relationship, the affirmation of personal significance and group identity, and the inter-relation of each of these tasks to the other. All these productive tasks together constitute a livelihood (Wallman, 1984). Understanding livelihood begins with understanding how people structure their means of living—how they use capabilities, assets, and activities in a resilient manner to sniff around and look for opportunities, to diversify by adding enterprises, and to multiply activities and relationships for stability. It basically encompasses people's capabilities, assets, income and activities required to secure the necessities of life. Livelihoods can also be defined as a set of activities a household engages in on a regular basis in order to generate adequate cash and non-cash income to maintain a minimum desired standard of living, both on a day-to-day basis and over a longer period of time. People who live with livelihood know and closely assess their assets. Assets include many things: skills, capabilities and talents, ability to work, time, health, networks of relationships, etc., as well as resources such as money or land. Assets and resources are combined with opportunities to construct a livelihood that focuses on living in the environment, rather than on income and consumption. Livelihood is a dynamic and complex process that combines activities to meet various needs at various times. It can mean having a portfolio of jobs rather than one. It may mean managing a portfolio of crops or livestock, instead of a monoculture of one or two. It could mean developing a portfolio of enterprises and activities for different seasons and looking at the entire family with all their relationships as part of the process instead of focusing on a "breadwinner".

In other words livelihood can be defined as adequate stock and flow of food and cash with an individual or a family to meet its basic needs. Livelihood security then means secured ownership of, or access to, resources and income-earning activities, including reserves and assets to offset risks, ease shocks and meet contingencies. There are four principal ways of acquiring livelihoods by the rural households:

1. *First is the production-based livelihood.* A large proportion of the small and marginal farmers gain livelihoods through production on small pieces of land.
2. *Second is the labour-based livelihood.* Most of the small landholders and landless rural households derive livelihoods by selling their labour.
3. *Third is the exchange or market-based livelihood.* Those rural households which produce surplus food and non-food agricultural products or non-farm goods earn their livelihoods by selling these surpluses in the market.
4. *The fourth set of livelihoods is transfer-based entitlements.* The households without any income-earning asset or able-bodied persons to work depend for their livelihoods on transfers from the government or other social organizations.

The term is also well recognized as humans intrinsically develop and implement strategies to ensure their survival. A livelihood can sometimes generate enough income, but may not be desirable or dignified, such as being a beggar. In other cases, a livelihood may generate sufficient income and may even be reasonably dignified, but may not offer adequate opportunities to participate in the wider social, cultural or political aspects of the community one lives in. In yet other cases, it may be adequate, dignified and offer opportunities to participate in social, cultural or political life, but may not be sustainable, as it may be based on fast-dwindling of natural resources.

Sustainable Livelihood Framework

In order to better understand how people build up and sustain livelihoods, the UK Department for International Development (DFID), building on the work of practitioners and academics, developed the Sustainable Livelihoods Framework (SLF). This framework is an analytical tool, useful for understanding the many factors that affect a person's livelihood and how those factors interact with each other. However, the sustainable livelihoods idea was first introduced by the Brundtland Commission on Environment and Development as a way of linking socioeconomic and ecological considerations in a cohesive, policy-relevant structure. The 1992 United Nations Conference on Environment and Development (UNCED) expanded the concept, especially in the context of Agenda 21, and advocated for the achievement of sustainable livelihoods as a broad goal for poverty eradication. It stated that sustainable livelihoods could serve as 'an integrating factor' that allows policies to address 'development, sustainable resource management, and poverty eradication simultaneously' (UNDP, 1997). Most of the discussion on Sustainable Livelihood (SL) so far has focused on rural areas and situations where people are farmers or make a living from some kind of primary self- managed production. In a classic 1992 paper, Sustainable Rural Livelihoods: Practical concepts for the twenty-first Century, Robert Chambers and Gordon Conway proposed the following composite definition of a sustainable rural livelihood: "A livelihood comprises the capabilities, assets (stores, resources, claims and access) and activities required for a means of living—a livelihood is sustainable which can cope with and recover from stress and shocks, maintain or enhance its capabilities and assets, and provide sustainable livelihood opportunities for the next generation; and which contributes net benefits to other livelihoods at the local and global levels and in the short and long-term". Of the various components of a livelihood, the most complex is the portfolio of assets out of which people construct their living, which includes both tangible assets and resources, and intangible assets such as claims and access. Any definition of livelihood sustainability, the authors argued, has to include the ability to avoid, or more usually to withstand and recover from, such stresses and shocks. More recently the Institute for Development Studies (IDS) and the UK Department for International Development (DFID) have been putting into operation the Sustainable Livelihood (SL) concept and approach.

At present context, Sustainable Livelihoods Framework is one of the most universally used frameworks for understanding livelihoods. The adoption of a livelihood approach within DFID resulted from the publication of the 1997 UK Government White Paper on International Development, where it was declared that the overriding aim of DFID is the elimination of poverty in poorer countries. DFID's definition of sustainable livelihood follows the one developed by IDS and which in turn is a modified version of the original definition elaborated by Chambers & Conway. The core principles of DFID to underpinning the approach are listed below (*Source*: Ashley & Carney 1999):

- *People-centred*: Sustainable poverty elimination will be achieved only if external support focuses on what matters to people, understands the difference between groups of people, and works with them in a way that is congruent with their current livelihood strategies, social environment, and ability to adapt.
- *Responsive and participatory*: Poor people themselves must be key actors in identifying and addressing livelihood priorities. Outsiders need processes that enable them to listen and respond to the poor.
- *Multi-level*: Poverty elimination is an enormous challenge that will only be overcome by working at multiple levels, ensuring that micro-level activity informs the development of policy and an effective enabling environment, and that macro-level structures and processes support people to build upon their own strengths.
- *Conducted in partnership*: With both the public and the private sectors.
- *Sustainable*: There are four key dimensions to sustainability—economic, institutional, social and environmental sustainability. All are important—a balance must be found between them.

- *Dynamic*: External support must recognize the dynamic nature of livelihood strategies, respond flexibly to changes in people's situation, and develop longer term commitments.

Sustainable Livelihood (SL) approaches must be underpinned by a commitment to poverty eradication. Although they can, in theory, be applied to work with any stakeholder group, an implicit principle for DFID is that activities should be designed to maximize livelihood benefits for the poor (Ashley and Carney, 1999).

A central element of DFID's SL approach is the Sustainable Livelihood Framework (SLF). The framework is not intended to be an exact model of reality, but to provide an analytical structure to facilitate a broad and systematic understanding of the various factors that constrain or enhance livelihood opportunities, and to show how they relate to each other. It should further be noted that the framework as such does not lay down any explicit definition of what exactly constitutes poverty, which is context-specific and, therefore, must be investigated on a case-by-case basis with different groups (DFID, 1999).

This framework is an analytical device, useful for understanding the many factors that influence a person's livelihood and how those factors interact with each other. The SLF views livelihoods as systems and provides a way to recognize:

- The assets/resources people draw upon,
- The strategies people build up to make a living,
- The circumstance within which a livelihood is developed, and
- Those factors that make a livelihood more or less vulnerable to shocks and stresses.

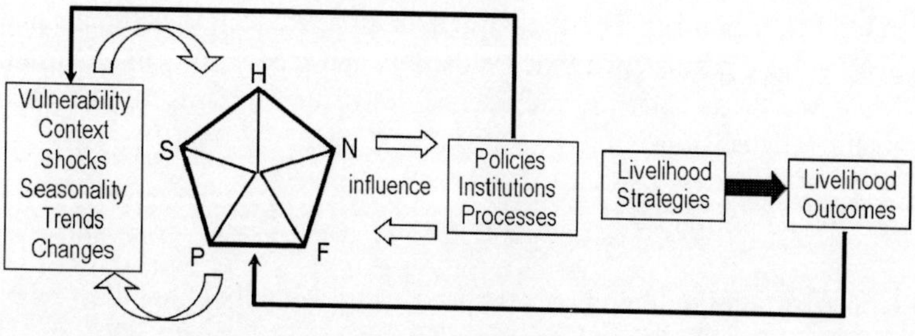

Source: DFID, 1999.

Fig. 2.1: Sustainable Livelihood Framework

The Sustainable Livelihood Framework is built around five principal categories of livelihood assets, graphically depicted as a pentagon to underline their interconnections and the fact that livelihoods depend on a combination of assets of various kinds and not just from one category. An important part of the analysis is thus to find out people's access to different types of assets (physical, human, financial, natural, and social) and their ability to put these to productive use. The framework offers a way of assessing how organisations, policies, institutions, cultural norms shape livelihoods, both by determining who gains access to which type of asset, and defining what range of livelihood strategies are open and attractive to people (Carney, 1998).

Livelihood Assets

Assets may be substantial, such as food stores and cash savings, as well as trees, land, livestock, tools, and other resources. Assets may also be insubstantial such as claims one can make for food, work, and assistance as well as access to materials, information, education, health services and employment opportunities. Another way of conceptualizing the assets or capitals, that people draw upon to make a living is to classify them into the following five groups: human, social, natural, physical, financial, and political capitals.

Livelihood Context

Livelihoods are formed within social, economic and political contexts. Institutions, processes and policies, such as markets, social norms, and land ownership policies influence our ability to access and use assets for a favourable outcome. As these contexts change they create new livelihood obstacles or opportunities. Livelihoods are also formed by the altering natural environment. The quality of soil, air and water; the climatic and geographic circumstances; the availability and accessibility of fauna and flora; and the occurrence and intensity of natural hazards all influence livelihood decisions.

Livelihood Strategies

Under certain livelihood context people utilize the livelihood assets or capitals to form livelihood strategies. The range and diversity of livelihood strategies are enormous. An individual may take on several activities to meet his/her requirements. One or many individuals may engage in activities that add to a collective livelihood strategy. Within households, individuals often take on different responsibilities to enable the sustenance and growth of the family.

Vulnerability Context

The potency of a given livelihood is not only considered by its productive outcomes, but equally by its resilience and flexibility to shocks, seasonal changes and trends. Shocks might include natural disasters, wars, and economic downturns. Availability of resources, income-generating opportunities, and demand for certain products and services may alter seasonally. More gradual and often predictable, trends in politics and governance, technology use, economics, and availability of natural resources, can pose serious obstacles to the future of many livelihoods. These changes impact the availability of assets and the opportunities to transform those assets into a "livelihood". Under such circumstances, people must adapt existing strategies or develop new strategies in order to survive.

Livelihood Framework

Here, a household is posited to have access to five types of capital: human, social, natural, physical, and financial. Human capital refers to the ability to labour, skills, intelligence and talent. Social capital includes trust, status, networks, local institutions and norms. Natural capital includes land, water, forests, minerals and agro-climatic conditions. Physical capital includes tools, plant and machinery, and roads, electricity supply, etc. Financial capital includes cash, savings deposits, insurance paid up, debts given to others and bonds and shares, if any in an enterprise. These five types of capital/assets give a household a livelihood platform, and access to this is either improved or let down by social relations such as gender and caste, or by institutions such as customs, land tenure or market practices. A household adopts different livelihood strategies in the context of demographic trends, technical changes and policies and programmes, as well specific shocks like a drought, an epidemic or civil unrest. These comprise a set of natural resource-based activities such as farming, livestock rearing or fishing, as well as other activities like trading. Coping strategies adopted in times of crisis include sale of assets, diversification and migration. If successful, these strategies lead to livelihood security at the level of a household, and more widely, for the community. In a happy scenario, the strategies are also sustainable environment.

DFID's SL approach is not a 'programming framework' in the sense that it obviously spells out the various steps to be taken in the planning of concrete SL programmes. Instead, it represents 'a way of thinking' about poverty, focusing on the livelihoods of the poor to facilitate the identification of issues or areas that should be addressed in a specific circumstance to reduce poverty. This is not to say that there are no strategic concerns influencing the choice of areas for intervention. For DFID, the two most important areas for effective contribution are (Krantz Lasse, 2001):

- Direct support to assets (i.e., providing poor people with better access to the assets that act as a foundation for their livelihoods); and
- Support to the more effective functioning of the structures and processes (policies, public and private sector organizations, markets, social relations, etc.) that influence not only access to assets but also which livelihood strategies are open to people.

Generally speaking, the idea is that if people have better access to assets they will have more ability to influence structures and processes so that these become more responsive to their needs (Carney *et al.*, 1999).

Poverty, Employment and Income

For understanding the livelihood scenario in the country, we need to first take a close look at the present employment situation, trends and quality of employment, followed by the existing level of income and poverty scenario of the country. It is significant that the percentage decadal population growth during 2001-2011 has registered a sharp decline since independence. For 2001-2011, decadal growth rate has become 17.64 per cent with a decrease of 3.90 per cent. Although in absolute term, the population of India has increased by about 181 million during the decade 2001-2011. It is expected that the annual growth rate would be in the same order of magnitude for the next few years of this decade, and persons added in the last two decades would need jobs or employment.

The decline in overall growth of employment during 1993-94 to 1999-2000 was largely due to the lower absorption in agriculture. The share of agriculture in total employment dropped from 61 per cent to 57 per cent and further dropped to 52 per cent in 2004-05. Following the same trend India has crossed the historic point that is less than 50 per cent of the total employment would be in the agricultural sector. While the manufacturing sector's share increased marginally during this period, trade, the hotel and restaurant sector contributed significantly more to the overall employment than in earlier years. The other important sectors whose shares in employment have increased are transport, storage and communications apart from financial, insurance, real estate, business and community, social and personal services.

Majority of India's working population are in the unorganized sector. Income levels and income security in the unorganized sector are much lower than in the organized sector. Another characteristic feature of the employment situation in the country is that the percentage of workers employed on regular salaried employment (16%) is small. The bulk of the workforce is either self-employed (53%) or employed in casual wage employment (31%). Income levels and income security for the self-employed and the casual wage employed are much lower.

Poverty is another aggregate which reflects the prevailing livelihoods scenario in the country. A paper by Arjun Sengupta *et al.* of the National Commission for Enterprises in the Unorganized Sector (NCEUS) used consumption expenditure data to show that around three quarters of India's population are poor and vulnerable and their numbers were a staggering 836 million as of 2004-05, of this, 21.8 per cent of the people can be regarded as poor or extremely poor. It is the fact that, four groups of people—extremely poor, poor, marginal and vulnerable—constituted about 77 per cent of the population in 2004-05. Most of them are living with below the international level of poverty of $2 per day—the common man, who has been bypassed by the high levels of growth.

As per Planning Commission of India, the percentage of persons below the Poverty Line in 2011-12 has been estimated as 25.7 per cent in rural areas, 13.7 per cent in urban areas and 21.9 per cent for the country as a whole. The respective ratios for the rural and urban areas were 41.8 per cent and 25.7 per cent and 37.2 per cent for the country as a whole in 2004-05. It was 50.1 per cent in rural areas, 31.8 per cent in urban areas and 45.3 per cent for the country as a whole in 1993-94. In 2011-12, India had 270 million persons below the Tendulkar Poverty Line as compared to 407 million in 2004-05, that is a reduction of 137 million persons over the seven years period.

It is important to note that although the trend decline documented above is based on the Tendulkar poverty line which is being reviewed and may be revised by the Rangarajan Committee, an increase in the

Table 2.1: Percentage and Number of Poor Estimated by Tendulkar method, using Mixed Reference Period (MRP)

	Poverty Ratio (%)			*Number of Poor (million)*		
	Rural	*Urban*	*Total*	*Rural*	*Urban*	*Total*
1. 1993-94	50.1	31.8	45.3	328.6	74.5	403.7
2. 2004-05	41.8	25.7	37.2	326.3	80.8	407.1
3. 2011-12	25.7	13.7	21.9	216.5	52.8	269.3
Annual Average Decline: 1993-94 to 2004-05 (percentage points per annum)	0.75	0.55	0.74	—	—	—
Annual Average Decline: 2004-05 to 2011-12 (percentage points per annum)	2.32	1.69	2.18	—	—	—

Source: Planning Commission, GOI, 2013.

poverty line will not alter the fact of a decline. While the absolute levels of poverty would be higher, the rate of decline would be similar.

Although the Indian economy has grown steadily over the last two decades, its growth has been uneven when comparing social groups, economic groups, geographic regions, and rural and urban areas. Despite significant economic progress, one quarter of the nation's population earns less than the government-specified poverty threshold of 32 per day (Ghosh, 2012). Since the early 1950s, Indian government initiated various programmes and schemes to facilitate the poor attain self-sufficiency in food production. These have included ration cards and price controls over the supply of basic commodities, particularly food at controlled prices, available throughout the country. Various employment generation programmes also were introduced for poverty alleviation and rural development. However, these efforts prevented famines, but did little to eliminate or reduce poverty in rural or urban areas between 1950 and 1980. After 1991, in India the poverty has been declined at a record rate due to rapid economic growth rate of the country. Another factor anticipated is India's launch of social welfare programmes such as Mahatma Gandhi National Rural Employment Guarantee Act (MGNREGA) and Mid-Day Meal Scheme in Government Schools. It has been found in various studies that MGNREGA helps reduce rural poverty gap (intensity of rural poverty), seasonal poverty, but not overall poverty.

Livelihood and Vulnerability Context

Vulnerability context is a vital factor while discussing poverty, income and rural livelihood generation. There is a close association between poverty and vulnerability, and social identity. The two social groups who are at the bottom of the pyramid by this classification are the Scheduled Castes/Scheduled Tribes (SCs/STs), who form the bottom layer, and the Muslims, who are in the next stratum. The next group is the OBCs. Another vulnerable and marginalized section is the women. In spite huge contribution in the society women who face huge social and economic discrimination and deprivation. This does not mean that the other groups are in far better and improved situation. Even for those who do not belong to any of these groups, the incidence of poverty is 55 per cent.

The depth of poverty is not identical across social groups even within the category of poor. What are most significant are the facts that this systemic and hierarchical segmentation along social groups is also reflected across economic groups represented by consumption expenditure classes, low education and informal work status. Within these economic groups, the only change in ranking is within the intermediate category of OBCs and Muslims in terms of per capita consumption. The latter has a marginally higher per capita consumption than the former among the poor and vulnerable but this edge is absent when all economic groups are combined.

The Scheduled Castes (SC) who account for over 16 per cent of the population, remain backward in economic and social development and are vulnerable to various forms of discrimination. Mostly landless and assetless with little access to basic amenities, the incidence of poverty, illiteracy and ill health among them is significantly higher compared to the rest of the population.

The Scheduled Tribes account for about 8 per cent of the population of the country but comprise a significant proportion of the poor and illiterate in the country. The STs are the aboriginal or indigenous inhabitants of India, concentrated in the central and north-eastern parts of the country. For centuries they have been living a simple life based on the natural resources and developed a cultural pattern congenial to their physical and the consequent social environment. The livelihood structure was also primitive in nature and based on local resources. Co-operative and collective endeavour has been a strongly developed feature of their economy. While landlessness is not a major problem for the STs, most of the land owned by them is of substandard quality. Moreover, their isolation from the mainstream on account of geographical location often renders them victims of the development process.

Women are the integral part of the society as they contribute in both productive and non-productive household activities. In spite of these women face economic insufficiency and social discrimination. Women enjoy poor decision-making power and less control over cash. These make women more vulnerable from both social and economic angel.

Agriculture and Rural Livelihood

The rural sector constitutes the basic foundation of India's economy. The agricultural sub-sector occupies a place of pride in India's economy and will continue to do so in the projected future. Agriculture contributed 34.7 per cent to GDP at current price in 1980-81, but its share has been declined over time. By 2006-07, it had declined to 17.5 per cent at current price and further decline to 13.9 per cent at current price in 2012-13.

Table 2.2: Share of Agriculture in GDP

Sl. No.	*Item*	*2009-10*	*2010-11*	*2011-12*	*2012-13*	*2013-14*
1.	Growth in GDP in Agriculture	0.8	8.6	5	1.4	4.7*
2.	Share in total GDP—Agriculture	14.6	14.6	14.4	13.9	13.9*

Source: Central Statistics Office (CSO) and Directorate General of Commercial Intelligence and Statistics (DGCI&S).

Notes: *Quarterly Estimates of GDP as of 30 May 2014.

The declining share of agriculture in the GDP does not mean a retrogression of agriculture; it only means that the secondary and tertiary sectors of the economy are growing at a high rate. Similarly, though the share of agriculture sector in GDP has been declined over time, the proportion of population dependent upon agriculture and allied activities has been more or less stagnant, or declined at a very slow rate. It is estimated that the agriculture sector supports more than half billion people and provide employment to 52 per cent of India's total work force (GoI, 2008). This means that agriculture is the prime source of rural livelihood and employment of India.

In addition, a structural change in the composition of agriculture, showing diversification into horticulture, livestock, and fisheries, is noticeable. The horticulture sector contributed 30.4 per cent of agriculture GDP, while the livestock sector contributed over 4.1 per cent of the total GDP in 2012-13.

Agriculture Based Micro Enterprises and Rural Livelihood

Agriculture and allied activities support livelihoods of nearly 70 per cent of India's rural population (Hiremath, 2007). In recent years, land-based livelihoods of small and marginal farmers are increasingly becoming unsustainable, since their land has not been able to support the family's food requirements and fodder for their cattle. As a result, rural households are forced to look at alternative means for supplementing their livelihoods. In this context, natural resource-based micro-enterprises have emerged as alternative livelihood opportunities in rural areas. Varying socio-economic and environmental trends including declining crop prices, swelling labour forces, migration and urbanization increased the demand for alternative employment and off-farm livelihood opportunities.

Micro-enterprises are the keys to generate employment opportunities as well as income earning avenues to both landless, women and landholding people in the rural areas. Micro-enterprises are now given special attention for several reasons.

- In some areas these play an important role to generate household income, employment and economic production in the rural areas.
- Secondly, these have to play a potentially key function in supplying resilient and flexible services in the rural areas.
- Thirdly, compared to land-based agriculture, they have a propensity to generate relatively good income and hence offer flexibility to household economic conditions in the rural areas.
- Finally, being comparatively less technology oriented these activities support a proportionately larger section of the unskilled labour force especially the landless, women and landholding people and also create larger number of livelihoods per unit of output in the rural areas.

Therefore, the poverty alleviation in rural areas requires a greater understanding of the interactions of agriculture and allied enterprises and their implications for the household economy.

Approaches for Agriculture Based Micro-Enterprise Development

Wide ranges of approaches and strategies have been taken for agriculture based micro-enterprise development. Some of the key initiatives are:

Watershed Development

Small-scale entrepreneurship through watershed development plays a significant role in poor people's lives and is one of the keys to lifting people out of poverty. Some of the activities are the backbone on which the rural society survives in rural areas. Watershed development primarily aiming sustainable management of natural resources contributing for overall agriculture development and livelihood promotion in rural areas. Initial poverty eradication efforts in India concentrated on supply of agricultural technologies, inputs and services that were often 'production' orientated. However, they were largely inappropriate to the needs of the poor and the benefits were mostly captured by the rich. Later, the approach changed towards 'capacity-building' in sector organizations to provide people and organizations with the skills and resources to perform an improved job. The concept of livelihoods and livelihoods analysis emerged in the mid-nineties closely associated with poverty reduction strategies. This approach was useful to identify and prioritize the needs of the community in enhancing their livelihoods.

Market Development

Although micro-enterprises operate in very informal, unregulated environments, the fortunes of most of these activities are connected by supply chains through production channels and the incense of competition, to mainstream commercial markets. These interrelationships increasingly link related enterprise activities performance to the behaviour of other actors in economic networks. Most times production activities of allied enterprises are supported by local markets to fulfil local demand. However, monopoly does not arise as diverse actors are involved in the production processes. Thus, most often, micro-enterprise activity serves as a strong social capital, within the community, builds strong social network.

Technological Intervention

In the livelihood analysis, technology assumes greater significance as having at least four interrelated constituents, viz., technique (machines and equipment), knowledge (know-how and skills), organization (systems, procedures, practices and support structures), and product (design, specification) (Scott, 1996; Pauli, 1999). Agriculture and allied enterprise activities enhance rural livelihood system through locally available technological backstop. In principle, poor people stand to gain from technological change—generating easier access to information, higher productivity, lower inputs costs, less wastage and better environmental management. However, the pace and volatility of change can be a problem, particularly when allied activities are left behind the agricultural development or forced to take greater risks in order to keep pace with increasing vulnerability. As a result, the livelihood outcomes that allied enterprise owners practice, is likely to be increasingly determined by these activities capacity to generate and manage technological change. In the long run, an effective analysis of the factors that influence technological change in and around agriculture and allied enterprises is important for understanding the livelihood strategies and options for poor people who work in these activities.

Livelihood and Rural Non-farm Sector

The rural livelihood structure in India is predominantly based on agriculture and other activities related to agriculture sector. Hence, a huge number of rural populations are mainly depending on agriculture sector both for its employment and livelihood. At the same time various non-agricultural activities are also playing a significant role in providing the opportunities of employment and incomes to the labour force belonging to both farming and non-farming households.

In spite of a reduction in the growth rate of population, the labour force growth reached 2.25 per cent per annum during the Eleventh Plan period in India. This is attributed to change in the age structure of the population and an increase in the population in the most active working age group of 15-59. Growth or decline in the Labour Force Participation Rates (LFPRs) depends on certain factors. With the increasing thrust on education, LFPRs in the age group 15-19 years will decline. On the other hand, with improved health and longevity, LFPRs in the older age-groups, particularly 50+ years, will increase by 7.9-8.9 per cent during the Twelve Plan period which implies the need for an increase in the pace of creation of additional work opportunities commensurate with the growth of labour force.

Table 2.3: Growth in Population and Labour Force Projection by Age-group

Population/labour force	*2002-2007*	*2007-2012*	*2012-2017*
Population (all age-groups)	1.63	1.41	1.2
Population (15-59 years)	2.41	2.08	1.7
Labour force (15-59 years)	2.42	2.15	1.78
Population (15+)	2.57	2.26	1.93
Labour force (15+)	2.51	2.25	1.92

Source: Planning Commission, Government of India, Tenth Five Year Plan 2002-07.

Note: (1) Data for respective years are per cent per annum and (2) Labour force projections here are on the basis of labour force participation rate for each quinquennial age group remaining unchanged.

Rural non-farm sector is the prime source for providing employment and income to this huge labour base in rural areas. Rural non-farm economy, in recent times, is considered as an effective approach for decentralization of economic activities to rural India. However, the sector has been competing with a number of factors like inadequate rural infrastructure, particularly roads, electricity and communication facilities, lack of sufficient skilled labour and adequate access to credit, information and training facilities, etc. There are two alternative approaches to define rural-non-farm activities (Saith, 1992). The first is the locative approach in which the primary criterion is that a RNF activity is performed in a location which falls within a designated rural area. The second is based on the linkage approach where an industrial enterprise generates significant development linkages with the rural areas. Rural-Non-Farm-Sector (RNFS) includes all economic activities, *viz.,* various household/ non-household and traditional/modern manufacturing activities manufacturing, handicrafts, processing, repairs, construction, mining and quarrying, transport, trade, communication, community and personal services etc. in rural areas. The rural non-farm economic sector comprises of wide ranging activities which are directly or indirectly associated to and supporting to various agricultural and non-agricultural related economic activities, excluding activities related to the agricultural production, performed in rural areas. Rural-Non-Farm-Activities (RNFAs), thus, play an important role to provide supplementary employment to small and marginal farm households, reduce income inequalities and rural-urban migration. The rural non-farm sector is being accorded wide acknowledgement for the following reasons:

- It provides employment to a huge population especially to the rural women folk who are the most marginalized and vulnerable section of the society.
- Rural non-farm sectors prevent rural people from migrating to urban industrial and commercial centres.
- It reduces the rural-urban economic gap that tends to influence other aspects associated with the life and aspiration of the rural people.
- Rural industries are generally less capital-intensive and more labour absorbing.
- Rural industrialization has significant spin-offs for agriculture development as well.
- Rural non-farm sector also ensures equitable distribution of income among the people.
- The earnings of regular workers in the rural non-farm sector are much higher than that of agricultural workers. Casual labourers earn higher wages in non-agricultural activities than in agriculture.

The non-farm sector is performing an significant role in the overall economy of the State in terms of both providing employment opportunity to different categories of skilled and unskilled labour force and contributing in the incomes of both farm and non-farm households. The contribution of non-farm sector has been consistently rising in the creation of additional employment and the generation of income in different geographical locations over the years due to decreasing man-land ratio and an overall decline in the net cultivated land area, beside a considerable decline in per capita net domestic production being originated from agriculture related activities. The consequences of these all-adverse performances of farming economies have universally been well recognized in terms of a significant decline in the concentration of workforce in agriculture and allied activities and its subsequent shift in non-farm sector during the recent past.

Gender and Rural Livelihood

Gender equality and women empowerment have been for a long time considered as a moral and legal issue. Recently, these issues have taken on a very different connotation mainly in terms of economic efficiency (Sanga, 2007). Gender unbalance development hinders the economic efficiency particularly through sub-optimal allocation of resources and ultimately it not only aggravates income and poverty but also leads to greater deprivation and dissatisfaction of social needs such as nutrition, health and education (Kelker, 2005; Sanga, 2007).

A person's livelihood is comprised of 'the capabilities, assets (material and social) and activities required for a means of living. A livelihood is sustainable when it can cope with and recover from stresses and shocks, and maintain or enhance its capabilities and assets both now and in the future, while not undermining the natural resource base' (Chambers and Conway, 1992). Rural livelihood is a key area for understanding how gender operates in limiting or expanding men and women's access, options and choices regarding the use of resources and their material conditions, and ultimately their ability to voice concerns and influence their positions in life. However, it is very difficult to understand the gender and livelihood scenario as it includes various issues like feminization of agriculture, increased participation of women in non- farm activities, internal and international migration of women, and other structural changes.

According to World Bank *et al.* (2008), more women compared to men work in the agricultural sector, though their roles are unrecognized. Many of the women may work as contributing family workers. Jackson and Rao (2004) argues that India, or provinces within India such as Kerala, are experiencing a feminization of agriculture. However, not many rural women in India own land and not many women are owners of agro-processing farms producing high value agricultural product (World Bank *et al.*, 2008). Women tend to be contributing as family workers or casual agricultural labour. This indicates that women's presence in agriculture in the Asia-Pacific does not mean a shift towards female ownership of agricultural farms. In rigid forms of patriarchal systems, such as in South Asia, the absence of male support makes it difficult for women to access agricultural input and produce markets, information and government services. Sometimes this has also led to internal family conflicts.

The feminization of the labour force is a global phenomenon and India is also experiencing the same trend. Female participation in paid formal work has increased globally while male employment had remained stagnant (Elder and Schmidt, 2004). This is due to changes such as rising levels of female education, decline in the average family size, and the changing aspirations of women and their families. It is also influenced by changes in structural factors such as, a decline in agricultural production, growing landlessness, withdrawal of agricultural subsidies, declining levels of male employment and male wages as a result of the dismantling of state owned enterprises and structural adjustment policies (Chen *et al.*, 2004). According to Kabeer (2007), the informalization of paid work and the changing nature of demand in the labour market also influenced the feminization of employment. This is due to the following reasons: (1) female labour is free of the fixed cost (i.e., employer provided benefits, social security) associated with male employment in the organized sector; (2) male breadwinner ideology still influences the view that women are secondary earners, thus low pay is justified; (3) gender discrimination and segregated markets curtail women's options and reduce their reserve price (Elson, 1999; Kabeer, 2007). In addition, there has been a sectoral shift in female labour. The feminization of employment indicates that demand for women's labour is present. Being able to earn an income and other things associated with work such as mobility, create opportunities for women to exercise agency and choice at an individual level. However, the type of work women are being recruited for is important. The structural factors such as occupational segregation and male breadwinner ideology, which create demand for women's flexible labour, may not necessarily strengthen women's voice and collective bargaining power in the market. Women's voice is a crucial factor for highlighting women's livelihood concerns and in promoting women's interests both at the local level and within the national policy making processes. At the local government level, which is a key arena for influencing rural livelihoods, India, has reserved seats for women. India introduced gender reservations for all tiers of local government in 1992. One-third of the panchayat seats are reserved for women only through competition, and one-third of the council heads are also reserved. In West Bengal, female-led councils undertook road building projects at a higher rate compared to male-led councils, since the jobs were likely to go to females. The evidence here suggests that the presence of women in decision-making bodies can make a difference in addressing women's livelihood concerns (Chattapodhaya and Duflo, 2004). According to the World Bank (2008), community driven development or CDD and self-help groups are effective ways for increasing women's participation and voice in matters related to rural livelihoods. These create space for women to participate in the development and implementation of projects. Hence, women's engagement in the agriculture labour markets and informal sector, which depicts women's labour force participation, has increased in the region, that indicates women have established their right to work. However, further intervention is required to expand women's livelihood options, address gender power relations and increase women's participation and voice. The discussion below highlights the activities that can be undertaken by different actors for addressing the various issues related to gender sensitive livelihood promotion in rural areas:

- The Government should prioritize enacting gender sensitive laws, implementing measures to create a dynamic rural economy, providing social security, and creating social safety nets during periods of crisis. All have far reaching impact on improving rural women's livelihood opportunities and promoting gender equality.
- Government policies must focus on creating a good investment climate through securing property rights, improving communications and transport, and removing barriers to accessing finance.
- Rural public works, such as employment guarantee schemes, helps to keep poor women afloat during lean agricultural periods.
- Better targeting systems need to be created to identify vulnerable households and remove them out of poverty.
- Gender sensitive governance reforms are crucial for improving State responsiveness towards women in agriculture. This requires institutional and legal changes such as the decentralization of agricultural services and functions.
- Community driven projects created by the State for agriculture or natural resource management can create scope for women (and men in disadvantageous positions) to participate in how resources are managed at the local level.
- The extension of the legal rights framework for female agricultural and informal workers is a key step towards ensuring decent work conditions for women and men.
- The activities and policies that should be prioritized in this area are: (a) capacity development of rural women (and rural women's collectives/collectivities); (b) provision of information, credit and access to input, produce, product markets to rural women (and women's collectives); and (c) regulation.
- Capacity development of female entrepreneurs requires context-based skills/training programmes, that not only include literacy and numeric, but also confidence building measures and ways to access market intelligence.
- Providers of rural finance must move beyond providing access,

and should consider how access can enable women and men to challenge gender power relations and gender-biased structures.
- For female traders, particularly micro-traders, information technology and skills training may increase their productivity and competitiveness.
- 'Building rural women's voice is a key area for promoting gender equality in various arenas related to rural livelihood.
- Network and umbrella alliances created by women's organizations can create successful campaigns for the concerns and needs of female farmers and informal workers.

The above discussion highlights various issues, actors and functions related to gender sensitive rural livelihood promotion. It reveals that a wide range of actions require empowering women individually and collectively through establishing women's livelihood rights, increasing their capability, strengthening their participation and voice.

Migration and Rural Livelihood

Migration has been significantly reshaping the rural social and economic structures of the country. The livelihood activities of rural families are no longer restricted to farming and are increasingly being diversified through rural-to-urban and international migration. With the development of trade and industry and the awareness produced by the mass media, rural poor are shifting towards the urban areas in search for better livelihood opportunities and to improve their standards of living. The lack of employment opportunities in the rural areas and better employment prospects and infrastructure facilities in the urban areas stimulate rural people to migrate to urban areas. It has been found in various research work that distress migration occurs due to lack of physical assets and human capabilities, initial condition of extreme poverty, low social status, lack of availability of gainful work and low bargaining power of the poor who are driven from their homes in search of work both in rural and urban areas. They end up as domestic servants, construction workers, rickshaw pullers, workers in small and informal manufacturing units of urban centres, workers in quarries and mines, brick-kilns, farm labourers, etc. The regional imbalance is also a factor responsible for migration. The causes of migration are usually explained by using two broad categories, namely, push and pull factors. Studies conducted in the sphere of migration in India—found that poverty, job searching and family influence have been the main push factors for out-migration, while availability of better employment opportunity, prior migrants and availability of better educational facilities have been identified as the key pull factors behind migration. To be more specific, for rural India, poverty is still considered to be the main push factor for illiterates and moderately educated migrants.

Researchers have found that migration can be internal (within the country intra-State, inter-State, rural-urban, rural-rural, urban- urban and urban-rural) and international. Unskilled labourers from resource-poor areas as well as areas having extreme poverty migrate to the rural and urban centres where there is demand for such labour. The migration patterns have also been different: in some cases cyclical, systematic and in others, sporadic and chaotic. In the absence of effective regulation of employment conditions, the migrant workers are more vulnerable. However, the generation of diversified livelihood opportunities, employment guarantee and reduction of rural-urban disparities can reduce the migration in a sustainable manner.

Climate Change and its Impact on Rural Livelihood

Climate change is leading to increase in temperatures, rising sea levels, decreased snow cover, increase in the frequency and severity of some weather events, etc. The UN Framework Convention on Climate Change refers to climate change as a change that is attributable directly or indirectly to human activity that alters the composition of the global atmosphere in addition to the natural climate variability observed over comparable periods of time. It mainly refers to a statistically significant variation in either the mean state of the climate persisting for an extended period, usually decades, or in its variability.

India with its fifteen agro-climatic zones, diverse crop seasons and farming systems is very prone to climate change. It has become a major challenge for agriculture, food security and rural livelihoods for billions of rural people in India. Increased uncertainties in climatic variability have become a major challenge for sustaining agriculture as well as its allied sectors in the face of already declining natural resource base. Agriculture is the main livelihoods system of most of our people and along with allied sectors like forestry, livestock and fisheries. Over 650 million Indians depend on climate-sensitive sectors like agriculture, forestry and fishery for their livelihoods. Agriculture is part of the problem and part of the solution. Food security and livelihoods depends on sustainable agriculture. Achieving food security requires adequate food availability, access and absorption. Agriculture plays a vital role in contributing to all the three components of food security. India's food production is likely to be affected by the climate sensitivity of its agriculture. This in turn will impact on poverty and livelihoods.

Agriculture is the sector most vulnerable to climate change due to its high dependence on climate and weather. Climate change is likely to destabilize the agricultural production in India. According to Ninan *et al.*, "agricultural productivity is sensitive to two broad classes of climate induced effects—(1) direct effects from changes in temperature, precipitation, and carbon dioxide concentrations, (2) indirect effects through changes in soil moisture and the distribution and frequency of infestation by pests and diseases. The bad impacts of water availability due to change in rainfall, increased flooding in certain areas and recession of glaciers combined with increased water demand due to demographic development and climate change could threaten food security, destabilize the natural ecosystems including species that sustain the livelihood of rural households and impact the coastal system due to sea level rise and increased extreme weather events.

Land, water and forests are the main life support systems of the rural people. The livelihood security of the majority of Indians relies on land and water based occupations including crop and animal husbandry, forestry and fisheries. Competing and conflicting demands on land for different uses, declining factor productivity, increasing input costs, and degradation are all conjointly posing severe threats to livelihoods. In India, water availability is plagued by spatial and temporal variability and scarcity. Both these factors are projected to increase due to declining amounts and more skewed patterns of rainfall in the context of a rising population and climate change. The climate change is already making impact on the lives of the population particularly the poor. The short-term losses in the form of reduction in livelihoods and incomes due to impact of climate change on agriculture are well known. However, the scale of the potential adverse impact on human development is less understood and underestimated. Climate shocks affect livelihoods in many ways. They wipe out crops, reduce opportunities for employment, push up food prices and destroy property, confronting people with limited choices. On the other hand, the poor may have no alternative but to reduce consumption, cut nutrition, take children out of school, or sell the productive assets on which their recovery depends (UNDP, 2007).

However, the rural poor have taken various adaptive and coping mechanisms to reduce the adverse effect of climate change. Adaptation to climate change takes place through adjustments to reduce vulnerability or enhance resilience in response to observed or expected changes in climate and associated extreme weather events (IPCC, 2007). Adaptation measures can be divided into two categories: (a) individual or autonomous; (b) policy driven or planned. Autonomous adaptations are initiatives by private actors rather by governments due to actual or anticipated climate change. Planned adaptation is the result of policy decision by public agency or governments based on an awareness that conditions are about to change or have changed and that action is required to minimize losses or benefit from opportunities (Rosegrant *et al.*, 2010). These measures are intended to increase adaptive capacity by modifying farming practices, improving crops and livestock through breeding and investing in new technologies and infrastructure. Some of the specific examples of adaptation include grassland management to the actual environmental conditions as well as the practice of reasonable rotational grazing to ensure the sustainability of grassland resources (Li *et al.*, 2002). Changes in management of agriculture and allied activities could also enhance adaptive capacity. India has a long history of coping with extreme changes in weather. These coping strategies would be useful to have long term adaptation strategies. Rural poor also cope with increased climate variability. However, in spite of some commonalities, the coping strategies and indigenous knowledge vary by regions and States.

Evolution of Livelihood Promotion in India

Livelihood promotions are conscious efforts by an agency or an organization to promote and support livelihood opportunities for a large number of people (other than those directly or indirectly employed by them). Government of India has been one of the largest agencies involved in such livelihood promotion efforts. However, the cooperative sector, the corporate sector as well as the NGO sector has also contributed to promoting livelihoods.

Pre-Independence Effort—Human and Institutional Development

Philosophy on livelihood promotion evolved a great deal since the early days, with contributions from people like Rabindranath Tagore–conceiver of the Sriniketan Experiment, Martandam, Fr. Brayane of the Gurgaon

Project and Albert Meyer of the Etah project, all initiated livelihood promotion in their own ways. Mahatma Gandhi, one of the early livelihood thinkers of twentieth century, had a holistic vision of livelihoods, with a deep concern for both, the poor and for sustainability. Gandhiji suggested developing local economies by promoting inter-dependant activities, as a member of a mutually supportive community, eventually leading to "*gram swaraj*". During this period, the emphasis was on building human capital and imparting knowledge. It was thought that people were not getting good remuneration because they lacked the know-how to do better. To address this gap, efforts to impart knowledge and skills were made. Even in the years after independence, government policies and strategies were based on similar principles. Many educational institutes and research organizations were started during the First Five Year Plan. The Community Development Programme of the Government of India was also designed on these lines. However, the limitation of this approach became visible by Second Five-Year Plan when it had been realized that just the know-how was not enough, a variety of services to enhance livelihoods were also necessary. Therefore, an alternative strategy was evolved, which tried to integrate various aspects related to livelihood promotion.

Integrated Sectoral/Holistic Strategies

The first-two decades after independence rightly focused on development and stabilization of agriculture through irrigation. The large numbers of irrigation development projects were set up by various State governments which stabilized and enhanced incomes and generated wage employment for the landless farmers. Khadi and Village Industries Commission (KVIC) is the largest livelihood promotion efforts based on Gandhian thinking. Set up in the 1950s, KVIC is an example of integrated sectoral livelihood intervention. It can also be called the first government intervention in the non-agriculture sector. Similarly, the Green Revolution was another example of integrated sectoral livelihood promotion. Its main objective was to achieve rapid increase in agricultural production through the use of complementary inputs and services (package approach) at the farm level. Though Green Revolution started with introduction of high yielding variety seeds, infrastructure support was provided in the form of irrigation facilities, roads, warehouses, market yards, etc. This was supplemented with development of agricultural credit delivery system, support to fertilizer and other agri-input companies, and investments in agricultural universities for research and training. The Green Revolution was essentially confined to wheat and later paddy, and much later soybean.

Strategies for the Vulnerable Segments of the Population

Though all the above interventions based on the principle of integrated sectoral support could influence the livelihoods of millions of people, they needed heavy investments, and still left out the poor, the landless, the marginal farmers, women, tribals and people living in remote areas. The efforts concentrated on those who were left out of the benefits of mainstream development. Some took this even further to work with the poorest of the poor. However, this idea got politicized into the slogan of "*garibi hatao*" and bureaucratized through the launch of the nationwide programme for poverty alleviation—the Integrated Rural Development Programme.

Minimalist Credit

However, all these efforts were based on an integrated approach where the intervention would all services necessary for supporting livelihoods of the poor. They required perpetual ongoing subsidies and still did not generate sustainable livelihoods. All this gave rise to a new thinking, which said, the poor know how to manage their livelihoods, all they need is access to capital. This emerged the concept of micro-credit or micro-finance. The 1990s saw millions of households being covered by micro-credit programmes, all over India. The debate between minimalist credit and integrated sectoral promotion approaches began to converge in the 1990s. A number of the integrated programmes dropped many of their offerings and became more focused on credit. On the other hand, a number of the minimalist credit programmes, started providing a lot of other inputs.

Contingency Approach to Enterprise Promotion

In 1989 an alternate livelihood promotion strategy namely Contingency Approach to Enterprise Promotion had been proposed by Vijay Mahajan and Thomas Dichter. It has been argued that promoting enterprises was complex and a better approach was to identify the bottleneck and work on that. In many cases, credit could be the only constraint. In such cases, minimalist credit was right and does work well. In other cases, credit is needed but is not the main constraint, what is needed could be skills, inputs or markets. Their argument was, though a large variety of services are required, all of them are not required at the same time and in every case. Thus the offering should be contingent upon what is needed in the situation. They also asserted that only a specialized type of organization could do it. And as it is difficult to build competencies to address all these factors in-house, high level convergence and collaboration become necessary.

Rural Livelihood Promotion Approaches

In order to ensure that the poor benefit from economic growth as well as both rural and urban opportunities, it is essential to recognize that structural barriers, i.e., social, market and institutional, cannot be solved by policy shifts alone. Direct interventions have been necessary to create new economic spaces and bring about changes in how markets work locally, where the poor themselves are the main participants. Therefore, the rural livelihood promotions have a set of key objectives and related interventions based on common guiding principles. The poor need to be socially and economically mobilized to form their own institutions and investment in the creation of this institutional platform is fundamental for sustainable poverty reduction; this is the main principle of all the livelihood interventions. Livelihood interventions can be in many forms and go far beyond running an income-generation programme. Some of the approaches of livelihood interventions in India are:

Spatial Approach

Spatial approach aims in promoting livelihoods in a specified geographical area, such as a region, sub-region, command area or a watershed. Many livelihood interventions have a spatial a geographical boundary. It may be a single village, a watershed, a river basin, a block, taluka or a district or a region. The main difference between other approaches and a spatial (or area development) approach is that it tries to tackle all the sectors and segments of the population in that area. Under this approach, a leading intervention has been made to supporting locally inter-dependant economic activities. It also support livelihoods in a degraded watershed or degraded forest areas, such as Joint Forest Management Project. Cluster development is also an integral part of spatial approach where interventions have made in cluster enterprises, such as Ludhiana for hosiery, Badohi-Mirzapur for carpets, and Sualkuchi in Assam for silk sarees.

Segmental Approach

While spatial livelihood interventions try to cover a whole region or a sub-region, segmental approach focuses its attention on one specific group of vulnerable poor people: landless, or tribals, or women or any such other. Segmental approach aims to promote livelihood for marginalized and vulnerable section of the society such as marginal farmer, landless households, tribals, women and disables. Micro-credit programme for rural poor in India is a classic example of segmental approach for livelihood promotion. However, even this can be limiting since many of the poor have little in terms of human endowments—and need investments in nutrition, health, education, vocational training and organizing into producers' groups and cooperatives, before they can benefit from microfinance or livelihood promotion efforts.

Sectoral Approach

Though the production systems in rural India are highly fragmented and diverse, rural economy has flourished around a growth sub-sector and its related and support industries. Sectoral approach aims to promote livelihoods along a sector of the economy or a sub-sector such as agriculture, horticulture, animal husbandry, crafts, tourism, etc. The white revolutions supported by the National Dairy Development Board and egg production by National Egg Co-ordination Committees are prime examples of interventions in a sub-sector. However, it is difficult to ensure that the poor benefit by sub-sectoral strategies alone. A sub-sector intervention is an attempt to enhance the share of the primary producers in a Rupee of the ultimate Consumer. It tried to resolve the bottlenecks, so that the poor can participate in different parts of the value addition chain of a single commodity, such as oilseeds, milk, does it. There are several facets, which need to be looked into for the sub-sector to generate large number of livelihoods and smoothly pass the larger proportion of the value addition to the primary producers. These include:

- Market: demand conditions;
- Basic agro-climatic conditions or, natural conditions;
- Infrastructure;
- Capital in various forms;
- Technology, Knowledge, Research;
- People, their skills and attitude, and how they are organized;

- Policy and regulatory framework; and
- Inefficiencies in any of these elements can block flow of resources and hinder number of livelihoods supported by the sub-sector.

Holistic Approaches to Livelihood Promotion

The venture called livelihood promotion is very complex and multi-dimensional. Holistic approach to livelihood promotion aims to integrate all different facets regarding rural livelihood promotion. Though many development organizations have attempted to extend a wide variety of strategies, there are few, which have attempted to address it in its full range. One of the very good examples of them could be the BASIX which has emerged as one of the leading microfinance institutions in India. BASIX is established in 1996 and working with over 3.5 million customers, over 90 per cent being rural poor households and about 10 per cent urban slum dwellers. It is cited for its scale, creativity, commercial orientation, and collaborative philosophy in a sector often marked by limited operations, routine approaches, donor dependence, and territoriality.

However, BASIX conceives of itself, not as a microfinance institution, but as "a new generation livelihood promotion institution.

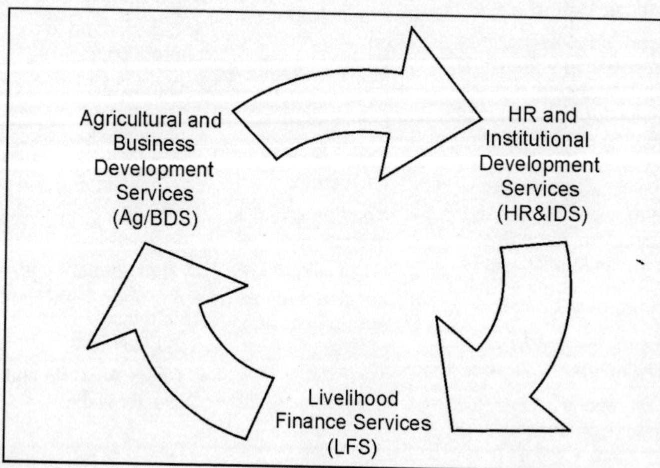

Fig. 2.2
Source: BASIX

The rationale behind this philosophy is as follows: Micro-credit in particular, and microfinance (including savings and insurance) in general, is helpful for the more enterprising poor people in economically dynamic areas. While, for poorest of poor in backward regions, a whole range of other livelihood promotion services (input supply, training, technical assistance, market linkages) need to be provided. Likewise, it is not possible to work with poor households individually and they need to be organized into groups, informal associations and sometimes cooperatives or producer companies, all of which requires institutional development services. Hence, BASIX adopted a strategy to provide a comprehensive set of livelihood promotion services which include Financial Inclusion Services (FINS), Agricultural/Business Development Services (Ag/BDS) and Institutional Development Services (IDS) to rural poor households under one umbrella. This strategy can be conceptualized in the form of a "Livelihood Triad", as shown in the diagram.

The Livelihood Triad includes the following services:

Livelihood Finance Services (LFS)	*Agricultural and Business Development Services (Ag/BDS)*	*HR and Institutional Development Services (HR&IDS)*
• Savings products include daily and monthly recurring and term deposit savings. • Loan products includes crop loans for seasonal input financing, agricultural term loans to purchase fixed assets, agri-allied loans for livestock farming, non-farm micro enterprise loans, and general purpose loans given to Self-Help Groups (SHGs) for on-lending. • Insurance, for lives and livelihoods. • Commodity futures, to reduce price risk.	• Identification of livelihood opportunities. • Productivity enhancement. • Market linkages - Input supply, output sale. • Local value addition. • Non-financial risk mitigation. • Local value addition through agro-processing.	• Formation of groups, federations, cooperatives, producer's organization, etc. of producers. • Capacity building of the partner organizations like producer organizations and NGOs. • Knowledge management and transfer of knowledge to multiple MFIs/NGOs. • Policy Analysis and Sector work.

Source: BASIX.

The livelihood triads have a dynamic inter-relationship. Clearly, BASIX's expansion into rural livelihoods promotion increases the need for collaboration with multiple, complementary organizations, and places a premium on BASIX's ability to facilitate the complex webs of relationships required to deliver a complete solution to the customer. In line with the demand for these capabilities and activities, BASIX has established a new area-level position: Area Executive (AE) for Livelihoods who is intended to be a subject matter expert in particular vertical solution. Products are "switched over" to commercial status and rolled out more broadly when fully developed, not necessarily when BASIX can charge for them. Agricultural and Business Development Service will be delivered by the existing Customer Service Agents (CSAs) who handle the Livelihood Financial Services (LFS). BASIX policy resolution also states that it will strive to yield a competitive rate of return to its investors so as to be able to access mainstream capital markets. In future BASIX will attract capital on a purely commercial basis and which has already begun to operate in this manner.

Life Long Learning (L-3) for Rural Livelihood Promotion

The concept of Lifelong learning assumes special significance in the life of deprived communities and in the dictionary of Commonwealth of Learning (COL). Since, the prevailing extension system is unable to cover and provide quality service to the rural community there is a need to look for various new strategies which could complement and reinforce the extension system. This situation of mismatch between the need and the supply of extension services necessitates the development professionals to evolve an alternative to remedy the mismatch. Life Long Learning for rural communities will not only fill the emptiness but also enhance the bargaining power of the rural communities. The process of Life Long Learning for livelihood promotion of rural community is based on the following principles:

(a) Facilitating self-directed personal strategic learning can enhance the quality of extension and create a demand-based development process.
(b) Technology-Mediated Open and Distance Education and Learning, which is abbreviated as "Tech MODE" that plays a major role in self-directed learning.
(c) Life Long Learning for rural Community assumes that

mobilizing the rural community and building cognitive social capital are essential preconditions for promoting self-directed learning.

(d) Combining modern ICT and local mobilization can integrate the vertical and horizontal transfers of knowledge, attitude and skill.

(e) This new approach to extension must be placed decisively in the framework of the entire social and economic value chain. The various stakeholders such as financial institutions, marketing agencies, industries and research institutions in that value chain need to come together to create a win-win framework. This helps communities to move away from the continuous dependence on donor-supported programmes and to adopt a self-sustainable, self-replicating, and self-generative extension process.

(f) The demand from rural communities for an integrated package of information to facilitate local knowledge management requires the knowledge creating institutions to work as a consortium to provide holistic locale-specific information.

Life Long Learning (L3) is a process that empowers vulnerable rural men and women by enabling them to (1) gain knowledge; (2) create their own self-directed learning process; (3) organise themselves to solve problems of marketing their products and food security; (4) improve their living conditions, and (5) increase their freedoms and independence through government support. This process can be conceptualised as Learning, Forming and Transforming. While gaining knowledge through self-directed learning process is named as Learning, organizing themselves to solve their day-to-day problems is termed as forming. Improving their living conditions and increasing their independence is conceived as transforming. In other words, L3 by educating (learning) the rural community attempts to bring them together (form into organization) to initiate the process of livelihood transformation.

Collaborative Polygon for Livelihood Promotion

In recent past, a new set of institutions have evolved for livelihood promotion in the rural areas which are termed as Livelihood Promotion Organizations. These Livelihood Promotion Organizations specialized entities are initially developed and promoted by an NGO or a commercial entity and later owned and managed by the community, registered as co-operatives or producer's company or federation, under the recent amendment to the Companies Act. These Livelihood Promotion Organizations have been playing a crucial role, supplementing the credit role of Bank and MFIs which includes identifying potential livelihood opportunities, motivating and mobilizing rural community, providing training and capacity building, organizing the poor into village level institutions and facilitate to participate in these livelihood opportunities, arranging for credit and infrastructure, establishing the value chain and the production processes, developing market linkages, bringing appropriate policy changes, stabilizing the pioneering units, and ensuring wider replication of the model for sustainability.

However, over the years, the economy has become specialized, dynamic and complex. So, on one hand input services requisite for supporting and sustaining large numbers of livelihoods have become more diverse and complex, on the other it has become necessary for agencies providing any of the input services to be more particular and specialized. For example, while setting up the Handicraft sub-sector in Santiniketan various agencies have recognized that the rural artisans needed inputs in design and some related skill development. Most of the raw materials were produced locally and so was the marketing of the cloth, which the artisans were accustomed in doing. However, with the development of

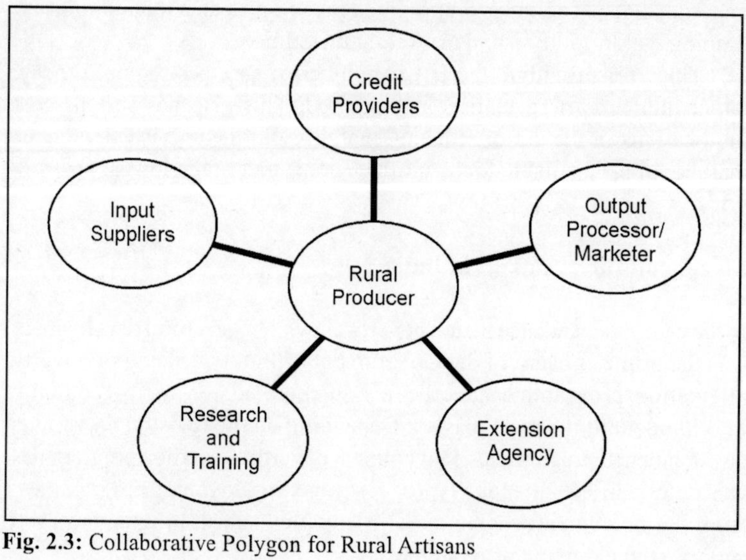

Fig. 2.3: Collaborative Polygon for Rural Artisans

the industry, today the raw material comes from distant markets. The products manufactured by the artisans also do not go to markets that she/he has information about nor has access to. Thus, the range of services required for supporting livelihoods have become wider: it includes supply of raw materials, marketing, in addition to helping them design.

But, earlier the designer could also help in skill building, as a trainer. But today, with the rapidly changing tastes for design, increasing competition, the designer has to become specialized in designing only to remain effective and efficient.

Another example is the setting up of the Honey sub-sector in Uttrakhand, Appropriate Technology India (ATI) and NGO has recognized that the rural people have traditionally practicing bee-keeping and needed inputs in improving the technology and some related skill development. The practice of bee-keeping was traditional in mountain and the raw material, i.e., the bee colonies were available locally and so was the marketing of the honey, which the producers were habituated in doing. However, with the changing scenario of climatic condition, unavailability of bee colonies and huge demand, today the bee-keeping practice has been transformed from traditional to commercial. The honey and other by-products manufactured by the rural producers have very limited idea about markets and quality proposition. Thus, the range of services required for supporting livelihoods have become wider: it includes supply of raw material, i.e., bee colonies, improving technology, capacity building and training, value addition and marketing in addition.

Thus, for providing the larger number of services required today, larger numbers of specialists are required. This also has serious cost implications in the era of reducing margins and the cherished value of making things available to the ultimate consumer at the lowest possible price.

Livelihood Interventions in India

In the post-independence period poverty alleviation and rural development was the prime concern of the Government of India. A plenty of poverty alleviation programme have been implemented for socio-economic development of the rural masses. Depending on the revision on various developmental programmes, Government poverty alleviation programmes can be classified into four types: (i) wage employment programmes; (ii) self-employment programmes; (iii) minimum needs programmes; and (iv) area development programmes.

- *Wage Employment Programme*: Wage employment programmes give employment while generating useful public goods. In 1977, the national Janata Dal government adopted this scheme and expanded it to the whole country as the National Rural Employment Programme (NREP). However, in the implementation of this programme, the landless were often unable to access the scheme, in order to create remedy for this; the Rural Landless Employment Guarantee Programme (RLEGP) came into being in the mid-1980s. Unlike NREP, it guaranteed employment to the landless poor. There were two area specific wage employment programmes. One is the Nehru Rozgar Yojana (NRY), which addresses wage employment issues in urban areas. The other was the Employment Assurance Scheme (EAS), which provided wage employment in resource poor areas. In the late 1980s, these two merged to form the Jawahar Rozgar Yojana (JRY). In effect till the early 2000s, JRY was essentially a Food-for-Work programme. The latest form of wage employment programme is the National Rural Employment Guarantee Scheme (NREGS) which offers 100 days of guaranteed employment to the rural unemployed poor. The defining feature underlying this programme is that it is based on the National Rural Employment Guarantee Act: a law passed in 2005 that guarantees that the government will provide 100 days of employment.
- *Self-Employment Programme*: The Antyodaya programme in 1978 in Rajasthan was the pioneer to a nationwide self-employment promotion programme. In 1980, the central government upscaled it to an all-India level as the Integrated Rural Development Programme (IRDP). Under IRDP, each village collectively chose the five poorest households who were then given financial assistance by banks and subsidies by the government, so that they could begin their own businesses/ enterprises. A few years later, assessments of the programme showed that the IRDP was unable to reach women, so the Development of Women and Children in Rural Areas (DWCRA) programme was begun. Assessments also found that there were only a few kinds of livelihood activities that the poor wanted to engage in, so a training programme was set up to help them diversify. This was the Training Scheme for Rural Youth for Self-Employment (TRYSEM). In the late 1990s, the individual

based approach of these programmes was supplanted by a group-based approach. It was recast as the Swarnajayanti Gram Swarozgar Yojana (SGSY), and continues till today. Yet its results have been quite disappointing, both in terms of incremental income for the poor and in terms of repayment of bank loans. The SGSY programme is now implemented as National Rural Livelihood Mission (NRLM).

- *Minimum Need Programme*: The thought behind the minimum needs programmes was that in order to access livelihood opportunities, the poor needed to have some minimum standard of resources. These programmes focused on building roads, ensuring drinking water and sanitation, and providing adequate housing. Each of these three had its own programme: the Pradhan Mantri Gram Sadak Yojana (PMGSY) for road infrastructure development, the Accelerated Rural Water Supply Programme to ensure that all groups of habitations with no more than 1,000 houses each, were provided with safe drinking water, and the Indira Awas Yojana, which provided subsidized housing for the rural poor. In 1995, the minimum needs programme was expanded to include providing old-age pensions, support to widows, disabled, and pregnant and lactating mothers. This was done through the National Social Assistance Programme.
- *Area Development Programme*: Area development programmes collaborate the three approaches above in a focused manner for resource poor areas. The Drought Prone Areas Programme (DPAP), Desert Development Programme, and Border Areas Development Programme, Tribal Area Development Programme (TADP) are examples from the 1970s. However, some areas proved to be chronically poor, and this understanding led to the Rashtriya Sam Vikas Yojana (RSVY) in 2003. Here, the 100 poorest districts were chosen and the government started investing in their development. However, investing in just one district did not alleviate poverty, and the government started the Backward Regions Grant Fund in 2005 to invest in the poorest districts.

National Rural Livelihood Mission (NRLM)

In spite of this rapid economic growth rate majority of the rural population in India continue to live below the poverty line. The key challenge is to ensure that the economic growth is inclusive and it leads to significant reduction of rural poverty. Despite significant efforts of Government rural poverty continues to be a major challenge. Programmes directly targeting poor families and supporting their livelihoods promotion hold a major promise to trigger pro-poor growth. However, the past record of implementation of these programmes has not been very successful and the pro-poor growth that they were supposed to generate has actually not taken place.

There was a significant shift in focus when in 1999 the Integrated Rural Development Programme (IRDP) was transformed to Swarnajayanti Gram Swarojgar Yojana (SGSY). The strategy of self-employment through organizing poor into Self-Help Groups (SHGs) became the cornerstone of the new strategy. An overview of the implementation of SGSY over the last ten years throws up a mixed picture. There is a widespread acceptance in the country of the need for poor into SHGs as a pre-requisite for poverty reduction. However, it has also brought into focus shortcomings like vast regional variations in mobilisation of rural poor, insufficient capacity building of beneficiaries, insufficient investments for building community institutions, weak linkages with the banks leading to low credit mobilization, lack of repeat financing and lack of dedicated manpower to implement the programme. The focus on single livelihoods activity has not met the multiple livelihoods requirements of the poor. Furthermore, several States have not been able to fully utilize the funds received under SGSY, indicating a lack of appropriate delivery systems and lack of building necessary absorption capacity among the rural poor. Absence of aggregate institutions in the form of SHG federations precluded the poor from accessing higher order support services for productivity enhancement, marketing linkage, risk management, etc. Several evaluation studies have also shown that the scheme has been relatively successful in alleviating rural poverty wherever systematic mobilization of the poor into SHGs, their capacity building and skill development was taken up in a process-intensive manner. In other places the impact has not been significant.

It was in this background that the Ministry of Rural Development (MoRD), Government of India (GoI) set up a committee under the Chairmanship of Prof. R. Radhakrishna (Committee on Credit Related Issues under SGSY). The committee gave its recommendations in the year 2009. The Ministry held widespread consultations on the recommendations and accepted the major recommendations of the Radhakrishna Committee. The Ministry secured the approval of the

Planning Commission and the Finance Ministry for restructuring the SGSY as National Rural Livelihood Mission (NRLM). The Ministry of Rural Development, Government of India has launched National Rural Livelihood Mission (NRLM) by restructuring Swarnajayanti Gram Swarozgar Yojana (SGSY) replacing the existing SGSY scheme, effective from April 1, 2013.

The basic purpose of National Rural Livelihoods Mission is to put in place a dedicated and sensitive support structure from the national level to the sub-district level which will focus on the poor, build and sustain their organizations at different levels. This will provide the poor a platform for collective action based on self-help and mutual cooperation and they become a strong demand system, build linkages with mainstream institutions, including banks, and Government departments to address the various dimensions of poverty. The core belief of NRLM is that the poor have innate capabilities and a strong desire to come out of poverty. This intrinsic capability of the poor is unleashed only when they are organized into institutions which are truly owned by them, provided sufficient capacity building and handholding support. NRLM also believes that the programme can be up scaled in a time bound manner only if it is driven by the institutions of the poor.

National Rural Livelihood Mission (NRLM) is the flagship programme of Government of India for promoting poverty reduction through building strong institutions of the poor, particularly women, and enabling these institutions to access a range of financial services and livelihoods services. NRLM is designed to be a highly intensive programme and focuses on intensive application of human and material resources in order to mobilize the poor into functionally effective community owned institutions promote their financial inclusion and strengthen their livelihoods. NRLM complements these institutional platforms of the poor with services that include financial and capital services, production and productivity enhancement services, technology, knowledge, skills and inputs, market linkage, etc. The community institutions also offer a platform for convergence and partnerships with various stakeholders by building environment for the poor to access their rights and entitlements and public service (RBI, 2013).

Basic Differences between NRLM and SGSY

There are some basic differences in principles, strategy and delivery mechanism which are:

1. National Rural Livelihood Mission (NRLM) is promoting a major shift from purely 'allocation based' strategy to a 'demand driven' strategy wherein States have the flexibility to develop their own plans for capacity building of women SHGs and Federations, infrastructure and marketing, and policy for financial assistance for the SHGs.
2. NRLM identifies the target group of poor through a 'participatory identification of the poor' process instead of using the BPL list as was done in SGSY.
3. NRLM promotes the formation of women SHGs on the basis of affinity and not on the basis of a common activity, as it used to be under SGSY.
4. Unlike SGSY, the NRLM has taken a saturation approach and ensures all the poor in a village are covered and a woman from each poor family is motivated to join the SHG.
5. NRLM has its own support structure for planning, implementation and monitoring which was lacking in SGSY.
6. NRLM provides continuous handholding support to SHGs, and their federations. This was missing in SGSY. Handholding support is provided to a great extent by building capacities of the SHGs/federations and by building a cadre of community professionals from among the poor women.
7. The objective of NRLM is to ensure that SHG s are enabled to access repeat finance from Banks, till they sustain their livelihoods and decent living standards. This was missing in SGSY, where the emphasis was on one time support (*Source*: RBI, 2013).

Key Features of NRLM

1. ***Sensitive Support Structure of National Rural Livelihood Mission*****:** The major drawback in SGSY was lack of dedicated manpower for the process intensive work envisaged under the programme. All evaluation studies have pointed out this as critical shortcoming. Hence, the major innovation under NRLM is the setting up of sensitive and dedicated support structures at the National, State, district and sub-district levels. The district level units for managing the activities of NRLM will have suitable linkages with District Rural Development Agencies (DRDAs). They will have appropriate linkages with the PRIs.

2. ***Universal Social Mobilization*****:** To begin with, NRLM would ensure that at least one member from each identified rural poor household, preferably a woman, is brought under the Self-Help Group (SHG) network in a time bound manner. Subsequently, both women and men would be organized for addressing livelihoods issues, i.e., farmers organizations, milk producers cooperatives, weavers associations, etc. All these institutions are inclusive and no poor would be left out of them.

3. ***Participatory Identification of Poor (PIP)*:** The experience from SGSY suggests that the current BPL list has large inclusion and exclusion errors. To widen the target groups beyond the BPL list and to include all the needy poor, NRLM will undertake community based process, i.e., participation of the poor process to identify its target group. Participatory process based on sound methodology and tools (social mapping and well-being categorization, deprivation indicators) and also locally understood and accepted criterion ensures local consensus that inadvertently reduces the inclusion and exclusion errors, and enables formation of the groups on the basis of mutual affinity. The most vulnerable households like the Particularly Vulnerable Tribal Groups (PVTGs), single women, women headed households, persons with disability, landless, migrant labour, etc would receive a special focus. NRLM will ensure adequate coverage of vulnerable sections of the society such that 50 per cent of the beneficiaries are SC/STs, 50 per cent are women, 15 per cent are minorities and 3 per cent are persons with disability.

4. ***Promotion of Institutions of the Poor*:** Strong institutions of the poor such as SHGs and their village level and higher level federations are necessary to provide space, voice and resources for the poor and for reducing their dependence on external agencies. They empower them and also act as instruments of knowledge and technology dissemination, and hubs of production, collectivization and commerce. NRLM, therefore, would focus on setting up these institutions at various levels. In addition, NRLM would promote specialized institutions like Livelihoods collectives, producers' cooperatives/companies for livelihoods promotion through deriving economies of scale, backward and forward linkages, and access to information, credit, technology, markets, etc. The Livelihoods collectives would enable the poor to optimize their limited resources.

5. ***Demand Driven*:** NRLM adopted a demand driven strategy. States have the flexibility to develop their action plans for poverty reduction which include a seven year Perspective Plan and a detailed Annual Action Plan. The overall plan is within the allocation for the state based on *inter se* poverty ratios.

6. ***Universal Financial Inclusion*****:** NRLM would work towards achieving universal financial inclusion, beyond basic banking services to all the poor households, SHGs and their federations. NRLM would work on both demand and supply side of Financial Inclusion. On the demand side, it would promote financial literacy among the poor and provides catalytic capital to the SHGs and their federations. On the supply side, it would coordinate with the financial sector and encourage use of Information Communication & Technology (ICT) based financial technologies, business correspondents and community facilitators. It would also work towards universal coverage of rural poor against loss of life, health and assets.

7. ***Revolving Fund and Community Investment Support Fund*****:** A Revolving Fund would be provided to eligible SHGs as an incentive to inculcate the habit of thrift and accumulate their own funds towards meeting their credit needs in the long-run and immediate consumption needs in the short-run. The C.I.F would be a corpus and used for meeting the members' credit needs directly and as catalytic capital for leveraging repeat bank finance. The C.I.F would be routed to the SHGs through the Federations. The key to coming out of poverty is continuous and easy access to finance, at reasonable rates, till they accumulate their own funds in large measure.

8. ***Provision of Interest Subsidy*****:** The rural poor need credit at low rate of interest and in multiple doses to make their ventures economically viable. In order to ensure affordable credit, it is proposed to provide subsidy on interest rate above 7 per cent per annum for all SHG loans availed from mainstream financial institutions, based on prompt loan repayment.

9. ***Training and Capacity Building*****:** Training and capacity building of the poor ensures that they are provided with the requisite skills for managing their institutions, managing their livelihoods, for enhancing their credit absorption capacity and credit worthiness. A multi- pronged approach for training and continuous capacity building of the targeted families, SHGs, their federations, government functionaries, bankers and other key stakeholders is envisaged. Particular focus has given to develop and engage community professionals, community resource persons for capacity building of SHGs and their federations and other collectives.

10. ***Infrastructure Creation and Marketing Support*****:** NRLM seeks to ensure that the infrastructure needs for key livelihoods activities of the poor are met with. Particular attention needs to be given to activities for providing marketing support to SHGs which include support for market

research, market intelligence, technology, extension and developing backward and forward linkages.
Source: MoRD, 2013 and RBI, 2013.

Decentralization, PRIs and Rural Livelihood

Decentralization is generally considered to be a positive step towards ensuring participation of poor and marginalized groups in decision-making processes at the local level. In the Indian States of Karnataka, West Bengal and Andhra Pradesh (AP), efforts to establish and empower local institutions have been shown to enhance rural livelihoods. In AP and Karnataka, encouragement of watershed user associations by State governments has improved the management of groundwater, and enhanced the resources on which dry land farmers depend. In Karnataka and West Bengal, the empowerment of local democratically-elected bodies—the Panchayats—has enhanced participation in decision-making forum, particularly among castes and classes that have been traditionally marginalized by local political processes. In West Bengal, the State government's dual commitment to democratic decentralization and social welfare has produced a series of pro-poor policies, including stronger land tenure, higher agricultural wages and better access to rural credit.

Panchayati Raj Institutions (PRIs) enhanced the capacity of local bodies to take up various activities regarding livelihood promotion more efficiently and assessing the need at village level through decentralized planning process. The roles of PRIs in rural livelihood promotion are briefly discussed below:

- The State Government has already entrusted the responsibility of identifying beneficiaries of land reforms on the Panchayat Samiti. While the said responsibility has continued, the Panchayats are more associated with improving land of the beneficiaries of land reforms so as to improve their productivity and helping those beneficiaries for accessing various inputs like bank credit, etc.
- Development of degraded land, irrigation facilities and checking of soil erosion, etc., of the beneficiaries of land reforms have been taken up on a priority basis using fund available from NREGA or other programmes for sustaining agricultural productivity.

- The PRIs are already engaged in development of agriculture and allied activities. Their capacity have been augmented further in assessing availability of natural resources and in improving its utilization for generating maximum economic gains keeping in mind the need for generating as much employment as possible and ensuring availability of food on a sustainable basis.
- Although land belongs to private individuals and crop planning is done in the private domain the Panchayats along with the State Government will work for necessary crop diversification and intensifying agricultural output. The role of the Panchayat is to provide supporting infrastructure to ensure optimum and sustainable utilization of land and water.
- In order to improve the cropping intensity the PRIs have worked for providing micro and minor irrigation and will also mediate with the State extension machinery for improved agronomic practices for higher yield. In order to introduce new crops or improving cropping intensity the Panchayats of all the three tiers are at liberty to act concurrently with the State Government for providing mini-kits to the poor farmers. The PRIs have similarly promoted activities related to horticulture, sericulture and cultivation of different commercial crops.
- Promotion of agro-forestry and social forestry have been already devolved on the Panchayats for taking up plantation in all possible areas excepting those which are declared forests.
- Water conservation by storing surface water is an important activity to which the Panchayats are already associated. This will be intensified further for growing at least two crops in the command area of such water bodies, which will be actively promoted by providing mini-kits to all poor farmers having land in the command area. There is an increasing trend of SHGs West Bengal taking lease of land for growing second crop and all such groups will be assisted to grow second crop and augment their income. The water bodies will be also intensively utilized for pisciculture.
- The Panchayats have been entrusted with the responsibility of taking up water and soil conservation measures out of various programmes including wage employment programmes and the watershed development programmes. Priority has been given for rain water harvesting for meeting as much of the demand of water as possible.

- The Panchayats have also worked for expansion of livelihood opportunities in the secondary and tertiary sectors by developing appropriate infrastructure, arranging skill training for the people, particularly those from the poorer and weaker sections of the community.
- Panchayats of all tiers have also played their roles in development of tourism in their respective areas and to extend necessary support to the Tourism Department for promotion of tourism in the State by showcasing traditional local art and cultural activities of unique nature, rare specimen of flora and fauna, places of scenic beauty, phenomena of ethnic diversity, places and relics of historical, cultural and religious importance, etc., that may entertain people and may have educative value.
- The responsibility of the Panchayats has reached a new dimension with the introduction of the National Rural Employment Guarantee Act 2005 as a right based and demand driven employment generation programme. The GP is the implementing agency for most of the schemes and the PS are entrusted with implementation of larger schemes. The PS and the ZP will oversee the planning and implementation of works and will ensure that demand for employment is met in respect of its area and will provide support to the lower tiers for achieving the objectives.
- The Panchayats have been fully entrusted with the implementation of the watershed development programmes under the centrally sponsored *Hariyali* schemes as well as other watershed development programmes.
- Organizing the poor in SHGs and empowering them have been a major strategy for improving participation of the poor in the affairs of the Panchayats. That has also helped the poor to be the prime mover for their own development by drawing support from the Government, including Panchayats. Role of the Panchayats in this context have been to facilitate the process and to ensure convergence of all the interventions at the community level through the SHGs, wherever possible.

The role of PRIs in rural livelihood promotion is highly diversified and multifaceted. PRIs have been addressing various developmental issues for promotion of sustainable rural livelihood.

Conclusion

Livelihoods are dynamic in nature and also are influenced by external and internal conditions making inter-dependent influencing factors more complex in nature. Inequitable access to livelihoods opportunities leads to social unrest and violence and political instability. The ratio of urban income to rural income rose from 1.6 in 1951 to 4.5 in recent times. Unequal development made some States like Punjab, Haryana and Maharashtra far richer as compared to States like Bihar and Orissa. Investment goes to the richer States for enhancing the development of infrastructure, skill building, higher technical education, etc.

There is almost saturation in agriculture employment forcing people to shift to secondary sectors which again require certain skill sets to survive. Due to uneven development of the secondary sector people are forced to migrate to a far location, as we have seen in the case of Bihar where people migrating to other States and cities and the violence in recent times in different parts of the country. Some of the major challenges in primary sector are the low productivity, environmental impact on land and water resources, lack of access to formal financial system, poor forward and backward linkages, institutional set-up, technical knowledge and assistance, lack of storage and transport infrastructure, poor, ineffective and corrupt delivery mechanisms, etc. The organized sector is facing a shortage of skilled labour while the unorganized sector is full with migrant rural poor unskilled people willing to shift out of agriculture. Thus there is a huge investment required to build the skills of the workforce.

The last decade has seen a high growth rate of the economy. Evidence, both from field experience, studies and data, shows that the employment opportunities created is inadequate in spite of rapid growth. Although GDP growth has accelerated, it has not been accompanied by a commensurate increase in employment, leading to a worsening in the employment situation in the post-reform period. These considerations have led to a demand for greater attention to the employment objective.

References

ACCESS Development Services; 2008: *State of India's Livelihoods: The 4 P Report*. Ed. by Sankar Datta and Vipin Sharma, New Delhi.

Ashley, Caroline and Diana Carney; 1999: *Sustainable Livelihoods: Lessons from Early Experience*, DFID, London.

Bhatt Yogesh, Kumar, Tandon, Rajesh and Sharma, Prem, N.; 1998: *Building Farmers' Organisations for Integrated Watershed Management in India—A Trainers' Manual*, PRIA, New Delhi.

Carney, D. (ed.); 1998: *Sustainable Rural Livelihoods: What Contribution can we make,* Papers presented at DFID's Natural Resource Advisers Conference, July 1998. Department for International Development, London.

Chambers, Robert and Gordon Conway; 1992: *Sustainable Rural Livelihoods: Practical Concepts for the 21st Century*, IDS Discussion Paper 296, IDS, Brighton, UK, February 1992.

Chambers, Robert and Gordon, Conway; 1992: *Sustainable Rural Livelihoods: Practical Concepts for the 21st Century*, IDS Discussion Paper 296. Falmer: IDS.

Chattapadhya, Raghabendra and Esther Duflo; 2004: *Women as Policymakers: Evidence from a Randomized Policy Experiment in India*, Econometrica.

Chen, Martha, A. and Joann Vanek, Marilyn Carr; 2004: *Mainstreaming Informal Employment and Gender in Poverty Reduction*, Commonwealth Secretariat, London.

Datta, S., Mahajan, V. and Thakur, G.; 2004: *An Introduction to Livelihood Promotion*, New Economics Foundation (NEF), Ford Foundation, BASIX.

Dev, S. Mahendra; 2011: Climate Change, Rural Livelihoods and Agriculture (focus on Food Security) in Asia-Pacific Region, Indira Gandhi Institute of Development Research, Mumbai. http://www.igidr.ac.in/pdf/publication/WP-2011-014.pdf

DFID; 1999: *Sustainable Livelihoods and Poverty Elimination: Background Briefing*, DFID, London. (www.ids.ac.uk/livelihoods.html).

DFID; 1999: *Sustainable Livelihoods Guidance Sheets*, DFID, London.

Elder, Sara and Dorothea, Schmidt; 2004: Global Employment Trends for Women, *Employment Strategy Paper 2004: 8*, Employment Strategy Department, ILO, Geneva.

Elson, Diane; 1999: Labour Market as Gendered Institutions: Equality, Efficiency and Empowerment Issues, in *World Development*, 27(3).

Ghosh, Jayati; 2011: India's Official Poverty Line, *Guardian*, London, UK.

Hiremath, B.N.; 2007: The Changing faces of Rural Livelihoods in India. Paper presented at the National Civil Society Conference on *What it takes to Eradicate Poverty* held during December 4-6, 2007. Institute of Rural Management, Anand, Gujarat.

IDS, 1995: Discussion Paper 347, Brighton, UK, January 1995.

IFAD; 2005: Empowering women workers in India, Retrieved from *IFAD Making A Difference in Asia and the Pacific*, IFAD.

IPCC; 2007: Working Group II, *Impacts, Adaptation and Vulnerability*, Intergovernmental Panel on Climate Change. Fourth Assessment Report, Ed. by Parry, M.L.O.F. Canziani, J.P. Palutikof, P.J. van der Linden and C.E. Hanson. New York: Cambridge University Press.

IRP and UNDP; 2010: Guidance Note on Recovery Livelihood, India. Retrieved from http://www.unisdr.org/files/16771_16771guidancenoteonrec overyliveliho.pdf

Jackson, Cecile and Nitya, Rao; 2004: *Understnading Gender and Agrigarian Change Under Liberalization: The Case of India*, UNRISD (draft).

Kabeer, Naila; 2007: Marriage, Motherhood, Masculinity in the Global Economy: Reconfiguration of Personal and Economic Life, *IDS Working Paper 296*, Pathways of Women's Empowerment and IDS, Brighton.

Kelkar, Govind and Dev, Nathan; 2005: *Gender, Livelihoods and Resources in South Asia.*

Lasse, Krantz; 2001: *The Sustainable Livelihood Approach to Poverty Reduction: An Introduction*, Swedish International Development Agency. Retrieved from http://www.forestry.umn.edu/prod/groups/cfans/@pub/@cfans/@forestry/documents/as et/cfans_asset_202603.pdf

Ministry of Rural Areas and Employment; 1994: *Guidelines for Watershed Development*, GoI, India.

Ministry of Rural Development; 2013: National Rural Livelihood Mission Framework for Implementation, MoRD, GoI.

Nair, Abhishek and Singh, Pramod, K.; 2012: Workshop Report on Adapting Rural Livelihoods to Climate Change, IRMA, India.

Nazneen, Sohela; 2010: Rural livelihoods and gender, *Asia-Pacific Human Development Report Background Papers Series 2010/08*, UNDP.

Ninan, K.N.; and Bedamatta, Satyasiba: 2012: *Climate Change, Agriculture, Poverty and Livelihoods: A Status Report*, Institute for Social and Economic Change, Bangalore.

Paul, Sujit Kumar; 2011: Transformation of a Backward Village into a Model Village for Livelihood Development: A Study in Purulia District of West Bengal, *Jharkhand Journal of Development and Management Studies*, Vol. 9, No. 2.

Pauli, G.; 1999: *Towards Technology Strategy for Sustainable Livelihoods*, Prepared for the sustainable livelihoods unit of the UNDP.

Planning Commission; 2011: *Faster, Sustainable and More Inclusive Growth: An Approach to the Twelfth Five Year Plan (2012-17)*, New Delhi.

Planning Commission, GoI; 2013: *Press Note on Poverty Estimates 2011-12*, GoI Press Information Bureau, New Delhi.

RBI; 2013: *Master Circular on Priority Sector Lending: Restructuring of SGSY as National Rural Livelihood Mission (NRLM)—Aajeevika,* RBI, GoI.

Saith, A.; 1992: *The Rural Non Farm Economy: Processes and Policies*, International Labour Force, Geneva (mimeo), pp. 12-16.

Sengupta, Arjun, K.P. Kannan, G. Raveendran; 2008: India's Common People: Who are they, How many are they and How do they live?, *Economic and Political Weekly*, March 15, 2008.

Sen, Amartya; 2000: *Development as Freedom*, Oxford University Press, Oxford.

Scott, A.; 1996: *Appropriate Technology: Is it ready for—and relevant to—the Millennium,* ITDG Publishers.

Tideman, E.M.; 1996: *Watershed Management, Guidelines for Indian Conditions*, Omega Scientific Publishers.

UNDP; 1997: *Promoting Sustainable Livelihoods: A Briefing Note Submitted to the Executive Committee*, UNDP.

UNDP; 1999: *Developing Sustainable Livelihood Indicators: Reviewing Lessons Learnt and a Framework for Action*, Draft, UNDP.

UNDP; 2007: Fighting Climate Change: Human Solidarity in a Divided World, *Human Development Report 2007/08*, Palgrave Macmillan, New York.

Vijay, Mahajan and Tom, Dichter; 1990: *A Contingency Approach to Small Business and Micro-enterprise Development*; Small Enterprise Development.

William, Solesbury; 2003: *Sustainable Livelihoods: A Case Study of the Evolution of DFID Policy*, Overseas Development Institute, UK.

World Bank; 2006: *Inclusive Growth and Service Delivery: Building on India's Success,* World Bank, Washington D.C.

World Bank, FAO and IFAD; 2008: *Gender in Agriculture Source Book*, World Bank, Washington DC.

World Bank; 2012: *Inclusive Green Growth*, World Bank, Washington D.C.

3

Panchayati Raj Institutions and Decentralisation

Introduction

Decentralisation means the transfer of authority, legislative, judicial or administrative, from central to intermediate and local governments. The term 'decentralisation' has generally been used to refer to a variety of institutional reforms. It is considered as a change in the organisational framework in which political, social and economic decisions are made and implemented. Mahatma Ganjdhiji's idea on *Gram Swaraj* seems appropriate and timely in current period. Indeed, his political philosophies on *Gram Swaraj* have now come into existence in the form of Gram Panchayat, which is an effective instrument of grass roots governance and participative development. Evidences from Indian history suggest that the village Panchayats were responsible for local problem solutions within the village level. In the Vedic era, there was *Panch-Ayat*, which means a group of five people who were selected by the villagers and they were responsible for local governance. *Sabha*, *Samiti*, and *Vidath*—these terms are mentioned in the *Rigveda* as local self-units. The *Ramayana* and the *Mahabharata* both indicate about local self-governance in the Epic era. Terms such as *Gram*, *Maha gram*, *Ghosh* finds mentioned in the *Ramayana*. Kautilya's *Arthashastra* too states that *Sabha* and *Samiti* played a vital role in controlling the decisions of the king. Besides *Neeti Shastra* of Shukracharya also mentions village governance during ancient period. During the Sultanate period, the sultans divided their kingdoms into provinces like *Vilayat*, *Amir*. Village was the smallest unit and had sufficient powers for local self-governance. Panchayats were also prevalent in the villages in the medieval period. According to Maheswari (1985), the beginning of local government can be presumed from 1687, when the Madras City Corporation was established. The British period divided into four time lines, that is, from 1687-1881: local governments were established to share the burden of resources of the central and provincial governments, 1882-1919: local governments were viewed as local self-government, 1920-1937: local governments were established and people's representatives were controlling the provincial administration and from 1938- 1947: local governments were in the state of rejuvenation and reconstruction (Joshi and Narwani, 2002). After India's independence in 1947, the Village Panchayats were included in the Indian Constitution. According to Article 40 of the Indian Constitution, "the state should take steps to organise Village Panchayats and endow them with such power and authority as may be necessary to enable them to function as units of self-government." Rajasthan was the first State where Panchayati Raj was established on 2nd October 1959. This followed the establishments of the Panchayati Raj Institution as a unit of local self-governance in every State of India.

Decentralised governance has been conceived as a mechanism of local self-government for promoting healthy and sustainable development. It is expected to facilitate effective people's participation, enhance degree of transparency and ensure greater accountability. Decentralised governance is assumed to provide more effective and competitive delivery of services at the grass root level. Being closer to the people, decentralised governance is assumed to meet needs and preferences of the people (Crook, 2003; Bardhan and Mukherjee, 2000). The case for democratic decentralisation is also predicated upon the notion that greater participation in local political affairs will improve the quality and reach of government services, particularly one's aimed at improving the lives of poor and politically marginal groups in society (de Souza, 2000). For proponents of democratic decentralisation, a central challenge of improving the delivery of public services becomes one of 'crafting' (Ostrom, 1990) institutions which can maximize participation in political life. In the context of poverty reduction, access to the (myriad) resources and benefits that governments provide is associated with systems of governance that empower poor and vulnerable groups in society.

Although there is of course great variation among cultures, countries and regions, we can identify a number of roles that governments typically play in poor and predominantly rural areas:

- One is the provision of public goods, such as universal education and healthcare;
- Second is the provision of divisible goods, such as irrigation, agricultural extension and credit;

- Third is the determination and enforcement of laws regulating key economic inputs, such as land, labour and capital; and
- Fourth and critical element is the recognition and protection of rights allowing for organization, association and entitlement in the eyes of the state.

All of these, it is worth emphasizing, are problematic in the sense that they require systems of governance which ensure that public resources are being delivered efficiently and effectively (Johnson and Start, 2001).

However, there are some scholars who have expressed reservation about the efficacy of decentralised governance (Prud'homme 1995; Tanzi, 1995). Prud'homme argues that decentralised governance promotes inefficiency and scope for corruption due to an influence of interest groups and discretion of local officials. The long tenure of officials at the same place makes it easier to establish unethical relationships with the local people. Tanzi also argues that decentralisation promotes personalism and reduces professionalism. Personalism breeds corruption as officials pay greater attention to individual citizen's needs and disregard public interest, thereby defeating the philosophy of decentralised governance. However, the notion that improving participation through decentralisation will necessarily lead to improvements in people's well-being, is not entirely consistent with documented evidence. A recurring theme that emerges from a sizeable body of literature is the relatively weak correlation that exists between democratic decentralisation and poverty reduction (e.g., Blair, 2000; Crook and Manor, 1998; Crook and Sverrisson, 2001; Golooba-Mutebi, 2000; Manor, 1999; Moore and Putzel, 1999; Rahman, 2001; World Bank, 2000). In one respect, this reflects the difficulty of establishing a clear and rigorous link between changes in governance and improvements in well-being (Rahman, 2001). It also suggests a more sober conclusion about the ways in which democratic decentralisation is thought to affect the quality and availability of local economic opportunity. As Crook and Sverrisson's cross-country comparison (2001) concludes:

> "The notion that there is a predictable or general link between decentralisation of government and the development of more 'pro-poor' policies or poverty-alleviating outcomes clearly lacks any convincing evidence. Those who advocate decentralisation on these grounds, at least, should be more cautious, which is not to say that there are not other important benefits, particularly in the field of participation and empowerment."

Even the most successful forms of democratic decentralisation have been unable to overcome economic and political disparities, both within and among regions. This, in part, highlights the problem of raising public revenue in rural areas, in which economic surplus (and, therefore, taxable revenue) is typically poor. Decentralisation can also pose new problems of co-ordination and planning. As the Kerala experience has shown (Ghatak and Ghatak, 2002) too much devolution can lead to major duplications of effort and gaps among different government agencies.

Finally, there is a problem of local elite capture. As many studies (e.g., Blair, 2000; Crook and Sverrisson, 2001; Drèze and Sen, 1996; Manor, 1999; Moore and Putzel, 1999) have pointed out, one of the dangers of devolving authority is that it simply empowers local elites and, worse, perpetuates existing poverty and inequality. Whether the introduction of democratic principles—on its own—would overcome the historical and cultural factors that perpetuate political inequality is somewhat doubtful (Luckham *et al.*, 2000; Moore and Putzel, 1999). This, in turn, highlights the challenge of encouraging democracy in rural areas in which large number of people are dependent upon small numbers of local, powerful elites. It also highlights the challenge of encouraging 'empowerment' without addressing the rights and entitlements (particularly ones governing land and property) that underlie political structures in rural areas.

Where the spoils of government intervention are particularly good, one can predict with reasonable confidence that the costs of ensuring equitable distribution and of discouraging local corruption will be high. This is notoriously true of rural infrastructure projects, such as road building (Rao, 2000) or irrigation (Wade, 1985), in which markets for primary inputs, labour and public regulation (Wade, 1985) are strong. Here the corruption of local administrative bodies will depend on a number of factors:

- The ease of procuring spoils from the programme;
- The ability to avoid detection and/or sanction;
- The amount of money involved (i.e., some departments and programmes are more 'wet' than others);
- Systems of accountability, which would ideally expose and sanction behaviour of this kind.

This last factor is worth highlighting, both because it can be affected by public policy and because it is the misallocation or 'corruption' of public resources that often justifies the strongest calls for democratic decentralisation (e.g., Drèze and Sen, 1996; World Bank, 2000).

Perhaps the strongest argument in favour of decentralisation is the idea that the establishment of strong and accountable systems of governance will encourage a more equitable distribution of state- provided resources, which can be directed towards poor and vulnerable groups. An underlying hypothesis here is that democratic participation will yield strong mechanisms of accountability, which in turn, will improve the distribution of benefits to groups that are traditionally marginalized by market and state.

Moreover, the whole idea of decentralised governance is based upon some key factors like people's participation, accountability, transparency, and fiscal transfers (Braun and Grote, 2002; Tanzi, 2001; Romeo, 1999; Crook and Manor, 1998; Litvack *et al.*, 1998). These are interlinked and their effects on development cannot simply be measured. The critique of decentralisation is valid in those regions of the world where poverty and a dysfunctional democracy are rampant for various reasons. A large part of literature talks about issues of quality of citizens' participation and broader questions of democratic control. The critical democratic theorists have noted that the predominant mode of social organizations is not a vertical relationship of authority between selfish individuals and the *supra* state, but a series of horizontal associations embodying groups of individuals who are capable of regulating and expressing themselves as members of a community, rather than as self-promoting individuals (Roy Chowdhury, 1996).

Decentralised governance may be effective in some parts of the world, where people are active, vigilant, and participative. In such societies, civil society groups assume far greater roles in educating people and, ultimately, people themselves seek greater accountability (fairness) from elected members and officials in meeting their immediate needs. On similar lines, recently the theory of social capital has been receiving increasing attention and it has begun to generate a remarkable consensus regarding the role and importance of communities and local organisations in making decentralised governance effective (Sangita, 2002; Sundaram, 1997; Putnam, 1993; Slater and Watson, 1993).

Matching with the global trend, developing countries often initiate decentralised governance to promote development. India is not an exception to this trend. India has been experimenting with the decentralised governance process for quite some time. After India attaining Independence Mahatma Gandhi–Father of the Nation–strongly favoured far larger role for Panchayats as small republics, enjoying complete political autonomy. He was of firm belief that such an institutional arrangement provides opportunity for villagers to involve in planning, programme implementation and thereby play catalytic role in achieving faster development of village India. Article 40 was added to the Constitution due to Gandhi's insistence (Mathur, 1988; Manor, 1997). The Block as a centre of Community Development (CD) came into existence throughout the country in 1952. However, CD was replaced by the Panchayati Raj Institutions (PRIs) on the basis of Balwant Rai Mehta Committee Report in 1959 with a view to ensure people's involvement in development programmes. These institutions could not be stabilized due to irregular elections, inadequate powers, poor finances and lack of political will. The broad framework for decentralised governance has been laid down in India under the 73rd Constitution Amendment Act. This has ushered in a greater degree of uniformity in the structure (three-tier), composition (reservation for SC, ST and women), powers and functions (financial and planning) of these institutions with the objective of achieving faster social and economic development. The three-tier structures of the PRIs are Zilla Panchayat at the district level, Taluk Panchayat at the intermediate levels and Gram Panchayat at the village level. The 73rd Constitutional Amendment Act has given an impetus to Panchayats for promoting development in terms of infrastructure, education, health and poverty alleviation in rural India.

Further, with the passing of 73rd Constitutional Amendment Act in 1992, a new system of decentralised governance was brought into being. This institutional arrangement promised an alternative to the hitherto followed bureaucratic mechanism. Instead of strengthening the PRIs in true spirit, the State/Union governments from time to time initiated various programmes without making the PRIs effective. There are several parallel programmes in implementation which are directly funded by Union/State governments and monitored by State government officials. These actions undermined the role of PRIs. Empirical evidences from various Indian States have shown that the decentralisation exercises have succeeded, to some extent, in a few States such as West Bengal, Karnataka, Kerala, Maharashtra and Madhya Pradesh. If one has to understand the dilemma of decentralised governance, has to understand the nature of political process, political institutions, local organizations and their temperament towards the development.

Evolution of Decentralisation Concept in India

India is huge with many States having a population of more than 50 million, dwarfing most sovereign countries in the world. To democratically govern a country of this size requires several tiers of government. Even though decentralisation has been an issue of concern in India for over a century, until recently there were generally only two federated tiers of government Central and State. This section summarizes the process leading to the 73rd Constitutional Amendment and its key features. During pre-independence, all efforts were towards administrative decentralisation only. The first attempt was after the 1857 mutiny with the British administration coming under severe financial pressures. Initially the focus was on municipalities. The Resolution on Local Self-Government of 1882 set out principles of decentralisation which many believe, have influenced the debate to date. The resolution recognized the twin considerations of local government: (i) administrative efficiency, and (ii) political education; and sought to promote these. However, the resolution met with resistance, and what evolved in spite of various subsequent committees such as the Royal Commission on Decentralisation (1907), the Report of Montagu and Chelmsford on Constitutional Reforms (1918), and the Government of India Resolution (1918), etc., was a hierarchical administrative structure based on supervision and control that still pervades much of the rural space in India. After independence the scenario were changed and rural self-governance got special priority but its actual implementation took more decades. The debates in the Constituent Assembly on Panchayati Raj were more fundamentally grounded. There were two differing viewpoints—that of Gandhi and of Ambedkar. The fundamental difference in philosophies of these two thinkers was on parliamentary democracy—Ambedkar believed the unit of development should be the individual while Gandhi believed the unit of development should be the village. A compromise was forged and in 1948, PRIs found place in the non-justifiable part of the Constitution.

In India, decentralised governance has been experimenting and practicing for quite some time. In the Indian context, decentralisation enjoyed a traditional name 'Panchayat'. Mahatma Gandhi was inspired by an idyllic view of the village life and the village organization and formulated his ideas as a *sine qua non* for alternative polity of a free India. He observed that India lives in its village and its development process will start with village and villagers. Gandhi emphasized on the supremacy of the people and insisted in the people's democracy as sovereignty at the grass roots which he called "Panchayat".

Gandhiji says, "My idea of Village Swaraj (Panchayat) is that it is a complete republic, independent of its neighbours for its vital wants and yet interdependent for many others in which dependence is a necessity. Thus every village's first concern will be to grow its own food crops, and cotton for its cloth. It should have a reserve for its cattle, recreation and playgrounds for its adults and children. Then if there is more land available, it will grow useful money crops. The village will maintain a village theatre, school and public hall. It will have its own water works ensuring clean supply. Education will be compulsory up to the final basic course. As far as possible every activity will be conducted on cooperative basis. There will be a compulsory service of village guards, who will be selected by rotation from the register maintained by the village. The government of village will be conducted by the Panchayat of five persons elected annually by the adult villagers, male and female both possessing minimum prescribed qualifications. These will have all the authority and jurisdiction required. This Panchayat will be legislature, judiciary and executive combined, to operate for its year of office. Any village can become such a republic today without much Interference" *Harijan*, 26th July, 1942. His idea was to establish such a society where every individual got maximum freedom and opportunity to develop personality and character to the maximum. Therefore, he stated that decentralisation was essential for true democracy, in which everyone can participate in the decision making and implementation processes (Islam; 2003).

However, Gandhiji's plan of decentralisation failed to win acceptance in the operative scheme of the Constitution of India. Soon after independence the urban and the rural elite and their representatives in politics had disdained for Panchayats. They had started looking at elite dominant bureaucratic system as the British ruled in India. The Drafting Committee of the Constitution of India effortlessly did exclude Panchayat in the Constitution. Since, Ambedkar, Chairman of the Drafting Committee of the Constitution had a different view of the Indian rural society, who argued in the Constituent Assembly that "village communities have survived surely on a low, on a selfish level. I hold that these village republics have been the ruination of India. I am, therefore, surprised that those who condemn provincialism and communalism should forward as champions of the village. What is the village, but a sink of localism, a den of ignorance, narrow minded ness and communalism" (Constituent Assembly debates 4th, November, 1948). In his point of view, it would be dangerous to give power to the Panchayat, as he thought that it may control rural power structure, which would work to the detriment of the Harijans and the rural poor. Although, Gandhi looked at village Panchayat as mechanism of all kinds of development, very few of his followers agreed with such views. Even Pandit Nehru chiefly supported the view of Ambedkar, and expressed that no progress can be made from the village, as villagers are backward intellectually and culturally. Gandhi insisted on the inclusion of the Panchayat in the revised draft. Finally, Panchayats gained a provision in the Directive Principles of State Policy, which is not mandatory. Power was given to the State that if the State wants could empower Panchayats. As Article 40 says that, "the state should take steps to organise village Panchayats and endow them with such powers and authority as may be necessary to enable them to function as units of self-government".

In spite of this, Pandit Nehru also realized the importance of decentralised governance in India when he started leading a nation like India. He says, "India will progress only, when the people living in villages become politically conscious. Tile progress of our country is bound up with the progress in our village. If our villages make a progress, India will become a strong nation and nobody will be able to stop its onward march, if you flinch from your determination and get involved in mutual quarrels and petty factions, you will not be able to succeed in your mission".

Prime Minister Nehru inaugurated the Community Development (CD) programme that was launched under First Five Year Plan of India in the year 1952. CD was initiated mainly for promoting development in rural India under the bureaucratic system without taking cognizance of Gandhi's idea of Panchayats. During the implementation period it was observed that the goal of the CD was not successful because of lack of people's participation. At this point, it was so important to know to what degree had this challenge been met. A study team was appointed under the Balwant Rai Mehta in 1957 to examine the creativity for improving economic and social conditions in the rural areas. The committee's view was that without an institute at the village level, which could represent the entire community, assume responsibility and provide the necessary leadership, evoke people's initiative and mobilize their voluntary and spontaneous participation for promoting development, the real success would not come about at all. The team favoured democratic decentralisation through the setting up of PRIs to community. Its recommendation works should be was that, 'public participation is organized through statutory representative bodies'. The Committee viewed at establishing three-tier Panchayat Raj systems through out the country through necessary legislation in states and Union Territories. The Committee also attempted to translate article 40 of the Constitution and remarked that Panchayti Raj system as a means of involving people and their representatives in development programmes of the government (Report of the Committee, 1959). The Prime Minister Jawaharlal Nehru inaugurated Independent India's first Panchayati Raj on 2nd October, 1959 in Rajasthan. After long ages it was observed that Panchayat system was suffered from a number of weaknesses and another study team headed by Ashok Mehta Committee was set up in 1977. The committee viewed that PR system was not only meant for decentralisation of powers and people's participation but it was also supporting rural development and strengthening the planning process in the micro-level (1978). It was marked as turning point in the concept and practice of PRIs.

Again, a committee chaired by Dantwala (1978-83) viewed decentralised block level planning since the centralized planning strategy had failed to provide rural employment and ameliorating the conditions of the rural poor.

Furthermore, a committee was set up in 1982 chaired by Hanumanth Rao, which viewed that unless planning was made from the lower level the desired result might not have been achieved, there should have been decentralised planning process in district level and participation of peoples through democratic institutions for promoting the development programmes.

Later the G.V.K. Rao Committee was set up in 1980, which viewed that strengthening of ZP and District Level Planning, as well as a better integration of Block and lower level planning with lower level PRI's (integrating administrative structure with PR institution) was essential for rural development.

Of late, the 73rd and 74th Constitutional Amendment Act saw the birth of a new era in decentralised governance in India. This has brought out uniformity in the structure (three-tier), composition (reservation for SCs, STs and women), powers and functions (finances and planning) of these institutions to achieve economic and social development. The three-tier structure of Panchayati Raj with Zilla Panchayts at the District level, Block Panchayats at the intermediary level, and Gram Panchayats at the village level has been introduced.

The inducement behind the 73rd Amendment Act was to make Panchayats as good governance or an effective mechanism for economic development and social justice at grass roots level. This Act has brought forth a genuine spirit of democratic decentralisation in the country. The Acts have ushered in change by providing wide-ranging powers and functions to local level constitutional bodies and ordinary people for ensuring participation in planning and implementation for effective and efficient development. The important initiatives have been envisaged for the people's participation are as follows:

- Preparation of plans for economic development and social justice;
- Implementation of schemes for economic development;
- The power and function of Gram Sabha for reservoir of people's power;
- Regular elections to the Panchayats; and
- Proportional seat reservation for scheduled castes and tribes and women.

Milestones in Indian Decentralisation

1882: The Resolution on Local Self-Government.

1907: The Royal Commission on Decentralisation.

1948: Constitutional debates between Gandhi and Ambedkar on Gram Swaraj, 'self-rule'.

1957: Balwantrai Mehta Commission—an early attempt to implement the Panchayat structure at district and Block (Samithi) levels.

1963: K. Santhanam Committee—recommended limited revenue raising powers for Panchayats and the establishment of State Panchayati Raj Finance Corporations.

1978: Asoka Mehta Committee—appointed to address the weaknesses of PRIs, concluded that a resistant bureaucracy, lack of political will, ambiguity about the role of PRIs, and élite capture had undermined previous attempts at decentralisation, recommending that the District serve as the administrative unit in the PRI structure. Based on these recommendations, Karnataka, Andhra Pradesh and West Bengal passed new legislation to strengthen PRIs.

1985: G.V.K. Rao Committee—appointed to address weaknesses of PRIs, recommended that the Block Development Office (BDO) should assume broad powers for planning, implementing and monitoring rural development programmes.

1986: L.M. Singhvi Committee—recommended that local self-government should be constitutionally enshrined, and that the Gram Sabha (the village assembly) should be the base of decentralised democracy in India.

1993: The 73rd Amendment to the Indian Constitution—PRIs at district, Block and village levels are granted Constitutional status. The Gram Sabha is recognised as a formal democratic body at the village level. The 74th Amendment, granting Constitutional status to municipal bodies, is passed soon after.

1996: The Adivasi Act—Powers of self-government are extended to tribal communities living in 'Fifth Schedule' areas.

In consonance with the 73rd Constitutional Amendment Act 1992, different State governments have initiated new Acts on decentralisation. Like other States GoWB also has introduced new amendment Act 1994 on decentralisation. However, West Bengal had a long history of democratic decentralisation since 1977.

Decentralisation at Central and State Level

Bengal, the erstwhile province in British India, had a long tradition of working of the statutory decentralisation. The diverse experience of running these rural bodies was inherited by West Bengal, a truncated part of old Bengal province since independence and the new State has been experimenting with different types and methods of rural self-government since then (Mukhopadhayay, 1977). The rural administration of Bengal till 1957 was governed by three pre-independence Acts: (1) The Village Chowkidari Act of 1870; (2) The Bengal Local Self-Government Act of 1885; and (3) The Bengal Village Self Government Act of 1919.

In the British period, the villagers of Bengal were acquainted with the idea of Panchayat primarily in 1870 through the Village Chowkidari Act. It may be observed that this Panchayat had no Panchayati Raj Institutions and Rural Development semblance with the ancient Panchayat system that existed in India in different forms in the provinces of India in the pre-British and even in the early period. The Chowkidari Act was purely of British make and its scope was extremely restricted. These Panchayats appointed by the District Magistrates, were merely an agency for the assessment and collection of a local tax, which was levied for the support of the village police without having anything to do with the management of affairs of immediate interest to the villagers (Mukherjee, 1974).

The Bengal Local Self Government Act of 1885 established a network of rural local bodies at three levels, the District Board, the Local Board and the Union Board. The District Board had jurisdiction over a whole district. The local Board was meant for each sub-division and the Union Committees for selected areas within the subdivision. The main functions of District Board were maintenance and improvement of roads and other communications, primary education, health and sanitation, veterinary work, construction and maintenance of rest house, administration of ponds and ferries and relief of suffering in time of famine and serious distress. The function of Local Board was care and maintenance of village roads, management of ponds and charge of ferries. The function of Union

Committee was management and control over ponds, control over village roads, sanitation and supply of water. The Act of 1885 provided for a District Board for each district and a Local Board for every sub-division of a district and fixed their term of office at four years. These bodies were to be constituted by the government on the basis of informal election. In most cases the names of persons nominated by the government used to be made known to the village folk in a meeting presided over by the sub-divisional officer. And the people invariably were expected to approve those names.

The Local Board had no independent authority and jurisdiction of its own. The Local Boards in the district were designed to act as the agents of the District Board for undertaking the public works and duties assigned to them by the District Board at its direction. Consisting of not less than six members, the two-thirds of the Local Board's members had to be elected by the people directly on the basis of a restricted franchise, and the remaining one-third to be nominated by the Government. The elected elements, in fact, used to be chosen by the Government and their selection had to be approved by the people as they could ill-afford to reject a candidate having the blessing of the District Officer or the Sub-Divisional Officer.

The Union Committee was the lowest tier of the Local Self Government Act of 1885. For election to Union Committees, only male persons were entitled to vote who must have paid yearly one rupee or more as road access or license tax in respect of trade or industry in the area, or possess an annual income of Rs. 240 from any source or being a member of a joint Hindu family, was a graduate or licentiate or held a certificate as pleader or Mokhtar. A candidate must have paid not less than Rs. 5 for road access or license tax of not less than Rs. 20 or possessed clear annual income of Rs. 1000 from any source, or being a member of a joint family was a graduate or licentiate or legal practitioner (Mukherjee, 1974).

The Bengal Village Self Government Act of 1919 achieved the fusion of the Chowkidari Union and Union Committee, the two bodies hitherto responsible for Chowkidari (police) and municipal functions, respectively, in the newly created body at the village level known as the Union Board. The Union Board came to be invested, apart from police function, with the powers and functions necessary for the management of village community affairs, minor roads, water works, public health and sanitation.

The Act of 1919 was further amended by the West Bengal Act of 1947: In 1947 when nomination system to the Union Board was abolished.

There was further extension of franchise and women were allowed to vote and stand as candidates, for the first time, in the Union Boards' elections in 1950 (West Bengal Act 1950).

The first instalment of decentralisation of power to the democratically constituted Panchayats came at the beginning of the Second Five Year Plan when a number of Panchayats were formed in different parts of the State as an experimental measure to gain practical experience in democratic decentralisation. A draft of the Panchayat Bill was introduced in the West Bengal Legislative Assembly in 1956 which was enacted as the West Bengal Panchayat Act 1957. This Act abolished the Union Boards and established the two tier system of rural local government consisting of GP at the village level and Anchal Panchayat at the union level. This Act was a progressive development towards village self-government in West Bengal. It was having provisions for rural development, rural civics, rural justice, rural police, etc. In the old Act there was no provision for development work. This Act also introduced adult franchise, for the first time, in the rural self-governing bodies of West Bengal. Under the Village Self Government Act 1919 the franchise power was given only to male. Besides, a new concept called the Gram Sabha (at the village level—village assembly) was introduced. The Gram Sabha consisted of all persons whose names were in electoral rolls of the West Bengal Legislative Assembly. Each Gram Sabha covered a population of 700 to 1,200 persons, residing in one or two villages. Gram Panchayat was the executive of the Gram Sabha. The Act required this body to meet at least twice a year to consider the annual budget and the annual report of Gram Panchayat and to give directions to it for future guidance. The members of the Gram Sabha elected from among themselves, their representatives to the GP. The GP was the lowest tier in the whole structure of Panchayati Raj. Its membership varied between nine and fifteen. At the first meeting of the Gram Panchayat its members were to elect one Adhyaksha (President) and one Upadhyaksha (Vice President).

The West Bengal Zilla Parishads Act was passed in 1963 to provide for remodelling of Local Government with a view to associating the local authorities with development activities and bringing about democratic decentralisation and people's participation in planning and development. This was a landmark in the evolution of Panchayati Raj in West Bengal. This Act replaced the old District Board and also District Development Council by the ZP at the district level. It established a new body Anchalik Parishad (AP) at the newly created administrative level of the Community Development Block.

These two Acts (1957 and 1963) provided four-tier system of decentralised governance consisting of ZP, AP, Anchal Panchayat (AP) and GP. In accordance with the Mehta Committee Report the GoWB established ZP at the district level, AP at the Block level and GP at the village level. Only AP in between the Block and village was new contribution of GoWB. This was created to replace the old Union Board with whose functioning the rural people in Bengal had become quite familiar. Though the GP and AP were established during 1958-59, the full-fledged four-tier structure of Panchayati Raj was ceremonially inaugurated in West Bengal on October 2, 1964, the date being the birth day of Mahatma Gandhi (Mukherjee, 1974).

Even though the above said Act facilitated decentralisation, in practice it was merely playing lip services to the idea of people's participation. Meanwhile, the then Congress Government in the State went through a crisis (1965-66) of an unprecedented nature. The Congress Party was defeated and a United Front dominated by the Left Party came to the power in West Bengal in 1967 general election. The new ministry introduced a comprehensive Panchayat bill in the Legislative Assembly. But before this bill was enacted, Front government went out of office in 1970. When a new Congress led coalition government came to the power it promised a new Panchayat system in Bengal. At last, the West Bengal Panchayat Act was passed in 1973 (Ghosh, 2000). However, the then government took no steps to implement them. Elections were not held regularly. The Anchal and the Gram Panchayat elections had been due for periods varying from ten to fifteen years in 1977. Again, the Congress government went out of office in West Bengal in 1977. The CPIM led Left Front Government (LFG) came into power in Bengal and proceeded to pass a series of Amendment Acts of 1973 (Webster, 1992). Thus, major amendments to the Panchayat Acts were made in 1992, 1994, and 1997. The immediate purpose of the 1994 amendment was to bring the State Act in conformity with the Constitutional Amendment and in fact provisions of the 1992 amendments, particularly provisions relating to reservation of seats, were made in conformity with the constitutional amendment.

West Bengal is one of the forerunners in installing a 3-tier Panchayati Raj System (PRIs) for rural local governance in India. The present generation Panchayats in the State started its journey in 1978, i.e., 15 years ahead of the 73rd Amendment of the Constitution of India. Ever since their inception, the State has demonstrated strong commitment to rural decentralisation by ensuring regular elections to PRIs, entrusting them with increasing responsibility of implementing various rural development programmes and making the development bureaucracy part of PRIs. The state also ensured adequate representation of the socially backward classes—Scheduled Castes (SC), Scheduled Tribes (ST) and women in PRIs for their involvement in the process of socio-economic development.

That rural poverty declined in the State from 73 per cent in 1973-74 to 32 per cent in 1999-2000, that annual growth rate of foodgrain production was recorded at 6.5 per cent between 1981 and 1991 and that the highest rate of growth of wages was recorded between 1979-80 and 1992-93 is mostly attributed to the effective role of PRIs in the successful land reforms and in organizing the poor and augmenting their social and economic opportunities through various programmes. It is acclaimed that West Bengal Panchayats showed the way and inspired the constitutional amendment.

While the Panchayat system in West Bengal attracted even world-wide attention, some critics have observed the "concepts of Panchayats being institutions of self-governance" still "either missing or dimly perceived." Some others observe that PRIs function more as part of the delivery system of the State Government rather than as institutions of self-governance. The State Government itself identified areas in PRI functioning which needed systemic improvements, e.g., institutionalization of bottom-up planning approach ; intensification of people's participation and of local level organizations in PRI functioning; convergence of PRIs with all other development agencies; greater accountability of the development bureaucracy to PRIs; and the like.

The State Government, always open to new ideas, brought about need-based reforms in the Panchayat system from time to time from the very beginning. Some unique features are—

(a) Gram Sansad at village lavel/Gram Panchayat (GP) lavel, Block Sansad at Block lavel/Panchayat Samiti (PS) level and Zilla Sansad at District lavel/Zilla Parishad (ZP) level,
(b) District Council at each headed by the leader of the opposition,
(c) Gram Unnayan Samiti at the Gram Sansad level,
(d) Institutional involvement of opposition members in the Standing Committees of ZP and PS and in the Finance and Planning Sub Committee of GP,
(e) Determination of principles of subsidiarity for each tier of Panchayats,

(f) Mapping of activities to be performed by three tier Panchayats falling under 28 subjects (out of 29) listed in the Eleventh Schedule of the Constitution of India,

(g) Empowering the Standing Committees and Sub-Committees to prepare and implement their own work plan and budget,

(h) Opening Panchayat Window in the State Budget by the Departments who have substantial flow of fund to Panchayats,

(i) Annual self-evaluation of all the three tier Panchayat bodies through score-based schedules for assessment of their performances and providing incentive grant to the best performing GP in each Block, to the best performing PS in each District and to the best performing ZP in the State separately under two heads—(1) institutional functioning and good governance and (2) mobilization of revenue and utilization of resources on the basis of validated scores of self-evaluation and

(j) Double entry system of accounting for all the three tier Panchayats.

The PRIs in the State have grown over the years with more spontaneity and has made positive impact in order to achieve economic development and secure social justice for all. However, even now there is a long way to go for the West Bengal Panchayats to really become proper people's institution as vanguard of holistic development of rural people. This document visions such institutions and sets out strategy to accomplish the vision. (Roadmap for Panchayat in West Bengal: A Vision Document of Department of Panchayat and Rural Development, Government of West Bengal, 2009).

73rd and 74th Constitutional Amendment Act

Only in 1993, with the 73rd Constitutional Amendment, were local governments in rural areas at the district, Block and village levels, the PRIs, made an effective reality all over India. The 73rd Amendment is based on a political idea-decentralised democracy. In it citizen participation is seen as key in both decision making and effective service delivery. This goal of reclaiming the State by the citizen has become important at this stage of India's development, not just because the bureaucracy and political class have reduced the State to a rent-seeking State, but also because the State's delivery mechanisms are showing signs of atrophy. The 73rd Constitutional Amendment Act (CCA) was passed on December 22, 1992, on the basis of general consensus. After ratification by more than half of the State Assemblies and after obtaining the assent of the President the Act came into force on 24 April, 1993. There are some radical features in the Act (Mahipal, 1997). The 73rd Amendment gives village, Block and district level bodies a constitutional status under Indian law (World Bank, 2000). They try to address some of the problems encountered by PRIs in previous years, by:

(i) Granting PRIs Constitutional status,
(ii) Empowering socially and economically disadvantaged groups, i.e., Dalits (Dalits are broadly Scheduled Castes), Adivasis (Adivasi are Scheduled Tribes), and women,
(iii) Ensuring free, fair, and regular elections,
(iv) Keeping terms fixed,
(v) Identifying a list of items which would come under the jurisdiction of PRIs, and
(vi) Addressing the issue of PRI finance.

Some of the provisions of the new Act are mandatory in nature, which are to be followed by all the States.

Mandatory Provisions

1. *Constitution of Panchayats*: According to the Central Act, there shall be a three-tier system of Panchayats in all States: at the village, intermediate and district levels. However, in States having a population of less than 20 lakh, the intermediate level may not be constituted.

2. *Composition of Panchayat*: All the seats in a Panchayat shall be filled by persons chosen by direct election from territorial constituencies in the Panchayat area. Such elections shall be conducted under the supervision, control and direction of the State Election Commission, comprising the State Election Commissioner appointed by the State government. The Chairperson of the Panchayat at the intermediate level shall be indirectly elected by and from amongst the elected members of the Panchayats.

3. *Reservation of Seats*: Seats shall be reserved for both Scheduled Castes (SC) and Scheduled Tribes (ST) in every Panchayat. The number of such seats shall be, as far as possible, in proportion with the percentage of their population to the total population. Such seats may be allotted by rotation to different constituencies in a Panchayat. Again, one-third of

these reserved seats will be further reserved for women from these castes and tribes. Similarly, in case of general seats also, one-third of them shall be reserved for women belonging to any class or category. Such seats will also be allotted by rotation to different constituencies in a Panchayat. Such reservations will also apply to the offices of chairpersons on a rotation basis

4. *Duration of Panchayats*: A Panchayat shall have a term of five years and if it is dissolved for any reason, fresh elections shall be held within six months from the date of such dissolution. In case the remainder of the period is less than six months, it shall not be necessary to hold any election for constituting the Panchayat for such period. A Panchayat constituted following the dissolution of its predecessor as above, shall continue only for the remainder of the period for which the dissolved Panchayat would have continued.

5. *State Finance Commission*: The Governor of a State is to constitute a State Finance Commission within one year of the Act coming into force and thereafter every fifth year. The Commission is to review the financial position of the Panchayats and make recommendations to the Governor in the following respects:

(a) The principles which should govern–
   (i) The distribution of the proceeds of the taxes, duties, tolls, fees levied by the State between itself and the Panchayats and the allocation among the Panchayats at all levels their respective shares of such proceeds;
   (ii) The determination of the taxes, tolls, duties and fees which may be assigned to or appropriated by the Panchayats;
   (iii) The grants-in-aid to Panchayats from the Consolidated Fund of the States;

(b) The measures needed to improve the financial position of the Panchayats; and

(c) Any other matter referred to the Finance Commission by the Governor in the interest of sound finance of the Panchayats.

The Central Finance Commission (CFC) is also required to make recommendations to the President as to the measures needed to augment the Consolidated Fund of a State to supplement the resources of the Panchayats in the State on the basis of the recommendations made by the State Finance Commission.

6. *District Planning Committee*: The provision for constituting the

District Planning Committee was made under the Constitution (74th) Amendment Act 1992. Accordingly, there shall be a District Planning Committee at the district level to consolidate the plans prepared by the Panchayats and municipalities and to prepare a draft development plan for the district as a whole.

The subject Panchayati Raj Institutions belongs to the State List in the Indian federal system. Therefore, the Central Act has left a large area for the State legislatures to fill in. Suitable provisions were to be made in the Acts passed by them for the purpose; keeping in mind the overall objectives spelt out in the Central Act. Some other provisions are discretionary in nature where the States are given some choice in their implementation.

Source: The 73rd Constitutional Amendment Act 1992

Discretionary provisions are listed below:

1. Nomenclature of the Panchayats at different levels.
2. Nomenclature of the chairpersons at different levels.
3. Size in terms of population and area for determination of Panchayats at village and intermediate levels.
4. Powers and functions of the Gram Sabha.
5. Composition of the Panchayats at different levels: Provided that the ratio between the population of the territorial area of a Panchayat at any level and the number of seats in such Panchayat to be filled by election shall, so far as practicable, is the same throughout the State.
6. To provide or not for the representation of:
   (a) The chairpersons of village Panchayats in the Panchayats at the intermediate level, and of the intermediate level panchayats at the district level Panchayat;
   (b) The members of the Lok Sabha and the members of the State legislative assembly representing constituencies that comprise wholly or partly a Panchayat area at levels other than the village level;
   (c) The members of the Rajya Sabha and the members of the State legislative council where they are registered as electors.
7. The mode of election of the chairperson of a Panchayat at the village level.
8. The manner in which the seats of the members of the Panchayats at different levels shall be reserved for scheduled castes/tribes

and women, provided that the number of seats shall be allotted by rotation to different Panchayats at each level.

9. The manner in which the offices of the chairpersons at different levels shall be reserved for scheduled castes/tribes and women. Provided that the number of offices reserved shall be allotted by rotation to different Panchayats at each level,
10. To provide or not for reservation of seats in favour of backward class in any Panchayat or offices of chairpersons in the Panchayats at any level.
11. To endow the Panchayats at various levels with such powers and authority as may be necessary to enable them to function as institutions of self-government and to make provisions for the development of powers and responsibilities upon Panchayats at the appropriate level with respect to:
    (a) The preparation of plans for economic development and social justice;
    (b) The implementation of schemes for economic development and social justice entrusted to them, including those in relation to the matters listed in the Eleventh Schedule of the Constitution.
12. To decide the taxes, duties, tolls and fees for which a Panchayat is authorised and also lay down the procedure and limits for the same.
13. To decide limits and the conditions of the taxes, duties, tolls and fees levied and collected by the State government but assigned to the Panchayats.
14. To decide the amount of grants-in-aid provided to the Panchayats from the Consolidated Fund of the State.
15. To authorise the Panchayats at different levels to create a fund for crediting all money received by or on behalf of the Panchayats and also for the withdrawal of such money.
16. To provide for the composition of the Finance Commission, the qualifications shall be requisite for appointment as members thereof and the manner in which they shall be selected. The Commission shall determine their procedure and shall have such powers in the performance of their functions as the legislature of the State by law confers on them. The Governor shall cause every recommendation made by the Commission under this article together with an explanatory memorandum as to the action taken thereon to be laid before the State legislature.

17. To make provisions with respect to the maintenance of accounts by Panchayats and the auditing of such accounts.
18. To determine the conditions of service and tenure of office of the State Election Commissioner and to make provision with respect to all matters relating to or in connection with election to the Panchayats. It is provided that the State Election Commissioner shall not be removed from his office except in like manner and on the like grounds as a judge of the High Court. This condition of service of the State Election Commissioner shall not be varied to his disadvantage after his appointment. The Governor, when so required by the State Election Commission, shall make available such staff as may be necessary for the discharge of the functions conferred on it.
19. To make provision with respect to all matters relating to, or in connection with elections to the Panchayats.
20. To make provisions with respect to:
    (a) The composition and functions of the District Planning Committee;
    (b) The manner in which the office of the chairperson of the District Planning Committee shall be filled, provided that not less than four-fifths of the total number of members of the committee shall be elected by and from amongst the elected members of the Panchayat at the district level and of the municipalities in the district in proportion to the ratio between the populations of rural and urban areas.

At the village level, the most important provisions relating to participation and accountability are those governing reservations and the Gram Sabha. Under the 73rd Amendment one-third of all seats must be reserved for women. Likewise, reservations for Scheduled Castes (SCs) and Scheduled Tribes (STs) are made in proportion to their population. At the village level, the Gram Sabha, which constitutes all eligible voters within a Gram Panchayat area, is meant to serve as a principal mechanism for transparency and accountability. Among its principal functions are:

- To review the annual statement of accounts;
- To review reports of the preceding financial year;
- To review and submit views on development programmes for the following year; and

- To participate in the identification of beneficiaries for some government schemes.

This last provision is particularly important because it confers substantive authority over an area that is particularly prone to misallocation and corruption (Sections 3 and 4). As Jha (2000) has argued, "The 73rd and 74th Amendments.. are designed to promote self-governance through statutory recognition of local bodies. The latter are expected to move away from their traditional role of simply executing the programmes handed down to them by higher levels of government and to formulate and implement their own programmes of economic development and social justice".

In short, the 73rd Amendment covers many areas that would enable the Panchayats to improve the lives and well-being of poor and vulnerable groups. Moreover, it contains specific provisions that guarantee the participation of traditionally excluded groups, such as women, SCs and STs, and transparency for local institutions such as the Gram Panchayats and the Gram Sabha. However, as Mukherjee (1999) has argued, the ambiguity surrounding the concept of 'self government' and the substantial power that still rests with the State governments have prevented most States from devolving any substantive power to the Panchayats. Such findings are consistent with a wider literature on the problems most commonly associated with decentralisation in India (e.g., Crook and Manor, 1998; Jha, 1999; Mathew, 2001; Mukherjee, 1999; Oommen, 1999; World Bank, 2000).

Under 73rd and 74th Constitutional Amendments a series of ideal conditions under which local institutions have been shown to be more accountable to poor and politically marginal groups in society. These were:

- Active participation among broad elements of society, including voting, campaigning, attending meetings, running for office, lobbying representatives, etc.;
- Fiscal and political support from higher level authorities within government; and
- The existence of competitive political parties whose legitimacy depends at least in part on the support of the poor.

In order to consider these hypotheses in relation to India's decentralisation process, it is first necessary to establish whether the constitutional changes that transpired in 1993 were in fact decentralisation. The scholarly literature on Panchayati Raj tends to move in two fairly incongruous directions. One, which is firmly grounded in the liberal democratic paradigm, argues that the 73rd Amendment did indeed create the conditions for decentralisation in India, and the second is that this was a positive development.

Although there is some disagreement about whether and to what extent the reforms have been implemented, the general consensus within this thought is that the 73rd Amendment was a positive step for Indian decentralisation and that the only factor preventing successful devolution is the failure to implement fully the terms and conditions of the 73rd Amendment. A second thought is decidedly more critical of decentralisation in general and the 73rd Amendment in particular. A central assertion that underlies this second school is that the reforms put in place in 1993 are largely cosmetic, and that the ultimate distribution of power and resources in rural areas is dependent on the pre-existing pattern of social inequalities created by caste, religion, class, gender and other forms of rural domination.

Using the conventional classification of 'political, administrative and fiscal decentralisation', the World Bank's three-volume study of Indian decentralisation (World Bank, 2000) ranks India 'among the best performers' internationally in terms of political decentralisation, but 'close to the last' in terms of administrative decentralisation. Most States have held at least one round of elections since 1993. Reservations allowing the participation of women, Scheduled Castes and Scheduled Tribes have been respected. Finally, voter participation has been high. The World Bank study goes on to argue that although Indian States and the Union Government have been willing to recognize the Panchayats, to hold elections and to respect stipulations governing reservations for Scheduled Castes (SCs), Scheduled Tribes (STs) and women, they have been unwilling to vest them with sufficient 'administrative control over significant functions or fiscal autonomy', (World Bank, 2000). In most States, Panchayats have been handed a wide array of responsibilities without the necessary fiscal and administrative resources.

In its assessment of Indian decentralisation, the Task Force on Devolution of Powers and Functions upon Panchayati Raj Institutions (MoRD, 2001) found that 'most of the States' had satisfied only the basic requirements relating to the transfer of functions, functionaries, funds and financial autonomy to the Panchayats.

Vyasulu (2000) finds that State governments have devolved little finances and fiscal powers to the Panchayats. Instead, many have established 'parallel bodies' as a channel for development funding. Self Help Groups (SHGs) connected to the *Janmabhoomi* programme in Andhra Pradesh and the Rajiv Gandhi Watershed 'Missions' in Madhya Pradesh are two illustrations of this trend.

Similarly, Oommen's (1999) comparison of 12 Indian States concludes that the Conformity Acts have generally 'been an exercise in amending existing Panchayat legislation for the sake of satisfying the mandatory provisions of the 73rd Amendment.' In particular, he raises the following concerns:

- Village Panchayats have been delegated functions 'without adequate administrative, financial and technical support', (1999);
- With the exception of Kerala and West Bengal, Panchayats lack discretionary powers over spending and staff;
- There is insufficient clarity and differentiation of functions among Panchayats and other levels of government;
- States reserve the right to assign or withdraw functions to and from the Panchayats by 'executive fiat,' (1999);
- Panchayats at all levels have inadequate powers of taxation; and
- Panchayats lack autonomous budgeting powers.

Again, the question of fiscal autonomy is a matter of some debate. George Mathew has argued that Panchayats do not necessarily need their own revenues to operate effectively. Access to 'guarded' or 'fenced' transfers from higher level authorities can serve this purpose, so long as the Panchayats have the autonomy to decide how the money gets spent. Others, such as Oommen (1999) have argued that political autonomy is directly dependent on the ability to raise and spend public resources and Fiscal autonomy cannot be built into a regime of grants-in-aid. PRIs can play a genuine role in local development and self-rule only if they enjoy some degree of fiscal autonomy. This attribute is clearly more than relying on untied funds and rests on innovative resource mobilization, including project-tied loans, public contributions and the like.

Leaving aside the problem of raising revenues in poor areas, there is also a problem of inter- governmental transfers. As Jha (2000) has argued, the State Finance Commissions (SFCs) have encountered difficulties assessing the financial needs of local bodies, reflecting both a lack of clear guidelines governing the function of SFCs and a dearth of reliable information on sub-district revenues and incomes (Jha, 2000). For the

Panchayats, this has reinforced a situation in which local bodies (particularly village-level Panchayats) have been handed vast responsibility with insufficient authority to raise and spend revenues and resources.

Again, the political structures created during Independence and the political dynamics that unfolded in the 1970s and 1980s have combined to create a political environment that has been particularly hostile to Panchayati Raj. However, there are exceptions to this rule, and the exceptions can tell us something about the ways in which decentralisation can work in this relatively inhospitable climate.

Crook and Manor (1998) argue that decentralisation has helped to counteract the types of top-down processes that have traditionally sheltered public officials from scrutiny and accountability in India. The 73rd Amendment contains a number of provisions that aim to counterbalance patterns of inequality and discrimination in rural India. Theory, reservations and the Gram Sabha provide an important means of ensuring that marginal groups are incorporated into local politics and that representatives act in a way that is consistent with their formal responsibilities and the plural interests of their constituents. In practice, however, neither appears to have lived up to this (rather lofty) ideal. Studies of decentralisation have consistently highlighted the fact that the 73rd Amendment and earlier attempts at decentralisation have failed to prevent a local (and primarily landed) elite from controlling local Panchayats. Micro-level studies have shown that Gram Sabha often fail to fulfil their role as deliberative bodies or as a mechanism for accountability (Alsop *et al.*, 2000; Deshpande and Murthy, 2002; Nambiar, 2001). This is partly attributed to low levels of participation among the electorate as well as the non-cooperation of local officials. Examples of the latter include officials delaying or postponing Gram Sabha meetings, officials were not attending Gram Sabha, and, more generally, official decisions having no bearing on decisions reached during the Gram Sabha (Crook and Manor, 1998: Chapter 2; Deshpande and Murthy, 2002; Nambiar, 2001). Explanations for poor participation in the Gram Sabha include (e.g., Alsop *et al.*, 2000; Nambiar, 2001):

- Limited benefits of participation;
- Opportunity costs, particularly on the part of very poor groups;
- Fear of disrupting existing patron-client relations;
- Corruption;
- Agenda fixing;

- Factionalism; and
- Fear of exclusion from community.

The World Bank's study of 53 villages in Rajasthan and Madhya Pradesh (Alsop *et al.*, 2000) found that gender and education were important determinants of political participation, measured in terms of campaigning, attending rallies, supporting a candidate, influencing voters, contacting a public representative, and attending Gram Sabhas. Even when there are reservations to ensure that marginal groups have a place in the Panchayat system, there is evidence to suggest that these formal institutions have been usurped by more informal patterns of domination and power. Reservations for women, for instance, are notoriously prone to corruption by male relatives, excluded from formal participation by their lack of scheduled status (Vyasulu and Vyasulu, 1999). Similar patterns have been observed among SCs and STs, whose economic well-being is dependent on the patronage of local elites. Such findings highlight the difficulty of transposing a formal model of democracy onto societies in which power and politics are still determined by highly informal systems of inequality and domination.

Evolution of Panchayati Raj Institutions (PRIs)

India has a long history of traditional local governments, going back to more than 4000 years. This institution has survived numerous political changes and upheavals in the ancient and medieval periods till the advent of the British Raj. With the coming of the colonial administration, the patterns of the working of the local bodies underwent marked changes. The present pattern of urban and rural bodies reflects a distinct impact of colonial period. The modern structure of Panchayati Raj in India is evolved through a long historical phase.

Village administration was also a significant part of the Ancient Indian Political System. During the Vedic age, the Aryans had built up small villages and the administration of the area was looked after by the village councils. A system of giving taxes also prevailed in the ancient society. Taxes such as Pali, Sulk and Bhaga were collected from the people. The revenue was spent for the benefit of the subjects. The presence of local self-governance has found in *Veda*, *Upanishad* and other old manuscripts. The Concept of Panchayat has originated from the word *Panch-Ayat* or a group of five persons selected by the villagers. Basically, it indicates the system through which rural people are governed. The word *Panchayatan* been found in old Sanskrit scriptures, which means a group of five persons, including some spiritual man. The concept of *Panch Parameswar* is found in ancient manuscript. Terms like *Samiti* and *Sabha* had found in *Rig Veda. Sabha* and *Samiti* were the democratic structure at the local level or village level and the king used to get the approval of *Sabha* and *Samiti* regarding certain functions and decisions (Joshi, R.P. and Narwani, G.S., 2002). In the later Vedic period, the *Samiti* disappeared as a popular assembly while the *Sabha* sank into a narrow body corresponding to the kings Privy Council (Singh Raj, 1996). In *Rig Veda* and *Atharva Veda* there are references to the ancient nature of Panchayats. This system was started by the king *Prithee*. Administration of village was administrated under the supervision and guidance of *Mukhiya* in great extent reference as *Gramin* is obtained in Vedic literature. It is called *Grambhojak* in *Jatakkathas*. Volumes, inscriptions, copper-plates and notes of tourists from Vedic age to ancient age refer *gramin* in various different words. In this way, it was known by different names in different regions of India. It is referred as *Gramin* in North Indian, *Munund* in Telangana, *Mahattak* in Uttar Pradesh and *Gramukut* and *Gavunda* in South India. Names may be differed but he was the main officer of village. Generally, rank of *Gramin* was hereditary but in case of non-worthiness of heir, the rank of *Gramin* was allocated to worth member of his family. *Gramin* was the administration and military head of village. His main duty was to maintain peace and defence against external forces, administration and to collect taxes. The office of the village head man (*Gramani*) indicates the emergence of the village as a unit of administration.

Again according to a Tenth Century *Sukha Neetisar* in ancient India members of the Panchayat was elected by the common man. Panchayats were given utmost respect. Disbursement of land, collection of taxes, law enforcement was under its full control. Panchayat used to come to the rescue of villagers during the time of emergency. The head of Panchayat was seen as a man of justice. The elder son of the head used to inherit his father. This way Indian rural society from the ancient period had Panchayat system which worked in a traditional manner. Mentions of village administration are also found during the fourth century B.C. when republican federation existed in the society of India. The city of Vaishali had Panchayat for administering justice and courts. The republican character of the polity of Vaishali lasted for thousands of years.

The existence of Panchayat system in Epic year had been found in two great epics—*Ramayana* and *Mahabharata*. The administration was divided into *Pur* (city) and *Janapad* (villages). The village peoples were called *Janapadi* on those days. The villages were termed as their size, i.e., *Gram* (village); *Maha Gram* (Big Village); *Ghosh* (group of Villages). The existence of *Mandi* (local market) is also found in the *Ramayana*. In *Ramayana* of Valmiki, there are references to the *Ganapada* (village federation) which was perhaps a kind of federation of village republics (Ghosh, R. and Pramanik, A.K., 1999). The local bodies were called as *Shreni* and *Nigam*. The system of governance was divided into the rule of king (*Raj-Tantra*), the rule of people (*Praja-Tantra*) and rule of the wise men (*Vidvat-Tantra*) or educated and knowledgeable person (Joshi, R.P. and Narwani, G.S., 2002).

Panchayats were so powerful during the *Mahabharata* period that even king could not interfere in their working. They were called *Gana* or *Sabha.* Although, the system during that period was autocratic, even then the king has to except the decision of the members of the *Sabhas* on Panchayats (Bhuyan and P.C. Pradhan, 2010). As per the *Mahabharata,* over and above the villages, there were units of 10, 20, 100 and 1,000 village groups. *Gramik* was the chief official of the village. *Dashap* was the chief of ten villages. *Vishya Adhipati*, *Sath Gram Adhyaksha* and *Sahasra Gram Pati* were the chief of 20, 100 and 1,000 villages respectively (Joshi, R.P. and Narwani, G.S., 2002). Existence of local self-governance had been also found in *Manu Smriti* as well as in Chanakya's *Arthashastra.* In *Manu Smriti* and Chanakya's *Arthashastra* the head of the village was called *Gramik*. Chanakya established Panchayats in villages and they had all powers to deal with issues relating to social and religious behaviour. They could interfere and express their opinion in the day-to-day affairs of the *Sabha* (Singh, A.K.). The village Panchayat enjoyed a lot of autonomy. Most of the religious, cultural, and economic activities were handled with care and efficiency by them (Mahapatra, S., 2006). During the Mauryan period (322 to 195 B.C.), Gram Panchayat existed and were well organized. Village life was run by the Panchayats. They also worked as administrative units. Villagers used to organize works of public utility and recreation, settle disputes, and act as trustees for the property of minors. But, they had not yet evolved regular councils. The village council appeared to have evolved into regular bodies in the Gupta period. They were known as *Panchamandalas* in central India and *Gramajanapadas* in Bihar (Altekar, A.S., 1997). In Chandragupta Maurya's regime, the decentralisation of powers was adopted as administrative policy. The smallest unit of the governance was village and head of the village was known as 'Gramik'. The villagers elect *Gramik*. The term like *Gram Sabha*, *Gram Janpad* and *Panch Mandali* are also found from the record of Gupta period. Village governance is also found in the Shukracharya's *Neeti Shastra*. Self-governance in the villages was also developed by the Chola.

During the medieval and Mughal periods, village bodies were the pivot of administration. In India after the Tenth Century, when Muslim influence started increasing, there was a change in the traditional face of Panchayats. But new ruling system did not change outwardly. Tughlaks had instructed his men especially not to interfere in the working of Panchayats and also not to harm them. In the Mughal period, particularly in the regime of Sher Shah, the villages were governed by their own Panchayats. Each Panchayat comprised of village elders who looked after the interest of the people and administered justice and imposed punishment on defaulters. The headman of the village, a semi-government official, acted as a coordinator between the village Panchayat and the higher administrative hierarchy. Akbar accepted this system and made it an indispensable part of civil administration. In this period, each village had its own Panchayat of elders. It was autonomous in its own sphere and exercised powers of local taxation, administrative control, justice and punishment (Ghosh, R., Pramanik, A.K., 1999). But during the Mughal period, because of innumerable battles and of the exploitation by land revenue officials there was a decline in the power of Panchayats. The system of providing justice directly by the Muslim rulers was another reason for the decline of this system. This was a very crucial period for the existence of Panchayats (Singh, A.K.). The Mughals introduced elaborate administrative machinery with a hierarchy of officials, particularly in the field of revenue. The Mughal local administrative system lasted over centuries. It was with the collapse of the Mughals stronghold, the British established their hegemony in India.

To a large extent, however, the modern idea of the Panchayat, its nature and its functions, derives from the image of the Indian village community conjured up in the writings of Sir William Jones, Hector Munro, Mountstuart Elphinstone, John Malcolm and a variety of other colonial authors in the late eighteenth and early nineteenth centuries. References to Panchayats and Janapadas in ancient Vedic texts, translated into English for the first time by orientalist scholars.

British officials found it as an elemental unit of Indian society and politics. Its most succinct and influential expression may be found in Charles Metcalfe's defense of the *Mahalwari* system of revenue settlement adopted in the newly ceded and conquered territories of the North-Western

Province (later UP). Describing the fortified villages which sprung up around Delhi in the years after the collapse of Mughal power in 1761 Metcalfe wrote to the 1832 Select Parliamentary Committee on the East India Company's charter in brilliantly evocative terms:

> "The village communities are little republics, having nearly everything they can want within themselves and almost independent of any foreign relations. They seem to last where nothing else lasts. Dynasty after dynasty tumbles down; revolution succeeds to revolution; Hindoo, Pathan, Mogul, Mahratta, Sikh, English, are all masters in turn; but the village community remains the same... This union of the village communities, each one forming a separate state in itself, has, I conceive, contributed more than any other cause to the preservation of the people of India through all the revolutions and changes which they have suffered, and is in a high degree conducive to their happiness, and to the enjoyment of a great portion of freedom and independence" (Dewey, C.J., 1972).

The British came to India as traders. The primary focus of the British Raj was much to do with trade and little to do with governance and development. The local governments were hardly their first priority. The British government was much more interested in the creation of 'controlled' local body instead of local governance. In the British period centralized administration established instead of decentralised administrative system. Colonial administrators controlled over the area by their own employees. Gram Sabha based Panchayat system gets abolished day by day after starting civil court and criminal court by the colonial ruler. Development of road connectivity, water communication in rapid way by the British Government it was very easy for them to rule the whole country from central. But in course of time, British Government constituted institute for village administration. It is a true and historical fact that local self-governance in India, as a representative institution, was developed by the British (Mathew, 1995).

It was Lord Mayo, the then Viceroy of India (1869 to 1872), who felt the need to decentralize powers in order to bring about administrative efficiency and in the year 1870 introduced the concept of elected representatives in the urban municipalities. The revolt of 1857 that had put the imperial finances under considerable strain and it was found necessary to finance local service out of local taxation. Therefore, it was out of fiscal compulsion that Lord Mayo's resolution on decentralisation came to be adopted. The beginning of local governance can be presumed from 1687, when the Madras City Corporation was established. The subsequent history was summarized as following category.

1. 1687–1881: Local government was established to share the burden of resources of the central and provincial governments.
2. 1882–1919: Local government was seen as local self-government.
3. 1920–1937: Local Government was established in the provinces and people's representatives were controlling the provincial administration also.
4. 1938–1947: Local government was in the state of rejuvenation and reconstruction (Maheswari, R.S., 1971).

The major events and initiative by the British Government are described briefly.

Establishment of Bombay (1726) and Calcutta Municipal Bodies (1773): The Bengal Chowkidar Act of 1870: The Bengal Chowkidar Act of 1870 marked the beginning of the revival of the traditional village Panchayati system in Bengal. The Chowkidar Act empowered district magistrates to set up Panchayats of nominated members in the villages to collect taxes to pay the chowkidars or watchmen engaged by them.

Famine Commission (1880): The 1880 Famine Commission also indicated the necessity of the local bodies at the village level for famine relief work (Maheswari, R.S., 1971).

Ripon Resolution (1882): Lord Ripon made remarkable contribution to the development of Local Government. In 1882, he abandoned the existing system of local government by the officially nominated people. According to his local self-government plan, the local boards were split into smaller units to achieve greater efficiency. In order to ensure popular participation, he introduced an election system for the local boards.

The government resolution of 18th May, 1882, stands as a landmark in the structural evolution of local governments. It provided for local boards consisting of a large majority of elected non-official members and presided over by a non-official chairperson. This is considered to be the Magna Carta of local democracy in India. This resolution proposed the establishment of rural local boards where two-third of whose membership was composed of elected representatives. He brought in the concept of self-government in urban municipalities. He is treated as the founding father of urban local government. Ripon's resolutions followed a series of Committees, Commissions and Acts in this line. To stimulate the candidature of man of standing, courtesy title of '*Rai Bahadur*' and '*Rai Saheb*' were allowed to Indian members during their term of services on local bodies (Maheswari, R.S., 1971). During 1883-85, the local self-government acts were passed in many provinces. Local boards could be superseded in case of abuse of powers. The British bureaucracy did not think of Indians as mature and experienced enough for local self-government. Hence, Lord Curzon subsequently opposed such liberalism and increased government control over such local bodies (Maheswari, R.S., 1971).

The Royal Commission: In 1906, Dadabhai Naoroji, the President of Congress accepted the "Self-Government" as the political goal for the country. Royal Commission constituted by the Government in 1907 on decentralisation in 1909 and released its reports. The Royal Commission reported on decentralisation that paucity of funds and caste and religious disputes were the main obstacles in effective functioning of local bodies. The Commission recommended "it is most desirable alike in the interest of decentralisation in order to associate people with the local tasks of administration that an attempt should be made to constitute and develop village Panchayat for the administration of local village affairs". The Royal Commission on Decentralisation in 1909 elaborated further the principles of Ripon resolution. But this remained merely on paper. Ripon's scheme did not make much progress in the development of local self government institutions.

Montagu-Chelmsford Reforms of 1919: Montagu Chelmsford reforms were passed in the year 1919. This reform transferred the subject of local government to the domain of provinces. The reform also recommended that as far as possible there should be a complete popular control in local bodies and the largest possible independence for them, of outside control. By 1925, eight provinces had passed Village Panchayat Acts. However, these Panchayats covered only a limited number of villages with limited functions (Stephen, F. and Rajasekharan, 2001). But this reform could not get much result as far as democratization of Panchayats was concerned and lead to a lot of organizational and fiscal constraints.

Simon Commission (1930): In 1930, evaluation of the implementation of self-governance was done by Simon Commission. It reported that except Uttar Pradesh, Bengal and Madras, they did not find any progress in the rural areas. The condition of the local bodies deteriorated between 1919 and 1930. Hence, it was suggested by the Simon Commission to increase the control of the State over these local bodies.

Government of India Act (1935): Government of India Act (1935) is considered as another important stage in the evolution of Panchayats in British India. With popularly elected government in the provinces, almost all provincial administrations felt duty bound to enact legislations for further democratization of local self-government institutions, including village Panchayats. Although the popular government in the provinces governed by the Congress vacated office following the declaration of Second World War in 1939, the position as regards local government institutions remained unchanged till August 1947, when the country attained independence.

Even though the British government did not have interest in the village autonomy, they were forced to do so, in order to continue their rule in India and moreover to meet financial necessities. The Indian rural democracy had flourished till the arrival of British. It received a set back during the British rule. Self-contained self-sufficient village communities and their Panchayats ceased to get substance. They were replaced by formally constituted institutions of village administration. In the highly centralized system of British rule, village autonomy seems to have lost.

Panchayati Raj Institutions in Post-Independence Period

The Village Panchayats were a part of the ideology of Indian National Movement. Gandhiji had given the idea of '*Gram Swarajya*': "The Government of Village will be conducted by the Panchayat of five persons annually elected by the adult villagers, males and females, possessing minimum prescribed qualifications. These will have all the authority and jurisdiction required. Since, there will be no system of punishment in the accepted sense, the Panchayat will be legislature, judiciary and executive combined to operate for its year of office. Any village can become such republic today.... Here, there is perfect democracy based on individual freedom. The individual is the architect of his own government".

So the task of strengthening Panchayati Raj System fell on the Indian government formed after independence. It was clear that India a country of villages had to strengthen village Panchayats to strengthen democracy. Mahatma Gandhi who strongly believed in *Grama Swarajya* pleaded for the transfer of power to the rural masses. According to him the villages should govern themselves through elected Panchayats to become self- sufficient. But surprisingly, the draft Constitution prepared in 1948 had no place for Panchayati Raj Institutions. Gandhiji severely criticized this and called for immediate attention. It is thus, that Panchayat finds a place in the Directive Principles of the State Policy. A compromise was forged and in 1948, PRIs found place in the non-justifiable part of the Constitution as Article 40 which reads as under:

> "The State shall take steps to organize village Panchayats and endow them with such powers and authority as may be necessary to enable them to function as units of self government".

During the early independent phase, Mahatma Gandhi conceptualized the Village Panchayats as the primary grass root level democratic unit and people's participation was considered as necessary so that India's perception as a welfare state could be fulfilled. According to Gandhiji "Greater power of the Panchayat, the better for the people as true democracy."

The first organized effort to tackle the problem of rural India was made through Community Development Programme in 1952 and National Extension Service in 1953. The programme was based on an integrated approach to the various aspects of rural development. The objectives were to promote self-help and self-reliance among the rural people, to generate a process of integrated social, economic and cultural change with the aim of transforming social and political life of the villagers. This programme was intended to bring socio-economic development of the rural masses on democratic lines, but failed to take off along the expected lines due to the absence of an effective instrument for people's participation. The programme was more or less bureaucratic and excessively politicized. SDO-cum-BDO fulfilled the local demands like road drinking water wells, Panchayat Ghars, school building, etc. All schemes were treated as Government Schemes rather than people's programme (Joshi, R.P. and Narwani, G.S., 2002).

Committees, Commissions and Five Year Plan

The debates in the Constituent Assembly on Panchayati Raj were more fundamentally grounded. There were two differing viewpoints—that of Gandhi and of Ambedkar. The fundamental difference in philosophies of these two thinkers was on parliamentary democracy—Ambedkar believed the unit of development should be the individual while Gandhi believed the unit of development should be the village. Gandhi said in the issue of the *Harijan* of July 26, 1942 that "My idea of village *swaraj* is that it is a complete republic, independent of its neighbours for its vital wants, and yet interdependent for many others in which dependence is a necessity. Thus the village's first concern will be to grow its own food crops and cotton for its cloth. It should have a reserve for its cattle, recreation and playground for adults and children.. The village will maintain a village theatre, school and public hall. It will have its own waterworks ensuring a clean water supply. This can be done through controlled wells or tanks. Education will be compulsory up to the final basic course. As far as possible every activity will be conducted on a co-operative basis. There will be no caste, such as we have today with their graded untouchability. Non-violence with its technique of *satyagraha* and *non-cooperation* will be the sanction of the village community. ... The Panchayat of five persons annually elected by the adult villagers, male and female, possessing minimum prescribed qualifications will conduct the government of the village. These will have all the authority and jurisdiction required. Since there will be no system of punishments in the accepted sense, this Panchayat will be the legislature, judiciary, and executive combined to operate for its year in office. Any village can become such a republic without much interference". While Dr. B.R. Ambedkar said in the Constitutional Assembly Debates in November 1948, that "It is said that the new Constitution should have been drafted on the ancient Hindu model of a state and that instead of incorporating Western theories the new Constitution should have been raised and built upon village Panchayats and District Panchayats... They just want India to contain so many village governments. The love of the intellectual Indian for the village community is of course infinite if not pathetic... I hold that the village republics have been the ruination of India. I am, therefore, surprised that those who condemn provincialism and communalism should come forward as champions of the village. What is the village but a sink of localism, a den of ignorance, narrow-mindedness and communalism? I am glad that the Draft Constitution has discarded the village and adopted the individual as its unit". (Panth, A.H. and Bohra, O.P., 1995).

The Indian National Congress emphasized the issue of *Swaraj*, and organized movements for Independence under the leadership of Mahatma Gandhi. There was no idea among the top leaders about the status to be assigned to the local self-government. Dr. B.R. Ambedkar opposed the idea of Gandhi's *Village Swaraj*. He believed that the village represented regressive India, a source of oppression. During the drafting of the Constitution of India, Panchayati Raj Institutions were placed in the non-justiciable part of the Constitution, the Directive Principles of State Policy, as Article 40. After Independence, Panchayati Raj had to go through various ups and downs. To strengthen the local bodies of our country and after the independence, the constitutional assembly discussed the matter and at last the Constitution of India placed the issues in the Directive Principle of the State Policy and mandated that "Organization of Village Panchayats—The State shall take steps to organize village Panchayats and endow them with such powers and authority as may be necessary to enable them to function as units of self-government". (Constitution of India, Directive Principles of State Policy, Article 40). So, the Indian Constitution was failed to provide guidance on how to develop the PRIs. This responsibility fell to a series of national Committees that addressed issues of implementation of the Constitutional mandate.

The *First Five Year Plan* recognized the need for a disaggregated planning exercise through a process of democratic decentralisation incorporating the idea of a village plan and of District Development Councils. But the First Five Year Plan failed to bring about active community participation and involvement of the people in the Planning processes, which included Plan formulation, implementation and monitoring.

During *Second Five Year Plan* Prime Minister Jawahar Lal Nehru inaugurated the Community Development Programme (CDP) on 2nd October, 1952 under the major influence of the Etawah Project undertaken by the American expert, Albert Mayer. Community Development sought to motivate the rural people to take community-based approach for the improvement of the economic and social condition of their life. The Government was expected to provide general guidance and technical-cum-financial assistance in some Blocks in a phased manner. The Community Development Programme was followed by the National Extension Service in 1953. Some National Extension Service (NES) Blocks were earmarked as the lowest unit of administration. But unfortunately, both the programmes were failed due to wastage of funds, corruption, malpractices and favouritism. That failure compelled the National Development Council to appoint a committee headed by Balwant Rai Mehta in 1956 to critically review the CDP and NES and suggest measures for effecting economy and improving efficiency in implementation of schemes. At the same time, the Planning Commission also recommended that Village Panchayats should be strengthened and given the responsibility for taking over development administration.

The Balwant Rai Mehta committee believed that community development would only be effective when the community was involved in the planning, decision, and implementation process. The committee suggested that the basic unit of democratic decentralisation was to be at the Block (Samiti) level since the area of jurisdiction of the local body should neither be too large nor too small. The Block was large enough for efficiency and economy of administration, and small enough for sustaining a sense of involvement in the citizens. Further, the Zilla Parishad (ZP) should play an advisory role. The committee focused on the rural sector and recommended that the functions of PRIs should cover the development of agriculture in all its aspects, the promotion of local industries and other services such as drinking water, road building, etc. Balwant Rai Mehta Committee studied the Community Development Projects and the National Extension Service and the team felt that there should be a single representative and vigourous democratic institution to take charge of all aspects of development work in the rural areas. The Committee suggested the concept of democratic decentralisation should be based on planning and implementation of CDP and NES. The main recommendation of this committee were as under:

- Suitable administrative decentralisation for effective implementation of development programmes.
- Place decentralised administrative system under the effective control of elected representatives of people.
- Development Block covering about 100 villages and having a population of a hundred thousand should coincide with taluka/tehsil/sub-district unit.
- There should be three tiers—Zila Parishad at the district level to replace the District Board, Panchayat Samiti at the Block level and the Gram Panchayat at the village level.
- Panchayats should work under the overall supervision of the Panchayat Samiti, which would include their representatives.
- The three-tier Panchayati Raj system would be vested with power and functions. Resource will be largely devolved upon the Panchayat Samiti—the intermediate tier. The Panchayat Samiti will play a primary role in rural development process.
- Looking at the diversity of the socio-economic conditions, some States might modify the proposed system. They may prefer devolution of powers to the district level body.
- Composition of the Panchayati Raj bodies should be representative of all sections of people, by and large.
- Dynamic attitude should be adopted towards the functioning of the proposed new set-up. Further devolution of powers, functions

and resources from the State government should be done in future, looking to the success of the scheme.

- Effective training of people's representatives at the three tiers of the local bodies was also stressed.
- People's representatives would plan the community development and allied programmes as well as direct and supervise their implementation by the bureaucracy. Hence, they should develop the knowledge and attitude essential for it. Seminars, workshops and conferences and training course should be arranged adequately.

Source: R.P. Joshi and G.S. Narwani, 2002.

The National Development Council also agreed most of the recommendations of 1958. The Government of India convinced all the States to adopt participatory approach for rural development. The PRI structure was introduced in most parts of the country as a result of the Balwantrai Mehta Report. However, it did not develop the requisite democratic momentum and failed to cater to the needs of rural development. Reasons for this were: (i) political and bureaucratic resistance at the State level to sharing of power and resources with the local level institutions, (ii) the takeover of these institutions by the rural elite who cornered a major share of the benefits of the various welfare schemes, (iii) the lack of capability at the local level, and (iv) the absence of political will of the grass roots leaders (Rao C.H., 1989).

The Third Five Year Plan (1961-1966) reemphasized decentralised planning in various sectors, while the absence of proper planning mechanism resulted in poor planning process.

The K. Santhanam Committee in 1963 was appointed to look solely at the issue of PRI finances. Its recommendations have influenced the thinking and the debate to date on following issues:

- The Panchayats should have special powers to levy special tax on land revenues, home tax, etc.
- People should not be burdened with huge taxes.
- All grants and subventions at the State level should be consolidated and untied.
- A Panchayat Raj Finance Corporation should be set up which would look into the financial resources of PRIs at all three levels, provide loans and financial assistance to these grass root level

governments and also provide support for non-financial requirements of villages.

Source: A.H. Panth and O.P. Bohra, 1995.

These issues have been debated over the last three decades and have been taken up by the State Finance Commissions.

The Fourth Five Year Plan (1969-1974) again emphasized on shifting towards district planning. The Planning Commission also took interest in helping the States in initiating decentralised planning. However, a very little progress was made towards decentralizing the planning process during the Fourth and Fifth Five Year Plans.

The Ashok Mehta Committee was set up when the *Janata Party* government came to power at the Centre in 1977 to examine the functioning of PRIs and to suggest measures for making decentralised planning effective. The Ashok Mehta Committee was appointed in 1977 to find out the weakness of Panchayati Raj Institution. It was decided to appoint a high-level committee under the chairmanship of Ashok Mehta to examine and suggest measures to strengthen PRIs and decentralised planning process. The Committee made the following recommendations:

- More genuine and effective devolution of powers to Panchayati Raj Institutions should take place. The district is a viable administrative unit for which planning, co-ordination and resource allocation is feasible and technical expertise is available.
- PRIs as a two-tier system, with Mandal Panchayat at the base and Zilla Parishad at the top. Because Zilla Parishad had better resource and leadership.
- Well qualified civil servants should be appointed for better administrative at both Zilla Parishad and Mandal Panchayats.
- Below the Mandal Panchayat, there should be a village committee including the weaker sections of people. Representation of SCs and STs in the election to PRIs on the basis of their population.
- Political parties should take part in the elections of PRIs.
- A Panchayati Raj Finance Commission should be set up to fulfil the district demands to implement plans. Besides that the PRIs should also develop their own resources of funds by collecting taxes.
- The District level Panchayat should prepare the district level plans and those plans should be implemented with incorporation of Mandal Panchayat.

Source: R.P. Joshi and G.S. Narwani, 2002

The States of Karnataka, Andhra Pradesh and West Bengal passed new legislation based on this report. But 1978 onwards was an unstable period in State politics, and PRI institutions were unable to develop their own political dynamics.

The Sixth, Seventh and Eighth Five Year Plans were again emphasized on district planning within a multi-level planning framework. But proper administrative arrangements were not made to facilitate this process and there was also a lack of technical expertise and financial devolution in the successful process of democratic decentralisation.

The GVK Rao Committee was appointed in 1985 to again revisit the obstacles in the way of effective PRIs. It recommended that PRIs at the district level and below be assigned the responsibilities for planning, monitoring and implementation of rural development programmes and that the Block development office should be the spinal cord of rural development.

More thinking on PRIs was initiated by the L.M. Singhvi Committee in 1986. The Gram Sabha (village assembly) was considered the base of decentralised democracy. The PRIs were to be viewed as institutions of self-government which would facilitate the participation of the people in the process of planning and development. It recommended that local self-government should be constitutionally recognized, protected and preserved by the inclusion of a new chapter in the Constitution. It also viewed with dismay the irregularity of elections and engaged with the issue of the role of political parties in Panchayat elections, stating that a non-involvement should be consensual rather than through legislative fiat. The role of political parties in Panchayats has since then divided the advocates of PRI into two camps. On the one side are those such as Jayaprakash Narayan, writing within the Gandhian tradition of partyless democracy, who saw "self-government through faction-fighting will not be self-government but self-ruination", and on the other are those such as Asoka Mehta who support the involvement of political parties since it enables candidates, from weak economic backgrounds, to effectively compete with the backing of a strong organization (Wadhwani, M. and. Mishra, S.N., 1996).

Sarkaria Commission was inquiring about federal structure and Centre-State relations. But anyway this commission had made a comment on PRIs. That is, the local bodies are not functioning effectively, because elections to these bodies were superseded and also the Panchayat Raj laws are not uniform across the States. Constitutional status for PRIs was opposed by the Sarkaria Commission. But the idea gained momentum in the late 1980s especially because of the endorsement by the late Prime Minister Rajiv Gandhi who introduced the 64th Constitutional Amendment Bill in 1989. Rajiv Gandhi's commitment to the PRI route to rural development seems to have emerged through a series of workshops, he had as Prime Minister with District Collectors, where he got a sense of the insensitivity of District Administration and of wastage of funds for rural development. The 64th Amendment Bill caused much anxiety among opposition parties because they perceived it to support the partisan agenda of Rajiv Gandhi and it was defeated in the Rajya Sabha.

Various other committees were instrumental for the design of rural decentralisation in India, namely on decentralised planning (Mahapatra, 2012). The Planning Commission of 1966 issued guidelines for district planning. The M.L. Dantwala Group of the Planning Commission issued guidelines in 1978 for Block level planning. The report of the Economic Advisory Council of the Prime Minister on "Decentralisation of Development Planning and implementation in the States" was issued in 1983, and the Working Group on District Planning of the Planning Commission issued its report in 1994. The concern with decentralised planning stemmed from "the slow rate of benefits flowing from the infrastructure already built up, as indicated by the slow growth of productivity, and (...) insufficient percolation of benefits to the poor and the socially disadvantaged sections, despite the proliferation of several poverty alleviation programmes" (Rao H.C., 1989). Centralized planning, it was felt, had not solved the 'basic problems of poverty, unemployment and inequality' (Mishra, B., 1997).

In the Ninth Plan, democratic decentralisation became effective with the enactment of the 73rd and 74th Constitutional Amendment Acts. Most of the State Governments/UTs have enacted enabling legislations for three tier system by providing political power with adequate representation from the weaker sections and women. In case of some UTs only a two tier structure has been recommended. Most of the States have formed State Election Commissions and State Finance Commissions (SFCs) as stipulated.

At present, Panchayati Raj Institutions have Constitutional entities. The State Governments have to implement the three tier panchayats with adequate powers and authority to enable them to function as institutions of local self-government. The Eleventh Schedule has identified 29 subjects which have to be brought under the Panchayats. The Panchayati Raj Institutions are able to undertake the responsibility entrusted to them

Decentralisation—Chronology of attempts and Committee Reports:

Year	*Item*	*Ideas and Concepts*
First Plan 1951-56	Community Development Blocks	To break up the planning exercise into national, State, district and local community levels.
Second Plan 1956-61	District Development Councils	Drawing up of village plans and popular participation in planning through the process of democratic decentralisation.
1957	Balwant Rai Mehta	Village, Block, District Panchayat institutions established.
1967	Administrative Reforms Commission	Resources to be given/local variations accommodated, purposeful plan for area.
1969	Planning Commission	Formulated guidelines; detailed the concept of the district plan and methodology of drawing up such a plan in the framework of annual plans, medium-term plans and perspective plans.
1978	Prof. M.L. Dantwala	Block–Level planning to form link between village and district-level planning.
1983-84	CSS/Reserve Bank of India	Strengthen district plan/District Credit Plan
1984	Hanumantha Rao Committee	Decentralisation of functions, powers and finances; Setting up of district planning bodies and district planning cells.
1985	G.V.K. Rao Committee	Administrative arrangements for rural development; District Panchayat to manage all development programmes.
1986	L.M. Singhvi Committee	The Gram Sabha (village assembly) was considered the base of decentralised democracy; local self-government should be constitutionally recognized.
Ninth Plan	73rd and 74th Constitutional Amendment Act	Democratic decentralisation became effective; local governments in rural areas became an effective reality all over India

both financial and functional. It is necessary not only to ensure flow of funds to them from the States and from the Central Government *via* the Centrally-Sponsored Schemes (CSS), but also to give them independent revenue collection powers so that they can generate their own fund. The State Finance Commissions were set up with the objective of making the Panchayats financially viable. While resource mobilisations by Panchayati Raj Institutions (PRIs) are generally limited, it is imperative to provide PRIs with revenue-raising powers of their own to reduce their financial dependency on the State and Central Governments. There are taxes which can be collected by local bodies. On the other side, grants for specific schemes entrusted to the Panchayats will be given to them by the State Government. Funds from Centrally Sponsored Schemes will also be form of a grant but those would not be a part of the untied. Sixteen per cent of the net proceeds of all taxes collected by the State in a year will be transferred to local bodies. Some other taxes like entertainment tax will be handed over to the local government. The three-tiers Panchayati Raj

Institutions have been empowered to raise taxes, levies and tolls to increase their incomes. An untied grant to Panchayats by sharing of tax and non-tax revenues and the flow of programme funds to the Panchayats has been mandated.

According to the recommendations of the Tenth Finance Commission these elected local bodies would receive Rs. 5381 crore as grant-in-aid to supplement their resources over a four year period from 1996-97. However, the Eleventh Finance Commission considers this issue, the State Governments may ask for more resources provided that their elected bodies are by then functioning well and are able to plan and implement various development works entrusted to them. Along with financial autonomy, functional autonomy of the Panchayati Raj Institutions also is clearly delineated. Even in respect of the 29 subjects identified in the Eleventh Schedule it is necessary for the State governments to clearly identify what would be done by the three-tiers of Panchayats at their own level. Detailed instructions and guidelines would have to be issued by the concerned departments. Some States like Gujarat, Maharashtra, Karnataka, Kerala, Tripura, and West Bengal have already been issued the detailed instructions. One major task of the PRIs is the preparation of plans for economic and social development. The district development plans would have to be prepared by the District Planning Committee (DPC) which is mandated. But in many States the DPCs have not been set up. Gram Sabha would be responsible to prioritization and selection of beneficiaries for various programmes and schemes. In this way, the people's participation can be ensured. Thereafter, village level plans will have to be prepared which would be incorporated in the intermediate plans and finally merged into a district plan. The village level Panchayat is responsible to look after the roads, sanitation, drinking water, etc., at the village level. The intermediate level would be responsible for Primary Education, Women and Child Welfare and employment generation activities. At the Zilla Parishad level drinking water, rural roads, secondary education and the district component of employment would be implemented. The DPCs should not only consolidate plans from below but also should take decisions on the development of the district within the available resources.

Panchayati Raj Institutions became the safeguard for the weaker sections of our society. The 73rd Constitutional Amendment Act provides for reservation for Scheduled Castes/Scheduled Tribes in every Panchayat in the proportion of the population in the Panchayat area. On the other side one-third of the seats would have to be reserved for women in every tier of PRIs. In the process of democratic decentralisation, people can be involved through their elected representatives. Gram Sabha is a platform for empowerment of the weaker sections of our society and also fulfil their urgent needs. For this, more powers have to be vested in the Gram Sabha who has the authority to sanction and disburse benefits in open meetings. But this is not enough for people's participation at Gram Sabha meetings. Steps have to be taken to ensure that maximum people can attend Gram Sabha meetings and make the PRIs in actual people's institutions.

Panchayati Raj Institutions (PRIs) and Decentralisation in West Bengal

Structure of Panchayati Raj Institutions in West Bengal

Panchayati Raj Institutions Structure of West Bengal: In 1973, the West Bengal Panchayats Act was passed, annulling the previous laws. The four tier structure was replaced by the emerging all India pattern of Gram Panchayats, Panchayat Samiti and Zilla Parishad. The new Gram Panchayats were similar to the Anchal Panchayats Act of 1957 and consisted of a group of villages with a population 10 to 12 thousand. Following the Balwantrai Mehta Committee Reports recommendations, Panchayat Samitis were conterminous with blocks, and Zilla Parishads were coterminous with districts. The Act provided for the direct election of members of all the three tiers for a five years term. The Pradhans of Gram Panchayats were ex-officio members of Panchayat Samitis and the Sabhapatis of Panchayat Samitis were similarly ex-officio members of Zilla Parishads. The Act also provided for nominations of officials without voting rights into the standing committees of Panchayat Samitis and Zilla Parishad and local MLAs and MPs as ex-officio members of both Block and district tiers. As a framework for decentralisation governance, the 1973 Act was a great improvement on the previous legislation in ensuring organic linkage between various tiers, improving executive efficiency through a system of standing committees, and providing greater clarity regarding the functions. In June 1978, elections were held simultaneously for all tiers of the rural local bodies for the first time. The event heralded a new era for the Panchayati Raj system in West Bengal. Since then, elections to the local bodies have been held at regular five years intervals as stipulated by law, with the most recent elections taking place in 2013.

Gram Panchayat

A Gram Panchayat (GP) normally covers a cluster of villages. This is the lowest tier of Panchayati Raj Institution. On an average each GP covered a group of villages with a population 10,000-12,000 people. The members of GP are directly elected by the votes given by the all adult voters of that respective area or sansad. The Chairman of GP in known as Pradhan, Deputy-Chairman is called Upa-Pradhan. The GP members elect these two functionaries from amongst themselves and they can be removed by majority resolutions in the GP. The Act of 1973 provides administrative power to endow the GP with three sets of powers and functions: obligatory, delegated and discretionary. The total elected members would vary between seven and twenty-five depending upon the number of voters in the area. There would be a Secretary, a Job Assistant, a Technical Assistant, one or two Assistant and Tax Collectors, Village Chowkidars and a Gram Sebak as the officials of the GP.

Panchayat Samity

The middle-tier of Panchayati Raj Institution is Panchayat Samiti. This tier is converged with development Block. This tier replaced the earlier Anchalik Parishads. According to the West Bengal Panchayat Act, this consisted with the following representatives:

(a) Maximum of three members elected from each GP area on the basis of adult franchise,
(b) Two persons belonging to SC/ST and two women to be nominated by the State government,
(c) Pradhans of the GP within the block area, and
(d) Members of Lok Sabha and Bidhan Sabha within the Block area (not minister)

The Panchayat Samiti (PS) gives emphasis on direct election of members by voters, and at the same time, it provides for co-option and integration with other bodies. The combination enables the PS to emerge as the focal point of people representation in the Block. Panchayat Samiti headed by Sabhapati (Chairperson) and a Sahokari Sabhapati (Vice Chairperson). The BDO is now the executive officer of the PS.

Zilla Parishad

In the three-tier Panchayat system, the Zilla Parishad is the highest tier at the District level. According to the West Bengal Gram Panchayat Act of 1973, Zilla Parishad (ZP) had constituted by the following categories of members:

(a) Two persons to be directly elected from each Block of the district,
(b) The Sabhapatis of all the PSs of the district (ex-officio),
(c) All the MPs and MLAs excepting the ministers from the district, and
(d) Two persons from the SC/ST and two women members nominated by the State government.

The Chairperson of ZP is called Sabhadhipati and deputy-chairperson is known as the Sahokari Sabhadhipati. The members of the ZP elect these two functionaries from amongst the directly elected members only. The DM is the executive officer of the ZP and ADM is its additional executive officer. All district level officers are statutorily linked to the corresponding standing committees.

Gram Sansad

Gram Sansad means "a body consisting of persons registered at any time in the electoral rolls pertaining to a constituency of a Gram Panchayat delimited for the purpose of last preceding general election to the Gram Panchayat." (Section 16A of W.B. Panchayat Act, 1973)

The most vibrant constitutional institution at the village level is Gram Sansad, incorporated by the West Bengal Panchayat (Amendment) Act 1992. It consists of registered electors of a constituency within the area of a Gram Panchayat. Under the law, the Gram Sansad will take place twice a year, annual meeting in May and half-yearly meeting in November.

Attendance of at least 1/10 (10%) of the total number of members/ voters shall form a quorum for the Gram Sansad meeting. If there is no quorum in a meeting, the meeting shall be adjourned to be held at the same place and hour on the seventh day after the date of such meeting. Attendance of at least 1/20 (5%) of the total number of members shall form a quorum for the adjourned meeting.
Source: West Bengal Panchayat (Amendment) Act 1992

The Gram Sansad is an institution, which provides an opportunity to participate meaningfully in governance, to all the people willing and capable of participating in the development process. Formation of Self-Help Group (SHG) by help of Swarnajayanti Gram SwarojgarYojana (SGSY), women participation in the development process is rapidly increasing in GP areas. The voters incorporated in SHGs, mostly under SGSY and majorities are women.

District/Block/Gram Sansads were constituted to provide a forum for accountability of the bodies to the members of the Sansad and through them to the people in general. Adequate information on functioning of the Panchayat body should be made available to the members of the Sansad sufficiently before such meetings so that they may study and appreciate the same, raise appropriate questions and suggest possible ways of improving functioning of those bodies.

The Department of Panchayat and Rural Development, Government of West Bengal has issued an Order vide No.298/PN/O/I/3C-7/03 dated 21.01.2009 directing the PRIs to make pro-active disclosure regarding 13 categories of information which should be circulated in the form of a booklet for information of all members. All informations should relate to the previous financial year in respect of the Annual Sansad meeting and the first six months of the year in respect of the half yearly Sansad meeting. The items of disclosure are—

1. Action taken on the recommendations/proposals made in the previous Sansad meeting along with a copy of the resolution of that meeting. Constraints, if any, faced should also be clearly spelt out.
2. The accounts for the relevant period based on Form 27 of the Accounts Rules applicable, with explanatory note, when necessary.
3. Head-wise balance of fund lying unspent at the end of the period and percentage of available fund utilized during the period for all important schemes as well as grants from the State and the Central Finance Commission during the relevant period along with constraints, if any, in utilizing the fund.
4. Own resource mobilized by the body during the relevant period showing total collection against total demand proposing steps for improvement.
5. Availability and utilization of own fund during the period and important items of expenditure from own fund. Visible areas of

utilisation and the quantum of fund used for those should be highlighted.

6. Number of meetings of the general body and those held by different Sthayee/ Upa Samitis during the relevant period and attendance. For the Samitis which held meetings below statutory level, reasons should be given.
7. Observation of latest audit report both internal and that by the ELA and action taken on those reports, if not already placed before the Sansad. Failure to act on any observation should be explained.
8. Report of the District Council, if any, related to that body and action taken on that report. Failure to act on any issue shall be explained.
9. A brief note on the findings of the latest Self-Evaluation report, if not already placed before the Sansad. Major areas of strength and weaknesses in functioning of that body should be stated. Actions taken/proposed on areas of weakness should be explained.
10. List of important works completed or on-going during the relevant period.
11. Names of persons to whom individual benefits were extended.
12. Exemplary incidents of people's participation/voluntary contribution may be highlighted for replication for other areas.
13. No. of posts lying vacant and actions taken to fill up those posts.

Disclosure of information voluntarily is an important element for good governance by the Panchayat. As a practice the Panchayat body compiles report having relevant information about functioning of those bodies and circulates the same in the form of booklets in the Sansad meeting.

Source: Panchayat and Rural Development Department.

Gram Sabha

The Gram Sabha has been regarded as the 'soul' of Panchayati Raj. A Constitutional status was given to the Gram Sabha for the first time in 1993. Gram Sabha have given power to the people to ensure transparency and accountability in the system. All the adult voters of the Gram Panchayat area is the member of Gram Sabha. All State Panchayat Acts have provided for the Constitution of the Gram Sabha. Gram Panchayats is the executive committee of Gram Sabha.

Article 243(B) of the Constitution refers to Gram Sabha as " a body consisting of persons registered in the electoral rolls relating to a village comprised with the area of Panchayat at the village level". Regarding the power of the Gram Sabha, Article 243(A) of the Constitution states that, "A Gram Sabha may exercise such power and perform such functions at the village level as the legislature of a State, may, by law, provide". *Source:* Section 16B of W.B. Panchayat Act 1973.

The concept of Gram Sabha was introduced by the West Bengal Panchayat (Amendment) Act 1994. It consists of registered electors of a Gram Panchayat area. It is the duty of a Gram Panchayat to convene a meeting of Gram Sabha in December every year in West Bengal.

In West Bengal Gram Sabha meeting is held in the month of December to prepare the next year plan and budget, beneficiary selection, etc. The West Bengal government provided for a two-tier structure for facilitating direct democracy. Village (Sansad) based bodies are named as Gram Sansads. In every Gram Sansad there is a Gram Unnayan Samiti which is responsible for scheme selection on the basis of local need and priority. Gram Unnayan Samiti makes the scheme list and in the Gram Sansad meeting Sansad-wise scheme is selected. Two meetings of the Gram Sansad guides and advises the Gram Panchayats about schemes for economic development, identifying the beneficiaries for poverty alleviation programmes, giving suggestions regarding budget, audit report, yearly administration report and recording objections regarding failure to implement development schemes. Attendance of at least 1/20 (5%) of the total number of members/voters shall form a quorum for the Gram Sabha meeting. If there is no quorum in a meeting, the meeting shall be adjourned to be held at the same place and hour on the seventh day after the date of such meeting. Quorum for the adjourned meeting is not mandatory. After making the Sansad-wise plans, the Gram Panchayat make draft plan as per Upa-Samiti. In the Gram Sabha the final plan is prepared as per priority. And finally after approval of Gram Sabha, the Gram Panchayat make the final plan and budget and send those to the upper level for approval.

The West Bengal Panchayat (Amendment) Act 2010 amend Section 16B of the principal Act and the following proviso shall be added— "Provided that a Gram Panchayat may, in addition to annual meeting, hold extraordinary meeting of a Gram Sabha at any time if the situation so warrants or if the State Government, by order, so directs and for the

purpose of holding such extraordinary meeting, provision of this section shall apply."
Source: The West Bengal Panchayat (Amendment) Act 2010.

Upa-Samiti

According to 73rd Amendment of Panchayat Act, there are five Upa-Samitis (sub-committees) at Gram Panchayat level. Those are:

(i) Artho O Parikalpana Upa Samiti (Finance and Planning sub-committee);
(ii) Krishi O Prani Sampad Vikas Upa Samiti (Agriculture and Animal Husbandry Development Sub-Committee);
(iii) Siksha O Janaswartha Upa-Samiti (Education and Public Health Sub-Committee);
(iv) Nari Sishu Unnayan O Samaj Kalyan Upa-Samiti (Women Child Development and Social Development Sub-Committee); and
(v) Silpa O Parikathamo Upa-Samiti (Industry and Infrastructure Sub-Committee).

Standing committees have wide ranging powers. They include preparing proposals for execution of a scheme within the budgetary provisions of the Gram Panchayat. The Pradhan shall also not sanction any fund for a scheme, programme or project without considering the views of the members of the Upa-Samiti to whom powers have been delegated by the Gram Panchayat with respect to such scheme programme or project. The Standing Committees have also been given wide powers to call for information, inspect and immovable property of the Gram Panchayat or any work in progress. With effect from 2005-06, each Standing Committee is being given a separate indication of a budget, so that they can plan better within their mandates.

Formation of Upa-Samiti

After Pradhan selection of Gram Panchayat, within three months Gram Panchyat has to from Upa-Samiti. Pradhan and Upa-Pradhan (Ex-Officio) and directly elected member of Gram Panchayat and Ex-Officio member of Panchayat Samiti will be member of Upa-Samiti but not more than three. BDO will issue a notice after deciding Date, Place and Time minimum 7 days before to call a meeting, to select those three members of Upa-Samiti. After member selection BDO also call a meeting in the same way to select "Sanchalak". But no members will be selected for Artho O Parikalpana Upa-Samiti. Other Sanchalak of rest four Upa-Samiti will be Ex-Officio members of Artho O Parikalpana. Leader of opponent party member also will be member of Artho O Parikalpana Upa-Samiti. Minimum half of total member of Nari Sishu Unnayan O Samaj Kalyan Upa-Samiti must be women and also Sanchalak also should be women. If the numbers of Gram Panchayat member is below or equal 10 then the number of Upa-Samiti member should be 1. In case of number of GP members are 11 to 20 then the Upa-Samiti member should be 2 and Upa-Samiti member will be 3 when the number of GP member 21 or more. Upa-Samiti will take plans and execute them at Gram Panchayat level.

Constitution of Upa-Samitis

As per West Bengal Gram Panchayat Administration Rules 2004, every Gram Panchayat shall, as soon as may be within three months following the first meeting, constitute Five Upa-Samitis under sub-section (2) of section 32A of the West Bengal Panchayat Act 1973.

Sanchalak: Within one week from the date of Constitution of the Upa-Samiti, the members of the respective Upa-Samiti elect in a meeting one member from themselves as Sanchalak of each Upa-Samiti. The most important aspects in this regard is that the Sanchalak of the Nari O Sishu Unnayan Upa-Samity should be women.

Gram Unnayan Samiti

The Gram Unnayan Samiti at the level of Gram Sansad was introduced by the West Bengal Panchayats (Amendment) Act, 2003. Gram Sansad will constitute Gram Unnayan Samiti and elect the members by simple majority. It will be responsible for ensuring active participation of people at grass root level in implementation and equitable distribution of benefits of Rural Development programmes.

With the objectives of mandatory people's participation, the West Bengal Government established the Gram Unnayan Samiti. Its formation, responsibility and duties inched in West Bengal Panchyat Rules 70 to 74, 2004. All the voters of Gram Sansad area elect the Gram Unnayan Samiti. This Samiti is called as working committee of Gram Panchayat. It is mandatory to form Gram Unnayan Samiti in each Gram Sansad area. This Samiti plays a vital role in executing a small scheme at local level. *Source*: West Bengal Panchayats (Amendment) Act 2003.

Steps for Gram Unnayan Samiti Formation

- Gram Panchayat will call a special Sansad meeting for GUS formation.
- This meeting should be called before 15 days of the meeting mentioning date and time and also should disseminate the information about the meeting by loudspeakers, distribution of pamphlets and by beating of drums etc.
- Gram Panchayat Pradhan will be Chairman and in case of his/her absence Upa-Pradhan can or in absence of both, Gram Panchayat member of that particular Sansad can chair that meeting.
- 20 per cent quorum is must for that special meeting. If corum is not fulfilled in adjourned meeting then this meeting again adjourned and this process will go until the Gram Unnayan Samiti is formed.
- Gram Panchayat technical assistant or executive assistant or secretary or job assistant should act as presiding officer. And she/he will responsible for proceeding.
- If Block Development officer till needs, then BDO can recruit for an invigilator at Block level for that special Gram Sansad meeting.

There are two categories of membership in the GUS, Reserve posts and Unreserved posts. In reserve post following member can be held—

1. Elected Gram Panchayat member from that particular Gram Sansad area.
2. That person who gets second highest votes in last election from that Gram Sansad area.
3. Three representative from three Government registered NGOs or CSOs or other group-wise organizations.
4. Total three SHGs member from three SHGs of that Sansad area (one from each group).
5. One Government employee (Retd. or working) of that particular Gram sansad area.
6. One teacher (Retd. or working) who resides in that particular Gram Sansad area.

Source: West Bengal Panchayats (Amendment) Act 2003.

Ten voters or one per cent of the total voters of Gram Sansad area (which is maximum) will be selected as members in unreserved post.

Gram Unnyan Samiti shall meet three to four times in month to active the Samiti. In annual Gram Sansad meeting, the Sansad members shall evaluate the Gram Unnayan Samiti's work progress and renew their membership.

Gram Unnayan Samiti shall prepare a Five Year Plan and an Annual Action plan and necessary budget for economic and social development. Samiti shall identify the local needs after discussion with local people especially rural poor. Those needs are food security, natural resource and employment, education, health and nutrition, women and child development and infrastructure and service delivery.

Salient Features of West Bengal Panchayat Act 1973 and 73rd Constitutional Amendment Act

Constitution of Panchayats

As per 73rd Constitutional Amendment Act, Article 243B, "There shall be constituted, in every State, Panchayats at the village, intermediate and district levels in accordance with the provisions of this Part". Panchayats at the intermediate level may not be constituted in a State having a population not exceeding twenty lakh.

Composition of Panchayats: As per 73rd Constitutional Amendment Act, Article 243C,

1. "Subject to the provisions of this Part, the Legislature of a State may, by law, make provisions with respect to the composition of Panchayats: Provided that the ratio between the population of the territorial area of a Panchayat at any level and the number of seats in such Panchayat to be filled by election, shall, so far as practicable, be the same throughout the State.
2. All the seats in a Panchayat shall be filled by persons chosen by direct election from territorial constituencies in the Panchayat area, and for this purpose, each Panchayat area shall be divided into territorial constituencies in such manner that the ratio between the population of each constituency and the number of seats allotted to it, shall, so far as practicable, be the same throughout the Panchayat area.
3. The Legislature of a State may, by law, provide for the representation:
   (a) Of the Chairpersons of the Panchayats at the village level,

in the Panchayats at the intermediate level or, in the case of a State not having Panchayats at the intermediate level, in the Panchayats at the district level;

(b) Of the Chairpersons of the Panchayats at the intermediate level, in the Panchayats at the district level;

(c) Of the members of the House of the People and the members of the Legislative Assembly of the State representing constituencies which comprise wholly or partly a Panchayat area at a level other than the village level, in such Panchayat;

(d) Of the members of the Council of States and the members of the Legislative Council of the State, where they are registered as electors within:

(i) a Panchayat area at the intermediate level,

(ii) a Panchayat area at the district level, in Panchayat at the district level.

4. The Chairperson of a Panchayat and other members of a Panchayat whether or not chosen by direct election from territorial constituencies in the Panchayat area shall have the right to vote in the meeting of the Panchayats.

5. The Chairperson of:

(a) Panchayat at the village level shall be elected in such manner as the Legislature of a State may, by law, provide; and

(b) Panchayat at the intermediate level or district level shall be elected by, and from amongst, the elected members thereof."

Source: The West Bengal Panchayat Act 1973.

Reservation of Seats

As per 73rd Constitutional Amendment Act, Article: 243D;

1. Seats of Panchayats shall be reserved for—(a) the Scheduled Castes; and (b) the Scheduled Tribes in every Panchayat and the number of seats so reserved shall bear, as nearly as may be, the same proportion to the total number of seats to be filled by direct election in that Panchayat as the population of the Scheduled Castes and Scheduled Tribes in that Panchayat area and such seats may be allotted by rotation to different constituencies in a Panchayat.

2. Not less than one-third of the total number of seats reserved under clause (1) shall be reserved for women belonging to the Scheduled Castes or, to the Scheduled Tribes.

3. Not less than one-third (including the number of seats reserved for women belonging to the Scheduled Castes and the Scheduled Tribes) of the total number of seats to be filled by direct election in every Panchayat shall be reserved for women and such seats may be allotted by rotation to different constituencies in a Panchayat.

4. The offices of the Chairpersons in the Panchayats at the village or any other level shall be reserved for the Scheduled Castes, the Scheduled Tribes and women in such manners as the legislature of the State, by law, provide;

(i) Provided that the number of offices of Chairpersons reserved for the Scheduled Castes and the Scheduled Tribes in the Panchayats at each level in any State shall bear, as nearly as may be, the same proportion to the total number of such offices in the Panchayats at each level as the total population of the Scheduled Castes or of the Scheduled Tribes in the State bears to the population of the State.

Source: The 73rd Constitutional Amendment Act 1992, Article: 243D.

Duration of Panchayats

As per 73rd Constitutional Amendment Act, Article: 243E; "Every Panchayat, unless sooner dissolved under any law for the time being in force, shall continue for five years from the date appointed for its first meeting and no longer." Irregular election of Panchayat Raj Bodies was the general characteristics for some of the States. This provision resists the same.

Source: 73rd Constitutional Amendment Act, Article: 243E.

Powers, authorities and responsibilities of Panchayats: As per provision of the Article 243G of the 73rd Amendment of the Constitution, "the legislature of a State may, by law, endow the Panchayats with such powers and authority as may be necessary to enable them to function as institutions of self-government and such law may contain provisions for the devolution of powers and responsibilities upon Panchayats at the appropriate level, subject to such conditions as may be specified therein, with respect to:

(a) The preparation of plans for economic development and social justice, and

(b) The, implementation of schemes for economic development and social justice as may be entrusted to them including those in relation to the matters listed in the Eleventh Schedule."

Source: The 73rd Constitutional Amendment Act, Article: 243G.

Constitution of Finance Commission

As per provision of the Article 243-I of the 73rd Amendment of the Constitution. "The Governor of a State shall, as soon as may be within one year from the commencement of the Constitution (Seventy-third Amendment Act 1992), and thereafter, at the expiry of every fifth year, constitute a Finance Commission to review the financial position of the Panchayats and to make position, recommendations to the Governor as to:

(a) The principles which should govern:
  (i) The distribution between the State and the Panchayats of the net proceeds of the taxes, duties, tolls and fees leviable by the State, which may be divided between them under this Part and the allocation between the Panchayats at all levels of their respective shares of such proceeds;
  (ii) The determination of the taxes, duties, tolls and fees which may be assigned to, or appropriated by, the Panchayats;
  (iii) The grants-in-aid to the Panchayats from the Consolidated Fund of the State;

(b) The measures needed to improve the financial position of the Panchayats; and

(c) Any other matter referred to the Finance Commission by the Governor in the interests of sound finance of the Panchayats."

Source: The 73rd Constitutional Amendment Act, Article: 243I.

Elections to the Panchayats: As per Article 243K

1. The superintendence, direction and control of the preparation of electoral rolls for, and the conduct of, all elections to the Panchayats shall be vested in a State Election Commission consisting of a State Election Commissioner to be appointed by the governor.
2. Subject to the appointed of, law made by the Legislature of a State, the conditions of service and tenure of office of the State

Election Commissioner shall be such as the Governor may by rule determine. Provided that the State Election Commissioner shall not be removed from his office except in like manner and on the like grounds as a Judge of a High Court and the conditions of service of the State Election Commissioner shall not be varied to his disadvantages after his appointment.

3. The Governor of a State shall, when so requested by the State Election Commission, make available to the State Election Commission such staff as may be necessary for the discharge of the function conferred on the State Election Commission by Clause (1)
4. Subject to the provisions of this Constitution the Ligatured of a State may, by law, provision with respect to all matters relating to, or connection with, elections to the Panchayats.

Source: The 73rd Constitutional Amendment Act, Article: 243K.

Addition of Eleventh Schedule

As provided by the Section 243-O, after the Tenth Schedule to the Constitution, the following addition of Schedule shall be added, namely Eleventh Schedule (as per Article 243-G) which are as follows:

1. Agriculture including agricultural extension.
2. Land improvement and land conservation.
3. Minor irrigation, water management and watershed development.
4. Animal husbandry, dairying and poultry.
5. Fisheries.
6. Social forestry and farm forestry.
7. Minor forest produce.
8. Small Scale industries including food processing industries
9. Khadi, Village and Cottage industries.
10. Rural Housing.
11. Drinking Water.
12. Fuel and Fodder.
13. Roads, culvert, bridge, ferries, waterways, and other means of Communications. Rural Electrification, including distribution of electricity.
14. Non-conventional Energy sources.
15. Poverty alleviation programme.
16. Education including primary and secondary schools.

17. Technical training and vocational education.
18. Adult and Non-formal education.
19. Libraries.
20. Cultural activities.
21. Markets and fairs.
22. Health and sanitation including hospital primary health centres and dispensaries.
23. Family Welfare.
24. Women and Child development.
25. Social Welfare including welfare of the handicapped and mentally retarded.
26. Welfare of the weaker sections and in particular, Scheduled Castes and Scheduled Tribes.
27. Public Distribution System.
28. Maintenance of Community assets.

Source: The 73rd Constitutional Amendment Act, Article: 243O.

From the Eleventh Schedule it is unambiguously stated that the Constitution of India delegate a large task upon the shoulder of Panchayats in order to establish an active and 'real' government on local areas.

Duties and Responsibilities of Gram Panchayat

As per West Bengal Panchayat Act 1973, Section 19 the Obligatory duties of Gram Panchayat are:

(1) A Gram Panchayat shall function as a unit of self-government and, in order to achieve economic development and secure social justice for all, shall, subject to such conditions as may be prescribed or such directions as may be given by the State Government:
   (a) Prepare a development plan for the five-year term of the office of the members and revise and update it as and when necessary with regard to the resources available;
   (b) Prepare an annual plan for each year by the month of October of the preceding year for development of human resources, infrastructure and civic amenities in the area;
   (c) Implement schemes for economic development and social justice as may be drawn up by, or entrusted upon it.

(2) Without prejudice to the generality of the provisions of

subsection (*l*) and subject to such conditions as may be prescribed or such directions as may be given by the State Government, the duties of a Gram Panchayat shall be to provide within the area under its jurisdiction for:

(i) Sanitation, conservancy and drainage and the prevention of public nuisances;

(ii) Curative and preventive measures in respect of malaria, small pox, cholera or any other epidemic;

(iii) Supply of drinking water and the cleansing and disinfecting the sources of supply and storage of water;

(iv) The maintenance, repair and construction of public streets and the protection thereof;

(v) The removal of encroachments of public streets or public places;

(vi) The protection and repair of buildings or other property vested in it;

(vii) The management and care of public tanks, subject to the provisions of the Bengal Tanks Improvement Act 1939, common grazing grounds, burning *ghats* and public graveyards;

(viii) The supply of any local information which the District Magistrate, the Zilla Parishad' the Mahakuma Parishad, the Council or the Panchayat Samiti within the local limits of whose jurisdiction the Gram Panchayat is situated may require;

(ix) Organizing voluntary labour for community works and works for the upliftment of its area;

(x) The control and administration of the Gram Panchayat Fund established under this Act;

(xi) The imposition, assessment and collection of the taxes, rates or fees leviable under this Act;

(xii) The maintenance and control of *Dafadars*, *Chowkidars* and Gram Panchayat Karmees within its jurisdiction and securing due performance by the *Dafadars*, *Chowkidars* and Gram Panchayat Karmees of the duties imposed on them under this Act;

(xiii) The Constitution and administration of the Nyaya Panchayat established under this Act; and

(xiv) The performance of such functions as may be transferred to it under Section 31 of the Cattle Trespass Act 1871.

(3) A Gram Panchayat shall not omit or refuse to act upon any recommendations of a Gram Sansad relating to prioritization of any list of beneficiaries or scheme or programme so far as it relates to the area of the Gram Sansad unless it decides in a meeting for reasons to be recorded in writing that such recommendation or recommendations are not acceptable or implementable under the provisions of the Act or any rule, order or direction thereunder; such decision of the Gram Panchayat shall be placed in the next meeting of the Gram Sansad.

Source: West Bengal Panchayat Act 1973, Section-19.

As per Section 20 of West Bengal Panchayat Act 1973 other duties of Gram Panchayats are as follows:

1. A Gram Panchayat shall also perform such other functions as the State Government may assign to it in respect of:
   (a) Primary, social, technical, vocational, adult or non-formal education;
   (b) Rural dispensaries, health centres and maternity and child welfare centres;
   (c) Management of any public ferry under the Bengal Ferries Act 1885;
   (d) Irrigation including minor irrigation, water management and watershed development;
   (e) Agriculture including agricultural extension and fuel and fodder;
   (f) Care of the infirm and the destitute;
   (g) Rehabilitation of displaced persons;
   (h) Improved breeding of cattle, medical treatment of cattle and prevention of cattle disease;
   (i) Its acting as a channel through which Government assistance should reach the villages;
   (j) Bringing waste land under cultivation through land improvement and soil conservation;
   (k) Promotion of village plantations social forestry and farm forestry;
   (l) Arranging for cultivation of land lying fallow;
   (m) Arranging for co-operative management of land and other resources of the village;

(n) Assisting in the implementation of land reform measures in its area;
(o) Implementation of such schemes as may be formulated or performance of such acts as may be entrusted to the Gram Panchayat by the State Government;
(p) Field publicity on matters connected with development works and other welfare measures undertaken by the State Government;
(q) Minor forest produce;
(r) Rural housing programme;
(s) Rural electrification including distribution of electricity;
(t) Non-conventional energy sources; and
(u) Women and child development.

2. If the State Government is of opinion that a Gram Panchayat has persistently made default in the performance of any of the functions assigned to it under sub-section (7), the State Government may, after recording its reasons, withdraw such function from such Gram Panchayat.

Source: West Bengal Panchayat Act 1973, Section 20.

Discretionary Duties of Gram Panchayat

Section 21 of West Bengal Panchayat Act 1973: Subject to such conditions as may be prescribed, a Gram Panchayat may, and shall if the State Government so directs, make provision for—

(a) The maintenance of lighting of public streets;
(b) Planting and maintaining trees on the sides of public streets or in other public places vested in it;
(c) The sinking of wells and excavation of ponds and tanks;
(d) The introduction and promotion of co-operative farming, co-operative stores, and other co-operative enterprises, trades and callings;
(e) The construction and regulation of markets, the holding and regulation of fairs, *melas* and *hats* and exhibitions of local produce and products of local handicrafts and home industries;
(f) The allotment of places for storing manure;
(g) Assisting and advising agriculturists in the matter of obtaining State loan and its distribution and repayment;

(h) Filling up of insanitary depressions and reclaiming of unhealthy localities;

(i) The promotion and encouragement of Cottage Khadi, Village and small-scale including food processing industries;
   (1) promotion of dairying and poultry;
   (2) promotion of fishery;
   (3) poverty alleviation programme;

(j) The destruction of rabbit or ownerless dogs;

(k) Regulating the production and disposal of foodstuffs and other commodities in the manner prescribed;

(l) The construction and maintenance of rest houses, cattlesheds and cart stands;

(m) The disposal of unclaimed cattle;

(n) The disposal of unclaimed cropses and carcasses;

(o) The establishment and maintenance of libraries and reading rooms;

(p) The organization and maintenance of clubs and other places for recreation or games: (1) cultural activities including sports and games; (2) social welfare including welfare of the handicapped and mentally retarded; (3) welfare of socially and educationally backward classes of citizens and, in particular, of the Scheduled Castes and the Scheduled Tribes; (4) public distribution system; and (5) maintenance of community assets;

(q) The maintenance of records relating to population census, crop census, cattle census and census of unemployed persons and of other statistics as may be prescribed;

(r) The performance in the manner prescribed of any of the functions of the Zilla Parishad or the Mahakuma Parishad or the Council, as the case may be, with its previous approval, calculated to benefit the people living within the jurisdiction of the Gram Panchayat;

(s) Rendering assistance in extinguishing fire and protecting life and property when fire occurs;

(t) Assisting in the prevention of burglary and dacoity; and

(u) Any other local work or service of public utility which is likely to promote the health, comfort, convenience or material prosperity of the public, not otherwise provided for in this Act.

Source: West Bengal Panchayat Act 1973, Section-21.

Gram Panchayat Meeting

Every Gram Panchayat shall hold a meeting at least once in a month in the office of the Gram Panchayat. Such meeting shall be held on such date and at such hour as the Gram Panchayat may fix at the immediately preceding meeting:

1. The Pradhan or in his/her absence the Upa-Pradhan shall preside at the meeting of the Gram Panchayat; and in the absence of both or on the refusal of any or both to preside at a meeting, the members present shall elect one of them to be the President of the meeting.
2. One-third of the total number of members subject to a minimum of three members shall form a quorum for a meeting of a Gram Panchayat and no quorum shall be necessary for a adjourned meeting.
3. All questions coming before a Gram Panchayat shall be decided by a majority of votes and in case of equality of votes the person presiding shall have a second or casting vote.

Meetings of Gram Sansad (Section 16 A)

In terms of Section 16A of West Bengal Panchayat Act 1973:

- Every constituency of a Gram Panchayat shall have a Gram Sansad consisting of electors of the concerned constituency.
- Every Gram Panchayat shall hold within the local limits of the Gram an annual and a half-yearly meeting for each Gram Sansad at such place, on such date and at such hour as may be fixed by the Gram Panchayat.
- The annual meeting of the Gram Sansad shall be held ordinarily in the month of May and the half-yearly meeting of the Gram Sansad shall be held ordinarily in the month of November every year.
- A Gram Panchayat may, in addition to the annual and the half-yearly meeting, hold extraordinary meeting of a Gram Sansad at any time if the situation so warrants or if the State Government, by order, so directs for the purpose of holding such extraordinary meetings.
- Every meeting shall be presided over by the Pradhan and, in his

absence, by the Upa-Pradhan and in the absence of both, the member or one of the members, as the case may be, elected from the constituency comprising the Gram Sabha or, in the absence of such member or members, any other member of the Gram Panchayat shall preside over the meeting.

- One-tenth of the total number of members shall form a quorum for a meeting of a Gram Sansad.
- A Gram Sansad shall guide and advise the Gram Panchayat in regard to the schemes for economic development and social justice undertaken or proposed to be undertaken in its area and may, without prejudice to the generality of such guidance and advice:
  - (i) Identify, or lay down principles for identification of, the schemes which are required to be taken on priority basis for economic development of the village,
  - (ii) Identify, or lay down principles for identification of, the beneficiaries for various poverty alleviation programmes,
  - (iii) Mobilize mass participation for community welfare programmes and programmes for adult education, family welfare and child welfare.
  - (iv) Promote solidarity and harmony among all sections of the people irrespective of religion, faith, caste, creed or race, and
  - (v) Record its objection to any action of the Pradhan or any other member of the Gram Panchayat for failure to implement any development scheme properly or without active participation of the people of that area.

Source: West Bengal Panchayat Act 1973, Section-16A.

Gram Sabha Meeting (Section 16 B)

Every Gram shall have a Gram Sabha consisting of all electors pertaining to the area of the Gram Panchayat.

- Every Gram Panchayat shall hold within the local limits of the Gram Panchayat an annual meeting, ordinarily in the month of December every year, of the Gram Sabha after completion of the half-yearly meeting of the Gram Sansads.
- The Gram Panchayat shall, at least seven days before the date of holding the meeting, give public notice of such meetings by

beat of drums as widely as possible, announcing the agenda, place, date and hour of the meeting. A notice of such meeting shall also be hung up in the office of the Gram Panchayat. Similar publicity shall also be given in the case of an adjourned meeting.

- A meeting of the Gram Sabha shall be presided over by the Pradhan of the concerned Gram Panchayat or, in his absence, by the Upa-Pradhan.
- The Gram Sabha shall deliberate upon, recommend for, and adopt resolution on, any matter referred to in Sub-section (6) of Section 16A and Section 17A:
- The Gram Panchayat shall, on considering and collating the resolutions of the Gram Sansads, place before the Gram Sabha the resolutions of the Gram Sansads and the views of the Gram Panchayat together with its report on the actions taken and proposed to be taken on them for deliberation and recommendation by the Gram Sabha.

In pursuance of the provision of 73rd Constitutional Amendment Act, West Bengal Government lays more emphasis on meeting of Gram Sabha.

Source: West Bengal Panchayat Act 1973, Section-16B.

Decentralised Planning in West Bengal

Administrative decentralisation is not a new concept for West Bengal. Bengal Village Self Government Act of 1919, which provided for a two-tier structure of Union Boards at the lower level and District Boards at the higher level. After independence, the Act of 1919 was replaced by West Bengal Panchayat Act 1957, reflecting the constitutional directive to promote Panchayati Raj Institution. The Act provided for a Gram Panchayat in every village, which will function as the executive of Gram Sabha, consisting of all the voters on the electoral role in the village. There were two elected executive posts, one Adhyaksha or President and Upadhyaksha or Vice-President. The Act of 1957 was prepared before the publication of the Balwantrai Mehta Committee's Report, which provided a shape to the Panchayati Raj. The Community Development Project (CDP) Blocks were not integrated with the Panchayat system in West Bengal. This created problems in the proper implementation of CDP. To incorporate the Panchayat institutions with the CDP framework, the West Bengal Zilla Parishad Act of 1963 decreed that Zilla Parishads were

to be set up in the place of the existing District Boards. Thereafter, 15 Zilla Parishads and 325 Anchalik Parishads were formed. These two new institutions, along with the 19,602 Gram Panchayats and 2,926 Anchal Panchayats formed under the 1957 Act, constituted the basis of a four tier system of rural local government.
Source: West Bengal Human Development Report, 2004.

In the mid-1960s, the State faced severe economic crisis, particularly for the food distribution, which generated serious social unrest. It also was a period of general political instability with a split in the ruling Congress Party in 1965, the ascension to power of a United Front government in 1967, its dismissal and return to power in mid-term elections in 1969, President's rule from 1970 and the installation of a new Congress government in 1972. In these circumstances, elections to the Panchayats—most of which had been formed between 1959 and 1963—could not be held.

The West Bengal Panchayat Act was passed in 1973; the existing structure was replaced by Gram Panchayat at village level, Panchayat Samiti at Block or intermediate level and Zilla Parishad at the district level. The new Gram Panchayats were similar to the Anchal Panchayats of 1957 Act. As per the Balwantrai Mehta Committee Report's recommendations, Panchayat Samitis were coterminous with Blocks, and Zilla Parishads were coterminous with districts. As per this Act, election of members of all the three tiers for a five years term become mandatory. The Pradhans of Gram Panchayats were ex-officio members of Panchayat Samitis and the Sabhapatis of Panchayat Samitis were similarly ex-officio members of Zilla Parishads. The Act also provided for nominations of officials without voting rights into the Standing Committees of Zilla Parishad, and local MLAs and MPs as ex-officio members of both Block and district levels.

As per the 1973 Act was improved from the previous legislation by ensuring organic linkage between three tiers, improving executive efficiency through a system of Standing Committees, and providing greater clarity regarding the functions. However, elections to these bodies were not held until the Left Front Government came to power in West Bengal in 1977. In June 1978 elections were held simultaneously for all the tiers of the rural local bodies for the first time. Since then, elections to the local bodies are holding at regular five years intervals.

After 1978, the newly elected Panchayats prioritize on execution of land reforms. At first Panchayats took the initiative to find out the benami landholdings, ensured the identification of excess land and the declaration of vested land. And ultimately charge handed over to the bargadars. By doing this West Bengal Panchayat received success by attaching the poor people with the Panchayati Raj Institutions. In case of rural development projects which were implemented through Panchayats, the beneficiaries of land reform were given priority in the receipt of benefits from those projects. The new leadership after 1978 came out of the tradition of peasant upsurge and struggle for land reform of the past three decades. The occupational engagement of the members showed a very significant picture that 43 per cent of elected members were landless poor. By 1988, 58 per cent of Panchayat members were poor peasants or agricultural labourers. These result focused that the power structure shifted from moneylender (before 1978) to the weaker sections of the society.

One of the major objectives of the Panchayati Raj Institutions was involvement in the planning process. A number of reforms were introduced in the planning process from 1983 onwards to ensure the people's participation at the local level. At the apex the State Planning Board (SPB) and the State Planning Department were formed. At the district level there are two tiers: the District Planning and Coordination Committee (DPCC), more of a deliberative body, and the District Planning Committee (DPC) its executive arm. The DPCs prepare the plan, which is approved by the DPCCs. The Block Planning Committee (BPC) is the planning agency at the Block level.

The District Planning Committee (DPC) is the nodal institution for decentralised planning structure which is headed by the Chairperson of Zilla Parishad and the District Collector is its Member-Secretary. It has a mixed membership of non-officials and officials. The District Planning Committee was empowered to approve schemes up to Rs. 5 lakhs while schemes of higher value and inter-district schemes would require the approval of the State Planning Board (West Bengal Human Development Report, 2004).

The Block Planning Committee, headed by the Sabhapati of the Panchayat Samiti, comprised Chairpersons of all the Standing Committees of the Samiti and also of Gram Panchayats as well as the Block level officers of various development departments. The Block Development Officer (BDO) is its Member-Secretary. This Committee prepares Block level plans and approves Block level schemes that costing less than Rs. 50,000. Schemes involving more expenditure, and inter-Block schemes, had to be submitted to the DPC for approval.

Source: West Bengal Human Development Report 2004.

Functional Decentralisation and Gram Panchayat

In every GP there must be elected representatives called Gram Panchayat members (Five to Twenty-five). Among the members there are following categories of Office Bearers—

1. Pradhan (Head of the Office)–One
2. Upa-Pradhan–One: Every Gram Panchayat shall, at its first meeting at which a quorum is present, elect, in the prescribed manner, one of its members to be Pradhan and another to be the Upa-Pradhan of the Gram Panchayat.

Source: W.B. Panchayat Act 1973, Section 9

3. Sanchalak—Five (One for each Upa-Samiti): Within one week from the date of Constitution of the Upa-Samiti, the members referred to in clauses (a) and (b) of sub-section (3) of Section 32A of the Act shall elect in a meeting one member from themselves as Sanchalak of each Upa-Samiti.
4. Members—As general member.

Source: The West Bengal Panchayat Act1973; Section 32A.

Powers, Functions and Duties of Pradhan and Upa-Pradhan

Under Section 34 of West Bengal. Panchayat Act 1973:
The Pradhan shall—

(a) be responsible for the maintenance of the records of the Gram Panchayat;
(b) have general responsibility for the financial and executive administration of the Gram Panchayat;
(c) exercise administrative supervision and control over the work of the staff of the Gram Panchayat and the officers and employees whose service may be placed at the disposal of the Gram Panchayat by the State Government;
(d) for the transaction of business connected with this Act or for the purpose of making any order authorised thereby, exercise such powers, perform such functions and discharge such duties as may be exercised, performed or discharged by the Gram Panchayat under this Act or the rules made thereunder:

Provided that the Pradhan shall not exercise such powers, perform such functions or discharge such duties as may be required by the rules made under this Act to be exercised, performed or discharged by the Gram Panchayat at a meeting; and

(e) exercise such other powers, perform such other functions and discharge such other duties as the Gram Panchayat may, by general or special resolution, direct or as the State Government may by rules made in this behalf, prescribe.

The **Upa-Pradhan** shall—

(a) exercise such of the powers, perform such of the functions and discharge such of the duties of the Pradhan as the Pradhan may from time to time, subject to rules made in this behalf by the State Government, delegate to him by order in writing:

Provided that the Pradhan may at any time withdraw all or any of the powers, functions and duties so delegated to the Upa-Pradhan;

(b) during the absence of the Pradhan, exercise all the powers, perform all the functions and discharge all duties of the Pradhan;

(c) exercise such other powers, perform such other functions and discharge such other duties as the Gram Panchayat may, by general or special resolution, direct or as the State Government may, by rules made in this behalf, prescribe.

Source: West Bengal Panchayat Act 1973, Section 34.

Inter-Tier Demarcation of Functions

There is a lack of delineation of functions among the three-tiers of the PRI. No doubt, 29 items have been included in the Eleventh Schedule of the Constitution but it is not clear as to what functions are to be performed by each tier. It varies from State to State.

States which have drawn the list of functions and activities for different levels of Panchayats in a routine manner on the lines of subjects mentioned in the Eleventh Schedule. These States have also added some other functions.

Most of the States categorised the functions under two heads:

(a) Obligatory or mandatory functions, and
(b) Discretionary functions.

Some States drew their own list.
Source: The West Bengal Panchayat Act 1973.

The functional transfer of subjects as mentioned in the Eleventh Schedule has been clarified through a detailed Activity Mapping exercise, which has been completed for 28 subjects (out of 29 subjects) as per **Order** No(s). 6102/PN/O/ dated 7.11.2005; No. 3969/PN/O/ dated 25.07.2006 and No. 4769/PN/O/ dated 29.10.2007. Activity mapping for only one subject, i.e., technical and vocational education is yet to be published.

So far 11 departments of the Government have issued matching orders from their end for the purpose of devolution, namely:

(i) Forest,
(ii) Health and Family Welfare,
(iii) Women and Child Development and Social Welfare,
(iv) Water Investigation and Development,
(v) Micro and Small Scale Enterprises and Textiles,
(vi) Animal Resources Development,
(vii) Mass Education Extension and Library Services,
(viii) Fishery,
(ix) Power,
(x) Food Processing Industries and Horticulture, and
(xi) Panchayat and Rural Development Department.

In addition to those the Land and Land Reforms Department assigned responsibilities to the PRIs from the very beginning of the Panchayat system. The duties and responsibilities of Panchayat functionaries in respect of activities of Land and Land Reforms Department have been laid down in the West Bengal Land and Land Reforms Act 1955, West Bengal Estate Acquisition Act 1953 and West Bengal Land Reforms Manual 1991.

Devolution of Powers and Authority to the Upa-Samitis of Gram Panchayats

Constitution of Upa-Samitis

Under Section 32A of the West Bengal Panchayat Act 1973:

(1) Subject to such direction as may be issued by the State Government in this behalf, a Gram Panchayat shall as soon as may be within three months following the first meeting referred to in Section 9, constitute Upa-Samitis as referred to in sub-section (2) and delegate its powers, functions and duties to such Upa-Samitis, in such manner as may be prescribed.

(2) Without prejudice to the generality of any other provisions of this Act, a Gram Panchayat shall constitute in such manner as may be prescribed the following Upa-Samitis—

(i) Artha O Parikalpana Upa-Samiti,
(ii) Krishi O Pranisampad Bikas Upa-Samiti,
(iii) Siksha O Janaswasthya Upa-Samiti,
(iv) Nari, Sishu Unnayan O Samaj Kalyan Upa-Samiti, and
(v) Shilpa O Parikathama Upa-Samiti.

Such other Upa-Samiti as the Gram Panchayat may, subject to the approval of the State Government, constitute.
Source: The West Bengal Panchayat Act 1973; Section 32A.

Subjects to be dealt by Upa-Samitis: In order to ensure better functioning and devolution of power and authority of the Gram Panchayat five Upa-Samitis are formed (Section: 32A of W.B. Panchayat Act 1973) just as there are Sthayee Samitis at the upper two tier.

The Upa-Samitis of a Gram Panchayat shall deliberate Upan and deal with the subjects specified below:

1. *Artha O Parikalpana Upa-Samiti:* (i) Finance, (ii) Budget, (iii) Accounts, (iv) Audit, (v) Taxation, (vi) Resource mobilization, (vii) Establishment and office management, (viii) Preparation of Gram Panchayat Plans, (ix) Implementation, monitoring and evaluation of all Poverty Alleviation including Employment Generation Programmes, (x) Food Security and Public Distribution Programme, (xi) Preparation of resource inventory and database of the Gram Panchayat Planning, (xii) Disaster control management, (xiii) Management of haat, bazar, ferry service of Gram Panchayat, (xiv) Coordination of works assigned to different Upa-Samitis and any other work not entrusted with any other Upa-Samiti.

2. *Krishi O Pranisampad Bikas Upa-Samiti:* (i) Agriculture and agro-industries, (ii) Horticulture, (iii) Agri-marketing, (iv) Irrigation including small irrigation, (v) Water resources development, (vi) Social forestry, (vii) Soil conservation, (viii) Apiculture, (ix) Sericulture, (x) Animal

resources development, (xi) Fisheries, (xii) Watershed development, (xiii) Cooperative movement, (xiv) Provident Fund for Landless Agricultural Labourers, etc.

3. *Siksha O Janaswasthya Upa-Samiti:* (i) Literacy campaign, (ii) Sishu Siksha Karmasuchi, (iii) Madhyamik Siksha Karmasuchi, (iv) Primary education, (v) Mass education, (vi) Rural library, (vii) Mid-Day Meal Programme, (viii) Rural water supply, (ix) Rural dispensaries and health clinic, (x) Public health and sanitation, (xi) Immunisation and family welfare programmes, (xii) Prevention of communicable diseases, etc.

4. *Nari, Sishu Unnayan O Samaj Kalyan Upa-Samiti*: (i) Self-help groups formed under various programmes including Swarnajayanti Gram Swarozgar Yojana (SGSY), National Rural Livelihood Mission (NRLM), (ii) Integrated Child Development Scheme, (iii) National Social Assistance Programme, (iv) Social welfare and welfare of women and children, (v) Welfare of weaker communities including old and handicapped people.

5. *Shilpa O Parikathama Upa-Samiti*: (i) Cottage and small scale industries, (ii) Rural artisans, (iii) Infrastructure development, (iv) Indira Aawas Yojana, (v) Construction of rural roads, culverts and rural housing, (vi) Rural electrification and generating alternative energy resources.
Source: The West Bengal Panchayat Act 1973; Section 32A.

Powers of Upa-Samiti

(1) Every Upa-Samiti shall prepare schemes and perform the functions of the Gram Panchayat in relation to the subjects allotted to it within its budgetary provisions. It shall also be responsible for implementation of the works and schemes of the Gram Panchayat and those assigned to it by different departments of the State Government relating to the subjects specified above. Provided that the financial limits to which an Upa-Samiti is competent to execute works and schemes undertaken by the Gram Panchayat, shall be such as may, from time to time, be fixed by the Gram Panchayat or by the State Government.

(2) For every item of expenditure exceeding its financial limit, each Upa-Samiti shall prepare proposal and place to the Gram Panchayat for approval. It shall be the duty of each Upa-Samiti to carry out the decision of the Gram Panchayat on such proposal.

(3) An Upa-Samiti shall not alter the budgetary allocation of funds made by the Gram Panchayat according to the subjects allotted to it.
Source: The West Bengal Panchayat Act 1973; Section 32A.

Functions and Duties of Upa-Samitis

(1) When any scheme is assigned by any department of the State Government or by the Panchayat Samiti or by the Zilla Parishad or executed from its own resources, the Gram Panchayat shall forward the contents of the scheme to the appropriate Upa-Samiti for drawing up a detailed plan for its execution.

(2) While forwarding the scheme, the Gram Panchayat may, issue direction to the Upa-Samiti of the manner in which the plan for its execution shall be drawn up.

(3) The Upa-Samiti shall cause preparation of plan and estimate of the work by taking assistance of any official of the State Government, the statutory Board, the Corporation or any other official receiving the grant, financial assistance, or the remuneration from the State Government, who shall render all assistance in this regard as may be necessary and proceed to execute the scheme.

Source: The West Bengal Panchayat Act 1973; Section 32A.

Fiscal Decentralisation and Gram Panchayat in West Bengal

The financial resources of the Panchayats broadly comprise internal revenue mobilized by themselves through the exercise of tax and non-tax powers, and resources received from the State in the form of devolution and grant from both the State and then Union Governments.

Under Section 45 of the West Bengal Panchayat Act 1973 (West Bengal Panchayat Act XLI of 1973):

(1) For every Gram Panchayat there shall be constituted a Gram Panchayat Fund bearing the name of the Gram Panchayat and there shall be placed to the credit thereof—
   (a) Contributions and grants, if any, made by the Central or the State Government;
   (b) Contributions and grants, if any, made by the Zilla Parishad, [Mahakuma Parishad, Council,]Panchayat Samity or any other local authority;
   (c) Loans, if any, granted by the Central Government or the State Government;
   (d) All receipts on account of taxes, rates and fees levied by it;
   (e) All receipts in respect of any schools, hospitals, dispensaries-buildings, institutions or works vested in,

constructed by or placed under the control and management of the Gram Panchayat;

(f) All sums received as gift or contribution and all incomes from any trust or endowment made in favour of the Gram Panchayat;

(g) Such fines and penalties imposed and realised under the provisions of this Act as may be prescribed;

(h) All other sums received by or on behalf of the Gram Panchayat.

Source: The West Bengal Panchayat Act 1973; Section 45.

Gram Panchayats' Own Source of Revenue (Imposition of Tax & Non-Tax)

(i) Imposition of Tax (on Lands and Buildings) by Gram Panchayats: Articles 243 H, 243 I and 243 X empower the PRIs and municipal bodies to levy and collect the taxes. Under Section 46 of the West Bengal Panchayat Act 1973:

(1) Subject to such rules as may be made in this behalf, a Gram Panchayat shall impose yearly—

(a) on lands and buildings within the local limits of its jurisdiction, a tax—

(i) at the rates of one per centum of the annual value of such lands and buildings when the annual value does not exceed rupees one thousand, and

(ii) at the rate of two per centum of the annual value of such lands and buildings when the annual value exceeds rupees one thousand, to be paid by the owners and occupiers thereof.

(b) [Clause (b) was omitted by s. 12(1) of the West Bengal Panchayat (Amendment) Act, 1992 (West Bengal Act XVII of 1992).]

(2) The following lands and buildings shall be exempted from imposition of tax under sub-section (1), namely–

(a) lands and buildings, the annual value of which is not more than rupees two hundred and fifty;

(b) lands and buildings belonging to a local authority and used or intended to be used exclusively for a public purpose and not used or intended to be used for purposes of profits;

(c) lands and buildings used exclusively for religious, educational or charitable purposes.

(3) The State Government may, by notification, exempt either wholly or in part any other class of properties or classes of properties specified in the notification from the taxes or rates leviable under this section.

(4) [Sub-section (4) was omitted by Section 12(2) of the West Bengal Panchayat (Amendment) Act 1992 (West Bengal Act XVII of 1992).]

(5) Subject to such rules as may be made in this behalf a Gram Panchayat shall levy—

(a) on all transfers of improvable property situated within the local limits of the Gram, a duty in the shape of an additional stamp duty at the rate of two per centum or, as the case may be, the amount of the consideration for the sale, the value of the property in the case of a gift, the amount secured by the mortgage, the value of the property of the greater value in the case of exchange, or the value of the rent for the first ten years in the case of a lease, as set forth in the instrument;

(b) a duty in the shape of an additional stamp duty at the rate of ten per centum on all payments for admission to any entertainment.

(6) The State Government may make rules for regulating the collection of the duty on transfers of immovable property and duty on entertainment referred to in sub-section (5), the payment thereof to the Gram Panchayat and the deduction of any expenses incurred by the State Government in the collection thereof.

Source: The West Bengal Panchayat Act 1973; Section 46.

(ii) Imposition of Non-Tax (Levy of the Fees, Rates, Tolls, etc.) by Gram Panchayats.

Under Section 47 of the West Bengal Panchayat Act 1973:

(1) Subject to such maximum rates as the State Government may prescribe, a Gram Panchayat may levy the following fees, rates and tolls, namely—

(i) fees on registration of vehicles;

(ii) fees on plaints and petitions and other processes in suits and cases instituted before the Nyaya Panchayat concerned;

(iii) a fee for providing sanitary arrangements at such places of worship or pilgrimage, fairs and *melas* within its jurisdiction as may be specified by the State Government by notification.

(iv) a water rate, where arrangement for the supply of water for drinking, irrigation or any other purpose is made by the Gram Panchayat within its jurisdiction;

(v) a lighting rate, where arrangement for lighting of public streets and places is made by the Gram Panchayat within its jurisdiction;

(vi) a conservancy rate, where arrangement for clearing private latrines, urinals and cesspools is made by the Gram Panchayat within its jurisdiction;

(vii) fees on [registration] for running trade, wholesale or retail, within the jurisdiction of the Gram Panchayat unless such [registration] or such trade is prohibited under any law for the time being in force;

(viii) tolls on persons, vehicles or animals or any class of them at any toll-bar which is established by the Gram Panchayat on any road or bridge vested in, or under the management of, the Gram Panchayat;

(ix) tolls in respect of any ferry established by, or under the management of, the Gram Panchayat;

(x) *[Clauses (x) was omitted by Section 7(1) of the West Bengal Panchayat (Amendment) Act 2004 (West Bengal Act XVIII of 2004).]

(xi) a general sanitary rate where arrangement for the construction and maintenance of the construction and maintenance of public latrines is made by the Gram Panchayat within its jurisdiction;

(xii) a drainage rate where arrangement for regular clearance of common drains is made by the Gram Panchayat within its jurisdiction;

(xiii) *[Clauses (xiii) was omitted by Section 7(2) of the West Bengal Panchayat (Amendment) Act 2004 (West Bengal Act XVIII of 2004).]

(xiv) fees for use of burning ghat vested in, or under the management and control of the Gram Panchayat;

(xv) fees on registration for [shallow or deep tube- wells] fitted with motor-driven pump sets and for irrigation for commercial purpose, subject to such terms and conditions as may be prescribed.

[*Explanation*– In this clause, "commercial purpose" includes any purpose for which irrigation water is supplied to the land of any persons, other the owner of the shallow tube-well, on realisation of water rates, by whatever name called, from the owner of such land.]

(xvi) fees on the village produces sold in the village market organized by the Gram Panchayat to be determined by means of weight, measurement or by number or any two or more of them;

(xvii) fees on erection, exhibition, fixing or retaining upon or over any land, building, wall, hoarding, or structure, any advertisement for public display in any manner whatsoever, in any place whether public or private excepting those exhibited by the State Government in the public interest.

(2) The Gram Panchayat shall not undertake registration of a vehicle or levy fee thereof and shall not provide sanitary arrangements at places of worship or pilgrimage, fairs and *melas* within its jurisdiction or levy fee, therefore, if such vehicle has already been registered by any other authority under any law for the time being in force or if such provision for sanitary arrangement has already been made by any other local authority.

(3) The scales of tolls, and the fees or rates and the terms and conditions of imposition thereof, shall be such as may be provided by bye-laws.

(4) Such bye-laws may provide for exemption from all or any of the tolls, fees or rates in any cases.

Source: The West Bengal Panchayat Act 1973; Section 47.

Devolution of Fund

Gram Panchayats received fund/resources from the State in the form of devolution and grant from both the State and then Union Governments. Major devolution of funds:

1. *State Finance Commission* (*SFC*): Grants under Third State Finance Commission (SFC) will be divided into two segments:

- Fund under first segment (98%) will be termed as Bangla Gram Bikash Prakalpa. Fund under Bangla Gram Bikash Prakalpa will be allocated to the Zilla Parishads, Panchayat Samitis and Gram Panchayats in the ratio of 12:18:70.

- Fund under second segment (2%) will be allotted among PRIs of all tiers as Incentive Grant in proportion to the 'Own Source Revenue' collected by PRI body in excess of the collection of the last year. This incentive grant will henceforth be termed as Panchayat Sampad Bikash Prakalpa.

2. *Central Finance Commission (CFC):* Government of India has accepted the recommendations of the Thirteenth Central Finance Commission (CFC) for devolution of grants-in-aid. The General Basic Grant for the three tier Panchayati Raj Institutions (PRIs) and the Special Area Basic Grant for the Hill Areas of Darjeeling District will be given in two instalments in the month of July and January of every year up to 2014-15. The State will be eligible for the second instalment depending on the utilization of at least 75 per cent of the available fund under Thirteenth CFC for the entire State.

Scarcity of drinking water is a common problem of most of the districts during summer. Hence, fund for maintenance of the sources for drinking water @ Rs.1 lakh per Gram Panchayat has been estimated to be required annually and 50 per cent of such requirement has been allotted separately from the available fund of Thirteenth CFC to the Gram Panchayats.

After earmarking the required fund for the above mentioned purposes, the rest amount has been allotted to the Zilla Parishad, Panchayat Samitis and Gram Panchayats in the ratio of 12:18:70. Allocation of fund to the Panchayat Samitis and Gram Panchayats within a district has been made following the criteria laid down in the guideline of Third SFC.

3. *Mahatma Gandhi National Rural Employment Guarantee Scheme (MGNREGS)*: The Indian job guarantee scheme, enacted as Act by legislation on 25 August 2005. The law was initially called the NREGA but was renamed as the MGNREGA on 2 October 2009. The scheme provides a legal guarantee for at least one hundred days of employment in every financial year to adult members of any household willing to do public works related unskilled manual work.

From 1st April, 2013, an unskilled job card holder receives Rs. 151 for a day's labour and on complication of appropriate quantum of work as per the Scheduled of Rates (SoR) as in vogue (Memo. No. 1852(19)/RD/P/NREGA/18S-01/08; 06.03.2013 of P&RD Dept., GoWB).

The Central Government shall meet the cost of the following, namely—

(a) the amount required for payment of wages for unskilled manual work under the Scheme, and
(b) up to three-fourths of the material cost of the Scheme including payment of wages to skilled and semi-skilled workers subject to the provisions.

The State Government shall meet the cost of the following, namely–

(a) the cost of unemployment allowance payable under the Scheme; and
(b) one-fourth of the material cost of the Scheme including payment of wages to skilled and semi-skilled workers subject to the provisions.

4. *Backward Regions Grant Fund (BRGF)*: The BRGF is designed to redress regional imbalances in development. The fund will provide financial resources for supplementing and converging existing developmental inflows into identified districts, so as to:

(a) Bridge critical gaps in local infrastructure and other development requirements that are not being adequately met through existing inflows;
(b) Strengthen, to this end Panchayat and Municipality level governance with more appropriate capacity building, to facilitate participatory planning, decision-making, implementation and monitoring, to reflect local felt needs;
(c) Provide professional support to local bodies for planning, implementation and monitoring their plans; and
(d) Improve the performance and delivery of critical functions assigned to Panchayats, and counter possible efficiency and equity losses on account of inadequate local capacity.

Backward Regions Grant Fund (BRGF) consists of two funding windows, as follows:

(a) A Capability Building Fund, and
(b) A Substantially Untied Grant.

Criteria for Distribution of Funds: The substantially untied grants will be distributed among the districts concerned as follows:

(a) Every district will receive a fixed minimum amount of 10 crore per annum,
(b) 50 per cent of the balance allocation under the Scheme will be allocated on the basis of the share of the population of the district in the total population of all backward districts, and
(c) The remaining 50 per cent will be distributed on the basis of the share of the district in the total area of all backward districts.

Financial Autonomy

It means Share of Gram Panchayat's Own Fund (Tax and Non-Tax) in Gram Panchayat's total (include all funds) expenditure. The Financial Autonomy Ratio (FAR) shows the extent of reliance on own sources of funds which lead to autonomy. In this case the top ranker is the Gram Panchayat with the highest FAR. Higher autonomy may be appreciated but it could also mean that the flow of Government and other funds are inadequate for the development of a particular Gram Panchayat.

Conclusion

The 73rd Amendment Act has made Panchayats an institution of self-government. Article 243G of the Constitution envisaged Panchayats as Institute of Self-Governance (ISG), which means they should enjoy functional, financial and administrative autonomy in their working area. As per the Constitution, Panchayats shall prepare plan for economic development and social justice at local level. The District Planning Committee shall integrate the plan so prepared with the plans prepared by the urban local bodies at district level.

The success and failure of the Panchayats would depend on planning and implementation. It also depends on maximum people's participation at every stage of planning process, from proposal to implementation. People's participation in local level development has been exercised through the formulation of the panchayat level development plan, project coordination at intermediate and district levels of the Panchayats.

In West Bengal the Gram Panchayats have been given more powers in comparison with powers given to the Block/District Panchayats. They have 14 obligatory and 21 assigned functions, apart from a large number of discretionary functions. The Gram Panchayats have full power to approve works. The Panchayat Samitis also perform a large variety of functions related to 18 sectors. The Zilla Parishads have a wide range of administrative and financial powers. They are delegated with all the functions of 29 sectors under Schedule XI with 17 other items and 24 departmental schemes for implementation.

In West Bengal, the planning process of grass root level has some stages from proposal to implementation. At first, local area plans are prepared by Gram Unnayan Samiti and those plans are submitted in the Gram Sansad meeting. Then all local area plans of all Gram Sansads come into the Gram Sabha. Gram Sabhas are convening to identify the problems of development and identify the local needs. Special efforts are made for ensuring participation of the people. The most important guideline is to hold group-wise discussion in each Gram Sabha according to various development sectors. After the identification of the felt needs in the Gram Sabhas, the next step in the planning process is to make an objective assessment of the natural and human resources of the locality. The reports of the Gram Sabha discussion, including list of problems identified are consolidated for each development sector in the Panchayat.

After getting the final plan from Panchayats, the Panchayat Samiti and Zilla Parishad started preparing their annual plans. The plan proposal were consolidated at the district level and integrated with the Municipal plans. The task force constituted by the District Planning Committee (DPC) for the purpose has evolved broad strategy for district level development. The district plan is nothing but only the synthesis of the village plans. At present the rules favour the implementation of planned activities by the Zilla Parisad. The DPC forwards the integrated development plan for rural and urban areas of the district to the State. The State Planning Board is the State level-coordinating agency for planning.

There are lots of factors which are hampering the decentralisation process like local level political interference on the whole process of Planning and implementation, low demand from the grass root level people, low peoples' participation, limited fund to implement any plans and availability of fund at the flag end of the financial year, administrative and bureaucratic willingness is rare, ambitious and poor planning without considering the available resources, lack of awareness of the members, lack of technological know-how, proper budget estimation is not done institution cost carried from the programme cost and do not submit utilization certificate in time by the Panchayat office.

Successful planning and implementation of development programmes require adequate funds, appropriate policy framework and effective delivery mechanism with healthy environment for decentralisation. After

73rd and 74th Amendment, the Government is trying to change in planning process by adopting bottom up approach. But due to financial limitation, low peoples participation, local political influence in administrative all are creating barriers in the way of success of decentralisation and bottom up planning process. Implementation process is continued to follow top down approach. So, most of the time, plans prepared by the villagers are not implemented properly at grass root level. It has been observed that the plans are good on paper but are rarely good in implementation.

References

Alsop, R., Krishna, A. and Sjoblom, D.; (2000), Are Gram Panchayats Inclusive? Report of a Study Conducted in Rajasthan and Madhya Pradesh, Background Paper No. 3 of the World Bank's unpublished *Overview of Rural Decentralisation in India*, Volume 3.

Altekar, A.S.; (1997), *State and Government in Ancient India*, Motilal Banarasi Das Publications, New Delhi.

Bardhan, Pranab and Mookherjee, Dilip; (2000), *Decentralising Anti-Poverty Programme in Developing Countries*. De Ivery.

Website:www.httpi/lglobetrotter.berkeley.edu/macarthur/inequallty/papers/decdelpov.pdf

Blair, H.; (2000), Participation and Accountability at the Periphery: Democratic Local Governance in Six Countries, *World Development*, 28 (1): 21-39.

Braun, Foachim Von and Ulrike, Grote; 2002: Does Decentralisation Serve the Poor, Ed by Ahmed Ehtisham and Vito Tanzi, *Managing Fiscal Decentralisation*, London: Routledge.

Crook, R.C. and Manor, J.; (1998), *Democracy and Decentralisation in South Asia and West Africa*. Cambridge, Cambridge University Press.

Crook, R.C. and Sverrisson, A.S. (2001), 'Decentralisation and Poverty Alleviation in Developing Countries: A Comparative Analysis or, is West Bengal Unique?' IDS Working Paper 130. Brighton: Institute of Development Studies.

Datta, Prabhat; (2011), *Of Rural Decentralisation and People's Participation: Three Decade Experience in West Bengal*, Dasgupta & Co., Kolkata.

Deshpande, S.V. and Venkatesha, Murthy, G.B.; (2002), Pressures from Below: Decentralised Governance in Karnataka, *Economic and Political Weekly*, 4 May, 2002.

Dewey, C.; (1972), Images of the Village Community: A Study in Anglo-Indian Ideology, *Modern Asian Studies*, Vol. 6, No. 3, pp. 291-328.

Drèze, J. and Sen, A.; (1996), *India: Economic Development and Social Opportunity*, Oxford University Press, Delhi.

Dreze, Jean and Sen, Amartya; (2012), *India: Development and Participation*, Oxford University Press, New Delhi.

Ghatak, M. and Ghatak, M.; (2002), Recent Reforms in the Panchayat System in West Bengal: Towards Greater Participatory Governance, *Economic and Political Weekly*, 5 January 2002, pp. 45-58.

Ghosh, Rathna, Pramanik, Alok Kumar; (1999), *Panchayat System in India. Historical, Constitutional and Financial Analysis*, Kanishka Publication, New Delhi.

Ghosh, Buddhadeb; (2000), *Status of Panchayati Raj in the States and Union Territories of India*, Indian Institute of Social Sciences and Concept Publishing Company, New Delhi.

Golooba-Mutebi, F.; (2000), Reassessing Participation in Uganda, Paper presented at the conference, New Institutional Economics, Institutional Reform and Poverty Reduction, Development Studies Institute, *London School of Economics and Political Science*, 7-8 September 2000.

Islam, Md. Nazrul; (2003), Decentralised Governance and Development: A Gandhian Vision, *Gandhi Prasang*, V(2): 63-8.

Jha, S.; (2000), Fiscal Decentralisation in India: Strengths, Limitations and Prospects for Panchayati Raj Institutions, Background Paper No. 2, World Bank Unpublished *Overview of Rural Decentralisation in India*, Volume 3.

Johnson, C. and Start, D.; (2001), Rights, Claims and Capture: Understanding the Politics of Pro-Poor Policy, ODI Working Paper 145. London: Overseas Development Institute.

Joshi, R.P.; (1999), *Constitutionalization of Panchayati Raj: A Reassessment*, Rawat Publications, Jawahar Nagar, Jaipur-4 (India).

Joshi, R.P. and Narwani, G.S.; (2002), *Panchayat Raj in India: Emerging Trends Across the States*, Rawat Publications, India.

Law Department (Legislative), (2004), The West Bengal Panchayat (Gram Panchayat Administration) Rules, 2004. Kolkata, WB: Law Dept. (Legislative).

Law Department (Legislative), (2007), The West Bengal Panchayat (Gram Panchayat Accounts, Audit and Budget) Rules, 2007. Kolkata, WB: Law Dept. (Legislative).

Law Department (Legislative), (2009), West Bengal Act XLI of 1973: The West Bengal Panchayat Act, 1973 (As modified up to the 31st May, 2009). Kolkata, WB: Law Dept. (Legislative).

Law Department (Legislative), (2010), West Bengal Act VIII of 2010: The West Bengal Panchayat (Amendment) Act, 2010 (As modified up to the 31st May, 2010). Kolkata, WB: Law Dept. (Legislative).

Litvack Jennie, Junaid Ahmed and Richard Bird; (1998), *Rethinking Decentralisation in Developing Countries*, World Bank, Washington, DC.

Luckham, R., Goetz, A.M. and Kaldor, M., (2000), Democratic Institutions and Politics in Context of Inequality, Poverty, and Conflict: A Conceptual Framework, IDS Working Paper 104, Institute of Development Studies, Brighton.

Mahapatra, B.P.; (2012), *Local Self-Governing Institutions and Fiscal Decentralisation in India: Form to Function*, RULNR, Abstract 2193836, Research Unit, CESS, Hyderabad, India.

Mahapatra, Subhasmita, (2006), An ally on Panchayat Raj, in (ed) *Panchayt Raj Institutions in India, Issues and Challenges*, Discovery, New Delhi.

Maheswari, S.R.; (1971), *Local Government in India*, Orient Longman, New Delhi.

Maheswari, S.R.; (1979), *Few Perspectives on Rural Local Government in India: Ashok Mehta Committee Report*, Asian Survey, Vol. XIX.

Maheswari, S.R.; (1983), *Rural Development in India*, Sage Publications, New Delhi.

Mahipal; (1997), Panchayati Raj in India: Issues and Challenges, *Kurukshetra*. 97(8).

Manor, J.; (1999), *The Political Economy of Democratic Decentralisation. Directions in Development Series*, World Bank, Washington DC.

Mathew, George; (1995), *Panchayati Raj: From Legislation to Movement*, Concept Publications, Delhi.

Mathew, G.; (2001), Panchayat Elections: Dismal Record, *Economic and Political Weekly*, 20 January 2001, pp. 183-4.

Mathew, G.; (2001), Panchayats Powerless in AP, *The Hindu*, 17 April 2001.

Ministry of Law and Justice (Legislative Department), Government of India (GoI). (2005), The National Rural Employment Guarantee Act: The *Gazette*, Legislative Dept., GoI, New Delhi, India.

Ministry of Panchayati Raj (MoPR), Government of India (GoI); (2006), Backward Regions Grant Fund: Programme Guidelines, MoPR, GoI, New Delhi, India.

Ministry of Rural Department (MoRD), Government of India (GoI)', (2000), Panchayati Raj in India-Status Report 2000. MoRD, GoI, New Delhi, India.

Mohapatra, Bishnu; (2001), Social Connectedness and Fragility of Social Capital: View from an Orissa Village, *Economic and Political Weekly*, XXXVI (8): 665-72.

Moore, M. and Putzel, J.; (1999), Politics and Poverty: A background paper for the World Development Report 2000/1, Institute of Development Studies, Brighton.

Mukherjee, Subrata; (1974), *Local Self-Government in West Bengal*, Dasgupta & Company (Private) Limited, Calcutta.

Nambiar, M.; (2001), Making the Gram Sabha Work, *Economic and Political Weekly*, 18 August 2001.

Oommen, M.A. (1999), 'Panchayat Finance and Issues relating to Intergovernmental Transfers,' in S.N. Jha and P.C. Mathur (eds.) (1999) *Decentralisation and Local Politics: Readings in Indian Government and Politics* (2). London: Sage, pp. 142-72.

Ostrom, E.; (1990), *Governing the Commons: The Evolution of Institutions for Collective Action*, Cambridge University Press, Cambridge.

Panchayat and Rural Development Department (P&RD Dept.), Government of West Bengal (GoWB); (2008), Annual Administrative Report 2008-09, P&RD Dept., GoWB, Kolkata, WB.

Panchayat and Rural Development Department (P&RD Dept.), Government of West Bengal (GoWB), (2010), Information on West Bengal Panchayats: Their Members and Functionaries, P&RD Dept., GoWB, Kolkata, WB.

Panchayat and Rural Development Department (P&RD Dept.), Government of West Bengal (GoWB), (2008), SRD Annual Report 2007-08, P&RD Dept., GoWB, Kolkata, WB.

Panchayat and Rural Development Department (P&RD Dept.), Government of West Bengal (GoWB), (2009), Roadmap for Panchayat in West Bengal: A Vision Document. P&RD Dept., GoWB, Kolkata, WB.

Panchayat and Rural Development Department (P&RD Dept.), Government of West Bengal (GoWB). (2011). SRD Project Completion Report 2011 (ARIES Project Code: 107904-101 & 107904-102). Kolkata, WB: P&RD Dept., GoWB.

Panth, Ananth. S. and Om Prakash Bohra; (1995), Finance of PRIs, *The Indian Journal of Public Administration*. Vol. 41, No. 1, Jan.-March 1995, pp. 73-77.

Paul, Sujit Kumar; (2013), Decentralised Planning: Experience of West Bengal Panchayats, in Himadri Sinha and Anant Kumar (eds), *Governance of Commons and Livelihood Security,* Xavier Institute of Social Service, Ranchi.

Planning Commission, Government of India (GoI). (1997), Ninth Five Year Plan, 1997-2000, GoI, New Delhi.

Prud'home, Remy; (1995), The Dangers of Decentralisation, *The World Bank Research Observer*, 10(2): 201-20.

Putnam, Robert Leonardi and Raffaella, Y. Nanetti; (1993), Making Democracy Work: Civic Tradition in Modern Italy, Princeton University Press, Princeton, NJ.

Rahman, H.Z.; (2001), Rethinking Local Governance towards a Livelihoods Focus, *PPRC Policy Paper*, Dhaka: Power and Participation Research Centre.

Rao, G.B.; (2000), Strengthening of Panchayats: Beyond Contractor's Role, Paper presented at the Workshop on Role of Panchayati Raj Institutions in Natural Resource Management, 2 and 3 February, New Delhi.

Romeo, Leonardo; (1999), Systems Experimentation in Support of Decentralisation Reforms: Reflections on Local Development Funds, *Regional Development Dialogue*, 20(2): 134-157.

Singh, Raj; (1996), *Panchayat Raj Manual: A Socio-Historical-cum-Legal Perspective*, Anmol Publications, New Delhi, 1996, p. 10.

Slater, R.P. and Watson J.R.; (1993), Decentralised Planning and the Anti-Poverty Programmes. Some Possible New Direction. Ed. By Hooja, Rakesh and B. Yerram Raju, *Decentralised Planning in Multilevel Framework*, Rawat Publications, New Delhi.

Stephen, F., Rajasekaran, (2001), *An Empirical Study of Women in Local Self-Governance in Karnataka*, Search Publications, Bangalore.

Tanzi, Vto; (1995), *Fiscal Federalism and Decentralisation: A Review of Some Efficiency and Economic Aspects*. Ed. By. Michael Bruno and Boris Pleskovic, Annual World Bank Conference on Development Economies, The World Bank, Washington DC.

The Constitution (Seventy-Third Amendment) Act, 1992, Government of India.

Vyasulu, V.; (2000), Decentralisation, Democratisation, Finances, and the Constitution: Reflections Based on Local Reality, Paper prepared for the Panel on Decentralisation of the National Commission to Review the Working of the Constitution.

Wade, R.; (1985), The Market for Public Office: Why the Indian State is not Better at Development, *World Development*, 13(4): 467-97.

World Bank, (2000), Overview of Rural Decentralisation in India. Volume I, Unpublished report, World Bank.

World Bank, (2000), Overview of Rural Decentralisation in India. Volume II: Approaches to Rural Decentralisation in Seven States, Unpublished report, World Bank.

World Bank; (2000), Overview of Rural Decentralisation in India. Volume III:Background papers, Unpublished report, World Bank.

World Bank; (2000), *World Development Report 2000-01*: Attacking Poverty. Oxford University Press, Oxford.

World Bank; (2000), Multi-State Study of Panchayati Raj Legislation and Administrative Reform, Vol. 3, Background Paper 1: de Souza, Peter, 2000. New Delhi, India.

World Bank; (2000), *Overview of Rural Decentralisation in India*, Vol. 1, September 27, 2000. New Delhi, India.

4
Self-Help Group

Introduction

Over the last few years, "People's Participation" and "Empowerment" has become the buzz words in rural development and local planning. In this context, Self-Help Group (SHG) has emerged as the most successful strategy, in the process of participatory development and empowerment of rural people.

The most conspicuous feature of the term empowerment is that it contains within it the word power. So obviously, empowerment is about power and about changing the balance of power. Power is exercised in social, economic and political relations between individuals and groups. Power itself can be simply defined as 'control over resources' (physical, human, intellectual, financial) and 'control over ideology' (beliefs, values and attitudes) (Batliwala, 1994). In an intrinsic sense empowerment is not something that can be done from the outside; it is something that the people need to do for themselves. Changes in awareness and confidence are one's own and can be tremendously creative and transforming when they occur.

Empowerment is not an end in itself however, but a means to an end. It entails acquiring adequate knowledge and capacity, confidence, help and ideas to decide what is best for oneself and to act accordingly in fulfilling one's own potentials. Empowerment involves a participatory approach that enables people to emancipate themselves. It challenges the basic structure of subordination and is concerned with the transformation of the structure of subordinations. Empowerment is the dynamics of power—that is one's capacity to influence or control others. One group can have effective power to control other by having control over resources and ideology. Hence, the process of gaining control over the self, ideology and resources that determine power may be termed empowerment.

Empowerment lies at the very root of democratic society. It is the watchword especially in the context of poverty alleviation and rural development because rural poor are too unorganized and powerless to be individually able to better their lot in societies. The benefits of growth failed to trickle down to the poor who are often marginalized if not excluded from the mainstream of development process. Empowering rural poor enhances the self-confidence, dignity and self-determination capacity of the rural people to eliminate the implicit and explicit socio-economic disadvantages and thereby provides a means to improve the effectiveness of development policy initiatives and programmes. Micro-finance through self-help groups is one of the effective strategies for poverty alleviation and promotion of economic empowerment.

Despite having a wide network of rural banks in the country and implementation of credit linked poverty alleviation programmes, a large number of rural poor continue to remain outside the fold of formal banking system. Various studies suggested that the existing policies, systems and procedures often did not meet the needs of the hardcore and assetless poor.

The conception and implementation of such programmes of poverty alleviation may get success if it is based on the broad principles of 'social banking' and the key to success lies in the evolution and participation of community based organizations. Social banking can be described as the elevation of the entitlements of previously disadvantaged groups to formal credit even if this may entail a weakening of the conventional banking practices. In the process of pursuing the broader objectives of social banking, however, certain weaknesses crept into the system of banking in general and rural banking in particular. The efforts to improve distribution of formal credit among the landless and near landless population failed and bank credit, once again, remained concentrated in the hands of the landed population. Due to lack of provision of consumption credit, this system could not fully adapt the task of poverty alleviation. Finally, it may be said that the system resulted in the creation of non-profit making assets on account of poor repayment of loans.

With increasing criticisms of the State led credit system and its utilization for poverty alleviation, in recent years developing countries have moved towards new mechanisms of lending such as micro-credit and/or micro-financing. Micro-credit is the extension of small loans to entrepreneurs too poor to qualify for traditional loans. It has proven an effective and popular measure in the ongoing struggle against poverty, enabling those without access to lending institutions to borrow at bank rates and start small business. On the other hand, Micro-finance is the provision of thrift, credit and other financial services and products of very small amounts to the poor in rural, semi-urban or urban areas for enabling them to raise their income levels and improving their living standards. Clearly both are targeted to solve the problems of rural finance where large number of small borrowers require credit frequently and in small quantities. The only difference is that the latter is a broader concept as compared to the former. Recently, Micro-credit has been claimed to be a solution to most of the problems that originated out of the States efforts to alleviate poverty using the instrument of credit.

The extension and development departments are fast realizing the significance of providing financial services to the poor, providing opportunity to save and access credit. Credit, if appropriately delivered, is attractive to the poor, financially viable and self-sustainable. Extension departments and NGOs also realize the limitations of formal Banks and the strengths of informal money lending, which unfortunately is exploitative. Hence, efforts have been made to learn from banks and the moneylenders, and create alternative models for credit delivery; which are simple, efficient, non-exploitative, financially sustainable and self-managed. Accordingly, the idea of Self-Help Group (SHG) has developed.

Self-Help Group

The Self-Help Group may be defined as a collection of individuals belonging to certain households agreeing to work or are already working with a bond of common interest, needs, socio-economic condition, location, kinship to achieve a common goal. SHGs are voluntary associations of women residing in the same area, formed democratically and without any political association. The basic principles on which SHGs function are group approach, mutual trust, manageable small groups, group cohesiveness, spirit of thrift, demand-based lending, collateral free, and peer group pressure in repayment, skill training, capacity building and empowerment. NABARD defined Self-Help Group as a group of 20 or less people from a homogeneous class who are willing to come together for addressing their common problems. They make regular savings and use the pooled savings to give interest bearing loans to their members. The process help them imbibe the essentials of financial intermediation including prioritization of needs, setting self-determined terms for repayment and keeping book of records. It builds financial discipline and credit history that encourages banks to lend to them in certain multiples of their own savings and without any demand for collateral security.

Self-Help Group is a group of homogeneous people who can develop their socio-economic condition by their own help. In India this concept is not new one. We can find the concept of SHG in rural India in the form of foodgrain storage practice. The main feature of rural life is community living. We see that most of the time to control various kinds of activity we create various group like cultural group, sports group, etc., but the Self-Help Group is little different from these groups. In this group the members belong from homogeneous socio-economic condition. They are also participating in the process of development.

The Self-Help Groups and micro-credit organizations have a long history. In Vietnam, Tontines or Hui with 10-15 members involved in financial activities in cash or in kind have been in existence for generations. In Indonesia, credit unions, fishermen groups, village based bank like institutions, irrigation groups, etc., have been in existence since long. In the 1970s some countries like Bangladesh and Brazil started a unique experiment in small lending. This gave to the concept of Microfinance and Micro-credit. Bangladesh became to the world the role model and the foremost and most successful proponent of this method of lending.

It is their model which is being largely replicated elsewhere in the world, including increasingly in India. In 1976, Muhammad Yunus, the noble laureate founded the Grameen Bank to give loans to poor Bangladeshis. To ensure repayment, the bank uses a system of "solidarity groups". These small informal groups apply together for loans and its member acts as co-guarantors of repayment and supports one another's efforts at economic self-advancements.

The Self-Employed Women's Association (SEWA) in Gujarat (India), is a combination of Self-Help Groups and co-operations of women workers in the informal sector. It followed a multi-faceted empowerment approach; where all economic activities of the groups were linked with health and social issues.

It took the movement about two decades to gather momentum. In 1992 SHGs emerged as important players in the microfinance sector when NABARD introduced a pilot programme linking SHGs and banks (Self-Help group Bank Linkage Programme) to enable poor households access the mainstream banking network and meet their financial needs. The programme received a boost in the year 1997 at the World Micro Credit Summit in Washington D.C., (US), when a global target was set for supporting 100 million of the world's poorest families, especially women, with micro-credit by 2005.

Meanwhile, Ministry of Rural Development reshaped its policy towards self-employment and incorporates SHG as an important vehicle under Swarnajayanti Gram Swarozgar Yojana (SGSY) from April 1st, 1999 by merging all erstwhile programmes like Integrated Rural Development Programme (IRDP), Training of Rural Youth for Self-Employment (TRYSEM), Development of Women and Children in Rural Areas (DWCRA), Ganga Kalyan Yojana (GKY), Million Wells Scheme (MWS) and Supply of Improved Toolkits to Rural Artisans (SITRA).

The growth in SHG formations, sustenance and credit has been uneven. Self-Help Group concept been taken differently in different States of India. The objective, the methodology and the means of the Self-Help Groups are different, therefore, their result or the impact is also different. Broadly three categories are found—Movement, Mission and Programme Approach.

SHGs play today a major role in poverty alleviation in rural India. A growing number of poor people (mostly women) in various parts of India are members of SHGs and actively engage in savings (in actual term Thrift) and credit, as well as in other activities (income generation, natural resources management, literacy, child care and nutrition, etc.). The saving and credit focus in the SHG is the most prominent element and offers a chance to create some control over capital. The SHG system has proven to be very relevant and effective in offering women the possibility to break gradually away from exploitation and isolation. Almost all major donor agencies support SHGs in India in one way or another, and many success stories are available, describing how membership in a SHG changed the life of a particular individual or group for the better. Many NGOs are promoting the SHG mechanism and linking it to various other development interventions. Whereas, there is ample evidence that the SHG approach is a very effective, efficient and relevant tool for organizing and empowering the poor, do arise with design, development and introduction of programmes to promote Income Generating Activities (IGAs) that will generate sufficient, sustainable and regular income.

The approach towards poverty alleviation is based on the formation of Self-Help Groups at the grass root level. This brings about the necessity for organizing them in a group by which they set the benefit of collective perception, collective decision-making and collective implementation of programme for common benefits. This organization holds the power and provides strength and acts as an anti-dote to the helplessness of the poor. The group saving of self-help groups serves a wide range of objectives other than immediate investment. The approach has evolved over the years in India.

Need for the Self-Help Groups

The necessity of forming this group is a big question. We all know that a single stick will break easily but when a number of single sticks are put together it becomes unbreakable or it is very difficult to break. In the same way a single person cannot do everything which is necessary for socio-economic development but when they form a group the work becomes easier for them. Group members may discuss and find solutions to their common problems and gain confidence by developing managerial skills through SHGs.

SHGs are now being viewed as dependable vehicles for rural credit delivery. SHGs have a number of advantages over the traditional system. In the traditional banking system, there has been a strong focus on issues like economic feasibility and loan size, collateral and guarantees, productiveness of a loan, structured loans, unit costs, scheduled assets.

The SHGs offer a unique opportunity for dispensing cheap credit (complementing the existing banking system) at the doorstep of the poor with almost assured repayment at terms and requirements suitable to the poor. The SHGs follow collective decision-making on issues like meetings, thrift and credit decisions. The participative nature of the group makes it a responsible borrower. However, the most critical factor which stands out is the fact that lending through SHGs focuses exclusively on the poor, who have hitherto been circumvented by the formal system. They initiate an empowerment process amongst the poor, especially the women.

Banks find it easier to dispense credit through Self-Help Groups. The SHGs on the other hand are able to cater to the immediate and often emergent credit needs of the individual members. The members have the freedom, probably for the first time in their lives, to decide as to which member's credit needs are more emergent, what should be the interest rate, under what terms and conditions should the loan be dispensed, etc. This helps them acquire confidence to manage credit, use problem-solving skills, prioritize needs, and function in a democratic manner.

The SHGs also ensure that women emerge from being passive recipients of doles to active participants and actors in decisions concerning their own lives. Women pool their expertise and create a sense of ownership in their own collective. This also gives them confidence to act as an alternate social mechanism at the grass roots. Women begin to increasingly take charge of their own local development and local governance. The group becomes, probably the first organized (though initially, informal) space for poor, marginalized women to share and voice their concerns.

Savings and credit groups also provide a base for poor women to organize themselves, expand options for livelihoods and to participate actively in development. Importantly, the capacity of women is built up in spheres that were previously not their domain, for example, opening and operating bank accounts, visiting local offices, accessing loans, etc. This also presupposes a number of skills that women must acquire to be able to operate effectively in the SHG. The SHG thus, often provides a platform for women to become functionally literate, sharpen communication and conflict resolution skills, and acquire skills in democratic functioning and institution building, etc.

Empowerment of women can be promoted through Self-Help Groups and other forms of groups and collectives at the grass roots pioneered through microfinance movement. The latent leadership and entrepreneurial abilities of the poor can be harnessed through microfinance activities. Experience in Bangladesh has proved that enterprise development and large scale employment generation can be promoted in remote rural areas and many of the poors who were eking out a living through wage employment have become entrepreneurs due to a wide variety of services that they can access through the micro finance system.

Self-Help Groups for Women

Indian Society is male dominated and status of women is secondary in India. But from the Vedic age to the times of *Ramayana*, women were important in family as well as in society. 'Women' is the mother of the race is the liaison between generations. Nehru once said, "To awaken people it is the woman who must be awakened. Once she is on move the family moves, the village moves, the nation moves".

Women play a considerably equal role in the economic welfare of the family. In rural society which is very complex, no particular activity is specified to be performed either by men or women exclusively. In such a society, it is meaningless to think that women are competing with, and are being restricted by men, rather male and female roles are clearly distinguished and culturally valued. In essence, men and women are actors in a complex rural society which functions more or less smoothly. Both men and women perform complementary and more often, multiple roles to improve the welfare of their families.

The decades between 1917 and 1947 witnessed the emergence of a number of women's organization in the country. Their involvement in the struggle for political freedom had taken women a long way from the position they had reached under the reformers. They now assumed leadership for their abuse, and thus generated a truly women's movement.

The spirit, in which Mahatma Gandhi had involved women in the struggle for freedom, has now come to be firmly enshrined in the Constitution of Independent India. It promises to all its citizens, "Justice—social, economic and political, liberty of thought, expression, belief, faith and worship, equality of status and opportunity, and to promote among them all fraternity, assuring the dignity of the individual and the unity of the nation."

The legislative protection, thus, provided to Indian women has, consistently, been supported in each of the Five Year Plans by a series of provisions, financial allocations and programmes aimed at prompting the education of women and at providing for their development and welfare.

Notwithstanding these concerted efforts as well as various enactments which have tried to bring certain degree of emancipation of Indian women in legal sense, the legal position, however, is far from being satisfactory. Women are not enjoying these rights and suffer from a number of socially inexorable disabilities and inhibition. The position of women in rural areas is even worse. They usually do not exercise their rights owing mainly to ignorance and are, therefore, unable to achieve the legal equality with men. The other factor which precludes exercise by women of their rights is the nature of social structure. The social norms and values which govern human behaviour in rural areas do not favour women using their rights and thus create obstacles towards the enforcement of legislations which aim improving the status of women.

The most basic struggle of women revolves around trying to get enough to eat for their families and for themselves and procuring the most basic necessities of life such as food, water, fuel, fodder and shelter. This struggle is made even grimmer because as women they have very little control over the conditions and products of their labour. They have almost no say in deciding who gets how much of the families meagre resources.

For most men, even poor men, struggle does not take the same implications as for women. For men struggle is generally confined to the workplace, while home and leisure offer a contrast; whereas for almost every women, like her work, struggle too seems to occupy her entire life. For women, there is no clear division in their work and leisure, in paid and unpaid work, in work and non-work relations.

In the vast majority of cases, women's struggle remains an isolated one. This being the case, the odds are so heavily weighted against the one women that often after several attempts she despairs and sees no way out of her situation. Yet, the compulsions of survival and her aspirations for basic human dignity drive her on. What happens to women in this ever-conflictual situation they are facing depends on the individual situations of women, the support they receive from others of their kind and the balance of forces which are beyond their control and often against them. What in fact seems amazing is that despite these heavy odds, women continue to struggle—individually and collectively.

Often struggles of women at work are looked at or analyzed from the point of view of implications for social change. It is explicitly argued or implied that women's participation in collective struggles expresses their involvement in or commitment to the process of this change. Women's lack of participation or the lack of viability of women's struggles has often been equated with women's disinterest in the process of social change.

The Indian women suffer from hunger and poverty in greater numbers and to a great degree than men. At the same time, it is women who bear the primary responsibility for actions needed to end hunger: education, nutrition, health and family income. For that the Indian women should be empowered.

Empowerment is the means by which individuals, groups and communities to take control of their circumstances and achieve their own goals, thereby being able to work towards helping themselves and others to maximize the quality of their lives. Empowerment is concerned with the process by which people become aware of their interests and how those relates to the interests of others and also participates in decision-making process.

Empowerment as a process of a community or a group thereof gaining autonomy and control over one's life. As a result of the empowerment, the empowered should become agents of their own development, exercising choices, selecting their own agenda and changing their status in the society. In the context of gender and development, empowerment should be viewed more as a process than as an end product. It is dynamic process changing according to circumstances. It applies to the individuals as well as the collective. At the individual level, empowerment involves building up the self-image and self-confidence as well as the critical faculties to think decide and act. On a collective plan, empowerment means enabling women collectively to take control of their own lives, to set their own agenda, to organize each other and make demands on the State and the society for change.

Empowerment is a long process. It has to pass through different stages. In the *first stage*, women should be trained to look into the situation from different perspective and recognize the power relations that perpetuate their oppression. At this stage, women share their feelings and experiences with each other and build a common vision and mission. In the *second stage*, the women tried to change the situation by bringing about a change in the gender and social relations. In the *third stage*, the process of empowerment makes them more mature to realize the importance of collective action.

As empowerment seeks to alter the gender and power relations, there could be a certain social or gender conflicts. The process of empowerment could also face certain obstacles emanating from the patriarchal system, traditional beliefs and political system. The result of empowerment, however, will not be confined to women. The other member of the families will also benefit from the empowerment process.

The term 'empowerment' has gained significance and prominence recently among Policy-makers and Researchers. In the field of women's studies and social work it is viewed with a holistic perspective and it can be classified as social, educational, economical, political and psychological empowerment. Empowerment is concerned with how people may gain collective control over their lives, so as to achieve their interests as a group and a method by which social workers seek to enhance the power of people who lack it.

Empowerment can be activated through five strategies. Education to promote the level of awareness, knowledge, information and skill of a woman is an important part of the strategy. Awareness is a pre-requisite for challenging the force of oppression. It results in greater participation of women in decision-making within and outside the family. The economic approach to empowerment seeks to alter the economic status of women by attacking the forces which cause gender division of labour, gender gap in wages, lack of control for women over their material resources, etc. The economic approach emphasizes development of women's skills, promotion of their savings and investment and enlarged economic opportunities. The third approach namely, development approach attributes poverty to their powerlessness and the lack of adequate access to health care, education and services resources. Yet another approach believes that women's empowerment requires awareness of a complex factors causing disempowerment of women. This approach advocates collective organization of women as well as gender sensitization, gender planning and strategy and consciousness raising activities. More recently, an organizational approach has been advocated which believes that organized women can alter the gender and social relations in favour of women both in public and private lives.

Empowerment could take place at two levels, individual and collective. Individual empowerment is a process of personal empowerment involving self-esteem, dignity, self-respect and self-perception. But the problems affecting the collectivity of women require collective empowerment. Restructuring power relations, changing social values and norms require intervention at the collective level. Collective empowerment aims at transforming collective consciousness, values and attitude. The problem of securing better access to education skills and employment, material resources and political power can be tackled only at the collective level. This requires effective organization among women, mutual help and certain amount of sacrifice.

Empowerment of women may result in the emergence of single big mass group to protect the democratic values, to fight against the social evils, to fight for social justice, to work for the cause of all those who are deprived of it. But the way of empowerment is not free from hurdles. Patriarchal norms, traditional beliefs, economic system, political conditions make the task of empowering women more complicated. Since patriarchy is found to be very deeply entrenched both in men and women, empowering women has become an extremely complex task. Achieving gender equality and changing the present gender relations requires widespread changes in the thinking and structure of every institution of changes in the society. Women's empowerment can only be achieved through integrated and synergetic thinking and action.

Women are more vulnerable than men to extremes of poverty and its consequences. For poor households, the women's capacity to work, her health, her knowledge and her skills, endowments often are the only resources to call upon for survival. The poorest families are the most dependent upon women's economic productivity. There is an inverse correlation between household economic status and women's labour force participation and their proportional contribution to total family income. Making women more productive and effective income earners will reduce their dependence and enhance their status in the family and the society. The main objective of the poverty alleviation programmes is helping the poor to overcome their condition of poverty through self-reliant development.

The proportion of population below poverty line has declined over the last decade but the number of people who are poor has increased.

Improvement in the quality of life has not percolated down to the poorest of the poor. Society benefits by converting poor from being social liability to social assets. The return to investment in education, health and employment get converted into productive human resources. Poverty indirectly put pressure on the environment, because poor exploit the environment for survival purposes. Persistent poverty threatens the social order and sometimes causes social instability.

The endeavour to improve the status of women needs to be placed in the context of the welfare activities of the government. Poverty alleviation programmes provide the structural context within which solutions are sought for their problems. Several policy documents, in particular the Report of the Committee on the Status of Women in India (1974), the Blueprint of Action Points and National Plan of Action for Women (1976), brought pressure on the government to recognize them as active participants in development.

The chapter on women and development in the Sixth Plan resulted in the introduction of schemes, specifically orientated to their needs, and the incorporation of special components in various schemes. The IRDP, TRYSEM and NREP stipulate that one-third of the beneficiaries should be women. While the Sixth Plan attempted to meet their needs in the areas of education, health, employment, industries, science and technology and welfare, the Seventh Plan further stepped up these efforts. To operationalise the governments concern for equity, strategies were spelt out to improve women's economic status and to empower them with greater say in decision-making.

The Seventh Plan witnessed the setting up of the Ministry of Human Resource Development (1985). The Department of Women and Child Development of this ministry has been entrusted with the responsibility of implementing and coordinating programmes of women's welfare and development. The Central Social Welfare Board was brought under the purview of this department. Since its inception, the department has initiated programmes with a view to promoting five major objectives—generation of employment and income; imparting education and training; building greater awareness; provision of support services; and legal assistance (GoI, 1988). While the Department of Women and Child Development has the largest number of schemes for women, the Ministries of Agriculture, Health and Family Welfare, Industries and Commerce and Labour also have special components in their programmes. In addition, several apex organizations, such as Khadi and Village Industries Commission (KVIC), NCDC and other corporations provide funds, training and marketing support for several socio-economic schemes. While the government provides subsidies, the banking sector, including NABARD, IDBI and the nationalized banks, is engaged in providing credit.

The government has come under heavy weather because of the ineffectiveness of most schemes. Admitting the inadequate flow of assistance to women through IRDP, for example, the government initiated the Development of Women and Children in Rural Areas (DWCRA) schemes in 1982. The Central and State governments, along with the UNICEF, are the funding partners of this scheme. The DWCRA is being implemented as a pilot project in 500 Blocks in 50 selected districts in different States. Although, the DWCRA has not been entirely successful, it has initiated several worthwhile programmes, as some studies show (GoI, 1988). Another experimental activity that merits attention is the Women's Development Programme (WDP) of the Government of Rajasthan. In a unique experiment—the government, voluntary groups and research institutions have come together to elicit the involvement of women at the grass roots. With the help of development workers at the level of Gram Panchayats, *Prachetas*, managing a cluster of ten villages, this initiative has networked women and has encouraged them to participate in grass root developmental activity. Thus motivated, the women activists brought pressure on various delivery systems, such as primary health centres, schools and ration shops to function more effectively. What the DWCRA and WDP highlight is the need for organizational strategies based on an understanding of the specific social milieu in which women find themselves. If it were not for their specific efforts, the riddle of resources never reaching needy women would not have been resolved at all. The knowledge that women have been denied developmental inputs because they are assetless or have no formal status within the household has come to light only through these grass root experiments. For example, it is known that a large number of poor households are headed by women. These households have not been able to avail of any benefits from government schemes, as the delivery systems recognize men and not women as heads of households. The banks are reluctant to give loans to women even though the Reserve Bank of India has made it clear that guarantees are not required for loans up to Rs. 5,000. They are kept out by cooperative societies as well. Membership in most agricultural cooperatives is restricted to those who have rights to land either as owner or as tenant. Women are denied membership because they are assetless and have no such rights (GoI, 1988).

The division of work between men and women is an area which has had few structural interventions. The development schemes of the government have done little to deviate from time-hallowed traditions. The KVIC provides a clear example of how the conventional division of labour between the sexes continues to hold sway. When it comes to women, the KVIC thinks it appropriate that they should take up food processing, tailoring and spinning yarn on the *ambar charkha*. These are activities in which women have always been engaged. And because they have always been women's work, these forms of labour are unskilled and poorly paid. Innovative schemes which break away from tradition and teach women to weave, drive automobiles, operate farm implements or work on the potter's wheel are hard to come by. It is clear that most poverty alleviation schemes have been cast in the mould of tradition. The outcome is social engineering, which is *ad hoc* and piecemeal. Equity and the empowerment of women cannot be achieved by economic programmes without first attaining a social breakthrough.

Emergence of Self-Help Group

The approach towards poverty alleviation should be Self-Help Group. Others should help the poor to help themselves. It is felt that individual effort is too inadequate to improve their fate. This brings about the necessity for organizing them in a group by which they get the benefit of collective perception, collective decision-making and collective implementation of programmes for common benefits. The organization holds power and provides strength; it can be an antidote to the helplessness of the poor.

Constitution of India in its fundamental rights has provisions for equality, social justice and protection of women. These goals are yet to be realized. It was being hoped that the strategies would be realized through the National Policy for empowerment of women. Remarkably Self-Help Groups were considered to be one of the strategies to mark the beginning of major process of empowering women.

Participation of women is vital and a critical pre-conditions in the new educational order which emphasises the process rather than more fulfilments of targets. There is a tide in the affairs of women creating a new environment for them to learn at their own pace, set their own priorities and seek knowledge and information to make informed choices. This essentially involves enabling rural women especially from socially, economically disadvantaged and marginalized groups to address and deal with problems and isolation and lack of self-confidence, oppressive, social customs and struggle for survival all of which inhibit their learning. It is in this process that rural women become empowered. Empowerment does not mean giving more powers to them, it only means giving them their long denied due.

All over the world there is a realization that the best way to tackle poverty and enable the community to improve its quality of life is through social mobilization of poor, especially women into Self-Help Groups. Ever since independence, a number of schemes have been launched for the upliftment of women in our country. Indian government has taken lot of initiatives to strengthen the institutional rural credit system and development programmes.

Despite having an extremely wide network of formal credit system, it has been observed that a large segment of the society among the poorest of the poor remained outside the purview of the banking system. Thus, in the context of the inadequacies of the formal financial system to cater to the needs of the rural poor, one major innovation that is being tried out to help the rural poor is the attempt to promote Self-Help Group (SHG). It is in this backdrop that the innovations like formations of SHGs were called for in banking practices and financing through SHGs have now become a business proposition for the present day. The linking of SHGs with bank finance was launched by NABARD in 1992 and the programme has made steady progress.

Membership Criteria

Poor people especially women are the main target group for the Self-Help Group formation. Poor are those people who have lack of Power, Opportunity, Outlook and Resource. So, to uplift their socio-economic condition it is necessary to achieve Power, Opportunity, Outlook and Resource and it is possible when they come under a single umbrella. For easy understanding we can divide in the following groups:

- Landless and marginal farmers.
- Rural entrepreneurs.
- Poor women.
- Hawker, small businessman, fisherman and daily labour and the like.

But priority for the group formation is given to women and also to the backward and schedule caste and tribal people of between 18 to 60 years old. Because those younger than 18 years cannot get the facility from the bank and those more than 60 years old people are not able to work hard.

Goals and Objectives of SHGs

The main objectives for making SHGs are to eradicate poverty and raise the income of people in need.

- To make a habit of savings.
- To gain self-reliance and self-respect.
- Change attitudes and thinking power.
- To sort out problems and find solutions.
- Creating adequate environment for group activity.
- Capital formation.
- To improve decision-making power.
- To be free from superstition.
- To establish equal rights and equal distribution.
- To be free from money indebtedness.
- To create a habit of loan repayment.
- To make plans for income generation and proper implementation of that plan.
- To create linkage with development agencies.
- Eradication of illiteracy and dissemination of light of education.
- Deaddiction.
- Generation for health-awareness.
- Cultural development.
- Ensuring active participation in the process of development.
- To raise voice against any kind of violence.
- And overall development of the society.

Self-Help ⇒ Self-Reliance ⇒ Empowerment ⇒ Poverty Eradication

A graphical diagrammed showing the way of poverty eradication. It is a bottom up approach for overall development.

Some Rules for SHG Formation

(A) *Members more than 6 but less than 20:* Legislative problems may arise if the members are more than 20 in a group. According to 1956 Company Act, Sec. 2, if the members are more than 20 they have to register themselves. On the other hand more than 20 members can create problems in the process of decision-making. To avoid such problems ideally a group should comprise of 20 or less members. But the members must be more than 6 for collective work.

(B) *One member from one household/family:* Another feature of the group is that only one member may come from one family only. If more than one member comes from a single family they may try to dominate the others. So a rule may be created that groups cannot be formed with blood relatives.

(C) *Members of the group may come from the same socio-economic condition:* Same mentality grows in a same socio-economic condition. If the group is of marginal farmers then it is necessary that all members will be marginal farmers. If there is a mixed economy in a single group then there is a chance that those better-off may try to control the weaker sections.

(D) *Never sexually mixed group*: Either the group should constitute of females or it should comprise of male members but mixed groups are never created. Because the male members try to dominate female members due to sex biases.

(E) *Members from the same village:* The members must belong from the same village so that the members are likeminded. Another advantage is that, in a short notice they can gather in a place and contact each other.

(F) A person is not allowed to take membership in more than one group.

(G) Avoid giving membership to any politician or moneylender.

Steps for Group Formation

First Step: For group formation:

- Visit the poor families in the village.
- Talk to them.
- Speak to the womenfolk.
- Rapport building.
- Win the trust of the people.
- Area selection.
- Identification of willing familes.
- Bank selection.

- Make an idea about self-reliance and self-workability.
- An idea about the savings as expenditure in family.

Second Step: Selection of members:

- Economically poor.
- Same Caste.
- Same Occupation.
- Helpful mentality.
- Neighbourhood family.
- Make query about previous loan/if yes, then arrangement for loan repayment/after loan repayment include as a member.
- One member from single family.
- Member from willing family.

Group Formation

- Arrange a meeting with the selected members.
- Select a name for the group.
- Make a decision about monthly subscription.
- Group must contain more than 6 members and less than 20 members.
- Selection of bank.
- Make a rubber stamp in the name of the group.
- Election of group leader, assistant group leader and treasurer.
- Taking passport size photograph of the Leader, Assistant Leader and Treasurer.
- Arrangement of cash book, ledger book, minute book and resolution book.
- Making personal pass book.

Selection of Group Leader and Assistant Leader and Treasurer

- He/she must be literate.
- Having capacity for group management.
- Having enough time for group work.
- He/she must be capable of travelling alone.
- Honest and peace-loving.
- Sympathetic.
- Family must be willing to support his/her work.

- Self-reliant and self-dependent.
- Must have basic arithmetic skills.

Activities of Leader

- Meeting organization and management (minimum one meeting in a month).
- Opening of group passbook in the local bank and making linkage with the bank.
- Noting down the decision which is taken in the meeting.
- Collection of member's subscription.
- Savings in the bank and withdrawal from the bank.
- Giving loan and collecting repayment of loan.
- Maintaining the paper works.
- Linkage with various developmental organizations.
- Arrangement of training programme according to need.
- Take responsibility to make every member active.
- Take an initiative that every member participates in the discussion.
- Publish account report in the meeting.
- Making personal Passbook in the name of every member.
- Write monthly savings and loan amount.
- Take an initiative for abolition of addiction and superstition.
- Bank deposit within ten days of any month.
- Regular connection with the members.
- Taking the final decision after consulting with all the members.
- Making rules and regulations for group management.
- Arrangement for awareness generation camp and skill development training on regular basis.

Activities of Treasurer

- Proper accounts record maintenance after each meeting.
- Personal savings records to be included in the member's personal Passbook.
- Regular audit at the time of money transaction.
- Cash counting in front of all the members and tally with the cash book.
- Lock the cash box and the key should be kept with another person who is reliable.

- Cashbook, ledger book, and loan money record book maintenance.
- Authorized signatory for withdrawal money from money bank.

Activities of Assistant Group Leader

- Proper management of the meeting.
- Verify the attendance of members.
- If any member becomes absent for more than two meetings then taking information about the reason behind the absence.
- If anybody is unable to submit the monthly savings money and loan money then the Assistant leader is responsible for investigation.
- Making linkage with the financial institute.
- Group meeting management in case of absence of group leader.
- Minute book maintenance.
- Taking initiative for team work.
- Cooperate with the leader for group sustenance.

Activities of Group Members

- Regular attendance in each and every meeting.
- Giving opinion.
- Timely payment of savings and loan money.
- Taking personal accounts from the leader and writing down in his/her own copy.
- Sometimes visit to the bank.
- Knowing and taking about group accounts clarification from the leader.
- Active cooperation with leader in group management.
- Addiction is prohibited at the time of meeting.
- Obediently follow the group rules and regulation.
- Giving opinion at the time of discussion for taking decision on rate of interest on loan money, etc.
- Making a family bond within the members.

Some Important Rules and Regulations for Group Management

- The group must have a name.
- There should be a rubber stamp in the name of the group.

- They have to make an account in the name of the group, and in the nearest bank.
- The group must have a leader and Assistant leader for group management.
- The leader, assistant leader and treasurer are authorized for any kind of bank transaction.
- Group cannot be formed with less than 6 members and more than 20 members.
- Minimum one meeting in a month should be conducted. It will be better if more than one meeting is possible.
- Make a fixed date for meeting.
- Every decision can be finalized in the meeting and the final decision should be recorded in the resolution copy.
- Every member has to participate in the meeting and they have to take an important role in decision-making.
- Decisions should be finalized on the basis of support by majority.
- If any member is absent at the meeting without any reason, he/she must pay penalty to the group and the money goes to the group or to the savings.
- Leader and assistant leader cannot take any kind of decision on their own without any discussion with the members.
- Every member has right to place his/her opinion in any discussion.
- No one is allowed to place his/her personal clashes with others member in the group meeting.
- Anybody is restricted to attend the meeting with unsound mind. On doing so, she/he must be penalized.
- The group has to create an emergency fund by equal distribution of money by the members. In any emergency, members can withdraw money from this fund and she/he is responsible for repayment within 15 days, otherwise she/he will have to pay interest on the amount.
- Every member is responsible for deposit of their savings money within first 5 days of that month and note down the amount in his/her personal book.
- Monthly subscription must be equal for every member.
- The total subscription money has to be deposited in the bank within the first 10 days of that month.
- For taking loan from the group money, the member is needed to apply to the leader mentioning the amount of money, cause, and time for repayment.

- The loan can be sanctioned in the group meeting with clear discussion about rate of interest.
- Deposit the loan money with interest to the leader within the first five days of the month.
- Nobody can receive new loan without repayment of previous loan.
- The loan can be disbursed on the basis of priority in case of more than one application.
- Decision for withdrawal of money from bank decided in the meeting and the decision with cause has to be recorded in the resolution copy. At the time of withdrawal the Xerox of resolution copy must be submitted to the bank.
- Group leader and assistant leader are responsible to discuss about the accounts in the meeting.
- Every member has to bear equal share for any kind of expenditure for group management.
- There are two different copies for group, one for monthly savings and another for loan. The record must be transparent and up-to-date. One able member is responsible for record maintenance.

Some Common Problems for Group Management

- Sometimes the group leaders and assistant leaders are capable to put their signature only. So they are unable to write down the daily report. They have to depend for accounts and calculation on other persons.
- Sometimes members are unable to deposit their monthly subscription on regular basis due to poor economy.
- Leader and assistant leader become engaged for whole day when they go to the bank. So they are unable to earn those day's wages which they earn by the daily wage.
- Sometimes the male persons of the village interferes in the group work.
- Sometimes personal clashes become a barrier for group management.

Causes for Group Dissolution

- By becoming a member without taking permission from the guardian (from husband).

- High ambition and expectation from the group.
- Dependent on family for monthly savings.
- Joining a group without clarifying the rules and regulations of the group.
- Misunderstanding between the members.
- Interference of moneylenders.
- Discussion about personal clashes at the time of group meeting.
- Political influence.
- Lack of cooperation to the leader from the members.
- If leader is not humble.
- Lack of faith on leaders/assistant leaders/ treasurers.
- Irregular meetings.
- Absenteeism in the meeting.
- Irregular savings.
- Unwillingness to repay loan.
- Unavailability of loan when more than one member applies for loan.
- Lack of interest for regular monitoring and audit from the forming agent.

A Self-Help Group is a voluntary group, formed to attain some common goals; most of its members have similar social identity, heritage, caste or traditional occupations and come together for a common cause and manage resources for the benefit of the group members. These groups are called 'solidarity groups' as they provide monetary and also moral support to individual members in time of difficulties.

Formation of Emergency Fund and its Uses

To meet the immediate need this emergency fund is created. The members can take some amount of money as a loan for short period of time from this created fund.

Formation of Fund

1. The fund will be created on the basis of equal quantity of money at a time. The amount must be decided in the meeting.
2. The collected money is kept in the box and this money cannot be deposited to the bank.
3. This fund also creates by any donation.

4. This fund also creates by the profit money, which is earned by any kind of group activity.
5. The fund must contain minimum of Rs. 300.

Uses of the Fund

1. Members can take loan from the fund in any emergency need.
2. At the time of giving loan it should be informed to the nearest members and after that it will be informed in the group meeting.
3. The time frame for loan repayment is 15 days. After 15 days the loan receiver has to pay this loan money with interest within one month form the date of loan received.
4. This loan can be received in the day as well as at night also.
5. The fund always contain some amount of money, it should not be nil. Because another member may feel need in emergency.
6. The loan can be given an amount of maximum 40 per cent of the total money.
7. Generally one member cannot take loan twice without repayment of previous loan.
8. Any body submits the monthly subscription by taking loan from the emergency fund but she/he must be responsible for repayment within 7 days.

Social Development through the SHGs

The SHGs are also responsible for economic development as well as social development. In the group meeting they can discuss about the local social problems and they can solve the problem in a teamwork. They can take initiatives on the following social problems;

1. Illiteracy.
2. Large family size.
3. Dropout.
4. Social abuse.
5. Unhealthy environment.
6. Addiction.
7. Castism.
8. Dowry.
9. Superstition.
10. Child marriage.

11. Divorce and Separation.

Self-Help Groups can move for the above mentioned problem to empower the destitute and giving security to the abused.

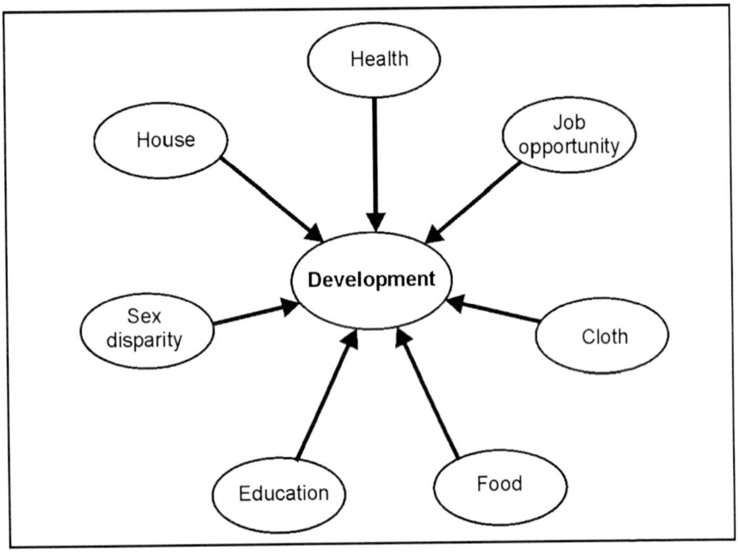

Fig. 4.1: SHGs model for Social Development

Through the SHG all the factors for development can be arranged.

Rules and Regulations for Savings

Time

The time for the meeting can be weekly, quarterly or monthly. The meeting can be arranged according to need.

Savings Amount

Sometimes it has been seen that, it became a problem for savings amount. To avoid that kind of problem, a fixed amount can be applicable for all the members. At first the amount may be minimum but in course of time it must be increased in amount. Large amount can be made for large capital. Large capital is helpful for entrepreneurship development.

Time for Submitting the Subscription

Meeting can be started by submitting the member's savings money. After submitting the savings money every member has to note down their amount in the passbook and cashbook. If anybody is unable to submit their savings money in a month, he/she can submit his/her savings money at a time in the next month. To avoid the irregular savings, fine system can be conducted in the group.

Withdrawal of Savings

The members can withdraw his/her savings but it is very dangerous for the group. Thereafter, the group has to make some regulation on withdrawal of savings money. The rules may be that after one year any member can withdraw 10 per cent of his/her savings, after two years it will be 20 per cent and after three years the withdrawal amount may be of 40 per cent. The rules for withdraw must be rigid otherwise fund will be nil at a time.

Rules and Regulations for Loan

Proving loan at the time of need is very essential factor for SHGs. In past days, due to complex rules and regulation poor people were unable to receive loan from any financial institution so they received loan from the local moneylender and they become trapped under the moneylender. Moneylender provides them loan in a high rate of interest and poor people were unable to repay. As a result moneylender abused them. But now, the poor people can get loan easily by making SHGs. SHGs provide loan from their own savings. But SHGs has some rules and regulations for giving loan to their members. The rules and regulations are as follows:

- After a certain period SHG can give loan because at first they have to make a reasonable amount.
- Inter loaning system can be conducted after the regular savings from each member.
- One member cannot take next loan before repayment of earlier loan.
- Loan can be given after a clear discussion.
- Loan can be given on priority basis.
- The amount of loan money can be fixed for all or it will be according to the need.

- There must be two guarantors at the time of loan receiving.
- Any outsider can take loan after clear discussion with the all members of the group. But it is advised that, no loan for any outsiders is better.
- Loan can be given without group meeting in case of emergency.

Interest Rate for Loan

Interest term is not so good to hear but it is very necessary for running the SHGs. Because there are so many reasons for taking interest on loan. Firstly, it makes an extra pressure for repayment of loan otherwise the members become careless for repayment. Secondly, interest is another source for increasing the fund. Thirdly, when group will take the loan from the bank they will have to give interest. Fourthly, to meet the regular work like transportation cost at the time of bank transaction, arrangement for cashbook, register, personal cashbook copy, etc.

Service charge or interest may be fixed after discussion with the every member.

- The service charge or interest may be rupees 12 in a year, i.e., rupee one in a month or rupees 24 in a year. But it should fix without creating any problem for the members.
- According to the priority the interest rate can be changed like for health loan for which the rate of interest will be lesser than the productivity loan.
- The rate of interest may be different for outsiders.
- Discount on interest may be considered according to the situation.
- Clear calculation must be maintained in the record-keeping book.

Loan Repayment

At the time of giving loan the group must be clear about the loan repayment. All the members can fix the instalment system for loan repayment. Poor people are unable to submit their interest or loan money at a time, so to make this process the instalment system can be developed. Another thing is small amount is not a headache for loan takers. It will make a saving habit, which is very good for economic development. In case of medical loan, the time for repayment can be extended.

Calculation of Instalment

For easy understanding an example is given below:

If anybody has taken Rs. 500 as a loan for one year and decided that he/she has to repay through ten instalments. The rate of interest is 24 per cent.

The calculation is:

Total interest: $24 \times 500/100$ = Rs. 120, in ten instalment, $(500 + 120)/10$ = Rs. 62.

So he/she has to pay rupees 62 in every instalment.

Another calculation is:

Rs. 500 for 2 years to repayment.

In 100 rupees there are rupees 2 as an interest

So in rupees 500 there are 2*500/100 = rupees 10 as an interest in a month

Suppose in the first month the repayment amount are rupees 50 from the loan money and rupees 10 as an interest.

Then the next month the capital become 500–50 = rupees 450. And the interest may be calculated on rupees 450. This process is called as a reducing balance.

The group can accept any one process, which is easiest for them.

Leave or New Membership of Group

Rules for new membership or leave from the group can be decided according to the situation. If anybody who wants to go out then he/she can get his/her savings amount and sometimes with deposited interest.

In case of new membership he/she has to apply through a particular format. The group can take decision about the depositing amount at the time of membership. The format may be as follows:

APPLICATION FOR NEW MEMBERSHIP

1. Name : ....
2. Father's/Husband Name :..
3. Address :..
4. Permanent Address :.......... ....

I am the resident of this area. I want to be a member of this "...................." Group. About the rules and regulations I know well.

After knowing all the rules and regulations I am applying for the membership.

I promise that I would follow all the rules and regulations of the group. If I want to leave any time from the group I will clear my all dues to the group.

I also promise that I will never do that type of work, which opposed my group.

Above the given information are true to the best of my knowledge.

Signature of the Applicant

On the basis of group discussion, we are including the applicant as a member within our group. All the informations of Application is correct.

Signature of the Secretary

Membership Annulment

- If any member creates any problem or is trying to oppose the rules and regulations of the group he/she can be dismissed from the group.
- If any member without information is absent and it continues for five meetings he/she will be dismissed from the group.
- If any member did not deposit his/her savings money without any reason for long time he/she will be dismissed.

In case of dismissed from membership the decision will be taken in the group meeting. If entire members are willing for that then two-third supports can dismiss that member.

Group Dissolution

The decision to dissolve the group will be taken unanimously.

If the decision is not unanimous then 75 per cent support can dissolve the group.

At the time of dissolution of group all the savings money should be distributed equally among the members.

Personal Passbook

The following format can be adopted to maintain the Personal Passbook.

Name of the Members : ……………………………………
Father's/Husband's Name : ……………………………………
Age : ……………………………………
Present and Permanent Address : ……………………………………
Name of the Group : ……………………………………
Number of members : ……………………………………
Daily or monthly income : ……………………………………
Occupation : ……………………………………

Date	*Personal Savings*			*Loan*	*Loan repayment*			
	Deposit	*With-drawal*	*Total*	*Amount. of Loan*	*Loan Amount*	*Service Charge*		*Penalty*
						Interest	*Total Interest*	
1	2	3	4	5	6	7	8	9

Total loan repayment	*Loan due*	*Signature of Group leader*
10	11	12

Meeting Resolution Book

Name of Group : ……………………………………
Address; Name of the Village : ……………………………………
Block : ……………………………………
District : ……………………………………
Total number of members : ……………………………………
Date of group formation : ……………………………………

Sl. No.	*Name of the members*	*Age*	*Father's / Husband's name*	*Occupation*	*Signature or thump impression*
1.					
2.					
3.					

1. Description about resignation and dismissed from the membership:……………………………

2. Reason behind the resignation:..
3. Date of dismissed from the membership:...........................

Cashbook

Name of the group
Month: From.../..../.... To ..../..../....

Deposit

Date	*Sl. no Voucher no.*	*Name of member*	*Deposit amount*	*Given interest*	*Loan Re-payment*	*Penalty*	*Others deposit*	*Withdrawal from bank*	*Total deposit*
			Total deposit	*Total interest*	*Total loan repay-ment*	*Total penalty deposited*	*Total others deposit*	*Total with-drawal from bank*	*Overall deposit*

Expenditure

Date	*Sl. No. voucher No.*	*Name of member*	*Loan amount*	*Instalment*	*Date of repay-ment*	*Others expen-diture/ loan*	*Savings at bank*	*Overall expen-diture*
			Total amount of loan			*Total expen-diture at meeting*	*Total savings amount at bank*	*Total expen-diture*

If the withdrawal is from the bank then it will be in deposit bank column and if the money deposit is in the bank then it will be in expenditure bank column.

Application for Loan at Bank

At the time of application for loan from the bank the group has to submit an application form with the Xerox copy of resolution book, cashbook and ledger.

Ledger: Savings Ledger

Name of the member:

Sl. No.	Date of savings	Amount of savings	Savings amount till date	Withdraw from the savings	Rest amount	Signature of group leader

Loan Ledger

Sl. No.	Date of loan received	No. of instalment	Date of instalment submission	Loan repayment		Dues
				Capital	Interest	

Audit

From the ledger anybody can get an idea about the accounts of the group.

Quarterly/Half Yearly Audit

After every three months or six months the group has to audit their accounts by any outsider or NGO representative.

Easy Process of Audit

1. At the time of audit the auditors have to tally between member's personal passbook and cashbook.
2. Tally between total savings of any member with ledger.
3. Match between record books with the ledger.

Dividend

The interest on personal savings can be deposited in the name of the members within the group fund otherwise the group can give dividend to the members from the interest.

Monitoring

To run the group properly, monitoring is very important. At the time of monitoring the following points have to be noticed:

- Number of members.
- Socio-economic condition of the members.
- Regular meetings.
- Rate of attendance at the meeting.
- Participation in the discussion.
- Participation at the time of taking any decision.
- Able to find out the social justice and injustice.
- Obey the group rules and regulations.
- Literacy rate among the members.
- Leadership development.
- Regular savings.
- Timely loan repayment.
- Loan for economic empowerment.
- Proper maintenance of passbook, cashbook and ledger.

A format is given below for monitoring the group activity

Month: .... Panchayat/Block name...........

Sl. No	Name of group	No. of members	No. of meetings	Rate of average attendance	Savings		Amount of grant
					Total	Monthly	
1	2	3	4	5	6	7	8

Loan received		Interest payment		Other source of income		Loan repayment		Total savings	
Total	This month	Total	This month	Total	This month	This month	Total dues	Amount in bank	Hand in group
9	10	11	12	13	14	15	16	17	18

Formation of Cluster and Federation

At present the SHGs are also three-tier system, i.e., Self-Help Group at the village level, cluster at the Panchayat level and Federation at the Block level.

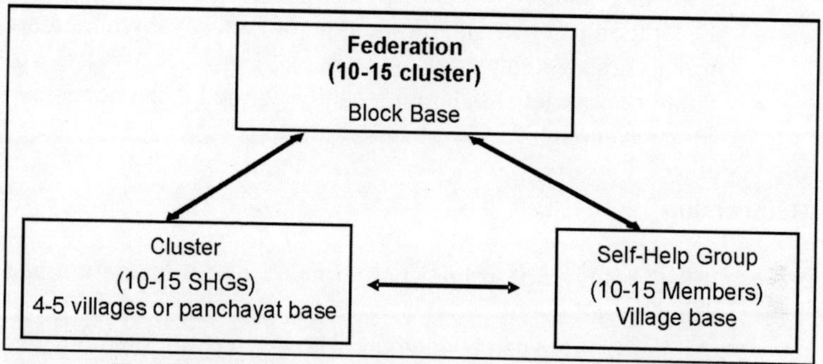

Fig. 4.2: Relation between SHGs, Cluster and Federation

Need of Federation

To empower the poor people and to solve the socio-economic condition the federation formation is very necessary.

Objectives

- To exchange the information and connection between more than one group for solving problems.
- Making linkage with the government offices for reaching facility to the group.
- Income generation of the group members.
- Empower the rural poor women.
- Help to the group by making linkage with the government.
- Participate in the decentralized planning process for making plans for the Gram Panchayat.
- Awareness generation to the group members.
- Making linkage between more than one side-by-side groups for sustenance.
- Socio-economic development for the deprived people.

Where We Can Form Federation?

That Block that have more than 100 groups and one Panchayat having 20-30 groups within this Block there we can make the federation.

- We can make the federation with all those groups of a Gram Sansad area to participate in the Sansad planning and implementation.
- Federation can be made in the type of Panchayat where more groups are available.
- Gram Sansad level federation can be formed if the number of group is enough.

Membership

- All the self-help groups can be member of a federation in a Panchayat.
- All those group can be member who are performing more than 6 months.
- Membership for a federation is depending on willingness.

Structure of Federation

Management Committee (Parichalan Samiti)

- To manage the federation activity there are 7 to 11 members to make a committee.

Structure

- Every group select two representatives, one can be any designated member, another one any general member.
- The representative of the group select 7 to 11 members for management committee. Two representative of a same group cannot be member of management committee.
- All these members are elected members of management committee.
- The convenor of the *nari o sisu unnayan upasamiti* can be a member, as a nominated member.
- Management committee can select three designated member, i.e., President, Secretary and the Treasurer. The selected members have no election power.
- After two years this committee can be reformed.

Federation Formation Process

First meeting for federation formation:

- Head of the department should call the first meeting.
- Sabhapati of the Panchayat Samiti, BDO, Nodal Officer of Block and Gram Panchayat Pradhan must have to attend the meeting.
- All the SHGs of the Panchayat will call for the meeting.

Activity

1. Discuss about the need for making the federation, structure and activity of a federation.
2. Choosing a name of the federation.
3. Information collection about the membership of the groups.
4. Fixation of an amount as a subscription for maintenance of the federation.

Meeting for Formation of Management Committee

One week after this meeting call will be given for making the management committee.

Two representatives of all the willing group will attend the meeting. Nodal officer will call the meeting.

Activity

1. Making rules and regulations of the federation
2. Making management committee of the federation
3. Collection of membership subscription

First Assembly of the Management Committee

This assembly can be arranged in the same day.

Activity

1. Executive member selection.
2. Taking decision about opening the bank account.
3. Detail about rules formation of the federation.

Activity of Federation

1. Keeping information about the groups like population, disabilities, occupation, resource, etc., of the members.
2. Collecting information about the savings, loan benefited members, etc.
3. Monitoring of group activity:
   - Role of group members to response to their social nature.
   - Regular savings and utilization of the fund.
   - Record maintenance.
   - Timely loan repayment.
   - Role of the group leader.
   - Regular meeting.
   - Benefit tracking by the members.
4. Invention of socio-economic needs.
5. Arrangement for training.
6. Making linkage with the helping institutions.
7. Help the Panchayat in decision-making.
8. Resource invention and economic development.
9. Small entrepreneurship development.
10. Solve the types of problems which are unable to be solved by the groups.
11. Taking parts in planning for area development and implementation process.
12. Encourage the villagers to participate in the Gram Sansad and Gram Sabha meetings.
13. Awareness generation among the poor.
14. Financial guidance to the groups.
15. If possible act as a financial institution and provide loan to the groups.
16. Mutual solution for the cluster level or group level problems.
17. Support to the government programmes.
18. Taking initiative for rural development.
19. Support to the weak groups.
20. Internal monitoring and supervision of the groups.
21. Help in forming new groups.
22. Financial support in case of emergency.

Rules and regulations of federation for proper management:

- The members of the management committee should distribute the activity according to their capacity.
- Every federation have to make their own rules and regulations.
- The federation have to take a name.
- The federation will conduct the meeting for regular management. The general assembly meeting will be held once in a year. Management committee meeting will be held twice in a month. Sometimes according to necessity the meeting can be called.
- Following rules have to made by the federation:
    1. Joining of new group in the federation.
    2. Terminate the membership.
    3. Fixation of membership subscription, collection method and its responsibility.
    4. Bank account management.
    5. Yearly planning.
    6. Selection of management committee and designators and duration of the committee.
    7. Activity fixation of designators.
    8. Financial arrangement.
    9. Put up the yearly report and accounts.

Before the federation formation the copy of the rules and regulations have to be passed in the general meeting.

Financial Arrangement

- To run the federation, the monthly membership subscription and admission fees have to be passed in the general meeting.
- Federation has to increase the fund by taking self-endeavour through creating income generation activities.
- Bank account is needed to open in the name of the federation.
- Two designators from the three will be authorized for management of the bank account.
- The management committee will decide the expenditure purpose.
- The income expenditure budget has to be sanctioned from the general meeting once in a year.
- A rule for collection of membership subscription has to be fixed in the general meeting.
- Federation can make the emergency fund for emergency purpose.

Activity of the Management Committee

- Regular meeting.
- Record maintenance.
- Accounts maintenance.
- Direct or indirect linkage with the groups.
- Work distribution according to the capacity.
- Personal fund formation.
- Observe the group activity and monitoring.

Monitoring and Supervision of the Federation Activity

- Nodal officer will be the responsible person for monitoring and supervision.
- Panchayat level advisory committee can be formed for helping activity of the federation.
    1. Panchayat Pradhan.
    2. Convenor of the *nari o sisu upasamiti.*
    3. Representative of the bank/cooperative.
    4. Government employee at the Panchayat level.
    5. Respected person of the area.
    6. Representative of the NGOs.
    7. Nodal officer/in-charge officer.

All those above mentioned are the members of the advisory committee.

- Linkage with the advisory committee.
- Federation has to be self-appraisal at a regular interval.

Capacity Building of the Federation Management Committee

The capacity of the federation management committee can be build by the two processes, i.e., continuous support in the federation activity and another one is arrangement of regular training.

- *Continuous support*: The advisory committee will be given the support at the Panchayat level to run the federation smoothly.
- Regular training:
    1. Training for the government officers, NGOs, Panchayat representative and bank officers.

2. Training for members of the management committee.
3. Training for the members of the SHGs, group leader.

District rural development cell is responsible for arrangement of the training at the Panchayat Samiti level and Zilla Parisad level.

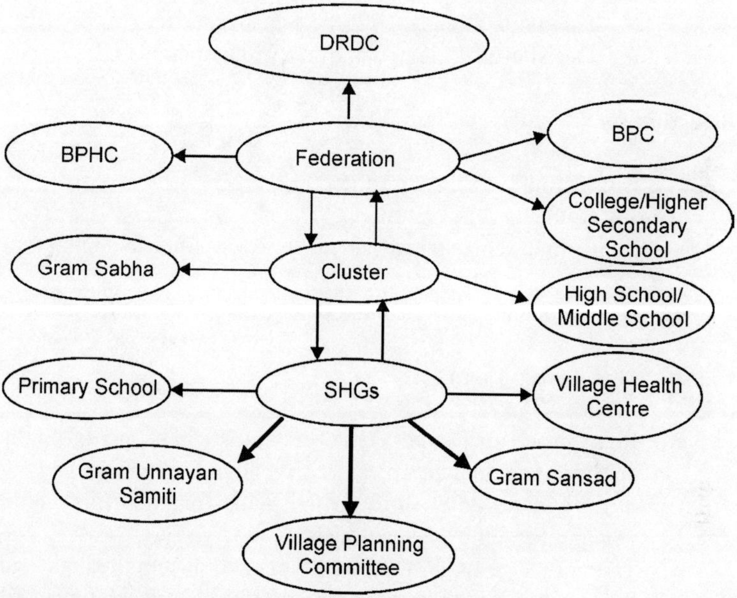

Fig. 4.3: A Schematic Representation of the Federation

Grading of the SHGS

First Grading

- First grading will be held after six months of the group formation.
- The objective of the grading is to observe the groups about the preparation for income generation.
- At the time of grading, BDO, Sabhapati, Panchayat Pradhan, Bank Officer, and other Block Officer will be in the grading team.
- At the time of grading the team should take care of the personal savings of the group.
- Following points have to be noticed at the time of grading:
  1. Regular meeting and attendance in the meeting.
  2. Membership.

3. Clear rules and regulations of the group.
4. Regular savings.
5. Loan amount from the group fund.
6. Rate of loan repayment.
7. Record maintenance.
8. Group initiatives in any kind of social activity.
9. Facilitator attendance at the time of meeting.
10. Decision-making power of the group members.

Selection for Giving Revolving Fund

- If the group scores more than 90 per cent – Selected without any confusion.
- If the group scores more than 60 per cent – Selected but have to keep in observation.
- If the group scores less than 60 per cent – Will not be selected.

Selection for Giving Loan

- If any group gets 80 per cent or more than 80 per cent from the appraisal then the group can receive loan for entrepreneurship development. After drafting the plans for entrepreneurship development, they can get the loan.
- The groups getting 60 to 80 per cent score from the appraisal, they cannot get the loan for entrepreneurship development but they can get revolving fund or cash credit.
- The groups have to give another appraisal after six months whose score is less than 60 per cent.

What is Cash Credit?

- Cash credit is a one kind of loan service which is given by the bank.
- In case of revolving fund, one time to four times of the total amount of the group fund, bank will sanction in the name of the group as a cash credit.
- The facility of the cash credit is that the withdrawal amount is loan amount. Rest amount can be withdrawn at any time.
- Bank will open an account in the name of the group and they will provide a checkbook to the group. The group can withdraw loan through this check book.

- Interest on cash credit is calculated everyday.
- Bank generally receives interest after every three months.

What is Revolving Fund?

- This is a fund which helps in income generation among the group members by transacting it as a loan and receives interest form the loan. Someone can develop small-scale income generation activity through this fund.
- Revolving fund has two parts—one is District Rural Development Cell and another one is Bank.
- First grading can be done after six months from the group formation.
- Total amount of the group is (savings + interest collection+ bank interest on savings- group maintenance cost). DRDC provides revolving fund depending on the group total money.
- The amount given by the DRDC is entrusted to the bank in the name of the group.
- Bank will provide one to four times of the total group amount.
- Money from the bank and DRDC jointly makes the cash credit.
- Bank will receive the interest but the group has not to pay any interest on DRDC amount.
- Second grading will be held six months after the first grading.

Group Promise

- We convey that, we will follow the discipline, unity, courage and toil.
- We increase our fund by regular savings and receiving loan from the bank.
- We will increase our income by taking loan and proper utilization of loan from group.
- We will take care of children's health and education.
- We will follow the family planning.
- We will form government recognized women Self-Help Group.
- We will participate in the Gram Sansad for village development.
- We will make the linkage with the bank, Panchayat and other government offices.
- We will give our support to the others at the time of emergency and we become a social agent for change.

- We shall develop our society and economy.

Self-Help Group: Some Emerging Issues

The experience in developing countries shows that provision of small credit to the poor through the linkage process has contributed to the process of rural development by creating conditions that are conducive to human development. It is reported that significant changes in the living standards of SHG members have taken place in terms of increase in income levels, assets, savings, borrowing capacity and income generating activities. Moreover, the participation of women in the economic activities and decision-making at the household and society level is increasing and is making the rural development process participatory, domestic and sustainable. The primary strength of the programme is that its foundations are based on poor people's own resources, where they save and contribute to group funds. Collective savings have been used as the basis for group formation at the hamlet level. The impact of converting individual savings into group funds not only provides the rationale for group formation but also enables the social utilisation of poor people's resources for their own development.

The members of each group belong to the same caste and same socio-economic status. Individually each member saves ranging from Rs. 25 to Rs. 50 per month. The group members deposit the money to the local Bank on regular basis and maintain a good record of their saving as well as other discussions. The programme, from one perspective, has promoted a savings movement among the poor where groups compete with one another on how much they can save. It is also found that some of the groups have increased the monthly subscription rate per head per month from the beginning. The social impact of this has been a tremendous enhancement of confidence among the poor that they can save and use their own resources to solve their own problems.

The leaders are selected by the group members themselves. The Panchayat, Banks and other developing agencies arrange intensive training on different aspects of leadership relating SHG to all such leaders. Every group has an opportunity to change its leader. The process of selecting leader has been ensured in such a manner that a woman who can play effective leadership roles for the benefit of group members is chosen. There is clarity among the majority of members on the necessary qualities, roles and responsibilities of a good leader. This investment in leadership building among the women has provided the social base and energy to the entire developmental programmes beyond the actual savings-credit programme. Seeing the successful leadership capacity and good interaction among the village people and also active participation in community activity, the villagers elect Self-Help Group leaders as Panchayat member. Most of the group members are actively participating in Panchayat activity. Normally, the group members organize meetings once in a week. Group participation is one of the major elements of SHG. Interaction in meeting help to develop friendship, express solidarity with the problems of others, nurture leadership and enhance one's own capacity in development. Women find a new identity through SHGs and provide efficient social support system to the community. Self-Help Groups are a potential source to empower and institutionalize participatory leadership among the marginalized and to identify, plan and initiative development activities.

One of the important strategies followed is to promote and sustain learning opportunities among women. The Blocks organize several self-oriented-cum-employment generation training and awareness generation programmes for different groups in different locations as per the needs of the community. All the members took part in different training and awareness programme, which help them to tackle the problems in their lives and their work. Through the training and awareness programmes they realize that they have knowledge and capacity and that they are able to be creative if they take initiative. Through these awareness and training programmes the group members is gathering knowledge and applying it in their day-to-day life. Almost all the members are trained on different income generating schemes as per their needs. Most of them have started the income generating activities after completion of the training. These group members are taking physical and financial help from their own groups.

The group members are directly involved for the social development of their respective villages. Liquor intake behaviour of most of the village are very high. After the formation of groups the women group members of the groups discuss this particular issue among themselves and started campaigning against drinking. Now the liquor sellers are compelled to stop the liquor selling in many villages. So, the group members have brought a revolution against drinking in the locality. The Groups are also directly involving themselves in Government programmes in various levels. The literate SHG members are also involved to educate their illiterate partners. In this way all the group members are involved in many such social and community development activities. These groups help women to establish a common participatory platform to raise their voice and solve their problems. Participation of women come out in open and discusses their problems, helps to bring about awareness on various issues and makes them self-reliant.

For each group formed under collective savings, the savings are immediately put to use as credit to individual group members. The groups immediately see the benefit of pooled savings as it solves their emergency credit needs for which they had to access earlier to moneylenders. The group members take loan from their own fund. Repayment is also good. The groups also take loan from the banks as per their need for starting various income generating activities. The loan has been taken by the individual members for income generating activities, consumption purposes, for immediate contingency purposes, for medical treatment, education for their children, also for the betterment of their future generation and so on. Inter group lending within the village has also been started. Such types of work develop the friendship among the group members, enable people to utilize their own resources and also develop cooperation among the community. The credit cycle also trains the groups in the management of a financial system. It forces them to establish group norms for lending and repayment, and enables the group to take decisions, where choices have to be made on who should get priority in credit. By first using their own funds, where ownership is more and stakes are higher, it brings into the system a greater sense of diligence and accountability. All the above features ensured a strong community-based financial system that realises on people's own resources, that teaches them efficient financial management and that meets their need for small consumption credit on a timely and accessible basis. The rate of interest for repayment is higher than the bank but much less than the moneylenders. The motive to charge higher rate of interest than the bank is that, through this lending the group members can increase their own fund. The group members are also taking loans from the banks for various purposes. Some groups want to deposit a good amount of money, and then they want to take loan or to start some income generating activities from that group fund. All the groups have their emergency fund. Normally they use to keep this fund in the custody of the group leader so that the group members even the villagers can get the money for emergency needs. Hence, it makes clear that the groups have a specific vision. In well-established SHGs, members contribute substantially to their family development in the form of getting credit for education of children, health needs and even for marriages, construction of houses and creating assets. Self-Help Groups enhance equality of status of women as participants, decision-makers and the beneficiaries in the democratic, economic, social and cultural spheres of life. SHGs encourage women to save and utilize savings to build self-reliance and confidence and provide great access to and control over resources.

Conclusion

Sustainability of the groups not only depends on saving, credit and economic activities. The members will have to involve all sorts of activities including social activities with active participation of all members. Participation of women in SHGs makes a significant impact on the sustainability of groups. Group cohesiveness, group integration among the members is a positive impact of SHG. The saving habit and credit management have created self-reliance in women as they have their own resource base. The group activities encourage mutual dependency among the members. Economic dependence of women on their husbands or other male members has reduced to a large extent because of the SHG. The active participation of group members shows that they can train others in capacity building, generate their own resources, and ask help of the government for social, economic and physical development of their communities. Their economic independence has elevated their level to involve them in the developmental activities of the village. They are enjoying a decent role in the decision-making process. The women are trained to identify their needs and necessities and accordingly they are participating in rural welfare activities after becoming the member of SHGs. This has developed the participatory approach in the villages.

After the SHG formation, due to regular meeting and training, awareness regarding health and hygiene is increasing day by day among the members. Knowledge level on various issues like immunization, family planning, nutrition, hygiene, childcare and mid-day meal has been increased among the SHG members. One interesting point emerged that the ICDS workers, health workers, government officials use SHG meeting as a platform to discuss on various issues which helped the members to raise their awareness. The SHG members need to improve their hygiene practices. Housing condition of the SHG members are now better equipped. Many SHG members are trying to get latrine facilities which indicate higher level of awareness on sanitation among them. The level of awareness on government programmes has also been increased. A large portion of members are aware about BPL and APL, pulse polio programme, mid-day meal, Integrated Child Development Scheme (ICDS), National Rural Employment Guarantee Act (NREGA) and Swarnajayanti Gram Swarozgar Yojana (SGSY), Old age pension, Government health programmes, etc. Training programme has an important role to develop the capacity of the SHG members. After formation of SHG, the members participate in several activities like training, *mela*, SHG conference, GP level meet, exhibition, etc.

Due to the above activities, SHG members are able to raise their additional monthly income of the family. Several assets like purchase of land, purchase of cattle for rearing, construction or modification of house, purchase of household items like TV, cycle, radio, torch, utensils, chair, almirah, etc., installation of tube-wells, etc., were created by the members. Even they invest the money for business purpose also. The involvement of SHG members towards self-employment like handicraft, business has been increased and percentages of housewives and daily labour have decreased. But the changes in occupations or occupational diversifications are very prominent among the SHG members. Due to the increase in income and awareness the SHG members are now spending money for other durable consumer goods, education, health, for asset creation and savings purposes. Bank loans and inter loan amount has been increased for the SHGs. Before forming the groups, the members never took any loan from bank. But now many of the members depend on bank for money which results decreased trend of dependency on moneylender.

Self-Help Groups enhance the equality of status of women as participants, decision-makers and beneficiaries in the democratic, economic, social and cultural spheres of life. In all stages of economic and social activities involvement of women becomes essential. The SHGs bring out the supremacy of women in moulding the community in right perspective and explore the initiative of women in taking up entrepreneurial ventures. The SHGs empower women and train them to take active part in the socio economic progress of the nation and make them sensitized, self-made and self-disciplined. The Group approach helps to remove social limitations of women such as superstition and dormant role in decision-making and also inculcated a great confidence in the minds of rural women to succeed in their day-to-day life.

References

Avasthi, P.K. *et al.*; (2002), Working and Impact of Self-Help Groups on

Economic Status of Women in Watershed Areas of Madhya Pradesh, *Indian Journal of Agricultural Economics*, 56(3), June, 2002.

Bagchi, Jasodhara (ed.); (1995), *Indian Women: Myth and Reality*, Sangam Books (India) Private Limited: Hyderabad.

Basu, Kishanjit and Krishan, Jindal (eds.), (2000), *Microfinance: Emerging Challenges*, Tata McGraw-Hill, New Delhi.

Bhagyalakshmi, J.; (2000), Women in Development. *Employment News*. Vol. XXV, No. 3, April 15-21, 2000.

BIRD; (2001), *Sustainable Microfinance Challenges Facing MFIs*, Report of a workshop organized by SIDBI and BIRD, Lucknow, 15-17 January, 2001.

Chandra, Aravind and Shah, Anupam; 1987: *Non-formal Education for All*. Sterling Publishers, New Delhi, India.

Dasgupta, K.; (2001), An Informal Journey through Self-Help Groups, *Indian Journal of Agricultural Economics*, July-September, 2001.

Dasgupta, Sugata and Murthy, L.S.N.; (1983), *Panchayati Raj Institution in West Bengal,* National Institute of Public Cooperation and Child Development, New Delhi.

Desai, Neera and Patel, Vibhuti; (1985), *Indian Women: Change and Challenge in the International Decade 1975-1985,* Popular Prakashan, Bombay.

Dubey, J.P.; (2006), Continuing Education: Changing Perspective. *Indian Journal of Adult Education*. Vol. 67, Nos. 1-2, January-June 2006.

Dwaraki, B.R., Narayanaswamy, N. and Ramesh, N.; (1996), *Towards Creating A Participatory Self Help Credit Cooperative*, Institute of Rural Management, Anand, Gujarat.

D'lima, Hazel; (1983), *Women in Local Government*. Concept Publishing Company Pvt. Ltd., New Delhi.

Everett, Jana Matson; (1979) *Women and Social Change in India*, Heritage Publishers, New Delhi.

Faizi, Amir Afaque Ahmad; (2009), *Self-Help Groups and Marginalized Communities*, Concept Publishing Company Pvt. Ltd., New Delhi.

Fernandez, A.P.; (1995), Rural Management System, Self-Help Group Concept, *MYRADA,* Bangalore.

Ghadially, Rehana,(ed), (1988), *Women in Indian Society*, Sage Publication, New Delhi.

Goela, Usha; (1992), Programmes for the Development of Women in the Government of India, in *Women's Issues—An Indian Perspective,* Ed. By Lakshmi Mishra, Northern Book Centre, New Delhi.

Government of India; (2001), *National Policy for the Empowerment of Women, 2001*, Department of Women and Child Development, Ministry of Human Resources, New Delhi, India.

Haragopal, G.; (1980), *Administrative Leadership and Rural Development in India*, Light and Life Publishers, New Delhi.

Harper, M.; (2002), Self-Help Groups and Grameen Bank Groups: What are the Differences, in Fisher, T. & Sriram. M.S. (ed.), *Beyond Micro-Credit: Putting Development Back into Micro-Finance*. Vistaar Publications, New Delhi.

Karmakar, K.G.; (1999), *Rural Credit and Self-Help Groups,* Sage Publications, New Delhi.

Karmakar, R. and Ghosh, B.; (2002), Role of women in the Self-Help Group: An emerging possibility to co-operativization at grass root, *Man in India*, Vol. 82.

Kumari, Archana; Verma, R.K.; (2010), *Women Political Leadership in India: Some Important Dimensions*, Serials Publications: Delhi.

Kundu, Amit; (2008), Impact of SGSY Scheme on Self-Help Groups of West Bengal, *Afro Asian Journal of Rural Development*, Vol. 41, Jan.-Dec., 2008.

Lalneihzovi (ed.); (2007), *Women's Development in India*, Mittal Publications: New Delhi.

Mahajan, Vijay; (1999), Is Micro Credit the Answer to Poverty Eradication? *Adult Education and Development,* Institute for International Co-operation of the German Adult Education Association, Vol. 53, 1999.

NABARD; (1992), Credit Needs of the Rural Poor—Role of Self-Help Groups and their linkage with Formal Credit Institutions, NABARD, Mumbai.

NABARD; (1995), Role of Self-Help Groups and their linkage with Formal Credit Institutions, NABARD, Mumbai.

NABARD; (1998), Self-Help Group Concept, *Vijaya Bank*—NABARD, Bangalore.

Narayanaswamy, B., Samanta, R.K. and Narayana Gowda, K.; (2007), *Self-Help Groups—Key to Empowerment of Rural Women,* The Women Press, Delhi.

Pandya, Rameshwari, (2008): *Women in Changing India*, Serials Publications: Delhi.

Paul, Kakali and Paul, Sujit Kumar; (2005), Economic Empowerment of Tribals Through Self-Help Groups, in *Economic Development Issues and Policies*, Ed. by Prof. N. Narayana, Serials Publications, New Delhi.

Paul, Sujit Kumar; (1999), Women in Development—A Participatory Approach. *Bulletin of the Cultural Research Institute*, Backward Classes Welfare Department, Government of West Bengal, Vol. XX, No. 3.

_______ (2004) Women Empowerment through Self-help Group. *Journal of Extension and Research*, Vol. VI, No. 1&2, January 2004.

_______ (2006), Women Participation in Development: The Shifting Paradigm through Self-Help Group, in *Gender Inequality and Women Empowerment*, Ed. by R. Paramanik & A.K. Adhikary, Abhijit Publication, New Delhi.

_______ (2008), "Self-Help Group: The Association for Rural Indian Women", in Suzanne Arcand *et al.* (eds). *Violencesfaits aux Femmes*, Presses de I'Universite du Quebec, Canada.

Prasad, Kiran; (2006), *Women in Rural Development*, The Women Press.

PRIA; (2004), *Potential of SHGs for Enhancing Participation of Women in Local Self Governance*, New Delhi.

Puhazhendi, V. and Satyasai, K.J.S.; (2000), *Microfinance for Rural People: An Impact Evaluation*, NABARD, Mumbai, India.

Sa-Dhan; (2001), *Microfinance Regulation in India*, Sa-Dhan, New Delhi.

Sen, Manab; (2003), *Self-Help Groups and Microfinance: An Alternative Socio Economic Option for the Poor*, SIPRD, Kalyani, Nadia, W.B. 741235.

Suguna, B.; (2006), *Empowerment of Rural Women through SHGs*, Discovery Publishing House, New Delhi.

Sunder Raj, D.; (2004), SHGs and Women's Empowerment. *Social Welfare*, Vol. 50, No. 10, January 2004.

United Nations Development Programme, (1995), *Human Development Report*, Oxford University Press, New Delhi for UNDP.

Weedon, C.; (1987), *Feminist Practice and Poststructuralist Theory*. Oxford: Blackwell.

Yunus, Muhammad with Alan Jolis; (1998), *Banker to the Poor: The Autobiography of Muhammad Yunus founder of the Grameen Bank*, The University Press Limited, Dhaka.

5
MGNREGA and Rural Development

Introduction

After attainment of independence from British rule, a sequence of schemes, one after another, operated both in National level and in States with an aim to provide wage employment to the labour-intensive workers in rural areas. Government adopted rural employment scheme for the workers privilege to labour-intensive jobs considering the issue of right, each given a distinct title along with a specific set of objectives and financial allocations.

The National Rural Employment Guarantee Act (NREGA) (Now Mahatma Gandhi National Rural Employment Guarantee Act) (MGNREGA) 2005 is landmark legislation in Indian history of social security legislation after independence. This act was enacted after successful struggle for the Right to employment guarantee legislation. Its importance is obvious in various perspectives. At first, it is a bold and unique step in the provision of rural employment in India and also in the world at large. Secondly, it is the first initiative about the right to work as an enforceable legal right. In India, where labour is the only economic asset for millions of people, gainful employment is a prerequisite for the fulfilment of other human rights such as the right to life, the right to food, and the right to education. The indispensable characteristic of this legislation which separates it from other scheme is its ratification through the parliament of India. This legislation has been bringing about noiseless revolution in rural India.

After independence rural India was suffering from unemployment and poverty. To reduce the poverty and generate employment opportunity, Government of India was taking one after other policies and programmes to solve both the problems but the success is not up to the level. Reduction of the poverty and unemployment was an important goal for the Planning Commission. Therefore, the objective of NREGS is to enhance the livelihood security of people in rural areas by generating wage employment through works that develop the infrastructure base of that area. Initially it was very tuff for Government of India to provide employment to huge population where 72 per cent households belonging from the rural areas and the rural economy depends on agriculture. But the government strongly believes that country's progress depends on rural areas and to develop the rural areas, it is very necessary to generate rural employment. After that the President of India has given his assent to the National Rural Employment Guarantee Bill 2005 and it has become an Act with effect from 7th September 2005, "to provide for the enhancement of livelihood security of the households in rural areas of the country by providing at least one hundred days of guaranteed wage employment in every financial year to every household whose adult members volunteer to do unskilled manual work and for matters connected therewith or incident thereto". The success of Maharashtra Employment Guarantee Scheme (MEGS), which was running in Maharashtra over last 30 years, was the main guide for implementation of this revolutionary programme in all over the India. In last three decades, Government of India launched lots of programmes like National Rural Employment Programme (NREP, 1980), Rural Landless Employment Guarantee Programme (RLEGP, 1983), Jawahar Rozgar Yojana (JRY, 1989), Employment Assurance Scheme (EAS, 1993), Jawahar Gram Samridhi Yojana (JGSY, 1999), Sampoorna Grameen Rozgar Yojana (SGRY, 2001), and National Food for Work Programme (NFFWP, 2004). The National Rural Employment Guarantee Scheme (NREGS) is now very effective step for employment generation by the Government of India.

Problems of Earlier Wage Employment Programmes

- Lack of awareness.
- Lack of community participation.
- Lack of planning.
- Quality of assets created was not always of requisite standards.
- Reports of false muster roll.
- Problems in Payment: often less than prescribed wages and Disparity between payment to women and men.
- Contractors persisted.
- Diversion of funds.
- Weak monitoring and verification system.
- No comprehensive data base.
- Inadequate Capacity of implementing agencies.

- Multiple wage employment programme running in parallel.
- No Public Accountability.

India's economy has been experiencing a high growth rate in the last two decades. Inspite of this high economic growth, India has suffered from several economic distortions. The national economy is predominantly rural in nature and reflected in the very high proportion of its population living in rural areas. It was 89 per cent in 1901, 83 per cent in 1951, 74 per cent in 1991, 70 per cent in 2001 and 68.84 per cent in 2011. The incidence of poverty in the country is still very high. As per Planning Commission of India data the percentage of persons below the Poverty Line in 2011-12 has been estimated as 25.7 per cent in rural areas, 13.7 per cent in urban areas and 21.9 per cent for the country as a whole, with the bottom 10-15 per cent poor regularly suffering from starvation, largely emanating from the lack of adequate purchasing as well as consumption power. Rural India has been facing various technological and infrastructural deficits. Majority of people are living in the villages and there is a need to improve the quality of life.

Rural poverty and its eradication has been part of the discourse since independence. A plenty of programmes since then have been planned and implemented in rural India to eradicate poverty, with varied impacts. The potential beneficiaries may find that the income from cultivation of small plots falls short of subsistence requirements. Specifically, through a work-requirement, these programmes are expected to exclude the more affluent sections. In this regard a new programme called MGNREGA was started by the Government of India. As, India is second largest populated country, the problem of poverty and unemployment are rampant; in this regard the wage employment programme like MGNREGP go long way in solving these problems.

The Mahatma Gandhi National Rural Employment Guarantee Act 2005 (MGNREGA) enhance the livelihood security of the households in rural areas by providing 100 days of employment in a financial year to any rural household whose adult members are willing to do unskilled manual work. The Act has enacted on 5th September, 2005 come into force with effect from February, 2006 in 200 districts initially as National Rural Employment Guarantee Act (NREGA) and later renamed by an Amendment as the Mahatma Gandhi National Rural Employment Guarantee Act (MGNREGA), on 31st December, 2009. The Act is a significant step towards legalization of the right to work. It has also enhanced people's livelihood on a sustained basis, by developing the economic and social infrastructure in rural areas. The choice of works seeks to address the causes of chronic poverty such as drought, deforestation and soil erosion. Effectively implemented, the employment guaranteed under the Act has the potential of transforming the geography of poverty. MGNREGA is the most significant act in the history of Indian polity in many ways like grass root level participation and governance of every citizen and beneficiary through democratic process, multi-layered social audit and transparency mechanism by involvement of civil society, comprehensive planning at village level towards sustainable and equitable development, etc.

Historical Background

In the post-independence period, poverty alleviation and rural development has become the prime concern of the Government of India while the wage employment programme has taken as an important strategy for rural development. The increased population size and labour force, seasonal employment, high rate of migration, poor asset and infrastructure, technological backwardness and increased vulnerability in rural areas demand for employment and income to improve the quality of life.

India has a long history of employment generation schemes, in which the central and State governments work toward livelihood security in rural areas by providing employment. The country's previous wage employment programme's outreach was greatly expanded between 1989 and 2005, and eventually culminated in NREGA on September 7, 2005. NREGA was enacted on 5th September, 2005 and implemented through National Rural Employment Guarantee Scheme. In the beginning NREGA began with 200 poor Indian districts in Phase I (2006-07) and was extended to an additional 130 districts during Phase II (2007-08). Since April 2008, the act has covered the whole India with the exception of districts that have a hundred per cent urban population and was renamed the Mahatma Gandhi National Rural Employment Guarantee Act (MGNREGA) in October 2009 by an amendment.

India's Eleventh Five Year Plan (2007-2012) points to MGNREGA as one of the main planks of rapid poverty reduction strategies in India. MGNREGA's focus has been on rural areas because 68.84 per cent of India's population, and most of the poor, reside in the countryside. The contribution of agriculture to national income has fallen dramatically in recent years but more than 600 million Indians still depend on farming (Shah, Mihir, 2008).

Objectives of MGNREGA

The mandate of the Act is to provide at least 100 days of guaranteed wage employment in a Financial Year (FY) to every rural household whose adult members volunteer to do unskilled manual work. The objectives of the programme include:

- Ensuring social protection for the most vulnerable people living in rural India through providing employment opportunities.
- Ensuring livelihood security for the poor through creation of durable assets, improved water security, soil conservation and higher land productivity.
- Strengthening drought-proofing and flood management in rural areas.
- Aiding the empowerment of the marginalized communities, especially women, Scheduled Castes (SCs) and Scheduled Tribes (STs), through the process of a right based legislation.
- Strengthening decentralization, participatory planning through convergence of various anti-poverty and livelihood initiatives.
- Deepings democracy at the grass root by strengthening the Panchayati Raj Institutions (PRIs).
- Effecting greater transparency and accountability in governance system.

Source: MGNREGA Sameeksha, 2012

MGNREGA has become a powerful tool for inclusive growth in rural India through its impact on legal protection, social safety nets, livelihood security and grass root governance. It brings a new era of technology and financial inclusion for rural communities.

Specific objectives of the MGNREGA are:

1. To provide minimum one hundred days of guaranteed employment, in a financial year to every household in the rural areas whose adult members are willing to do unskilled manual work subject to the conditions lay down by the Act.
2. To augment livelihood resource base of the rural poor through creation of durable assets for employment generation in a sustainable manner.
3. Strengthening rural governance through decentralisation and processes of transparency and accountability.

Funding Pattern of the Scheme

This Scheme shall be implemented as a Centrally Sponsored Scheme on cost sharing basis between the Centre and the State as provided in the Act. The Central Government shall meet the following cost:

1. The amount required for payment of wages for unskilled manual work for the scheme,
2. Up to three-fourths of the material cost of the scheme including payment of wages to skilled and semi-skilled workers.
3. Such percentage of the total cost of the scheme as may be determined by the Central Government towards the administrative expenses.

The State Government shall meet the following cost:

1. The cost of unemployment allowance.
2. One-fourth of the material cost of the Scheme including payment of wages to skilled and semi-skilled workers.
3. The administrative expenses of the State Council.

Nodal Agency

The Panchayats and Rural Development Department, Government of the concerned State shall be the Nodal Agency for implementation of the scheme.

Type of Works Permissible

(a) Water conservation and water harvesting;
(b) Drought proofing including all the components of watershed development, afforestation and tree plantation, labour intensive fencing, nursery raising and other related activities;
(c) Irrigation canals including micro and minor irrigation works;
(d) Provision of irrigation facility to land owned by households belonging to the Scheduled Castes and Scheduled Tribes, and also the beneficiaries of land reforms;
(e) Renovation of traditional water bodies including desalting of tanks;
(f) Development of land owned by households belonging to

Scheduled Castes and Scheduled Tribes, beneficiaries of land reforms, the beneficiaries under the Indira Awaas Yojana, and small and marginal farmers (last in priority) including development of layouts for beneficiaries of rural housing schemes, development of play grounds, development of land for village markets and for creating other durable community assets;

(g) Flood control and protection works including drainage in water-logged areas including creation of temporary drainage structures during rainy season;

(h) Rural connectivity to provide all-weather access including earthwork on the roads to be covered in the Pradhan Mantri Gram Sadak Yojana (PMGSY), and

(i) Any other work, which may be notified by the Central Government in Consultation with the State Government.

Different Steps under MGNREGA

- Registration of families.
- Distribution of job cards.
- Receipt of work application and issues of dated receipts.
- Selection of the public work to be taken up in a particular GP.
- Development and approval of technical estimates and issuance of work order.
- Allotment of work to applicants.
- Implementation and supervision of work.
- Payment of wages.
- Payment of unemployment allowance.
- Evaluation of completed work.

Registration

The adult member of every household who resides in any rural areas and are willing to do unskilled manual work under the Scheme shall be entitled to apply for registration to the Gram Panchayat.

Job Card

The Gram Panchayat shall issue a job card within a week to the registered household after making such enquiry as it deems fit. All the payments made shall be entered in the original job card only. No payment shall be made without the job card.

Employment

Any registered adult member of the household may apply for allotment of work in plain paper or in the prescribed form to the Gram Panchayat. If a Gram Panchayat is not in a position to provide employment under the self of works within the Gram Panchayat and employment needs to be given outside the Gram Panchayat, the Gram Panchayat shall inform the Programme Officer within six days of receiving an application for providing work. While, providing employment, priority should be given to women so that at least one-third of the beneficiaries shall be women, who have registered and requested for work. If a rural disabled person applies for work then works suitable to his/her ability and qualification shall have to be given as far as possible. Employment shall be provided within the radius of five kilometres of the village where the applicant resides.

Unemployment Allowance

According to the Act "If an applicant for employment under the Scheme is not provided such employment within fifteen days of receipt of his application seeking employment or from the date on which the employment has been sought in the case of an advance application, whichever is later, he/she shall be entitled to a daily unemployment allowance in accordance with this section". Unemployment allowance shall be less than one-fourth of the wage rate for the first thirty days during the financial year and not less than half of the wage rate for the remaining period of the financial year.

Responsibilities of the Gram Panchayat

"The Gram Panchayat shall be responsible for identification of the projects in the Gram Panchayat area to be taken up under a Scheme as per the recommendations of the Gram Sabha and the Ward Sabhas and for executing and supervising such works." In 7th September, 2005 *The Gazette of India* published the general information regarding the National Rural Employment Guarantee Act by the Ministry of Law and Justice. After this enactment, West Bengal Government issued a notice (No. 684-RD/NREGA/18S-1/06 dated 02/02/2006) regarding this scheme. In West

Bengal, West Bengal Rural Employment Guarantee Scheme framed as per section 4(1) of the National Rural Employment Guarantee Act, September 2005 (NREGA), came into force from February 2006 to give effect to the provisions of the Act. Various transparency and accountability measures and provisions for social audits are available with this Act.

Planning

The Operational Guidelines of MGNREGA (MoRD, 2008) states, "Planning is critical to the successful implementation of the Rural Employment Guarantee Scheme (MGNREGA). A key indicator of success is the timely generation of employment within 15 days while ensuring that the design and selection of works are such that good quality assets are developed. The need to act within a time limit necessitates advance planning. The basic aim of the planning process is to ensure that the district is prepared well in advance to offer productive employment on demand". The unique feature of MGNREGA is its bottom-up architecture-planning and selection of works and their implementation are to be done in a participatory manner under the leadership of the Gram Sabha (GS) and the Gram Panchayat (GP). However, few reports record that this actually happens on the ground. Work priorities tend to follow orders from the State or district headquarters and do not reflect the needs and aspirations of the people as they should. The hope was that greater water security and drought-and flood-proofing would be realized. While there have been a few successes in this regard, these remain oases of excellence. Section 13 of NREGA makes Panchayats the principal authorities for planning. The process of planning under Section 16 of the Act, the GS is to make recommendations on the works to be taken up under MGNREGA. The Gram Panchayat is to prepare a shelf of projects and annual plans on the basis of GS recommendations (MoRD, 2008). The MGNREG Act specifies that at least 50 per cent of the works in terms of cost should be executed by the GPs. Section 6.3 of the Operational Guidelines indicates that the Gram Panchayat is the single most important agency for executing works. It says, "The other implementing agencies can be Intermediate and District Panchayats, line departments of the Government, Public Sector Undertakings of the Central and State Governments, Cooperative Societies with a majority shareholding by the Central and State Governments, and reputed NGOs having a proven track record of performance. Self-Help Groups (SHGs) may also be considered as possible Implementing Agencies" (MoRD, 2008).

The Operational Guidelines also states that every State have to develop labour budget based on a projection of employment demanded by rural households. This is important and must form the basis for the preparation of the annual plan. In practice in almost all States, the employment provided in the previous financial year is the basis for projection of the labour budget of the current year.

From the year 2015-16, as a part of Labour Budget exercise Government has decided to give special focus on backward blocks while conducting the labour budget exercise. For this purpose, an intensive participatory planning exercise has been recommended and to be conducted in 2,500 backward blocks.

Payment Procedure and Unemployment Allowance

Every person working under the Scheme is entitled to wages at the wage rate notified by the Central Government under Section 6(1) of the MGNREGA. State Governments and the programme authorities make all efforts to publicize the notified wage rates in simple language and through means that are easily accessible to the local community. The Act also provides that equal wages should be paid to both men and women workers, and the provisions of the Equal Remuneration Act 1976. Timely payment of wages has emerged as one of the main challenges of Mahatma Gandhi NREGA over the last few years. According to Section 3(3) of MGNREGA, workers are entitled to being paid on a weekly basis, and in any case within a fortnight of the date on which work was done. Weekly Muster Roll is a necessary and primary condition to ensure payment of wages within 14 days after start of work.

A significant reason for delay of wage payments is non-availability of sufficient funds at district/Block/GP level. Often it happens that while in some districts/Blocks/GPs in a State, there is shortage of MGNREGS funds, in others there is surplus fund lying unutilized. Once the MGNREGS fund is allotted to a district/Block/GP, it is very difficult to transfer funds across districts/Blocks/GPs. Fund allocation, hence becomes an arduous task in implementation of MGNREGS. To meet this challenge, the States must adopt an integrated fund management system called e-FMS (Electronic Fund Management System) which ensures that idle funds are not lying at any level. Under e-FMS, the MGNREGS fund is a centrally pooled fund maintained at the State level. All Project Implementing Agencies (PIA) across the State are the users of this centralized fund and have access to this pooled fund (with certain restrictions). PIAs make electronic transactions through the centralized fund, for the purpose of wage/material/administrative payments (with certain ceilings). All electronic transfers are realized in a span of 24 hours. Based on this principle of Centralized fund and decentralized utility, the e-FMS ensures timely availability of funds at all levels and transparent usage of MGNREGS funds. This improves efficiency of the programme on the whole and also has a positive effect on timely payment of wages.

Provision of unemployment allowance is another important aspect of the MGNREGA. The operational guideline of MGNREGA stated that if an applicant is not provided employment within fifteen days of receipt of his/her application seeking employment, he/she shall be entitled to a daily unemployment allowance. In the case of advance applications, employment should be provided from the date that employment has been sought, or within 15 days of the date of application, whichever is later. Else, unemployment allowance becomes due. The unemployment allowance has been paid as per Section 7 of the Act. The allowance given not has been less than one-fourth of the wage rate for the first thirty days and not less than one-half of the wage rates for the remaining period of the financial year.

Convergence

Convergence is an evolving process and while broad principle can be laid out at the centre, the actual contours of convergence will be determined by the resources at Central, State, District and programme level. With this perspective, convergences have made between MGNREGA and different Ministries and Departments, implementing programmes with complementarities with MGNREGA. Some of the Ministries and departments converged with MGNREGA are:

- Ministry of Agriculture—Indian Council of Agricultural Research;
- Ministry of Environment and Forest;
- Ministry of Water Resources;
- Department of Land Resources;
- Pradhan Mantri Gram Sadak Yojana—Rural Roads;
- Ministry of Agriculture;
- Minister of Drinking Water and Sanitation (NBA);
- Ministry of Women and Child Development (Anganwadi centre);

- Ministry of Commerce & Industry (Schemes of Rubber Board); and
- Ministry of Textile (Sericulture Board).

Mode of Convergence

To fully identify the possibilities of convergence, it may be necessary to make a beginning with selected programmes, so that the experience of implementation may further inform and refine strategies for convergence. Some of the basic principles of guideline related to convergence under MGNREGA are:

1. Funds may be made available from other schemes to meet cost of an identifiable part of the project that could result in enhanced durability of assets created/proposed using MGNREGA funds.
2. Funds may be made available from other schemes as livelihood component for putting to use for livelihood, assets created/ proposed using MGNREGA funds.
3. The third mode could be to provide for technical inputs from concerned departmental officials. The inputs could be either in the form of supervision by technical staff during work execution for improving the quality of assets created/proposed or for capacity building for using assets under MGNREGA for livelihood.
4. Gap feeling, meaning pooling together funds of MGNREGA and other schemes and deploying pooled funds for creation of an asset.
5. A combination of two or more of the above modes is also possible.

While exploring options for convergence, special care have been taken to ensure that MGNREGA funds do not substitute resources from other sectors or schemes. MGNREGA funds are intended to create additional employment and this will not happen if the employment currently generated by other programmes is substituted by the MGNREGS.

In operational terms, convergence of different programmes with MGNREGS will require coordination between the converging programmes and MGNREGA at stages of planning, implementation and management. Para 16(4) of the MGNREG Act stipulates that every Gram

Panchayat shall, after considering the recommendations of the Gram Sabha and the Ward Sabhas, prepare a development plan and maintain a shelt of possible works to be taken up under the Scheme as and when demand for work arises, the projects that are identified for convergence with MGNREGA should be discussed in the Gram Sabhas located in the project area. MGNREGA component of the work taken under convergence should be implemented by Gram Panchayat or other implementing agency, as prescribed in the Act. Other implementing agency should follow the norms prescribed in the respective programme guideline. Planning for works and managing the convergence would require institutional arrangements for proper coordination at District, Block and village level. The institutional platform for such dovetailing will be the Gram Sabha at the village level, and then the Gram Panchayat.

Accountability and Social Audit

Social audit in the recent development scenario has conceived as a key instrument of social accountability. Eventually, the implementation of MGNREGA in India, for providing alternative livelihoods to rural poor has widely recognized essence of 'social audit' for ensuring accountability and transparency in implementation process. MGNREGA, which was implemented through legislation in 2005, is believed to have potential for addressing income needs and unemployment problems in rural India, if transparency in implementation would be maintained through an appropriate institutional mechanism. Keeping this in mind, the transparency and public accountability rules have been framed as a part of MGNREGA. Social audit is a process whereby Government programmes are monitored directly by the people concern. The process has the potentialities to implement development programmes more effectively within a prescribed institutional framework. Taking the cognizance from the fact, the provision included in MGNREGA with an objective to foreground accountability through a decentralized participatory institutional framework. Under such provision, powers have been vested to local self-governing institutions for ensuring accountability in each stage of implementation, by organizing Gram Sabha (Village Assembly). Gram Sabha under the banner of 'Social Audit Forum/ committee' is empower to organized village level meetings as public hearing through a well designed activity plan. However, organization of such process in a diversified socio-cultural and political scenario and within so-called decentralized institutional framework has faced stiff challenges in India.

Salient Features

The salient features of the Act are:

- *Right-based Approach*: MGNREGA belongs to a long history of wage employment programmes. The most significant features of the MGNREGA are that it creates a Rights-based framework and that it is a law. Its main instruments for articulating a Rights-based approach are documents like Job Cards-workers' documents for asserting his rights, exercise of choice by workers, time-limits for fulfilling guarantees by the Government, social Audits, compensation/penalties.
- *Registration of Household*: The primary step is the registration of household at Gram Panchayat. Adult members of a rural household who are willing to do unskilled manual work at a fixed wage rate are eligible to apply for registration either in written, or orally to the Gram Panchayat. The basic unit for registration is a household. The Act mandates 100 days of employment in every financial year to each household in rural areas.
- *Job Card*: The registered households are then issued with a Job card after due verification of place of residence and age of the household members (only adult members are eligible for employment). Job card is a proof or basis of identification for demanding employment. Normally a job card is to be issued within 15 days of registration. Every Job card has a unique identification number. For demanding employment in Gram Panchayat or in Block is to be made against the respective Job card number. Authority is also responsible for updating the Job card regularly and confirms payment to the beneficiaries on a regular basis.
- *Demand for employment*: Employment seekers have to submit a written application seeking work in the Gram Panchayat or Block office stating the time and duration for which work is sought. The GP or Block office will have to issue a dated receipt of the written application for employment. The authority has to guarantee of providing employment within 15 days.

- *Planning and approval of the work*: The planning and approval of work has to make through decentralized planning process. Gram Sabhas (GS) are vested with the task of preparing shelf of projects. Plans and decisions regarding the nature and choice of works has to be made in financial year along with order in which planned works are to be taken up, selection of site, etc., are all have to be prepared in open forum of Gram Sabha and rectified by the Gram Panchayat (GP).
- *Unemployment Allowance*: As per the MGNREGA the authority will have to provide employment within 15 days from the date of employment application. In case if the authority failed to provide employment then they will have to provide an unemployment allowance to the beneficiary.
- *Work Allocations*: Some of the issues are to be considered while allocating work to the beneficiaries. The Act stated that work should be provided within the 5 kilometres of radius from the native villages. In case, if work is provided beyond 5 km, an extra wage of 10 per cent will have to be given to the beneficiaries as additional transportation and living expenses. Priorities should be given to the women so that one third of the beneficiaries under this scheme will be women.
- *Payment of Wages*: Payment of wage in a regular basis is also an important component of this Act. The Gram Panchayat and Block offices are responsible for documentation of muster roll and preparation of payment details. The wages are to be paid as per the State-wise Government of India's notified MGNREGA wage. The payment of wage as per the Scheduled of Rate (SoRs) is another criterion for wage payment. The wage should be paid on weekly basis and not beyond a fortnight in any case. Payments are to be made through single or joint Post Office/Bank account of beneficiaries.
- *Cost Sharing*: Both of the Centre and the State are part of the financial obligations. The Central Government bears 100 per cent wage expenses of unskilled manual labour and 75 per cent of material expenses, including wages of skilled and semi-skilled workers.
- *Worksite Management*: The MGNREGA prohibits the utilization of contractor, machinery and other agents in the implementation process. This ensures the direct and regular flow of benefits to the target groups under the scheme. The Act also mandates that

in the total cost of work undertaken in a Gram Panchayat, the wage expenditure to the material expenditure ratio should be 60:40. This ensures the integrity of the Act as well as focus on employment generation. Workers have to be provided with certain on-site amenities. Worksite facilities like shed, crèche, drinking water, first aid are also made mandatory in working site.

- *Transparency and Accountability*: Transparency and accountability are the two important features of this Act. The MGNREGA mandates transparency and accountability by engaging common people in entire process from planning and budgeting to monitoring and evaluation of the work. The decentralized planning and implementation process is one of the main comment of this Act. Social audit is another component of this Act. Every GP has to maintain all the record and Gram Sabha has to scrutinize all the documents and records under the scheme on a regular basis. All the accounts and records related to the scheme should be available for public scrutiny.

MGNREGA and a Paradigm Shift

The MGNREGA marks a paradigm shift from previous wage employment programmes implemented in India's history. MGNREGA unlike any other in its scale is structural design and thrust. It has an integrated natural resource management and livelihoods generation perspective within a legal framework. The transparency and accountability mechanisms under MGNREGA create extraordinary accountability of performance, especially towards immediate stakeholders. Some of its other unique aspects are outlined below:

- MGNREGA have unique structural design which is decentralized, bottom up, people-centred, demand driven, self-selecting, and right-based.
- It provides a legal guarantee of wage employment.
- It is a demand driven rather supply driven programme where the provision of work is triggered by the nature of demand for employment by the work-seekers.
- It has legal safeguard for compensation as unemployment allowance, in case of failure to provide work on demand or delay in payment of work undertaken.

- It is free from the problem of targeting (identification and selection) beneficiaries as it has a unique self-targeting mechanism.
- This provides an additional incentive for the States to leverage the Act to meet the employment needs of the poor. The State Government have some relaxations as the programme incentivises States to provide employment as 100 per cent cost for unskilled labour and 75 per cent cost of the material is borne by the Government of India.
- MGNREGA is demand-driven rather allocation-based like other wage employment generation programme and so the transfer of resources from GoI to States has done on the demand for employment in each of the States.
- The entire process of MGNREGA is based on a decentralized matrix structure with an effective delivery mechanism which indicates the value of participation of wage seekers, Gram Sabha and Gram Panchayats for successful implementation of the programme.
- Social audit, a new characteristic of the programme makes it more accountable and transparent towards the common people.

MGNREGA and Some Facts

- Enacted as a Rights-based legal framework for guaranteeing a basic livelihood security to rural households and this is a law.
- Belongs to a long history of wage employment programmes.
- The implementation of the Act has yielded encouraging results in augmenting employment, increasing wage earnings, stemming distress migration, enhancing productivity and promoting equity, specially gender equity.
- Brings a new era of technology and financial inclusion for rural communities.
- Designed as a social safety net and has the potential to transform rural India into a more productive, equitable, connected society.
- Formulation of Rights based laws as policy instruments.
- A classic example of the shift from a policy based on the perception of development as a welfare activity of the Government to a policy that recognizes basic development needs as rights of the citizens, compelling commitment of resources by the Government, even challenging some of its existing systems.

- MGNREGA came in the context of radicalization of State policy, foregrounding its obligation as a law.
- Built on the pivotal authority of the local bodies, the Act strengthens grass root democratic processes.
- Transparency and public accountability are integral to it, expressed through social audits, proactive disclosures and free access to all records.

MGNREGA as a Right Based Approach

MGNREGA belongs to a long history of wage employment programmes and enacted as a Rights-based legal framework for guaranteeing a basic livelihood security to rural households. It is actually the formulation of Rights based laws as policy instruments. MGNREGA came in the context of radicalization of State policy, foregrounding its obligation as a law. It is a classic example of the shift from a policy based on the perception of development as a welfare activity of the Government to a policy that recognizes basic development needs as rights of the citizens, compelling commitment of resources by the Government, even challenging some of its existing systems. It is built on the pivotal authority of the local bodies which strengthens grass root democratic processes. It is designed as a social safety net and has the potential to transform rural India into a more productive, equitable, connected society. Transparency and public accountability are integral to it, expressed through social audits, proactive disclosures and free access to all records. The implementation of the Act has yielded encouraging results in augmenting employment, increasing wage earnings, stemming distress migration, enhancing productivity and promoting equity, especially gender equity. Some of the right based features of MGNREGA have been mentioned below:

- The procedure of application for wage employment is the basic principle for assertion of rights. It actually ensures the primary level participation of the people in the process through claiming right to employment under the Act. Wage seekers have also the right to apply for registration in their local Gram Panchayats.
- Job Card is the basic instrument to demand work and is also the worker's record of rights.
- The Act also mandates the right to ask for employment as and when needed is acknowledged through a dated receipt issued by the village based local body. MGNREGA made the demand factor a conscious strategy as a Right to obtain employment.

- The right to receive employment is guaranteed through time-lines: fifteen days to allocate employment, fifteen days to make payments is also a major component of the MGNREGA.
- The Act also provides a third set of prescriptions relate to safeguards against violations of rights through providing unemployment allowance to the worker in case of delayed employment allocation.
- Rights under the Act are further safeguarded though social audits and proactive disclosure under MGNREGA.
- It provides a wage equal to the minimum wage prescribed for agricultural labour, under the Minimum Wages Act.

While the Rights-based framework of the law is one of its significant features but it possesses the maximum challenges in its realization. Rights can be ordained but their actualization is not the consequence of ordains. Rights do not stay restricted to a space that can be carved out and protected from their raw environment. The basic instruments for exercising Rights in MGNREGA depend on the capability of the worker which is lacking. More over lack of organization makes difficulty in enforcing the Rights.

Reason for Acceptance around the Country

Since major elements of MGNREGA have been taken from previous wage employment programmes, the question that arises is what makes them effective and acceptable widely now in a way that they were not before?

One important factor has compelled Government to enforce the right to work as an Act despite several dilemmas. Government has recognized 'Rights' not just as workers' demands, nor as just a sequence of actions, but essentially as a need of workers have that the Government is obliged to accomplish. The law creates space for innovation, flexibility and decentralized process enabling States to deal with several problematic issues, locally, and these local innovations have been the basis for its effectiveness and acceptance. In fact, local innovation has been the main outcome of the legal design and the tool for its efficiency. The factors which are responsible for effectiveness and acceptance of MGNREGA are discussed below:

1. *Policy context*: The data of the Planning Commission of India reveals that the percentage of persons below the Poverty Line in 2011-12 has been estimated as 25.7 per cent in rural areas, 13.7

per cent in urban areas and 21.9 per cent for the country as a whole. The respective ratios for the rural and urban areas were 41.8 per cent and 25.7 per cent and 37.2 per cent for the country as a whole in 2004-05. It was 50.1 per cent in rural areas, 31.8 per cent in urban areas and 45.3 per cent for the country as a whole in 1993-94. There is a reduction of 137 million persons over the seven years period from 2005-06 to 2011-12. However in 2011-12, India had 270 million persons below the Poverty Line as compared to 407 million in 2004-05 and that is an alarming situation. Another factor, the decline in overall growth of employment during 1993-94 to 1999-2000 was largely due to the lower absorption in agriculture. The share of agriculture in total employment dropped from 61 per cent to 57 per cent and further dropped to 52 per cent in 2004-05. Following the same trend India has crossed the historic point that is less than 50 per cent of the total employment would be in the agricultural sector. Extensive erosion and degradation of natural resource base over the last fifty years have resulted some of the worst natural disasters adversely impacting on agricultural productivity and employment opportunities thereof. Growing poverty and unemployment have lead to fragmentation of land and increase in number of agricultural labours. At the same, there has been an increase in the percentage of operational holdings under small and marginal farmers. The policy response to a circumstance of poverty, unemployment and inequality has focused on inclusive growth. MGNREGA is one the policy measures which contributes to inclusive growth through right based employment generation and livelihood security. MGNREGA is classic example of the shift from a policy based on the perception of development as a welfare activity of the Government to a policy that recognizes basic development needs as rights of the citizens, a compelling assurance of resources of the Government, even challenging some of its existing systems.

2. *Political context*: MGNREGA is widely accepted because it is a law backed by political will and it has excited the political thoughts of the State. With its thrust on employment provided locally, and its large scale, direct reaching out to the poor, the Act enjoys high priority in the Central Government's agenda. The political support to the Act has been high in spite of the fact that the party in power in the State is different from the one in

the Centre. Public involvement of State's political leadership with the scheme under the Act ensured required support to the scheme for its implementation in the State.

3. *Framework of Law*: The most important fact that the programme is governed by law has made it different from other wage employment programmes. It successfully imposed a thought that there is a law and therefore, work must be provided to the local labour that may be in need of it.
4. *Decision-making space to States*: The MGNREGA provides flexibility to the State Governments to make schemes under the Act. States are to formulate schemes as per the framework given by the Act and the schemes are to be the instruments for the Act. The State can also make its own Act, incorporating the features of MGNREGA. Therefore, the design of the Act places the onus and ownership on the States. Further, and even more important, it leaves decisions and control with the State, even while funds for implementation are from the Centre.
5. *Decentralized planning and role of local bodies*: The entire planning process under MGNREGA is decentralized in nature and its success highly depends on people's participation. The local bodies, Panchayati Raj Institutions (PRIs) have a principal role in planning, implementation and monitoring. This is specially important at the village level, where the local body, the Gram Panchayat has the unique advantage of being located in the local village community as well as being the main institutional outreach of rural development.
6. *Financial support:* The Central government is the major stakeholder for providing financial assistance. The Central Government committee provides 90 per cent of the cost, and in addition hundred per cent of administrative expenses up to the permissible limit, for implementing the MGNREGA.

   Another important component is the demand-based budget. The budget is based on the principle of demand. A preliminary budget provision is made, but the initial budget is open to augmentation according to the labour demand that may rise. It has been a transformation from fixed allocation based budget to demand based budget.
7. *Demand-based strategy:* The MGNREGA is generally applicable to anyone who demands employment under it. The single eligibility criterion is that the applicant should be a local

residence in a Gram Panchayat. The rural people may demand work at any time of the year for any number of days up to the guaranteed employment of a hundred days in a year and finance for providing employment is being given to the implementing authority. This has been the first employment generation programme which is free of long bureaucratic procedure.

8. *Administrative Support:* The Act requires a highly develop and efficient administrative support for implementation. The Centre has the authority to determine administrative expenses which it has to fund fully. Dedicated personnel has to be deployed for managing critical programme components like ICT, social audits, works, grievance redressal at the block, district and State levels.
9. *Transparency and Accountability:* Transparency and Accountability are two important component of the Act. Transparency and accountability have been mandated in the Act through a framework which includes documents and processes. These includes:
   - Job card is a valid document for demanding employment.
   - The Right To Information (RTI) has been integrated with MGNREGA.
   - The social audits conducted by the village assembly (Gram Sabha) which go beyond the RTI to fix accountability and seek correctives.
   - The payment to the worker under the MGNREGA has been transacted through the bank or post office account. It is a significant measure for ensuring transparency and accountability.

Progress and Impacts of MGNREGA

Employment, Income and Livelihood Security

MGNREGA has succeeded to provide a stable source of income and livelihood security for the poor, vulnerable and marginalized section of the society. Overall, evidence reveals that MGNREGA does provide basic income assurance to a large number of beneficiaries. Various empirical studies have revealed that the MGNREGA has huge impact on the rural areas in terms of poverty alleviation and generation of income opportunities. There are a number of distinct ways in which MGNREGA is likely to impact on poverty, the most direct and obvious way is by providing extra work opportunities and income to the poorest in the rural areas (Dutta, P. *et al.*, 2012). Net household income has been increased around the country. Some researcher also stated about importance of MGNREGA as supplementary income sources. MGNREGA income is also being used by rural households for starting their own enterprises. It has been suggested that the concepts of the multiplier and accelerator could be usefully applied to MGNREGA. On the one hand, MGNREGA increases the purchasing power of workers creating demand for commodities. This has been regarded as an important contributor to soften the impact of the world-wide recession on the Indian economy. At the same time, by generating incomes for small and marginal farmers, both through direct benefits to them as workers and by improving the productivity of their lands, MGNREGA stimulates private investment on these farms. Effectively a wage employment programme can thus be transformed into a source of sustainable livelihoods generating self-employment. This would permit reductions in allocations for MGNREGA over time, not only because landed labourers get back to their own farms, but also because of a general rise in demand for labour in the rural economy (Shah, 2009).

MGNREGA has huge impact on monthly per capita expenditure also. It has been found from various studies that the MGNREGA has caused a significant increase in monthly per capita consumption expenditure of households. Expenditure on non-food consumables increased while expenditure on transportation decreased significantly due to the MGNREGA. This was most likely because the MGNREGA stipulates that employment be provided within 5 kilometres of the residence of participants. MGNREGA seems to provide poor households the capability to survive economic shocks and deal with inflation.

MGNREGA has also contributed to ensuring a higher intake of food and food availability. The expenditure on consumption of nutritious food has increased. In assessing the impact of MGNREGA on poverty, it is important to also look at the relationship between MGNREGA and market wages. Literature suggests that employment generation programmes like MGNREGA, that can put upward pressure on agriculture wages, are likely to be some of the most effective ways of improving the welfare of the poorest.

Research suggests that welfare costs of economic crises and climate shocks are excessively high for the poor who lack the means to protect themselves from adverse income and employment shocks. This could further strengthen existing inequalities, create persistent poverty and slow down the pace of poverty alleviation. Through its impact on income, consumption, food security and employment, MGNREGA appears to be helping in protecting the poor and vulnerable. The programme also raised the probability of holding savings for a rural household and the per capita amount saved increased in rural areas.

High Involvement of Marginalized Community

The majority of the MGNREGA workers belong to the most disadvantaged sections of society who seek employment. MGNREGA is succeeding as a self-targeting programme, with high participation from marginalized groups including the SCs and STs. At the national level, the share of SCs and STs in the work provided under MGNREGA has been high. The percentage of work share among the SC and ST were 22.96 per cent and 15.95 per cent in the financial year 2013-14 while it is 20.86 per cent and 20.72 per cent in the financial years 2014 -15 (as shown in the Table 5.1). This trend is definitely a positive indication.

Table 5.1: MGNREGA Work Status in Percentage (FY 2013-14 and 2014-15)

Working Community	*FY 2013-14*	*FY 2014-15 (till Aug)*
SCs	22.96	20.86
STs	15.95	20.72
Others	61.09	58.42

Source: MGNREGA MIS

The Act also allows work like irrigation, horticulture, development of private land belonging to the SCs and the STs or below poverty line families, the beneficiaries of land reforms, the beneficiaries under the Indira Awas Yojana (IAY) of the GoI, the beneficiaries under the Scheduled Tribes and other traditional forest dwellers, small and marginal farmers land. The rejuvenation of cultivable waste land and transforming it into cash crop and fodder sources under MGNREGA is also being a prime strategy for many States. MGNREGA can play a significant role in raising the agricultural productivity of these farmers who will then be able to return to farming and will no longer need to depend on the Scheme for their survival. This is a step in the direction of moving from unskilled manual labour to skilled farming practices.

Impact on Gender and Social Empowerment

The issues of gender equity and social empowerment are being the prime focus of majority of programmes implemented by both Central and State Governments. MGNREGA is not an exception. As a rural wage employment generation programme, MGNREGA recognized the importance of incorporating gender equity and social empowerment in its structural design. Various provisions under the Act ensure that women have equitable and easy access to work, decent working conditions, equal payment of wages and representation on decision-making bodies.

At the national level, the participation of women in the Scheme has surpassed the statutory minimum requirement of 33 per cent. The women representation was 53.09 per cent and 51.58 per cent in the financial year 2013-14 and 2014-15 (till the August 2014) respectively as per MGNREGA MIS data. Significantly, female share on works under MGNREGA is greater than their share of work in the casual wage labour market across all States (Dutta *et al.*, 2012). Women are participating in the Scheme much more actively than they participated in all forms of recorded work (Ghosh, J., 2009). However, the large inter-State variation in women participation has remained an issue for the implementation. Some of the States like Kerala, Tamil Nadu, Andhra Pradesh, Rajasthan, Himachal Pradesh have high women participation while States like Assam, Mizoram, Jammu & Kashmir, Uttar Pradesh have very low women participation. MGNREGA has reduced the traditional wage discrimination in public works. Equality in wage rates is also an important factor to be positively affecting participation of women in this Scheme. States with comparatively higher wage differential in informal labour market (other than MGNREGA) are probable to have a greater participation of women in MGNREGA, which assures wage equity.

Improved access to financial resources and paid work has a positive impact on the socio- economic status of the women in rural areas. Many researchers have found that women enjoy their freedom in collection and spending of MGNREGA wages, indicating greater decision-making power at household level. The money has been utilized largely for consumption purpose like avoiding hunger, repaying small debts, paying for their child's schooling and bearing medical expenses.

Another significant fact about MGNREGA is better access to credit and financial institutions among the women. The mandatory transfer of wage payment through bank accounts has ensured that a greater number of women are brought into institutional finance from which they had been largely excluded (Ghosh, 2009). Research suggests that qualitative and quantitative improvements in gender equations across various spheres (social, political and economic) coupled with positive changes in self-perception gradually result in the empowerment of women and social change.

Environmental sustainability and livelihood security are two major factors need to be flourished while considering the impact of MGNREGA on gender. Women are more severely affected by climate change and natural disasters because of their social roles (providing daily essentials like food, fuel, fodder, water, etc.). Migration again leads to extra burden for women since in cases of extreme circumstances men likely to migrate leaving the women-folk behind to look after their property. MGNREGA, through the creation of sustainable rural resources, water conservation and forestry, has contributed to ecological restoration and make environmental benefits through increased livelihood security, especially for rural women, to climate change and other shocks.

Women empowerment is the inevitable push factor for growth and development of a nation like India. In India women represent a major share of poor population. The Government has formulated different programmes/schemes to uplift the women from poverty and vulnerability of life. One such women sensitive programme is Mahatma Gandhi National Rural Employment Guarantee Act (MGNREGA). MGNREGA has provided a unique opportunity to the rural people of India to earn their own income without any discrimination of caste or gender. The Act gives priority to women while providing employment and it mandates that at least one-third of the beneficiaries should be women who have registered and requested for work under the Act. Most remarkable feature of MGNREGA is that it pays women the same as men, something that was virtually unimaginable in rural India. MGNREGA plays a significant role to meet the practical as well as strategic requirements of women's participation. It has become a fire of light in the empowerment of the rural women and contributed for the livelihood security, improved economic conditions and standard of living by creating equal wages to male and female workers. The role of MGNREGA on women empowerment can be seen in terms of:

Economic Empowerment: In the area of economic empowerment, there is no doubt that MGNREGA has made dramatic changes in the economic status of women in the village. It has provided employment to women in more than half the households in the village at a wage rate that is much higher than the prevailing wage rate in the local economy.

Decision-making power on expenditure: MGNREGA has increased the income of women workers and as a result, their ability to choose the consumption goods and their decisions on expenditure have increased.

Women now have the freedom to spend money in their own way or jointly with their husbands.

Intra-household decision-making: Women play a key role in raising the financial resources for their family but their contribution remains uncounted because, they perform a significant amount of unproductive work. Women enjoy less freedom in domestic decision-making in rural areas. MGNREGA has major impact in transforming some unproductive work into productive work and has widened the scope of decision-making role of women at household levels.

Community-Level Effects: In spite of the 73rd Constitutional Amendments women's participation at the local and district level of governance system remains low. But, after the implementation of MGNREGA women participation has increased in many areas.

Emergence of Social Capital: The introduction of MGNREGA has promoted collective strength of women in several spheres of village life. The first major impact is that women from different areas now know each other, interact with each other and help each other. Another interesting aspect of the collective strengths of women is that new leaders have emerged in the village.

Creation of Durable Assets

The sustainable asset creation has strengthened the livelihood resource base of rural areas lead to sustain rural livelihood structure. The works under MGNREGA are basically related to water (water conservation, flood control, irrigation, drought proofing, renovation of traditional water bodies and micro-irrigation), and related to rural connectivity. It has huge potentiality to benefit rural communities by improving irrigation facilities, enhancing land productivity and connecting remote villages to input and output markets.

However, the quality of assets created was not up to the mark. It has faced criticism on the quality and sustainability of the assets generated under it. Critics of the Scheme argue that since employment generation is the primary objective of the Act, the works undertaken are labour-intensive, these works tend to be non-durable and have limited use (Bassi, N. and Kumar, D.M., 2010).

MGNREGA allows for asset creation, such as water conservation works, provision of irrigation facilities, land development, etc., on public land. Though the MGNREGA is demand-based and implementation of one kind of work does not exclude the other, there has been some argument on the effectiveness and success of works undertaken on public land in comparison to works on private land. Studies show that while private assets are preferred by beneficiaries, public assets benefited a larger area and more people, leading to higher returns on investments.

Most assets created under MGNREGA are used for multiple purposes. This reflects the potential of MGNREGA to contribute to water and livelihood security in the village ecosystem. For assessing the development impact of MGNREGA assets, it is important to take into account the nature and multi-utility of each asset. In fact, MGNREGA may be viewed as the world's largest laboratory for community-based multi-use water services (MUS).

As mentioned by MoRD, MGNREGA with its inter-sectoral approach opens up opportunities for convergence with different programmes. The aim of convergence is to optimise public investments made under existing Schemes through suggested ways of linking and steering them towards a common/shared recipient end, both physical (area, infrastructure, natural resource) and human (person, group, agency).

Reduction in Migration

The impact of MGNREGA on rural labour markets has several dimensions that need careful consideration. For instance, the programme has increased rural labour participation rates by drawing into the workforce many who were not active workers, and making attractive and convenient work opportunities easily accessible. But it is also argued that the Scheme has created labour shortages by removing a block of labour supply from the residual labour market (Verma, 2012).

The impact of MGNREGA on agriculture labour has been the subject of considerable debate among researchers. It is hypothesised that government hiring of unemployed labourers would affect labour supply across peak and lean agricultural seasons directly through its effect on wages and indirectly through its effect on agricultural output (Basu, 2011).

However, it is difficult to suggest that this casual labour in MGNREGA is actually labour from the agriculture sector. The shortage in agricultural labour and their diversion from farms may be due to factors outside MGNREGA. In fact, post 2004-05, there has been a negative trend in labour force participation. A study found that high non-farm wages have had a more significant role in the diversion of labour from agriculture than MGNREGA (Indumati and Srikantha, P.M., 2011).

MGNREGA has reduced migration by providing work closer to home and decent working conditions. The World Development Report 2009 contended that a reduction in migration, as caused by MGNREGA, is posing a barrier to internal mobility thus limiting economic growth of these households. The reduction in distress migration may be more apparent in the case of households that need to migrate with their families; the entire family is forced to migrate to cities due to limited work opportunities. MGNREGA also provides supplementary income for family members who choose or are unable to migrate.

Challenges Emerge for MGNREGA

MGNREGA marks a radical change from earlier wage employment programmes in terms of its legal and demand-driven framework. However, there have been many constraints in infusing the system with the new culture of demand-driven, rights-based, decentralized decision-making. In general, the implementation of MGNREGA in a State can be expected to depend on the quality of grass root governance. States with better systems of governance and administration are more likely to have the ability to run complex programmes more effectively (Dutta *et al.*). On the other hand, poorer States have greater demand for work under MGNREGA. However, they also have higher rationing rates and greater unmet demand for work. This is perhaps because the State institutions are less capable of implementing MGNREGA. Some of emerging challenges regarding implementation of MGNREGA are discussed below:

Lack of Awareness about the Act

There is lack of awareness among potential beneficiaries about certain provisions and process of the MGNREGA. This limits them to get full benefit under the Act. Knowledge about the provisions of the Act is very important for exercising the demand to work and other entitlements like demanding work, unemployment allowance, social audit, etc., under MGNREGA. Low awareness level also hampers the effectiveness and efficiency of the work undertaken under the Act.

Poor Participation in the Planning Process: The MGNREGA mandates that the identification, selection and prioritization of activities to be taken up during a Financial Year (FY) under the Scheme, be done by the Gram Sabha. Planning and prioritization of the activities by the

Gram Sabha ensures that the development requirements of each village are addressed through active participation of the villagers. However, field studies reveal some constraints in this mechanism, viz.:

- Gram Sabhas are not frequently organized.
- The nature of participation in preparation of annual action plan is passive, accepting what was offered to them rather than proposing the plan. It is mostly a mere list of the demands of the Panchayats.
- The planning process becomes unable to meet the problem at grass root level.
- Political bureaucrats are finalized what to be sanctioned for proposed plan.
- Finally bottom-up planning practically come into top-down philosophy.

Poor Capturing Demand

According to the MGNREGA, an adult member of any rural household willing to do manual unskilled work should be provided work on the basis of demand. However, research suggests that in some instances, due to low awareness, limited capacity of the delivery systems and traditional social structures among other reasons, households are not being provided employment under MGNREGA. In other words, there is a rationing of demand; households that are willing to work and seeking employment under the Scheme are not being given work (Dutta, *et al.*).

The Act mandates every household that applies for work is to be issued a dated receipt. This receipt is the instrument for ensuring the household to get work within 15 days from the date they desire work to be provided. Hence, provision of timely work is crucial to ensuring livelihood and social security to the poorest. However, findings from the field suggest that this is not always the case.

Unemployment Allowance

The Act mandates that if an applicant is not provided employment within 15 days from his/her application, he/she is entitled to a daily unemployment allowance. But unfortunately in such cases unemployment allowances are not provided to the beneficiaries.

Timely and Full Payment of Wages

MGNREGA mandates that wage payment should be made to beneficiaries within 15 days of work being finished. However, delays in payment have been found in various field studies across the country. Delays on wage payments are a huge disincentive for beneficiaries who seek employment under the Scheme (Khera, 2011). It also dilutes the spirit of the Act which tries to provide social security to the poorest of the poor. There are various reasons behind the delay which are:

- Shortage of staff at GP level lead to late measurement of works which translates into late payment of wages.
- Lack of functionaries as well as administrative support is a real bottleneck in MGNREGA implementation, with serious consequences, especially for its bottom-up, people-centred architecture.
- Fund allocation and disbursement process takes huge time.
- Delay in updating expenditure records, delay in placing demand for additional fund by the district (which travels through the state to the GoI) and scrutiny of expenditure and release of funds by the GoI cause the delayed payment.

Leakages and Misappropriations in the Scheme

MGNREGA has received serious criticism on account of perceived misappropriations and leakages under the Scheme. Wage payments to beneficiaries are calculated on the basis of attendance and measurements listed on Muster Rolls (MR). MRs are supposed to be available at worksites and updated everyday. However, studies that have conducted MR verification indicate several irregularities in the filling and maintenance of these MRs. Fake entries in MRs have been found in field studies. In some cases Contractors are used to execute some work although MGNREGA prohibits the use of contractors for work and machinery. In some cases wage payments are made to workers who either have no JCs or those who did not actually undertake work at worksites. Double payments have also been noted.

Lack of Public Transparency, Accountability and Participation

The Act mandates that the Gram Sabha has to organize regular social audits of all the projects under the Scheme taken up within the GP. But it has been found that the social audits are not frequent and quality is very poor. The frequency and quality of social audits is a major constraint in effective implementation of the Scheme. Lack of bureaucratic interest, lack of proper idea about the Social Audit process among the facilitators and common people, political interference hamper the process. However, there are good practices where States have taken innovative steps towards developing and institutionalizing accountability tools into the governance system.

Corruption

Statistics clearly indicate that the poverty alleviation programmes have had a minimal effect on poverty levels in India due to corruption. The actual funds that reach the beneficiaries are very little compared to the funds allocated for welfare schemes. A systemic corruption and lack of transparency on the part of implementing agencies have made MGNREGA a major source of corruption in rural India. It is very interesting that many government employees were illegally provided job cards under the MGNREGA and this was in gross violation of the norms. The systemic corruption cases in rural areas have also showed that how the Panchayati Raj Institutions (PRIs) have bypassed the local people which were intended to play an important role in planning and executing this flagship programme to respond to the local needs of the people. Specially, the issue of fake job cards, job cards deposited in the custody of implementing officials or political party middlemen, delayed payment are being used for nefarious purpose of minting money illegally. Another corruption has highlighted that the official estimates of wages realized by workers are in fact inflated because the actual wages received by workers were much less than what is shown in the official documents. Again, this includes the reality that corruption of the local governments leads to the exclusion of specific sections of the society. Local governments have also been found to claim that more people have received job cards than people who actually work in order to generate more fund than needed, to be then embezzled by local officials and political leaders.

Muster Roll

In spite of having a clear guideline, the performance of measurement system under MGNREGA is very poor. It is often politically biased and technically wrong. It also left a long trail of fake muster rolls and embezzled money. The fake and wrong entries have made in muster role resulting dissimilarities in the actual work scenario and the work entered in the official document. The local political leader influences the misinterpretation in the master roll for gaining illegal monetary benefits. It is often found that, in many cases the wages paid according to the muster rolls had actually not been received by the concerned labourers. There are several cases of fake muster roll entries, over writing, false names and irregularities in job cards. Even the names of dead people who have not registered often feature in the master rolls.

Sale of Job Cards

The Job Card is the key document recording workers' entitlements under MGNREGA. The Job Card is the registered household's legal instrument for applying for work, which also ensures transparency and protects workers against fraud. However, in actual situation a deep corruption has emerged based on the job card. Bribes are paid in order to receive the job card. A fraud has also been suspected where people have been issued under the MGNREGS card who is either employed with another Government job and who are not even aware that they have a job card. It has been often found that the upper caste people sold their job card to the poor people who do not have any job card against some money. The local political leaders and officials are also engaged in such type of corruption and keep the job cards for monetary benefits. Sometimes bribes are paid to the local leaders for receiving the payment.

Work Culture

MGNREGA is a measure of social security. It is significantly raising the livelihood security and wage rate in rural areas. However, in some cases it hampers the rural work culture. The workers spend only three to four hours in the working site with minimum participation resulting in poor quality as well as quantity of work under MGNREGA. These have become a trend in rural areas and highly affected the agricultural sector. The demand of wage has been increasing day by day while the labours have become less productive, affected the cultivation of marginal and small farmers. The existing crop cycle is also hampered as some of the seasonal crop like oilseeds, vegetables and pulses are not possible to cultivate due to labour crisis.

Another fact which has been found in the rural areas is the degradation of social harmony among the landlord and rural labours. The cooperation and intra-group harmony have been an integral part of rural social structure in India but recently this cooperativeness has been reduced and an individualistic way of thinking has emerged in the rural areas which have highly affected the social and political balance of the areas.

Political Interference in the Implementation Process

In some States planning and implementation of MGNREGA is facing huge political interference which hampers the entire process. The selection of work and work site are politically biased. The political leaders take responsibility for implementing the work under MGNREGA. The Gram Sabha also has become a political platform and run by the interest of local political desires. High involvement of political parties causes poor performance and high level of corruption dilutes the impact of MGNREGA.

Most importantly, MGNREGA ensures that millions do not starve. By guaranteeing a minimal income for able bodied when no other work can be found, the programme helps citizens afford food for their families. There is also tentative evidence that the scheme has led to an increase in cultivated land, improved dietary habits, and reduced forced migration. Jean Dreze, one of MGNREGA's main advocates, claims the transition to a rights-based framework has led to a major decline in labour exploitation in rural public works. Wages are now higher, delays in wage payments are shorter than before, productivity norms set by employers are more reasonable, and complaints of harassment cases are rare. Hence, MGNREGA has a overall impact on the rural life of India.

However, some areas have emerged which should be addressed meaningfully for successful implementation of the programme and generate better impact through MGNREGA. The areas which need focus in the future are:

- States have not set up effective systems of recording demand. State should take some action to solve this problem. State Government have to ensure that MGNREGA MIS will record the demand of work.
- More focus should be given on decentralized planning process through the Gram Sabhas. The State should provide extra focus to enhance the engagement of people in the grass root planning process.

- To meet the demand and supply of employment a proper labour budget should be developed.
- The State should develop the administrative structure for proper implementation and monitoring the scheme.
- Apart from deploying additional staff, the State should ensure the timely payment of wage.
- A major criticism of MIS is that it does not capture transactions on real-time basis and all data entries are basically *post facto*. Another criticism is that there are delays in data reporting through MIS. These areas have to be developed to increase the efficiency of the MGNREGA MIS.
- Special focus should be given to the vulnerable groups such as persons with disabilities, primitive tribal groups, nomadic tribal groups, denotified tribes, women in special circumstances, senior citizens.
- Civil societies may be involved to improve the grass root participation in the planning process.
- Some protective measures should be taken to regularize the social audit. For instance capacities of the Gram Panchayats have to develop to conduct social audit in a proper way.

MGNREGA Outcomes

- The Act, has given evidence of positive outcomes, even while its performance across the country has been unequal.
- MGNREGA has opened opportunities for large scale employment of both skilled and unskilled manpower at Block/village levels in rural areas.
- There has been an increase in minimum wages for agricultural labourers in most States.
- It is the poorest of the poors and the most vulnerable groups who seek employment under the programme.
- The MGNREGA has been designed to allow women equity in both access to work and in the payment of wages.
- Equal wages between men and women have been a major incentive to women to work.
- MGNREGA ensures a positive trend towards women empowerment and identify them as an economic opportunity provider.
- Another aspect of understanding NREGA and women's assertion

is the growing contribution of women workers to the sources of their households' livelihood.

- Outmigration from villages has gone down.
- Assets created under MGNREGA have been conducive to the geographical-ecological environment, have been useful and have contributed towards natural resource regeneration.
- It designates a balance between human action and natural resources creating a sustainable economic security through green jobs.
- MGNREGA has also been able to contribute to ecological restoration through its design.
- Under MGNREGA, State governments are working to develop plans with a focus on afforestation and eco-restoration.
- MGNREGA through convergence with Pradhan Mantri Gram Sadak Yojana (PMGSY) is improving rural connectivity.
- Almost 88 million accounts opened in Banks and Post Offices for NREGA workers, makes this the largest financial inclusion of the rural poor.

Some Observations

The seeds of MGNREGA were planted long before in hope of getting smiles on the faces of rural poor through its upcoming flowers and fruits of asset creation and cool shade of guaranteed employment of hundred days. The programme addressed was bliss to the people for its unique feature and objectives and was welcomed with open hands by the rural India. It has its success stories in certain areas. Tamil Nadu is one of the mentioning States who have hoisted the flag of successful implementation of MGNREGA. It has been observed that the amble condition of employment promised by the programme resulted in a situation of discontent of different dimension among all the class of people.

Independent India attempted to adopt a number of schemes both at National and State level aiming to provide wage employment to the labour intensive workers and unskilled labourers at the rural level. MGNREGA is milestone in this process. The National Rural Employment Bill 2005 has effectively become an act from 7th September, 2005. As stated before, it was tabled after the implementation of several other programmes like NREP, 1980; RLEP, 1983; EAS, 1993; JGSY, 1999; SGRY, 2001; and NFFWP, 2004.

This legislation brought new hopes in rural India. The programme objected to provide minimum hundred days work or guaranteed employment in a financial year to every household in the rural areas whose adult members are willing to do unskilled manual work, through creation of assets by optimum resource utilisation and resource management, having regular monitoring with crystal clear transparency through social audits. "Weak Hands of Implementation" is a big responsibility in improper rearing of the programme. Majority of the zones in India is in hallucination regarding the recipes of MGNREGA. It is good to taste but has not proved to be nutritious for the rural population. The social and economic health of the rural poor is in emergency as the faulty implementation of MGNREGA has leaded a jerk in the strong spines of rural workforce. The cynical development through this act is foremost owing to lack of human resource for proper planning and management of the works to be done under each Panchayat. Thousands of hands are observed to be ready to receive the hundred days work, but the real scenario is starving from its proper implementation. A section of rural workforce saw rays of light through this programme. They expected to earn their bread and rice from income generated through MGNREGA as they belong to landless families and has to work either in the fields of landlords or migrate far in search for feeding themselves. Thereafter this programme is supposed to medicate the wounds of hunger of these workers but how far have succeeded in doing so in real terms, remains in a smoky sketch. The views of the poor landless section, the tribal, portray their living in an unstable condition though they have been facilitated by the programme. The reason lies in the fact that payment are denied to be in proper time and in certain cases proper amount as well. It has been in picture that payments are received by the people much later than the promised period of time. Thereafter, their crisis in the lean period of employment remains unaltered. Moreover, negotiation among the workers of higher castes and authority on the basis of their paid labour has been subjected by the different respondents of the opposite. " *Aki kajer jonne bamunra ashe daralei, kono kaj nakorei poisa, Amra kano kaj korbo"*— The comments of tribal workers obtain the view that the *high caste people* deny to work in the same field with them as they are section of people with more social prestige and thereafter working with the tribal in the same field crucifies their dignity. They have made negotiation in the aspect of payment, which is like, these high caste people who are official workers, "only in paper", gets a part of the total payment without giving any labour. This easy income through NREGA by this section of people creates gap and showcases caste discrimination in the society.

Moreover, the study receives a different impression in the sector of work culture from the small and middle class farmers. The section of marginal farmers who have small cultivable land are dependent on the agricultural labourers for their harvesting since they themselves remain involved in profession other than agriculture. The society views *"Weakening of the Bonds"* as well. Prior to the emergence of NREGA the rural community was solely engaged in the works as agricultural labourers. The migration opportunities of the unskilled or semi-skilled labourers from agriculture to guarantee employment has weakened and widened the bonds of relationship between the masters and labourers. The fragrance of labour—master relationship has its conversation from familiar to pure professionalism. There has been observed in the declination of dependencies on the labourers by their masters in the present day scenario. Previously, it was natural to expect from the labourers to do their works on their own eagerness and responsibility. But with their diversion of concentration to other works the responsibility of pulling out the labour rests solely on the shoulders of the masters. They are of opinion that the workers refuses to work in their fields as they are busy in NREGA work. These farmers are in a situation of dual deprivation. Foremost the workers refuses to work which make losses in their cultivation and later they are oppressed to pay extra wage along with food so that the workers agree for a particular handful of hours as they have strong objections in paying labour for the entire day. "*Ami takar sate khabar o dite raji, tao tara aste naraj. Saradiner jonne smay nei.........*"—This response depicts the helpless situation of the farmers who are dependent on labours for their cultivation. Their commercial attitude made its place not only in the terms of relationship but also in monetary matters. The wages provided to an agricultural labourer is compared to that of a Job Card holder. The masters are compelled to provide at least equal if not more to their labourers. The demand for increment of wages accelerated with time, is taking a strong shape in rural areas. Here again the middle class farmers face a hard situation. Owing to scarcity of workers the big farmers are capturing them with the demanded money in order to make their work done. This has resulted in the increase of labour wage which grows as a problem for the small and middle class farmers. It is beyond their capacity to hire labour in such high rates and so they struggle with a lack of availability of labour. The possible increasing wage rate of NREGA is more than informative news for the thinkers. The incoming of money in good quantity with a negligible extraction of labour will encourage the youth more than even before to shift the paradigm of work from agriculture. The persisting present scenario move to a future which eclipses the practice of agriculture. The groaning of this helpless section of farmers speaks of their hardships in herring labour and themselves are paying labour for their own cultivation. Thereafter, NREGA has been speedily changing the vision and mission of the rural areas. The spoon feed theory of employment by NREGA plays a significant step leading to conversion of rural work culture. The shift from the traditional agricultural labour to unskilled labour of these people has propentiated the work culture in an unbalanced reluctant landform. The present narrated condition has led to emergence of immense sufferings for the marginal farmers. The inclination of agricultural labourers into the guaranteed work with a replacement of better remuneration for less laborious work have mirrored them the situation of lack of labour for harvesting in their fields. On the other hand the cost of cultivation has also increased in a mentioning aspect. The situation leads this section of farmers to quit cultivation and transfer their occupation as labourers. The practice of traditional agriculture is into a sphere of question.

"*Chasher khorcha bere gache, r chash korbona..., Boshe-boshe taka peye jawa te chash bash r hobena...*" Many farmers feel that it is not possible to continue cultivating their lands as the labourers are getting full amount from MGNREGS without doing any work and this hampering the work culture of the labours. Certain similar responses are received who are oppressed to leave cultivation owing to the explained unavailable obstacles for cultivation. On the other hand observations enlightened the *changing behaviour of this workforce* as well. The question lies in search of a reason for such an occurrence. Emergence of unofficial dealings in work culture is a growing trend of the present century. A steady change has been noticed within the rural people regarding their criteria of choosing their work. The growing commercial attitude and greed among the people opens them to make deals and work for the individual or sector offering them with higher wage. In most of the cases of 100 days work, it has been viewed that they get money for the hours of paying labour more in this case, as per in comparison with an agricultural labour. The comparative luxurious feeding plated by NREGA have attracted the rural youth to such an extent that they are now dangerously neglecting the home made recipes of agriculture. The hard work, struggles throughout the day in field, which once were their identification are now have become options in case of unavoidable situations. The rural youth argue over part-time working in guaranteed employment rather than a full day wastage of their hard labour in these two spheres of work, with an average equal standards of payment, that have encouraged the rural workforce to accept this bold step. These 'ready to make' recipes of NREGA have challenged the existence of working capabilities of the people as they have been spreading rust in the bones of the rural workforce.

The greed, luxury and the acceptance of the famous concept "*Ye dil mange more……*" have led the rural work force to be in shady to access the longitudinal longevity of their happiness. This changing and replacing working patterns gives a smoky future of Indian work culture as unlike others the performance of this programme will also be history in near future.

Considering the area of NREGA it is shameful to say that the delivery activities of the Panchayat through this scheme is mere construction and reconstruction which was supposed to be asset creation. Thereafter, the areas will be saturated with such activities. Ruination of asset creative activities, shrinks the possible sustainable development in the society, and gave birth to, a self-dressed objective of *'just'* utilisation of the received money by the Panchayats. The then made up attitude have led to expel the thought of planning for asset creation, ultimately exhaling the fragrance of sustainable development, which was supposed to be another objective of the particular scheme.

"taka tar zero balance dekhate hobe ja asheche ..., Ki bhabe korbe amar janar dorkar nei ... " This is the opinion of a Panchayat Pradhan of a Gram Panchayat. The head of the Panchayats are forced to show the zero balance in their account due to the pressure of the higher authority. Rapidly the works, assets creation, development are all done in verbal discussions and computerized by skilled manual manipulators. The made up records shows a clean picture of performance of Panchayat is qualitative and quantitative aspect with proper and complete utilisation of the received money and mentioning number of mandays. But in reality the fate of the commoners lie in the broken roads, waterless ponds, barren unirrigated lands, and with days of unemployment. The scheme was also responsible to meet the cost of unemployment allowance but the response of the criteria remained in papers and its need in starving stomach. The eyes views unemployment and distress but the manipulative written record succeeds in hiding its manifestation. The mannerism of viewing a fact in the present society is pillared by authentic proofs. Thereafter, we are fortunate enough that mechanism of technology of present century gives a mark free finish in hiding our faulty administration. The moral of

implementers and future fate of the ones implemented upon, is mortgaged and sold time to time in auction.

Another interesting feature can be canvassed in this subject of study that is the concept of "*Money in the air*" have developed an increasing trend of '*epicureanism*' other than being lazy and opposing hard work among these youth, the rural workforce. According to Earnet Angels law "with the rise of income proportionate expenditure on food will decrease and proportionate expenditure on other personal needs will increase". Epicureanism is entertained by adopting urban habits, and indefensible affinity towards modern technology. This section of rural workforce is indicated to become unstable with additional energy of unproductive financial assistance by the government. The regular practice of income through negligible exercise of labour will lead them to an unorganised position which in future will cost their living when the scheme fails to provide money or lacks its funds.

Gradually the growing number of workers will face a hard rock living standard. The then scenario depicts a miserable picture of these labourers as when fail to receive or earn. These workers will have to starve for a handful of rice as they have already spoiled their working capacity in fields for that of being engaged in a much less laborious work of this programme for a long time. It might lead to a circumstance where these emerging changes in work culture closes their prospects of income of the workers either by fate on stagnation of the programme by their own lazy attitude of continuing their traditional profession as agricultural labourer.

Conclusion

The success of NREGS depends on overall proper implementation according the guidelines. Yet Government of India is trying to eradicate poverty and generate employment opportunity but till now the process is not satisfactory. Government has to improve the fund release process so that the work should not be stopped any more. Political leaders also have to understand the necessity of this Programme for overall development of the society. Strength of the Gram Panchayat by appointing staff is also very necessary to implement this scheme properly. To make this scheme successful it is very necessary that social audit team should work properly and rural people as well as beneficiary of this scheme also be needed to involve themselves in proper monitoring and physically verifying the scheme.

Undoubtedly, the MGNREGA can surely change the landscape of poverty in a specified area within a specific time frame. If properly implemented, this programme can also bring a sea change in the geography of poverty. In order to cope up various rebellious activities and movements, effective development can be the most confident way for retaliation. The water, the soil, the forest are associated with the life of mankind from the dawn of civilization. Thus proper utilization of these natural resources in an integrated and holistic way ensures overall development and peace. Undoubtedly, Purulia is marching towards its noble vision and mission.

References

Ambasta, Pramathesh, Shankar, P.S. Vijay and Shah, Mihir, (2008), Two Years of NREGA: The Road Ahead, *Economic and Political Weekly,* February 2008.

Bassi, N. and Kumar, D.M.; (2010), *NREGA and Rural Water Management in India: Improving Welfare Effects*, Occasional Paper No. 3-0910, Hyderabad: Institute for Resource Analysis and Policy, September 2010.

Basu, A.K.; (2011), Impact of Rural Employment Guarantee Schemes on Seasonal Labour Markets: Optimum Compensation and Workers, *The Journal of Economic Inequality*, USA: Springer, May 2011.

Central Employment Guarantee Council; (2010), Report of the Working Group on Planning and Execution, Government of India, New Delhi.

Datar, Chhaya; (2007), Failure of National Rural Employment Guarantee Scheme in Maharashtra, *Economic and Political Weekly,* August 2007.

Dreze, Jean (2005), Employment Guarantee: Promise and Demise; *Yojana*—A Development Monthly; Vol. 49, April 2005.

Dutta, P., Murgai, R., Ravallion, M. and Dominique, M.V.; (2012), *Does India's Employment Guarantee Scheme Guarantee Employment?*, Policy Research Paper, Washington, DC: World Bank.

Ghosh, Gopi Nath (2008), NREGS Transparency and Accountability; *Yojana*- A Development Monthly, Vol. 52, August 2008.

Ghosh, J.; (2009), *Equity and Inclusion through Public Expenditure: The Potential of the NREGS*, New Delhi: Paper for International Conference on NREGA, 21-22 January 2009.

Indumatib, S. and Srikantha, P.M.; (2011), Economic Analysis of MGNREGA in the Drought–prone States of Karnataka, Rajasthan and Irrigation–dominated State, *Agricultural Economics Research Review*, Vol. 24.

Khera, R.(ed); (2011), *The Battle for Employment Guarantee*, New Delhi: Oxford University Press.

Khera, R.; (2011), *Wage Payment: Live without Pay?' in The Battle for Employment Guarantee*, ed. R. Khera, New Delhi: Oxford University Press.

Ministry of Rural Development (MoRD); (2008), *The National Rural Employment Guarantee Act 2005 (NREGA): Operational Guidelines 2008*, Government of India.

Ministry of Rural Development (MoRD); (2009a), *Guidelines on expanding the scope of works under Schedule1 Para 1(g) to include construction of Bharat Nirman Rajiv Gandhi Seva Kendra (BNRGSK)*, Government of India.

Ministry of Rural Development (MoRD); (2009b), *Guidelines for implementation of works on individual land under NREGA*, Government of India.

Ministry of Rural Development (MoRD); (2012), *MGNREGA Sameeksha, An Anthology of Research Studies on the Mahatma Gandhi National Rural Employment Guarantee Act, 2005*, Ministry of Rural Development (MoRD), Government of India, New Delhi.

Ministry of Rural Development (MoRD); (2010), *Guidelines for Convergence: Leveraging NREGA for Sustainable Development through Inter-sectoral Convergence*, Ministry of Rural Development, 2009-10.

Ministry of Rural Development (MoRD); (2012), *Report of the Committee on Revision of MGNREGA: Operational Guidelines*, New Delhi: MoRD, 2012.

Narayanan, Sudha; (2008), Employment Guarantee, Women's Work and Childcare, *Economic and Political Weekly*, March 2008.

Notification No. 684-RD/NREGA/18S-1/06 dated 02/02/2006. Government of West Bengal, Department of Panchayats and Rural Development, Jessop Building (1st Floor) 63, NS Road, Kolkata. 700001.

Puri, Manohar (2006), The NREGA: Rural People to Grow with The Nation; *Kurukshetra—A Journal on Rural Development*; Vol. 54, No. 6, April 2006.

Shah, Mihir; (2008), Governance Reform Key to NREGA Success, The *Hindu*, 13/14/2008.

Shah, M.; (2009), Multiplier Accelerator Synergy in NREGA, *The Hindu*, 30 April, 2009.

Singh, Puran (2006), National Rural Employment Guarantee Scheme—A Task Ahead; *Kurukshetra- A Journal on Rural Development*; Vol. 54, No. 7, May 2006.

Singh, Raghuvansh Prasad (2008), Two Years of NREGA; *Yojana—A Development Monthly*, Vol. 52, August 2008.

The Gazette of India; Ministry of Law and Justice, September 7, 2005.

Verma, S.; (2012), *Labour Market Dynamics in Post-MGNREGS Rural India*, Unpublished report shared with the Ministry of Rural Development (MoRD).

West Bengal Human Development Report, 2004.

6
Tribal Development

Introduction

India, a welfare state, devoted to the idea of democratic socialism, aims at providing a minimum desirable standard of living to every citizen without any sort of discrimination. In order to meet this avowed objective, the whole developmental process is directed not only towards the advancement of resources, but also towards their equal distribution, so that every citizen of India can get the impact of development and his due share in the national wealth. This process involves safeguard of weaker and vulnerable section of society by state, in order to bring them closer to the normal living standard of their fellow citizens by overcoming their helplessness caused by their social and economic backwardness. Keeping this goal in view, various legislative and welfare measures for the upliftment of these sections have been envisaged in the Indian Constitution, in the form of various concessions and special benefit and protection are provided to them to raise their position in the social ladder as well as in their economic advancement.

The Tribal populations are the aboriginal or indigenous inhabitants of our country and are found in all parts of India. For centuries they have been living a simple life based on the natural resources and developed cultural patterns congenial to their physical and the consequent social environment. This community actually originates from one of the oldest ethnological section of population, lives in isolated areas as distinct group—both culturally and ethnically, and is usually backward—socially, educationally and economically. Because of distinct way of living, pattern of behaviour, customs and traditions, the programmes for their development ought to be in consonance with the social realities of their life. With these reasons, various Governmental Programmes/schemes—both from Central and State are being designed and implemented for the upliftment of their lot, so that they may join the mainstream of national life.

After independence, Government of India has provided special provisions for upliftment of Schedule Tribe (ST) and Schedule Caste (SC). Many Constitutional safeguards were provided for the welfare, development and protection of SCs and STs in the country like; Article 14—Equal rights and Opportunities, Article 15—Protection against discrimination on the grounds of caste, religion, race, sex etc., Article 46—Educational and Economic interests of Weaker sections, Article 275(1)—Grants-in-Aid for promoting the Welfare of STs and raising the level of administration, Article 330, 332 and 335—Stipulates reservation of seats in Lok Sabha, Legislative Assemblies and Services, Protection of Civil Rights (PCR) Act, 1955 and Prevention of Atrocities (POA) Act, 1989—Protection of STs and SCs from social discrimination like untouchability, exploitation and atrocities. Development programmes for STs have been formulated with the object of improving their social status and providing them with educational and economic opportunities through the efforts of Centre, State Governments and Voluntary Organisations. Since independence, the developmental efforts followed in the earlier five year and annual plans of the Centre and State governments adopted main strategies of social empowerment, economic empowerment and social justice through welfare and developmental schemes/programmes. Economic empowerment of STs has been carried out through provision of income generation activities like grants, loans, and subsidies, construction of infrastructure facilities for agriculture, irrigation and community welfare. The social empowerment is being carried out through educational development and promotion by the implementation of various schemes/programmes like Post-Matric Scholarship, Pre-Matric Scholarship to the ST students, Hostels for ST boys and girls studying in middle schools, higher secondary schools, colleges and universities, Coaching and Allied scheme by providing special pre-examination coaching, upgradation of merit for ST students by providing them facilities for all-round development through education in residential schools, Top Class education for meritorious ST students in reputed educational institutions for higher/technical education.

Concept and Definition of Tribe

Tribal are a self-control unit, they establish a society themselves, shares a common territory and demarcated as a special economic, political as well as social sphere. Different terms have been popularized by different authors for calling these groups. *Aborigines* or *Aboriginals* are the terms which connote that they were the first or original inhabitants of the land, having original habitat, native to the soil or indigenous. While Risley, Grigson, Elwin, A.V. Thakkar prefer this term, Dr. Ghurye calls them "so called" Aboriginies or Backward Hindus. The Hindi word *adivasi* is having the same connotation as *Aborigines*. Hutton calls them "Primitive Tribes". Some people, however, dislike the term aborigines or *Adivasi* and prefer the term *Vanavasi* (Forest Dwellers) or *Girijan* (Mountain Dwellers) which indicates the "nature" of their present habitat or that in the immediate past. The term "primitive" has also been used by different authors with different meanings. While some use it just to indicate tribal groups. Other used it to indicate a lower level of acculturation amongst tribal group. Thus a primitive tribal group should mean a relatively more backward tribal group which is still nearer to its original cultural level. The Government of India has recognized some tribal groups, as being "primitive", and special plans as well as grants are sanctioned for their development.

Classification of Tribal Population in India

For the sake of convenience and study the tribal people of India have been broadly classified on different bases.

Classification based on region: Geographical or regional distribution forms the first base. On this basis the following five regions are considered:

1. *North Eastern Region*: It consists of Assam, Arunachal Pradesh, Mizoram, Nagaland and Tripura. The tribes in this region include the Garo, Kuki, Mizo, Khasi, Munda, Sema, Nagas, Riyang, Miri, Apa-Tani, etc.
2. *The Sub-Himalayan Region*: It includes north and north-west India, Himachal Pradesh, the major tribe being Gujar, Gaddi, Theru, Jaunsari, etc.
3. *The Central and East India*: It consists of West Bengal, Bihar, Orissa, Madhya Pradesh and Uttar Pradesh. The tribes covered are Baiga, Bondo, Juang, Kol, Khond, Santhal, Uraon, Ho, Munda, Lepcha, Korwa, Bhils, Pahadiya, etc.
4. *South India*: It includes the States of Tamil Nadu, Kerala, Andhra Pradersh and Karnataka. The main tribes included are the Tod, Kol, Kadar, Chenchu, Koya, Gonds, Cholanaiken, Gadaba, etc.
5. *Western India*: Includes Rajasthan, Gujarat and Maharashtra and the tribes included are the Bhils, Garasia, Gonds, Kolams,

Pardhans, Korku, Koli, Thakar, Katkari, Warli, Pawra, Munda, Kol, Khond, Dubla, etc.

Classification Based on Language: Another classification is based on language spoken which is assigned to various language groups. These are:

1. *Austric Language Group:* The tribes speaking languages from this group include Kol, Munda, Khasi, Nikobari, Korku, Santhal, Gadaba, etc.
2. *Tibeto-Chinese Language Group*: For examples the Naga, Khasi, Kuki, Miri, Mizo, etc.
3. *The Dravidian Language Group*: The Gonds, Toda, Kolam, Koya, Pardhan, Uraon, etc.
4. *The Indo-European Language Group*: The Bhils, Warlis, Thakurs, Koli, etc.

Classification Based on Ethnic Root: One more classification is based on the ethnic roots of the tribes. The more predominant are:

1. *The Mongoloid Origin*: The Nagas, Mizo, Sema, Jaunsari, Apa-Tanis, Tharu, etc.
2. *The Proto-Austroloid*: This group usually speaks the so-called Kherwarian or Kaularian languages and includes the Munda, Ho, Bhils, Pahadia, Korku, Korwa, Baiga, Gonds, etc.
3. *The Negrito*: We usually recognize them as being of Dravidian origin and include Toda, Kota, etc.

Historical Background of Tribe

Tribal did not emerge automatically as a special group. From the ancient history they focus themselves as a special group of people having some backward features, with different types of name, somewhere as "*Santhal*", somewhere as "*Munda*", etc. About two thousand years from 800-600 B.C. of Indian history only few scattered references about the tribals are revealed. We cannot trace exactly and only have to belief on historical tales, myths, short histories of the locality or the region by the folk people who help us to know the unrecorded past of tribes. As because of tribal people migrate from one place to another place, so it is quite difficult to trace their original location of living. For instance Mundas before setting in the sixth century B.C. (Roy, 1992) had stayed a number of places. It is believed that Azamgarh (Eastern Uttar Pradesh) was the ancient home of Mundas.

Tribal are the integral part of the Indian civilization. Various involvements of Indian civilization were contributed by the tribal. They are existed from the time of Aryan and Non-Aryan of pre-historic era. After entering into India, Aryans found some others (non-Aryan people) and called them *Dasyus.* The word *Dasyus* means peoples who are not belonging from the Aryan category. The *Dasyus* of Vedic antiquity, non-Aryans, are of two types—Kolarians and Dravidians. The Mundas and Santhals of the present age are considered as the descendants of the non-Aryan Kolarians Stock.

On the other hand Gonds and the Kondhs (Kandhs, etc.) are considered as the representative of the Dravidians. Both the Kolarians and the Dravidians came into the land at a prehistoric period far interior to the Aryan from two opposite directions, the Kolarians from the East or North East, the Dravidians from the North West. It is tough that the Kolarians came first and after spreading in the present north eastern Himalayan region and Bengal, encountered the Dravidians which is currently somewhere in the Vindhya region. The Kolarins being broken up by the tide dispersal in the valleys and forests of Vindhya high lands. The Dravidians marched ahead and settled in the south.

The *Ramayana* also tells about some tribal people. It states about two types of tribal people one is Aryans and another is non-Aryans. Among the non-Aryans important tribes were *Rakshasas* and *Vanaras* both being the aboriginal tribes of Deccan. There are other tribes also they were *Nishadas*, the *Grdhrajs*, the *Sabaras*, the *Yaksas* and the *Nagas* (Vyas, 1967:24). The *Rakshasas* are regarded by (Vyas, 1967:13), as the earliest inhabitants of Sri Lanka. The members of Ram's army were the Vanaras, they usually reside in the jungles and *Guhas* and they helped Ram to rescue Sita.

Even not only in the *Ramayana*, the *Mahabharata* also tells about few tribes. It is also believed that Lord Shiva took the form of Kirata and meets Arjuna. Here, the form of Vedic period Kirata is known as the non-Aryan tribes, they reside in the mountains of Himalaya region. In *Mahabharata* the Kouravas army mentioned Mundas, as one of the most important constituents of their army.

From the early time of India it is shown that tribes are either compromising with the Hindu neighbours or went further in the deep forest. All through the contact for long centuries with the Hindu neighbours, the tribal find themselves assimilated to an extent with the Hindu culture. Ghurye (1963:18) had discussed in details and opines that almost all the so called aboriginal tribes of the region have a Hinduized section, small or large that they have been in fairly intimate contact with the Hindus for a long time, and they have common interest with the Hindus in the matter of religion and gainful occupation. Several studies indicate that in the Hindu period of Indian history due to interactional situation between them and their Hindu neighbours they have had to assimilate most of the major Hindu traditions. During this period they had more or less good mutual relation.

Features of Scheduled Tribes

Among the tribes, scheduled tribes are the most important part and second largest group of backward classes, unprivileged sections and are marginalized. They lived in forest, mountain, rocks, and valleys, commonly known as *Adivasis* and they are the original inhabitant of India. Gandhiji called them '*Girijans*'. The Constitution of India also referred to them as 'Scheduled Tribes'. According to the Scheduled Tribes Modification Order 1956, there are 414 different types scattered all over in various States of India.

The specification of tribes and the tribal communities as "Scheduled Tribes" arose only after the construction of the Constitution. The list of Scheduled Tribes was prepared in 1950. The primitiveness and backwardness were being tested to apply them for specifying Scheduled Tribes. The main characteristics which are common to all the Scheduled Tribes considered:

(i) *Tribal Origin*: Tribals have more kin-oriented societies, and the nature of social solidarity, they maintain, is mechanical. In their society, there is less hierarchy and no economic specialization. Tribe itself is a basic unit of society. It possesses four main qualities—*Distinctiveness, Smallness, Homogeneity* and *Self-Sufficiency*.

(ii) *Primitive way of living:* Tribal people possesses a primitive way of living, they reside in the hamlets and did not want to access something new. They follow their own cultural tradition to continue their territory. Now-a-days society is modern and every commodity is easily accessible. But the tribal are far away from this. Even they want to stay with their own primitive way, they don't want to put something new in their livelihood. But few of them emerge automatically and become the part of modern speedy society by lagging behind their own primitive way of living.

(iii) *Habitation in remote and less easily accessible areas*: Most of the time it has been seen that either tribal people reside in forest, mountains or far away from the society, even they did not accept themselves as a part of modern society. Either they have to depend on the fertility of the soil or forest product for their livelihood. Even they did not come to take the minimum need of their life, they eventually visited hospitals or Block offices or some other Government offices which are made for them.

(iv) *General backwardness in all respects:* Tribal shows their backwardness in case of education, health status, living standard, etc. They did not take education as a special need for livelihood development. Health status is also not improved due to consumption of mal-nutritious food, and also 'biri' and 'alcohol', even women also used to take these products without any hesitation. Average lifespan among the tribal is 50-60 years. Backwardness is seen in case of adopting techniques. They are not well equipped with the modern technology, modern system of living, etc. Even they did not show their interest to overcome from the problem they feel in every step of their life.

The term *"Tribe"* has not been defined in the Constitution of India. The term "Scheduled Tribe" was inserted in the Constitution vide Article 342 (i), which empowered the President of India to specify the tribes or tribal community by public notification. The scheduled tribes have been specified in 27 State/Union Territories under Article 342(i) of Indian Constitution.

Economic Situation of Scheduled Tribe

Tribals are considered as the special group of people whose socio-economic structure is different with the non-tribal or advanced group of people. They have a very simple technology which fits well with their ecological surroundings and conservative attitude. They practice different types of occupations to sustain themselves and live on marginal economy.

There are some basic features of the tribal economy these are as follows:

1. *Small Economy*: Small economy lies within the area where the number of community is hundreds or thousands. It is a fundamental characteristic of primitive life. Most (but not all) of the resource goods and service transactions take place within a small economy.

2. *Simple Technology*: In relation to the modern technology the tribal is much simpler and crude, Tools that are either made by themselves or are acquired for a fee from craftsman or from manufacturing groups.

3. *Geographical or Cultural Isolation*: The tribal people mainly live in the forest or scheduled areas and maintain their distinct culture. They are not agreeing to adopt the non-tribal trend for developing their economy.

The profit motive in economic dealing is generally absent. The role of an incentive is fulfilled by a sense of mutual obligation, sharing and solidarity. Co-operative and collective endeavour is a strongly developed feature of their economy. The rate of innovation, internal or induced is very low and consequently they are stable and make hardly any progress. There is an absence of technological aid in a tribal economy which results in inefficient, inadequate or even wasteful exploitation. The manufacture of consumer rather than capital goods is common and the same are consumed, nothing being saved or exchanged in trade.

Some Fundamental Characteristic of Tribal Economy

Forest Based Economy

Tribal economy is generally based on the forest and sea for coastal tribes. The simple technology and the absence of technological aids is the other structural feature of the tribal economy. Tribal people have a close and intimate relation with the forest. Their economy revolves around the forest. The tribal people fulfil their requirement from the forest with the help of simple equipments made by them; they did not depend on other technical aid. They collect honey, fruits, timber, leaves and other NTFP and MFPs. Even they make roof of houses by using forest products.

The Birhors of Bihar, the Chenchus of Andhra Pradesh, the Juangs of Orissa, the Kadars of Kerala, Paliyans and Panians of Tamil Nadu, etc., depend on the forest and in this area flora and fauna predominates as the primary source of food. Even the agriculturist tribe like Munda and Oraon, and the Ho of Chotanagpur depend on the forest, to an extent that is nearly half (46%) of their economy (Rai, 1967: 98).

The Bhils of Western India depend on forest for 'Mahua' and 'Biri' leaves to a great extent (Nath, 1960). The basket maker Mahalis of Bihar get the bamboo as raw material from the forest they inhabit. The pastoralist Gaddis of Himachal Pradesh depend on forest for the pasture of *dhar* for their flock consisting of goats and sheep (Pal Singh, 1965:11).

Simple Technology

Tribal used simple technology for cultivation, hunting, etc. They made their simple equipments by their own and used these equipments. They are actually far away from the modern technology adopted by the non-tribes.

The Birhor tribes, (a forest dwelling community) use ordinary jungle knife to procure forest raw meterials. Rope making is manually done. The hill cultivators like Malers and Ao-Nagas use very ordinary axe for felling trees. They mainly engaged in shifting cultivation which requires hard labour but gives less return. Munda, Oraon who are actually agriculturist tribe used plough which is made of single piece of wood and cannot plough deep. The artisan type Lohars use an ordinary type of *bhatti* and hammer for their work.

Absence of Profit in Economic Dealing

Profit making is quite absent in case of tribal. The barter system fulfil ones requirement but does not give any profit. The mutual obligation and extension in free of cost help the labour and give very marginal profit at all.

Community as Cooperative Unit

The co-cooperativeness is the main characteristics which have been seen in case of tribal people. They depend on the mutual interdependence. Among the Munda, Oraon, Ho, Santhal, Gond Bhil, etc., tribe has close economic relation. Most of them are involved in gazing the cattle, working in shifting and settled agricultural field, for their economic interest which is common for all.

The young boys go with their cattle jointly especially for defence and security. The tribes are seen in the muddy field jointly at the time of transplanting paddy. They transplant each other's field on a reciprocal basis. The Birhors exploits the forest for raw materials in group, and collect the fibres on the family level, trap the hares or monkeys collectively. The Chenchus of Andhra Pradesh collect honey in a group of 10 people.

In Jharkhand or Bihar tribes migrate jointly to West Bengal in search of jobs at the time of ploughing or harvesting jointly.

Unit of Production, Consumption and Pattern of Labour

The tribal people believe in the familial or domestic way of production. The family is unit of production. The family is engaged in this work. According to the sex and age the total work load has been distributed among themselves. Whether the member is husband or wife, parents or children together form the production unit. They produce what actually they need for their consumption. Even they get cooperation from the neighbours also. Generally heavy works are done by the adult male member of the family and females do the work which has not any typical work load like digging out the roots, collection of fire woods, etc.

The family is often unitary in its productive process so that the whole job from extraction of natural resources to procurement of the consumable goods is done by the family itself. The family is entitled and empowered to act as an autonomous unit. Among the hill cultivators like Maler of Santhal Pargana, each member of the family is engaged somewhere in the economic activity. The Artisan tribe Mahali engaged in basket making. The skill is transmitted from father to son. Husband, wife and their children all keep themselves attached to this work. Big baskets are mainly prepared by males. The Mahali female prepares winnowing fans and mat lining. The children help their mothers in their domestic chores.

The following description of the activities of the tribal men and women illustrate the extent of division of labour among the Indian Tribes. In the Ho tribe making of embankments, bows, arrows, nets and fishing implements, baskets, hunting, felling of trees, thatching of houses, harvesting, threshing, oil crushing, propagation and collection of lac, etc., are some of the jobs assigned to men. Woman carry loads, take the surplus produce for sale to the weekly market and engage themselves in rope making, fishing and preservation of fish, making walls, weeding transplanting paddy, fetching rearing of children. Children look after the birds, lend cattle, fish in shallow water, collect Mahua and lac and help their mother in rearing their younger siblings.

Gift and Ceremonial Exchange

Giving gift and hospitality is an important part of their economy. According to Dalton (1971:53) "The mode of transaction which does exist widely among the tribes is reciprocity, i.e., material gift and counter gift giving induced by social obligation derived typically from the kinship".

Periodical Market

Tribal people exchange their commodities made by themselves or purchase something new from the outsider market, somewhere it is known as *Hatt*, somewhere as *Bazar, Pithia, Shandies*, etc. Generally these markets are held within 5 to 10 km of the inhabitant areas. These markets are most powerful channels of communication in the tribal region.

Actually these places are not only for selling or purchasing goods or products. It is also a place of meeting with their native friends, villagers, relatives. Here people from different groups come, not only for economic purpose but also secular and religious activities in the tribal region takes place.

The mode of economic transaction is barter and native goods, i.e., produced in the region like foodgrains, local hand woven clothes, baskets, etc. and case for non native goods produced in the urban region or outside of the region like salt, cloths, readymade cloths, cosmetic soaps, etc. The whole business enterprise runs in the tribal area within the framework of the weekly market which is a regular phenomenon of the tribal life. Thus it can be easily concluded that the weekly market is the mirror of tribal culture in India in general

Interdependency

Level of interdependency is high among the tribal community. It is quite similar with the *Jajmani* system. The people belong to upper class is known as *Jajman* and the family or head of the family server is known as *Kamin* under *Jajman. Jajman* payed his kamin in cash or kind in daily/weekly/monthly basis prevailing in rural India though, it is not called for the *Jajmani* system as such.

In middle India the village Lohar or Kamar of Bihar and West Bengal sharpens the plough shares of the entire agriculturist like Munda (Vidyarthi, 1966) Oraon, Ho, Bhumij, etc., for which he receives some of paddy annually or some grain per plough or implement. The Mahalis and Doms fulfil the demand for bamboo baskets and other such materials of the area.

Constitutional Provision for Scheduled Tribe

It is quite a well-known fact that tribal people is a group who are recognized as the backward community of our society from the British colonial period. Even today also the tribal scenario has not changed up to the level of expectation.

The Indian Constitution specially provided certain Article in the Constitution for the improvement of the Tribal community from all aspects and also to protect them from the oppressions caused by the other people of the society. The protective rights granted by the Indian Constitution, 1950 to the tribal people can be classified under the following heads:

- Educational and Cultural Rights [Article 15(4), 29, 46 and 350].
- Social Rights (Article 23 and 24).
- Economic Rights (Article 244 and 275).
- Political Rights [Article 164(1), 243, 330, 334, and 371].
- Employment Rights [Articles 15(4), 16(4), and 16(4A)].

In addition to these rights Fifth and Sixth Schedule of Indian Constitution completely deals with the tribal people.

To Protect Educational and Cultural Rights of Tribes

Article 15(4)

(i) Prohibition of discrimination on grounds of religion, race, caste, sex, place, place of birth or any of them.
(ii) No citizen shall, grounds only of religion, race, caste, sex, place of birth or any of them, be subject to any disability, liability, restriction or condition with regards to:
  (a) Access to shops, public restaurants, hotels and places of public entertainment.
  (b) The use of wells, tanks, bathing ghats, roads and places of public resort maintained wholly or partly out of State funds or dedicated to the use of the general public.

Article 29

It guarantees to any section of the citizens residing in any part of India having distinct language, script or culture of its own, the right to conserve the same, i.e., language, script or culture. A minority community can preserve its language, script or culture by and through educational Institutions (Including Scheduled Tribes).

Article 46

The State shall promote with special care the educational and economic interests of the weaker sections of the people and in particular of the Scheduled Tribes and Scheduled Castes and shall protect them from social injustice and all forms of exploitation.

Article 350

The Constitution also gives rights to every person to submit a representation for redress of grievance to any officer or authority of the Union or a State in any of the languages used in the Union or in the States as the case may be.

To Protect Social Rights of Tribal

Article 23: Prohibition of trafficking of human being and forced labour.

Article 24: Prohibits employment of children below the age of 14 years in factories and hazardous employment.

To Protect Economic Rights of Tribal

***Article 244*:** Special administration of scheduled areas and tribal areas.

***Article 275*:** Special grants from the Union to certain states to undertakes schemes of development for promoting welfare of tribal.

To Protect Political Rights of Tribal

***Article 164(1)*:** Other special provisions like appointment of ministers to look after the tribal interest exclusively.

***Article 243*:** It deals with the reservation of seats for Scheduled Castes and Schedule tribes in the House of People and Panchayat.

***Article 334*:** Provides that nothing in this article shall effect any representation in the house of the people or in the legislative assemblies of the States until the dissolution of the then existing house or assembly as the case may be.

Article 371: It deals with the special provisions with respect to the States of Sikkim, North Eastern States.

In a significant judgment, a five judge bench of the Supreme Court has held that a person belonging to Scheduled Castes or Scheduled Tribes, bearing the same nomenclature (name) in two States is entitled to the rights, privileges and benefits only in the State of his origin but not entitled to those rights and benefits in other States where he migrates subsequently, though they are specified in the Scheduled Castes or Scheduled Tribes list of the State (Article 341 and 342).

To Protect the Employment Rights of the Tribal

Article 15(4)

Reservation in favour of Scheduled Tribes or Scheduled Castes for the purpose of advancement of socially and educationally backward citizens to make them equal with other segments of community.

Article 16

1. There shall be equality of opportunity for all citizens in matter relating to employment or appointment to any office under the State.
2. No citizens shall on the grounds of religion, race caste, sex descent place of birth, residence or any of them be ineligible for or discriminated against in respect of any employment of office orders of the State.

Article 16(4)

No one has the right to prevent the State of making any provision for the reservation of appointments or posts in favour of any backward class of citizens, which in the opinion of State is not adequately represented in the services under State.

Approaches of Tribal Development in India

The proper meaning of development should be development from various aspects. The two aspects for crucial change in any society especially for tribal are:

- Identification and Screening of existing resources, and
- Mobilization of those resources for utilization in a sustainable manner.

Even after screening and identifying the existing resources and allocating resources to viable projects, the question of motivation of tribal for change still remains. Along with this problem are the other bottlenecks in the programme implementation such as lack of political will among the elites or the decision-makers, leakage at all levels of functionaries, lack of interdepartmental co-ordination, and lack of committed personnel to work in tribal areas for implementation of tribal development programmes. Thus motivation of tribal and bringing about awareness among them becomes an imperative objective for any efforts of modernization of tribal. The most important task in all tribal development programmes is to development awareness and consciousness which includes diffusion of information about local administration, institutions, relevant legislations, rights and responsibilities of tribal citizens and the necessary informations regarding the changing programmes. Various endeavours have been taken for tribal development by the Government as well as by various Voluntary Organizations from the time of Pre-independence.

Pre-Independence Period

The approaches for tribal development in India on eighteenth century based on the certain events happened in various places of the country. Till the beginning of eighteenth century the tribals were allowed to inhabit independently by following their own way of living, their culture, traditions, etc. Outsiders were afraid of entering into the areas where the tribal inhabitants were administering for themselves. The programme of conservation and preservation of forests resulted in progressive encroachment on the rights enjoyed by the tribal. The extension of a centralized administration during British period resulted in exploitation of tribal by *Zamindars*, *Muttandars*, landlords, moneylenders and the forests contractors to the maximum. In 1765 the Chotanagpur become a part of territory conceded to the British. The situation aggravated further when the Maharaja of Chotanagpur began granting villages on temporary lease. These lease holders ousted the aboriginals from their village. The first entry of the British into the region took place in 1772 when the Maharaja requested them to help in revenue matters.

Their entry resented and the tribal become restless and revolted against the landlords several times during 1789, 1797, 1807, 1812, and 1820. These revolts were, however, suppressed. Various Tribal Development Approaches in pre-independence period are:

Administrative Reforms—Regulation XIII of 1833

The tribal revolution during 1832 converted the whole region. The suppression of riots was followed by a number of agrarian reforms to prevent tribal land from passing into the hand of non-tribals. The most important administrative reform was Regulation XIII of 1833, as a result of which Chotanagpur was declared a non regulated area, as it was considered that the regulations which were intended for the more advanced districts of West Bengal and Bihar were not suited to it. These reforms and administrative steps, however, more or less remained on paper as the tribal were totally uninformed about them and even if they knew they were too isolated to take any advantage of them (Dhebar Commission Report 1961:22).

Other Special Measures

The foundations of policy of special type of administration for under developed areas Embodied in Regulation 1 of 1796 and the idea of special arrangements for isolated tribal areas were influenced by incidents such as the disturbances of 1831, the Santhal rebellion of 1855 and other sporadic outbursts among the tribal people. The Ganjam and Vizagapatnam Act of 1839 prescribed simple and elastic forms of judicial and administrative procedures in tribal areas. Later all these areas were declared "Scheduled Districts" and their administration was conducted in accordance with Scheduled Districts Act 1874. Taking advantage of this Act, many protective regulations were enacted in various States.

The Santhal Rebellion of 1855-56 was the result of exploitation by merchants and moneylenders in their transactions with the Santhals, the misery caused by the inquisitorious system of allowing personal and hereditary bondage for debt, the unparalleled corruption and extortion of the police in aiding and abetting the moneylenders, and the impossibility of the Santhals obtaining redress from the courts (E.G. Mann, 1867). Similar outbreak of violence occurred in 1879 which is commonly known as the Rampa Rebellion in East Godavari district of Andhra Pradesh.

The Rampa Rebellion started in East Godavari district has rapidly spread to Visakhapatnam district. In the East Godavari Agency of Madras Presidency the conditions of the tribal populations were considerably improved as a result of the Rampa Rebellion (Haimendorf, 1985).

Agency Tracts Interest and Land Transfer Act 1917

The various orders passed from time to time with the view of ameliorating the conditions of the tribal population of the East Godavari Agency were ultimately consolidated in legislation known as Agency Tract Interest and Land Transfer Act 1917. In order to save the tribal from the exploitation of the moneylenders. The Act laid down that:

(i) Interest on any debt or liability shall not as against a member of a hill tribe be allowed or decreed at a higher rate than 24 per cent per annum nor shall any compound interest or any collateral advantage be allowed against him;

(ii) The total interest allowed or decreed on any debt or liability as against a member of a hill tribe shall not exceed the principal amount. Even more important were the sections restricting the transfer of land from tribal to outsiders. Haimendorf opined that "these sections of the Act of 1917 should, if fully implemented, have put a stop to all alienation of tribal land (Haimendorf, 1985);

Again a series of disturbances and movements took place such as Sardari agitation, Birsa movement, Thana Bahagath movement, etc., between 1887 and 1914. In the primary states, as the tribal were dissatisfied with the rulers who wanted to protect themselves in the name of protecting tribal. This resulted in creating "wholely excluded area and area of modified exclusion" as part of Government of India Act 1919. The administrations of these areas were removed from the purview of the legislatures but the limits of exclusion differed in their extent and degree.

Simon Commission (1928)

Slowly the tribal were drawn into National Freedom Movement creating anxiety on the part of the British administration to isolate the tribes from political contagion. Consequently, the 'excluded areas' and partially excluded areas incorporated in 1935 Act as per the recommendations of the Simon Commission (1928). This was the first landmark in affording political reservation to tribal and a few other sections of Indian population. Further, it was declared for the first time that no Act of then Federal Legislature or the provincial legislatures would be applied to these excluded areas except on the direction of Governor, who was empowered to make such exceptions and notifications as he considered necessary. It also enabled the Governor to make regulations of the peace and good government of the areas, but such regulations required the assent of the Governor-General. Reservation of seats for tribal was made in the local legislature of Madras, Bombay, Bihar, Assam and Orissa.

In drawing up the scheme of exclusion under Section 91 of the Government of India Act 1936, the Secretary of State indicated that the areas to be placed in the category of "Excluded areas" must be based upon strict necessity and be as limited as possible in scope consistently with the needs of the tribal population (The Government of India 1935). In regard to areas classified as "partially excluded" there should be no hesitation to include in the category any area containing a preponderance of tribal which was of sufficient size to make possible the application of special legislation ad special administrative treatment. In spite of these measures indebtedness and land alienation continued unabated and took new forms like debt bondage reducing many tribal to virtual slavery to non-tribal immigrants (Pratap, D.R., 1980). To mitigate this situation, the Madras Debt Bondage Abolition Act was passed in 1940 for tribals living in the agency tracts of the present Andhra Pradesh. The situation of tribal in Hyderabad State in the early 1940s as described by Christoph Von Furer was that large forest areas where tribal communities persisted in relative isolation from more advanced population. However, transfer of land from the tribal to non-tribal was an ongoing process. There were no officials especially concerned with the welfare of the tribes and no legislation protecting tribal interests comparable to the agency Tracts Interest and Land Transfer Act of 1917, of the neighbouring Madras Presidency. Many of the cases of exploitation and oppression of tribal communities written by Haimendorf were also published by Nizams Government under the title "*Tribal Hyderabad*" (Haimendorf, 1985, p. 41).

"The culmination of the entire tribal policy of Hyderabad State was the promulgation of an act known as the Tribal Areas Regulation 1356 Fasli (1946 AD). This regulation empowered the Government to make such rules as appear to them to be necessary or expedient for the better administration of any notified tribal areas in respect of tribal and of their relations with non tribal. The substance of this regulation was incorporated in the Tribal Area Regulation 1359 Fasli (1949 AD) and the rules giving effects to its provisions were issued by the Revenue Department under the title Notified Tribal Areas Rules 1359 Fasli on 16 November 1949. A schedule annexed to the tribal areas regulation notified the area to which rules were to apply" (Haimendorf, 1985:23). These rules provided great benefits to the tribal in Hyderabad State.

Mobile courts were initiated to redress grievances of tribal. A beginning was made to stabilize economic base, initiated new process of acquiring knowledge and acquaint the tribal with democratic decision making process by tribalising the new institutions.

Post-Independence Period

Tribal development approaches after Independence: Strategies for tribal development as expressed by the Jawaharlal Nehru was "We should avoid two extreme courses one was to treat them as anthropological specimen, and the other to be engulfed by the masses of Indian humanity." He also added that "They could not be left cut off from the world as they were and development to be pursued within the framework of five fundamental principles". These are:

(i) People should develop along the lines of their own genius and the government should avoid imposing anything on them. It should try to encourage in every way their own traditional art and culture.
(ii) The rights in land and forests should be respected.
(iii) The government should try to train the tribals to do administration and development work. Some technical personnel from outside, no doubt be needed, especially in the beginning. But introducing too many outsiders into tribal territory should be avoided.
(iv) The Government should not over administer these areas or overwhelm the people with a multiplicity of schemes. It should rather work through and not in rivalry to their own social and cultural institutions, and
(v) The result should be judged not by statistics or the amount of money spent, but the quality of human character evolved.

Various Tribal Development Approaches

Multipurpose Tribal Development Projects

In 1954, 43 multipurpose tribal development projects launched as a part of community development projects. Only 5.73 per cent of the total tribal population was covered by the development projects. The norm for the establishment of tribal development Blocks was considerably smaller both in terms of population and area coverage, compared to a C.D. Block. The following criteria were adopted for the creation of tribal development Blocks:

(i) Total population should be at least 25,000
(ii) Minimum tribal concentration of 62-63 per cent in the area.
(iii) Area should be 150 to 200 square miles
(iv) Viability of the area to function as normal administrative unit.

Elwin Committee 1959

The most significant programme for the development of tribal areas is the establishment of Special Multipurpose Tribal Blocks, in consonance with Articles 46 and 275 of the Constitution. The objective of these Blocks is to bring about radical changes in the economic and social standards of the tribals. Forty-three special Multipurpose Tribal Blocks were set up jointly by the Ministry of Home Affairs and the Ministry of Community Development and Cooperation in the most underdeveloped tribal areas. There was criticism on the work of these Blocks, so a committee was appointed under the chairmanship of Verrier Elwin in 1959 with the following terms of reference:

(i) To study the working of the special Multipurpose Tribal Blocks; and
(ii) To advice the Government of India on how to implement the initiative development programme of the Blocks more effectively and give the programme a proper tribal bias.

The report was accordingly submitted in 1960. These Blocks are now called Tribal Development Blocks. A suggestion to this effect was recommended by the Elwin Committee in 1960. Besides, the Committee also recommended the opening of 300 new Tribal Development Blocks covering areas having 55 per cent tribal population, But the GoI has decided to start 330 such Blocks covering areas having 66.6 per cent tribal population. The pattern of expenditure on these Blocks, during the Third Plan is Rs. 25,000 for vehicles, Rs. 75,000 for Project Office Personnel, Rs. 0.24 million scientific lines with greater emphasis on agriculture, health, communications, education, etc. The expenditure should be framed on the recommendations of Elwin Committee as: Scheme for Economic Development—60 per cent; Communication—25 per cent; and Social Service—15 per cent. In spite of certain shortcomings, these Blocks appear to be the best approach for the welfare of tribals. The committee had remarked: "The experiment has not failed, valuable experience has been gained".

Dhebar Commission (1960)

Dhebar Commission was appointed under the chairmanship of U.N. Dhebar who submitted a detail report in the year 1961. This report critically examined and assessed the 5 tribal situations prevailing after 10 years of planned development and made several practical suggestions and recommendations. Findings of the Commission:

(i) Slow pace of development and meagre investment in the tribal areas,
(ii) The protective pleasures were sporadic and inadequate which could resist exploitation and injustice, and
(iii) Simple administrative system of these areas.

Shilu Ao Committee (1969)

After the introduction of Dhebar Commission 1960 another Commission under the chairmanship of Shilu Ao (1969) was set up. The major findings of this Committee were:

(i) A tribal Block was too small to function effectively as a basic unit for planning and implementation.
(ii) The indebtedness, land alienation, educational backwardness and inadequacy of communication were identified as the basic problem of the tribal communities and these did not receive adequate attention in the frame of Tribal Development Block.
(iii) The tribal development Block failed to get any significant

support from the general development programmes including the Community Development (CD) programme.

Suggestions

(i) The Committee suggested vigorous action to implement the recommendations of the *Dhebar Commission* as these remained unattended till that time.

(ii) The team also suggested for preparing comprehensive tribal development programme with larger resources commensurate with the size of the problem and the overall national development effort.

Panchayat Raj System—Democratic Decentralization

The provisions of the Panchayats (Extension to Scheduled Areas) Act 1996 (PESA) is not applicable to Assam and Tamil Nadu States as there are no Scheduled Areas in these States. But, the Constitution (Seventy-third Amendment) Act 1992 is applicable to these States which equally applies to the Scheduled Tribe population. As such, some of the more important stipulations especially those relating to planning would need emphasis in the context of tribal sub-plan and poverty alleviation measures. The factual position in this regard in the States of Assam and Tamil Nadu is as follows:

Firstly, Article 243A provides that "A Gram Sabha may exercise such powers and perform such functions at the village level as the legislature of a State may, by law, provide".

Secondly, in respect of powers, authority and responsibilities of Panchayat, Article 243G provides that "Subject to the provisions of this Constitution the Legislature of a State may, by law, endow the Panchayats with such powers and authority as may be necessary to enable them to function as institutions of self-government and such law may contain provisions for the devolution of powers and responsibilities upon Panchayats at the appropriate level subject to such conditions as may be specified therein with respect to:

(a) The preparation of plans for economic development and social justice, and

(b) The implementation of schemes for economic development and social justice as may be entrusted to them including those in relation to the matters listed in the Eleventh Schedule".

Tribal Development Programmes in India

Five Year Plan and the Tribal Development Programmes

The First Five Year Plan period was started in 1951. Development programmes were started in 1952 as a Community Development Programme and 56 community development projects were started. But the First Five Year Plan did not play any specific and special role toward the development of tribal areas. Various programmes were initiated with particular reference to health, communication and housing. The programme was very comprehensive and the concept was equally applicable to the tribal areas with rest of the country but very soon the government realized that the task to be accomplished in the tribal areas was much more difficult. As most of these areas comprise hilly and forest regions and sparsely populated with poor communication and little institutional infrastructure.

During the Second Five Year Plan (1956-61) recognizing the socio-economic conditions, prevailing in the tribal areas, concrete developmental schemes were planned. A novel administration system was introduced, with creation of "Multipurpose Tribal Projects in certain selected Tribal Areas" Therefore, it was decided to supplement the Community Development Programme and accordingly 43 Special Multipurpose Tribal Development (TD) Blocks were started during 1954. Special emphasis was given to education in addition to health, agriculture, communication and housing programmes.

In the Third Five Year Plan (1961-66) the Tribal Development Blocks numbered 458 and the coverage of population was 32.50 per cent. The major emphasis was given on economic development along with education, health, housing and communication. At the end of third Plan it was reviewed and revealed that the programme did not have the desired impact. Therefore, it was decided to add a third phase of five years to Blocks and desist from establishing new ones. The Tribal Development Blocks covered all the areas having more than two-third tribal populations. However, exceptions were made in case of West Bengal and Karnataka where TD Blocks were not feasible due to their dispersed nature of tribal population.

Isolated tribal populations of Karnataka were covered by the *ad hoc* tribal development projects and in case of West Bengal, Tribal Development Blocks were established temporarily for two years in each area having sizable tribal population. The coverage of tribal population in these two States was lean. By the end of Fourth Five Year Plan (1969-74)

39.37 per cent of total tribal population were covered in 504 tribal development Blocks. On the whole, the areas with more than two-third tribal populations got the benefits of this development effort. Up to the end of Fourth Five Year Plan the remaining tribal populations were derived benefits from the general development programme.

A series of programmes were introduced during the Fourth Five Year Plan Period (1969-74). Special attention was directed to individual families in addition to area based programmes. These programmes were: The Small Farmer Development Agencies (SFDA), Marginal Farmers Development Agencies (MFDA), and Drought Prone Area Programme (DPAP). In the wake of establishment of these area specific and weaker group oriented projects, the programmes for tribal area were also intensified on a plot basis. Tribal Development Agencies (TDA's) were established on the pattern of SFDA. Six TDA's were started during Fourth Plan and two more were added in the Fifth Plan. The purpose behind setting up of these agencies was for massive investment exclusively for tribal folk from central funds while making State outlays for development of both tribals and non-tribals.

For making the tribal development programme more effective and meaningful these were reviewed by special committees and commissions from time to time. Their experiences and insights enabled the planners and policy-makers to think in terms of formulating an integrated tribal development strategy with requisite intimate linkages with the national strategy of socio-economic development.

A new phase of tribal development started since Fifth Five Year Plan and may be considered as a turning point in the history of tribal development. During this plan period the concept of Tribal Sub Plan (TSP) within the broad frame of state and central plan took concrete shape. The Fifth and Sixth Five Year Plan periods are also remarkable as it was the first time when anthropologists, development administrators and policy-makers joined together to review the earlier policies and programmes and devised way for launching the new one for the welfare of the tribals specifically.

The Tribal Sub-Plan strategy comprises:

(a) Identification of tribal majority areas in a State/UTs and launching there integrated tribal development projects having thrust both in socio-economic development of the areas and on betterment of the highly depressed tribal families (employment, income, education, etc.);

(b) Earmarking of appropriate funds for the TSP and ensuring regular flow into it from State outlay and also from the outlays as well as credit from financial institutions for backing up some of schemes launched under ITDP;

(c) Creations of appropriate administrative structure with appropriate personnel for implementation of ITDPs.

Briefly, the concept consists of identification of development Blocks within a State having more than 50 per cent tribal population launching of massive effort for tribal development in such areas called the Sub-Plan Area. For the preparation of tribal Sub-Plan the Planning Commission issued a set of guidelines to the States. The guidelines spelt out the long-term objectives of the tribal sub-plan as:

1. Narrowing the gap between the levels of development of tribals and other areas.
2. Speeding up the processes for social and economic development.
3. Building up the inner strength of the people.
4. Improving their organizational capabilities.

Thus, the guidelines laid down the criteria for identification of the sub-plan areas, approach and strategy for development and also the pattern of funding and formulation of programme in these areas. The guidelines also stated that the sub-plan areas in each State should comprise a number of viable projects. Such unit of planning is an Integrated Tribal

Table 6.1: Plan Outlay and Expenditure for Tribal Development Programme in India

Sl. No.	*Plan Period*	*Total Plan Outlay (Rs. in crores)*	*Tribal Development programme (In crore)*	*Percentage*
1.	First Plan* (1951-56)	1,960	19.93	1.00
2.	Second Plan* (1956-61)	4,672	42.92	0.60
3.	Third Plan* (1961-66)	8,577	50.53	0.60
4.	Annual Plan* (1966-69)	6,756	32.32	0.50
5.	Fourth Plan** (1969-74)	15,902	75.00	0.50
6.	Fifth Plan** (1974-79)	39,322	1,182.00	3.01
7.	Sixth Plan** (1980-85)	97,500	5,535.00	5.67
8.	Seventh Plan** (1985-90)	1,80,000	12,000.00	6.67

Note: *Expenditure, **Outlay.

Source: Ministry of Home Affairs, occasional papers on tribal development, 1996, pp. 1, 19-20.

Development Project (ITDP) in a State, comprising an aggregate of Development Blocks. The ITDP is being smaller than a district and bigger than a Block. The lowest unit of performance of the programme is the Development Block. It has a development team with the Block Development Officer as its leader. Programmes have to be planned for an ITDP in the shape of a sub-plan for the tribal region of the State. Guidelines laid down that the planning should be based on the needs of the area and the people, and hence, the process has to be commenced at the grass root level, i.e., the Development Block and funnelled upwards to the ITDP, State and National level.

Scheme of Development of Primitive Tribal Group (PTGs)

Among scheduled tribes, there are certain tribal communities who have been declining or are in stagnant population, low level of literacy, pre-agricultural level of technology and are economically backward. Total 75 such groups in 17 States and 1 Union Territories have been identified and categorized as Primitive Tribal Groups (PTGs). States/UT-wise list of PTGs is at Annexure. Most of these groups are small in number, have not attained any significant level of social and economic progress and generally inhabit in remote localities having poor infrastructure and administrative support. Therefore, they become the most vulnerable sections among the Scheduled Tribes and priority is required to be accorded for their protection, checking the declining trend of their population and for their development. Such an approach may also strengthen the few MADA and such micro-projects in operation in our country.

Objective

Since PTGs constitute the most vulnerable section among tribals who inhabit in isolated, remote and difficult areas in small and scattered hamlets/habitats, the scheme aims at planning their socio-economic development in a holistic manner by adopting habitat development approach and intervening in all spheres of their social and economic life, so that the quality of life of PTGs is improved and a visible impact is made.

Scope

The scheme will cover only the 75 identified Primitive Tribal Groups. The scheme is extremely flexible because it enables every State to focus on areas that they consider is relevant to their PTGs and their socio-cultural environment. Activities under it may include housing, land distribution, land development, agricultural development, cattle development, construction of link roads, and installation of non-conventional sources of energy for lighting purpose, social security including Janshree Beema Yojana or any other innovative activity meant for the socio-economic development approach for the comprehensive socio-economic development of PTGs, more particularly for the PTGs who are nomadic in nature. Efforts should be made to bring nomadic PTGs to the settled mode of life, will be carefully addressed. The funds under this scheme would be made available only for those items/activities which are very crucial for the survival, protection and development of PTGs and are not specifically catered to by any other scheme of State or Central Government or by guidelines governing the utilization of funds under Special Central Assistance to Tribal Sub-Plan and Article 275(1) of the Constitution. The general principle of convergence of funds and functionaries will apply.

All the 17 State Governments and the Union Territory of A&N Islands shall prepare a long term "Conservation-cum-Development (CCD) Plan" for each PTG of their State in the format prescribed by the Ministry of Tribal Affairs. This CCD Plan will be prepared by the State Governments/ UT Administration for a period of 5 years, i.e., for entire Plan period on the basis of requirement assessed through Baseline Survey and submitted to Ministry of Tribal Affairs at the start of Plan period. The CCD Plan shall clearly indicate the annual provisions for each financial year and also the agency involved in implementation of that activity. While preparing the CCD Plan, the State Government/UT Administration shall also keep habitat/hamlet development approach in view, more particularly for the nomadic PTGs. The State Government/UT Administration shall ensure proportionate flow of financial resources for all PTGs found in their State and the activities shall be taken with a proper mix of interventions through the State/UT Government and NGOs. The duplication of intervention in same area shall be avoided. The delivery mechanism has to be strengthened through innovative plans and procedures.

The CCD Plan submitted by the State/UT shall be examined and approved for entire period of 5 years by an Expert Committee constituted by the Ministry. At the field level, the CCD Plan shall be implemented under the supervision of a Committee constituted by the State Government for the purpose.

The State Government implementing agencies will furnish a schedule of activities to be undertaken with the first and subsequent release of funds, and the time likely for their continuance or completion to enable effective project progress monitoring. Ministry officials will undertake field monitoring and reviews.

Implementing Agency

(a) The scheme will be implemented in accordance with aforesaid CCD Plan prepared by the State/UT through various agencies of the State Government/UT Administration like Integrated Tribal Development Projects (ITDPs)/Integrated Tribal Development Agencies (ITDAs), Tribal Research Institutes (TRIs), and also Non-Governmental Organizations (NGOs). The State Government concerned will, however, be responsible for proper execution, implementation, supervision and coordination of the scheme, including identification of NGOs for the purpose.

(b) The Ministry of Tribal Affairs can also draw up plans for the PTGs involving reputed National level bodies, including Industry Associations, and the concerned State Governments/Agencies.

Pattern of Funding

It is a 100 per cent Central Sector Scheme. The funds will be released to States/NGOs in one instalment in accordance with the annual programme proposed for a particular financial year in the CCD Plan. Funds in favour of NGOs will be released directly by the Ministry of Tribal Affairs, in accordance with CCD Plan, of the State Government, and transferred to the bank account of the NGOs.

Integrated Tribal Development Project

A Tribal Development Block has been taken up as the smallest unit for inclusion in the new programme. A group of Blocks which generally comprises a tehsil, has been taken as the basic unit for planning and development of the new tribal development programme. The unit is known as Integrated Tribal Development Project.

The qualifying minimum size of the compact tribal majority area inclusion in the TSPs was reviewed with reference to the degree of tribal concentration obtaining in different States. A minimum population threshold of 20,000 was accepted as the smallest unit in Maharashtra, Andhra Pradesh and Assam. This norm was further relaxed to 10,000 in Tamil Nadu, Kerala and Uttar Pradesh. In case of West Bengal and Tripura it was necessary to go down further and identify groups of villages for special development programmes. In Karnataka and Daman, it was not possible even to identify sizable villages of tribal concentration. The new programme in their cases, therefore, was designed entirely for dispersed tribals.

The delineation of the areas of tribal concentration was taken up in the beginning of the Fifth Plan and completed by the end of 1976. Although the ITDP was conceived as comprising a group of Blocks, the actual size varied from State to State depending on the demographic structure of the tribal community in that region. The total numbers of ITDP established by the beginning of 1978 was 180. An ITDP with more than one Block is termed as Meso Project and ITDP comprising only one Block or less than one Block can be termed as Micro Project. Out of 180 ITDPs 121 are Meso units and remaining are micro-units. The Sub-Plans and ITDPs do not include the tribal majority States and UTs and whose cases the plans of the States or UTs, as the case may be, have been taken as plans for tribal development.

However, the guidelines laid down the principles for identification of sub-plan areas, the approach and strategy for their development and also the pattern of funding and formulation of programmes in these areas. The guidelines also stated that the sub-plan areas in each State should comprise a number of viable projects. For each such ITDP an itregrated area development plan focussing specific attention on the specific problems of the area and the tribal people was to be formulated. The sub-plan areas in each State thus comprise a number of viable projects.

The unit of planning an ITDP in a State, comprised an aggregate of development Blocks. The ITDP area being smaller than a district and bigger than a Development Block appears to be more feasible for planning. The lowest unit of execution of the programme is the Development Block. It has development team with a Block Development Officer as its leader. The programmes have to be planned for an ITDP in the shape of a sub-plan for the tribal region of the State. Guidelines lay down that planning should be based on the needs of the area and the people and, hence, the process has to be commenced at the grass root level, i.e., the development Blocks, and funnelled upwards to the ITDP, State and national level.

The Programme on Integrated Tribal Development Projects (ITDP) under Tribal Sub-Plan (TSP) is being implemented since the Fifth Five Year Plan and completed by the end of 1976. A Tribal Development Block has been taken up as the smallest unit for inclusion in the new programme. A group of Blocks which generally comprises a tehsil, has been taken as the basic unit for planning and development of the new Tribal Development Programme. This unit is known as Integrated Tribal Development Project.

Since an Integrated Tribal Development Project has been accepted as the unit of Planning and Implementation at the micro level, it was also desired that the administrative boundaries should not be changed unless considering essential for the preparation of TSP, the Planning Commission issued a set of guidelines to the States.

The Long-Term objectives of the TSP were:

1. Narrowing the Gap between the levels of Development at the tribal and other areas; and
2. Improving their quality of life.

The Immediate Objectives were:

1. Elimination of exploitation in all forms.
2. Speeding up the processes of social and economic development.
3. Building up the inner strength of the people.
4. Improving their organizational capabilities.

Administrative Structure

The Block administration is being reconstructed to remove existing deficiencies and improve its capacity to shoulder increasing responsibility for implementing the various schemes of Tribal Development hanged over to it by ITDP.

The administration of ITDP has its place within the district administration. It can play an effective part in integrated area project and then in its coordinated implementation largely through the Block administration. The ITDP administration and its multi-disciplinary team of officers have thus a deliberative, advisory and supervisory role to play.

Tribal Cooperative Marketing Development Federation of India Limited (TRIFED)

The Tribal Cooperative Marketing Development Federation of India Limited (TRIFED) came into existence on 06.08.1987 and got registered under the Multi-State Cooperative Societies Act 1984 (now the Multi-State Cooperative Societies Act 2002). It started functioning in 1988 under the Administrative control of the Ministry of Welfare, Government of India, (presently the Ministry of Tribal Affairs, and Government of India).

The main objective of TRIFED is to serve the interests of its members in more than one State for the social and economic betterment of its members by conducting its affairs in professional, democratic and autonomous manner through self-help and mutual cooperation for undertaking marketing development of the tribal products.

The main activities of TRIFED as per the Roadmap of Fifth Plan period from (2007-08 to 2011-12) assigns the following four main activities to TRIFED:

1. Retail Marketing Development,
2. Minor Forest Produce Marketing Development,
3. Skill upgradation and Capacity Building of ST Artisans and MFP Gatherers, and
4. R&D Development/IPR Activity.

Presently TRIFED is marketing tribal products through 40 outlets out of which 26 outlets are its own and 14 outlets on consignment basis in association with State level organizations promoting handicrafts. TRIFED also participates in various exhibitions and fairs to promote the tribal art. Another event is Tribal Artisans *Mela*. Tribals draw sustenance and income including their requirement for food, fodder, fruits, medicines, shelters, rituals, recreations and cultural activities from the forest.

"Minor forest produce" includes all non-timber forest produce of plant origin including bamboo, brush wood, stumps, cane, *tassar*, cocoons, honey, wax, lac, *tendu* or *kendu* leaves, medicinal plants and herbs, roots, tubers and the like. TRIFED envisages upgrading the skills of MFP gatherers For skill upgradation and Capacity Building of ST Artisans:

TRIFED Imparts Three Levels of Trainings

1. Primary Level Training (PLT),

2. PLT-cum-Design Workshop Training followed by Reinforcement Training (PLT-DWTRT),
3. Design Workshop Training (DWT), and
4. TRIFED has established a Quality Control Research and Development Centre at NSC Beej Bhawan, IARI Campus, Pusa Complex, New Delhi 110012.

Its R&D Centre is equipped with modern/sophisticated instruments to test and certify internal samples like Spices, MFPs like Honey and Tamarind, Dry fruits, Herbal Products, Processed Meat and fish products.

Tribal Sub-Plan (TSP)

A strategic policy initiative to secure overall development of the STs, was first introduced in the Fifth Five Year Plan. The focus of TSP is on "securing budgetary allocations for tribal development at least proportionate to their population, in order to bring them at par with other sections of society and to protect them from exploitation."

Main Objectives of Tribal Sub-Plan

1. Substantial reduction in poverty and unemployment of the STs.
2. Creation of productive assets in their favour and provide them with livelihood opportunities on a sustainable basis.
3. Human resource development of the STs by providing adequate educational and health services.
4. Provision of social, physical and financial security to them against all types of exploitation and oppression.

Tribal Sub-Plans Financed through the resources drawn from—

(a) State Plans.
(b) Special Central Assistance of Ministry of Home Affairs (Now Ministry of Welfare).
(c) Central and Centrally Sponsored programmes, and
(d) Institutional Finance.

Tribal Sub-Plan Approach Includes

(i) Integrated Tribal Development Projects comprising generally administrative units like Sub Divisions/Districts/*Tahsils/Taluks* with 50 per cent or more Scheduled Tribe population.

(ii) Pockets of having a total population of 10,000 or more and a Scheduled Tribe population of 50 per cent or more.

It was decided that tribal majority States like Arunachal Pradesh, Meghalaya, Mizoram, Nagaland, Lakshadweep, Dadra and Nagar Heveli may not need a tribal sub-plan as the entire plan of these States/Union Territories was primarily meant for ST population constituting the majority. For the second category of States/Union Territories tribal sub-plan approach was adopted after delineating areas of tribal concentration. A similar approach was adopted in the case of States and UTs having dispersed population by paying special attention to patches of Tribal concentration, keeping in view of their tenor of dispersal. To handle the tribal population coming within the new TSP strategy in a coordinated manner, Integrated Tribal Development Project (ITDP) for the substantial tribal areas, Modified Area Development Approach (MADA) for pockets having a total population of 10,000 and ST components of 50 per cent or more and special projects for primitive tribal group (Micro Projects) were conceived and adopted.

The seventeen States namely, Andhra Pradesh, Assam, Bihar, Gujarat, Himachal Pradesh, Karnataka, Kerala, Madhya Pradesh, Maharashtra, Manipur, Orissa, Rajasthan, Sikkim, Tamil Nadu, Tripura, Uttar Pradesh and West Bengal and Two UTs, viz., Andaman and Nicober Islands and Goa, Daman and Diu are implementing the Tribal Sub-plan through the approach of ITDP. Five per cent Tribal population was covered till the end of Fifth Five Year Plan. A new approach of MADA in Sixth Plan and micro project for primitive tribes has helped in bringing the coverage of tribal population about 75 per cent.

Modified Area Development Approach (MADA)

Modified Area Development Approach (MADA) came into force at the end of Fifth Five Year Plan in a group of villages having 10,000 inhabitants or more where 50 per cent are tribal. By the end of the year 2001-2002, 46 MADA projects covering parts of 47 Blocks of 17 districts and 5,67,071 tribal population. For their welfare individual benefit oriented schemes are implemented in the ratio of 70 per cent and 30 per cent outlay respectively under special central assistance provided by

Government of India. The achievements made under the scheme during 2001-2002 (till December 2001) were as follows:

(a) Amount utilized under S.C.A. for M.A.D.A. Blocks Rs. 82.80 lakh.
(b) Beneficiaries assisted Rs. 1403 ST families.

Special Central Assistance to Tribal Sub-Plan

The Special Central Assistance (SCA) is provided by the Ministry of Tribal Affairs to the State Government as an additive to the State TSP. SCA is primarily meant for family-oriented income-generation schemes in sectors of agriculture, horticulture sericulture and animal husbandry cooperation. A part of SCA (not more than 30%) is also permitted to be used for development of infrastructure incidental to such income generating schemes.

Special Central Assistance (SCA) is intended to be additive to State Plan efforts for tribal development and forms part of TSP strategy. The objective of the strategy is two folds:

1. Socio-economic development of STs.
2. Protection of tribals against exploitation of the above, SCA primarily funds schemes/projects for economic development of STs.

The GoI Guidelines Broadly Lay Down the following Norms

SCA is primarily meant for income generating family oriented schemes and infrastructure incidental thereto (not more than 30 per cent of the total outlay) wherever a scheme is provided for any Central Sector/ Centrally Sponsored Schemes (CSS), SCA should not be utilized for the same. Rather, the allocations available under specific schemes can be availed of Major infrastructure development should be supplemented from the TSP flow, rather than being catered out SCA like roads, electrification, etc. Schemes for funding demonstration units should not be financed out of SCA. Rather, the follow-up of demonstrations should be catered to looking for the Special disadvantaged tribal groups.

Tribal population below poverty line should alone be supported with SCA financed activities. In any specific schematic projects financed by outside agencies, both national and international, normally a part of the outlay is proposed as State Government contribution. Such contribution should flow from normally State Plan and not out of SCA.

Wherever, State Government Organizations like Tribal Development Cooperative Corporations (TDCCs) or Forest Development Corporations (FDCs) are dealing with schemes related to tribal welfare and development, the equity based should not be financed out of SCA, without prior approval of the GoI. This will lead to better monitoring of the concerned activities. Specific sectors related to the Tribal need to be givers a fillip by special schemes in the areas like sericulture, horticulture, etc., out of SCA.

Wherever, conjunctional flow of funds can be ensured from other on-going development programmes, this must be dovetailed so as to have a better spatial and demographic coverage.

National Scheduled Castes and Scheduled Tribes Finance and Development Corporation (NSCFDC)

National Scheduled Castes and Scheduled Tribes Finance and Development Corporation was bifurcated to form a separate National Scheduled Tribes Finance and Development Corporation (NSTFDC). It is a fully owned Government of India Undertaking and its managed by board of directors with representation from Central Government, State level agency, financial institutions and persons representing Scheduled Tribes, etc.

Objectives

1. To provide a linkage between SC/ST poor families and financial institutions.
2. To provide financial assistance at concessionary rates for income generating activities both in farm and non-farm requirement.

By the end of December, 96 NSFDC has assisted 2.13 lakh beneficiaries to the tune of Rs. 314.2 crore.

Educational Development of Scheduled Tribes

The percentage of literacy among the scheduled tribes which was 1.5 per cent at the time of independence has gone up to 47 per cent as per 2001 Census and female literacy rate increased to 34.76 per cent as per the 2001 Census. As the rate of literacy of the tribal people and SC people is comparatively low. Therefore, Government takes up the matter seriously and adopts a comprehensive approach for their educational development.

Educational Development during the British Rule

The British took over the educational organization of the time, as the most effective ones and extended their support to them. The system was completely dependent on the individual initiative of able and leading persons. Its social and economic characters were marked with wealth and power. The old indigenous rural academies of the *gurus* were admitted to the financial assistance of the Government. The authorities were obviously very selective at the initial stages of admitting any institution to financial assistance.

The role and responsibility of the Government in furthering the education of the people were being seriously studied by the imperial authorities of the British at the beginning of the Nineteenth Century. By the middle of the century the British democracy was moving nearer to State Policy of Education and was gradually becoming a state concern to British democracy at home.

The initiative of Sir George Campbell, the Lieutenant Governor of Bengal in 1871, to align the Government with the exclusive education of the existing upper strata of our caste and communal society remains there as a historic step in the matter of education. Sir Campbell may be regarded as the founder of the modern primary education in Bengal. The imperial concern for the education of the Indians of their choice was exposed in the setting up of an education commission in 1882 by the Government. The Commission recommended that the "elementary education of the masses, its provisions, extension and improvement should be that part of education to which strenuous efforts of the State should be directed in a larger measure than before".

After bringing primary education under Government supervision, the Government of Bengal appointed an expert committee to suggest a scheme for secondary and primary education which would free the students from the stereotype. They recommended that "object-lesson teaching should be introduced". Education broke from its traditional mooring and took the western shape and character of formal training. The Government measures were always directed in such a manner as to accommodate the prosperous and the prospective vernacular schools of the local initiative. The role of the rich, both rural and urban, in educational ventures could hardly be overestimated.

Educational Development in Post-Independence Period

For the development of education among the tribal community following initiatives were taken by the Government of India. These are:

1. *Rajiv Gandhi National Fellowship*: To provide financial assistance for ST students for pursuing higher studies leading to M.Phil. and Ph.D.
2. *Ashram Schools*: To promote education among STs living in remote areas.
3. *Book Grants*: Provide text books to the students or the equivalent value for purchasing books.
4. *Pre-Matric Scholarship*: Pre Matric scholarship programme has been initiated for the students who belonging from 5 to 10 class.
5. *Post Matric Scholarship Scheme*: This scheme is initiated for the students who have passed Matric examination and continuing their education either in class XI or graduation or students from any other technical courses or law students, etc.

Government of India has launched various educational programmes for the development of the Tribal Community. Post Matric scholarship is one of them which give extra support in the higher education of the tribal community. Besides the scholarship facility this scheme also provides many additional allowances like book bank facility, tour charges, hostel facility, etc. Post Matric Scholarship is totally centrally sponsored scheme under the Ministry of Tribal Affairs for the tribals. The main objective of this scheme is to provide financial assistance for the higher education of the tribal students after Matriculation.

Candidates who after passing one stage of education are studying in the same stage of education in a different subjects, e.g., B.Sc. after B.A. or B.Com. after B.A. or M.A. in other subject will not be eligible. Students who have completed their educational career in one professional line, wish to study for another profession, e.g., L.L.B. after B.T./B.Ed. will not be eligible. From the academic year 1980-81, however, studies in two professional courses are allowed.

Students studying in Class XI of Higher Secondary Schools which have a continuous school course of 12th class will not be eligible.

However, in cases where the X class examination of such courses is treated as equivalent to Matriculation and students after passing tenth class can join other courses, such students will be treated as post Matric students and will be eligible for the award of scholarships.

Students pursuing Post Graduate courses in medicine will be eligible if they are not allowed to practice during the period of their course. Students who after failing or passing the Under Graduate/Post Graduate examinations in Arts/Science/Commerce join any recognized professional or technical certificate/diploma/degree courses will be awarded scholarships if otherwise eligible. No subsequent failure will be condoned except courses in *Group 'I'*, and no further change in the course will be allowed.

Students who pursue their studies through correspondence courses are also eligible. The term correspondence includes distant and continuing education. Employed students who take leave without pay for the entire duration of the course and study as full time students will be eligible for scholarships.

From the academic year 1980-81, employed students whose income combined with the income of their parents/guardians does not exceed the maximum prescribed income ceiling are made eligible to Post Matric scholarships to the extent of reimbursement of all compulsorily payable non-refundable fees.

All children of the same parents/guardians will be entitled to receive benefits of the scheme. Scholarship holder under this scheme will not hold any other scholarship/stipend. If awarded any other scholarship/ stipend, the student can exercise his/her option for either of the two scholarships/stipends, whichever is more beneficial to him/her and should inform the awarding authority through the Head of the Institution about the option made. No scholarship will be paid to the students under this scheme from the date he/she accepts another scholarship/stipend. The student can, however, accept free lodging or a grant or *ad hoc* monetary help from the State Government or any other source for the purchase of books, equipment or for meeting the expenses on board and lodging in addition to the scholarship amount paid under this scheme. Students who have already received coaching in any of the pre-examination training centre with financial assistance from the Government will not be eligible. The students whose annual family income is less than Rs. 2,00,000 are eligible for this scholarship.

Livelihood Pattern: Transition from Traditional to Modernity

Livelihood development is defined as adequate and sustainable access to income and resources to meet basic needs. The livelihood pattern of the population throws a searching light on the economic and social life of the area. Livelihood approaches are a way of thinking about the objectives, scope and priorities for development. They place people and their priorities at the centre of development. They focus poverty reduction interventions on empowering the poor to build on their own opportunities, supporting their access to assets, and developing an enabling policy and institutional environment. The Sustainable Livelihood approach defines livelihoods as the capabilities, assets (including both material and social resources) and activities required for a means of living. Livelihood strategies are the combination of activities that people choose to undertake in order to achieve their livelihood goals. These include productive activities, investment strategies and reproductive choices. Livelihood approaches try to understand the strategies pursued and the factors behind people's decisions to reinforce the positive aspects of these strategies and mitigate against constraints. The choice of strategies is a dynamic process in which people combine activities to meet their changing needs.

The central aim of enhancing economic productivity of India is to improve the overall welfare of majority of Indian households who are living below poverty line. Livelihood development lies at the very root of a society. It is the watchword especially in the context of poverty alleviation and rural development because rural poor especially the tribal people are too unorganized and powerless to be individually able to better their lot in societies. The benefits of growth failed to trickle down to the poor who are often marginalized if not excluded from the mainstream of development process. Developing rural poor enhances the self-confidence, dignity and self-determination capacity of tribal people to eliminate the implicit and explicit socio-economic disadvantages and thereby provides a means to improve the effectiveness of development policy initiatives and programmes.

Agriculture is the primary source of income for the majority of the population of India. More than 76 per cent of the rural population depend on agriculture and allied activities. Agriculture dominates the economy to such an extent that high proportion of working population of India is engaged in agriculture. Therefore, in such a country, agricultural development should form the foundational for national development. Since the mid-sixties the traditional agricultural practices are gradually being replaced by modern technologies and farm practices in India and veritable revolution is taking place in our country. This marked the beginning of the new era of modernization of agriculture with increased emphasis on capital inputs. The introduction of modernization in farming, the extension of irrigation facilities and the revolutionary improvement in agricultural practices through the use of chemical fertilizer, HYV seeds, etc., have resulted in widespread increase of production. While traditional agriculture relies heavily on indigenous inputs such as organic manures, seeds, simple ploughs and other primitive agricultural tools, bullocks, etc., agricultural modernization thus involves the use of modern agrarian technology in the form of improved varieties of seeds, chemical fertilizer, pesticide, extensive irrigation and improved machineries has since long been introduced in the tribal and rural areas of West Bengal, primarily with a view to raise the level of income, standard of living and lifestyle of the rural and tribal people. It was also intended to raise the level of national income by increasing agricultural production.

Tribal population constitutes a considerable percentage in our country. The tribals in our country are known as *Adivasis* in the ordinary usage of the term. In general, it is applied to the people, who are considered primitive and who live in backward areas and do not know the use of writing. Tribe, in the *Dictionary of Anthropology* is defined as "a social group, usually with a definite area, dialect, cultural homogeneity, and unifying social organization. It may include several sub groups, such as sibs or villages. A tribe ordinarily has a leader and may have a common ancestor, as well as patron deity. The families or small communities making up the tribe are linked through economic, social, religious, family or blood ties". Broadly, tribe is an aggregate of people sharing social values, common dialect, territory and culture. Tribals are observed to be away from the modern civilization and remain in natural surroundings and in small, sometimes autonomous communities. However, with the process of extension of infrastructural facilities such as education, health, banking, transport and communication, the isolation of these people is gradually breaking and their contract with the outside world is expanding. The largest concentration of tribal people anywhere in the world, except perhaps Africa, is in India. There are about 250 tribal communities in India. Agriculture is the primary source of livelihood for the overwhelming majority of the tribal population in the country. The setting of problem of agricultural development in the context of agrarian transformation, has added importance concerning the tribals, because the role of both land

and forest claimed high place in resurgence of the tribal economy hitherto. May be that both these economic sectors shared the overall responsibilities to provide subsistence economy to the tribal people on the sustainable base, because of primitive technology of production operative in farming practices mainly followed by the tribal farmers as direct technology of extensive cultivation. Plot rotation is followed in shifting cultivation and crop rotation in settled cultivation. Agriculture based tribal economy is now a more important sector to break through the subsistence level of the downtrodden tribal people after the nationalization of forest, in the early fifties. Although not all the classes of the tribals are seeking their livelihood from settled cultivation as quite a large number of nomadic tribes are almost on the wheel of their bullock carts or on the back of their domestic animals and are on their move from one place to another as vagrant group of nomads. Therefore, they earn their livelihood by roaming from one place to another.

The economy of the tribals is primarily rural and agriculture based and allied activities constitute their mainstay. Agricultural modernization has since long been introduced in the tribal areas of West Bengal, primarily with a view to raise the level of income, standard of living and lifestyle of the tribal people The Santal is one of the largest tribal communities in India and also in West Bengal. The Santal of West Bengal is broadly known as an agriculturist tribe. In agrarian sector, the Santals are mainly marginal and small farmers and cultivate for their own consumption without hankering after profit. Very few among them practice commercial agriculture and others are involved as landless agricultural labourer or day labourer. Their involvement with the modes of production as well as production relations, also with their distribution and consumption patterns is somewhat different from other sections of Indian population. Some of the Santal families have adopted modern agricultural technology in the form of using shallow tube wells, chemical fertilizers, High Yielding Varieties of seeds, power tillers, tractors and so on. But this innovation can be found in a patch of Santal areas having tiny lands. Greater portion of Santal agriculture is, however, still to achieve the spectrum of modernization. But somehow, the Santals are getting the benefit of agricultural modernization one way or other. From this point of view, in the present study, attempts have been made to know the extent and nature of socio-economic changes among the Santals due to agricultural modernization. Attempt has also been made to grasp the nature of the tribals' outlook on life in the changing context.

Government Efforts for Tribal Development

Since independence, considering the general socio-economic backwardness of the tribal communities, Government of India has been planning and launching programmes to develop and integrate them with the mainstream of Indian national life. To sustain the Constitutional safeguards given to them, Government adopted so many programmes through the Plan periods. The Fifth Five Year Plan is considered as the turning point in the history of tribal development in the post Independent India for the launching of Tribal Sub-Plan. Initially it was an area development programme. But in the subsequent plan periods it was becoming a target group approach where individual family was to be benefited specifically from the programme to build up their economic base. The objective of assisting the targeted number of tribal families is to cross the poverty line and to increase the access to health, education and employment opportunities and thereby to improve their quality of life.

In the course of tribal development approaches in the post independent India the Fifth Five Year Plan may be mentioned as the turning point for the launching of Integrated Tribal Development Programme (ITDP). ITDP was launched in the year 1972. During Sixth Plan, emphasis was placed more on family oriented programmes than on infrastructure development. Thus, from the Sixth Plan period it was becoming a target group approach where individual families were to benefit specially from the programme. During the Seventh Plan Tribal Development with ITDP pattern was continued without any basic changes in the approach, pattern or structure. In this plan period thirty lakhs tribal families were assisted to build up their economic base. The Eighth Five Year Plan gave emphasis on development of essential infrastructure facilities to achieve the objective of assisting the targeted number of tribal families to cross the poverty line and to increase their access to health, education and employment opportunities. These families were selected on the basis of their absolute economic status, the poorest being given the first preference.

In West Bengal, ITDP was introduced in the year 1983. A good number of tribal population is under these schemes. Various kinds of schemes have been introduced for them. Some of the schemes are meant for agriculture; some are employment and income generating schemes. From the field investigation, it was noticed that some beneficiaries are conducting the schemes successfully and in some cases schemes have failed. However, there remain some factors for non-feasibility of the loans.

From the very beginning of the tribal development, it was realized that no development activity could be of benefit to the tribal population unless their exploitation was prevented and an integrated credit cum marketing services was developed in the sub-plan areas. Hence, elimination of exploitation was given priority in objectives of Tribal Sub-Plan. Priority was also given to do away with middlemen and the moneylenders. But elimination of exploitation has limited success. In spite of financial assistance through ITDP loans, private sources are also being used by the tribal people side by side. Private sources are still standing between the development agencies and the beneficiaries as an alternative.

Changes in Sources of Credit Needs

Though the tribals are getting benefit from institutional sources of Integrated Tribal Development Programme, most of the beneficiaries are taking loans from different informal sources. They used to borrow money from the private moneylenders; local assemblers (*aratdar*), and the landowners. Among them, the tenant cultivators are most numerous, followed by the agricultural labourers. Here, in most of the cases the landowners are the neighbouring Caste Hindu people, in whose land the landless tribals are working as agricultural labourers round the year, sometimes generation after generation, the share croppers sharing lands with them and at the rest of the time working as agricultural labourers on their lands. On the other hand some take loans from their friends or relatives. Some borrow money from other sources, like the owner of Saw Mill, Rice Mill, Brick Kiln, etc. where they work as labourers. So, inspite of having the benefit of getting loans from the government sources, the tribals take loans from various informal sources. The main reason behind it is that the government do not provide loan for consumption purposes, which is very much needed for their daily survival. On the other hand, the loan from non-institutional sources is easily available without any formalities.

Despite having a wide network of rural banks in the country and implementation of credit linked poverty alleviation programmes, a large number of rural poor specifically the tribals who constitute a significant number, continue to remain outside the fold of formal banking system. Various studies suggested that the existing policies, systems and procedures often did not meet the needs of the hard-core and assetless poor.

The extension and development departments are fast realizing the significance of providing financial services to the poor, providing opportunity to save and access credit. Credit, if appropriately delivered, is attractive to the poor, financially viable and self-sustainable. Extension departments and NGOs also realize the limitations of formal Banks and the strengths of informal money lending, which unfortunately is exploitative. Hence, efforts have been made to learn from banks and the moneylenders, and create alternative models for credit delivery; which are simple, efficient, non-exploitative, financially sustainable and self-managed. Accordingly, the idea of Self-Help Group has developed. The experience in developing countries shows that provision of small credit to the poor through the linkage process has contributed to the process of rural development by creating conditions that are conducive to human development. It is reported that significant changes in the living standards of SHG members have taken place in terms of increase in income levels, assets, savings, borrowing capacity and income generating activities. Moreover, the participation of tribals in the economic activities and decision making at the society level is increasing and is making the rural development process participatory, domestic and sustainable.

Changes in Indigenous to Modern Trends in Agriculture

Agriculture is the main source of income for the majority of the Santals. Earlier, they used to practice traditional method for agriculture. Their technology was indigenous. But now they are adopting modern technologies like shallow tube-wells, pumpsets, power tillers, threshers, sprayers, and so on. They are also using HYV seeds, chemical fertilizers, pesticides, etc. to achieve better yield. For irrigating their lands, earlier they were entirely dependent on monsoon rainfall and thus only one crop (monocrop) was cultivated. But the introduction of pump-sets and shallow tube-wells has brought changes in their modes of production. Now they are cultivating double crops sometimes triple crops. Those farmers who do not have pump sets or shallow tube-wells, they hire it from the other sources for irrigation purposes and get the benefit. Thereby, the irrigation facility is gradually increasing. Land tilling and threshing is being done in the mechanized way by most of the Santals. Earlier those were done by bullock power and manual labour. A substantial percentage of households have threshers and sprayers. On the other hand, all the Santal households are now using high yielding variety of seeds, chemical fertilizers, pesticides, etc. to increase their yield. There have occurred many changes in the aspects of their social organizations and cultural activities. A spartan glance can be given to get nature of changes taken place among the Santals due to the adoption of agricultural modernization. The cultivation of Santals was normally subsistence in nature. Now this tendency is decreasing. Commercial nature of farming has been gradually taking place among the mechanized farmers. The market orientation is also increasing among the Santals.

Income and Employment Generations

Income, employment and wealth generation is taking place among the Santal mechanized farmers. In the existing cropping pattern the Return Over Variable Cost per acre (ROVC/acre) is high, so the income is increasing. Due to the modernization in agriculture the cropping intensity is increasing and the farmers are engaged in cultivation round the year and get a substantial income from the occupation. Due to increase in income, the Santals are obtaining a substantial amount of wealth, which was negligible earlier. For the cultivation purpose, before the mechanization, they mostly used family labour. Hired labour was very few and the payment was in kind or in exchange. Now, due to the mechanization in agriculture, hiring in labour is gradually increasing and mode of payment is in cash not in kind. Family labour in agriculture has been steadily replaced by hired labourers among the mechanized tribals and occupational diversification is taking place more and more. The entry of agricultural modernization, education, better transport facilities and communication enabled the villages to develop certain skills. The Santals have definitely developed some skills which enabled them to give up their old work of hunting, gathering and cutting of wood. The skills which they have acquired are now being used for any development purposes.

Income distribution is crucial in the sense that this would give an overall idea of the level of living. Most of the mechanized farmers are marginal and small farmers. Very few percentages of households have large quantity of land. It has been found that the higher landholding households have higher average incomes. On the other hand, due to the mechanization in agriculture, the average income is higher among the mechanized households. Due to the higher annual income, the standard of living is better among them.

Change in Education

The tribals were very conservative in assessing the relevance of present education in life. They experienced that those who got education at the school turned out to be useless. After completing education they did not do any manual work, though the schools increasingly provide facilities to the tribal people. Having enjoyed the facilities, when a Santal turned home after completing his school education, he found himself completely alienated from his own village, his clan and his kin. He had little inclination to work in the field and to perform manual work. To a Santal, education, thus, became irrelevant. Relevance of school education for a Santal arises only when they are assured in entering into the government services. It is only from then he would allow his son to continue his education. The use of education as he understands today is for government employment only. They feel that the reservation in services is sufficient to get employment if one is just educated.

The Santals, despite their dismal views on education, have accepted schooling for their children. It is due to the hope that if educated they would get some opportunities of service as government reservation policy is there. The tribal mechanized farmers are getting the benefit of the government policy and the advantage of education more. The literacy and level of higher education is highest among the mechanized farmers even among the tribal women. The illiteracy is highest among the landless category of people. It has been found that the tendency towards higher education is increasing. Most of the old members of the tribal community are illiterate. But due to the effect of agricultural modernization, they are now coming forward. They are trying to give education to their children. Now they are aware about the government reservation policy and they think that if their children get education then they can get government services and be better off in the larger society.

Expenditure Pattern

Expenditure pattern is the most important indicator to understand the level of living. Earlier, the Santals used to expend most of their incomes for food. But due to the increase in income and awareness they are now spending money for other durable consumer goods, education, health care, etc. Savings tendency has also been developed. Food is the basic necessity of all living beings, and consists of several components. During the course of the study it has been observed that with an increase in income, the amount of money spent is proportionately lesser on grains, and more on oils and fats, vegetables, meat, fish and eggs. They are also spending the money for recreation purposes. After the satisfaction of demand for food, the mechanized farmers make efforts to fulfil the needs of clothing and housing. Other necessities like health, education, travel, fuel, ceremony, etc. come later. Some percentage of money is spent for luxury goods. The Santals are habituated in liquor. But after mechanization and increase of income the expenditure on intoxicants like liquor is gradually decreasing. The mechanized farmers are not only expending the money for consumption purposes but also expending some percentage of their income for education, health purposes and even for some other income generating activities, which is the most remarkable change. The conspicuous consumption expenditure is increasing with income augmentation among the mechanized farmers.

House Types (Wallart)

The tribals used to live in forests or river banks. Their housing conditions are normally not good, made by mud with thatched roof. Now, the housing condition is developing, as they are getting more production from agriculture. There are three types of houses found in the tribal villages—*kutcha*, *pucca* and mixed. The *kutcha* structure usually has mud walls, *kutcha* floor with mud plaster and the roof thatched with straw. The next stage of improvement in the structure is the replacement of thatch on the roof by corrugated iron sheets, cement flooring and the walls are made of bricks. These houses are mixed type. And finally the *pucca* houses are those which are made of brick, cement and masonry.

Almost all the non-mechanized and landless farmers live in *kutcha* houses. Among the mechanized farmers, many houses are mixed and a few percentage are living in *pucca* houses. Due to the agricultural mechanization and improvement of agriculture among the tribal farmers, the housing condition is improving.

Family Structure

Structurally, the Santal family is different from the regional family of the caste Hindus. The Santal, like other Mundari groups of tribes in India, is characterized by a segmentary social system based on kin groups-lineages and clans. Though the traditional nature of their segmentary social system has been attenuated to a great extent, the idiom of groups based on kinship is still of paramount importance for a proper understanding of the social structure of the Santal. Among the Santals, families formed of the marital union of a man and a woman and the children born of them constitute their primary kin group lineages, in term of their genealogical connection to a common ancestor. The lineage groups are again merged into still larger kin groups based on common descent. These descent groups locally termed as *paris*, together forms the society of the Santal.

Both types of families namely joint and nuclear have been found among the tribal people. Nuclear family is based on monogamy, i.e., marriage of one man with one woman. The married couple together with their children forms a nuclear family. On the other hand, when several individuals through the father's or the mother's line live together with their respective wives and children, they form joint family. The joint family must have a common head, common kitchen and share of common residence. Among the Santals, it has been found that the percentage of nuclear family is higher than the joint family. In the Santal community, when a grown up son marries, he separates from his parents and establishes his new family. The separation is complete when the son and the father do not work on the common farm; a separate piece of land is allotted to the son for his maintenance on which he alone operates. Nuclearisation or individualization is increasing slowly but steadily. Family structure is gradually diversified to nuclear one and attachment to the family is diminishing.

Health and Hygiene

Now-a-days the general health condition of the Santals is far better than before. Earlier they suffered from malnutrition and always were depended on indigenous medicine or *ojhas*. The sense of personal hygiene among the Santals is very poor. Malnutrition and uncleanly habits have made the Santals victims of several diseases. Main complaint is about their anaemic condition. During the rainy season, they generally suffer from ulcers, eye-ache and stomach-ache. Malaria is also rampant during this season. Both males and females suffer from these diseases. The only remedy they seek is from the tribal quacks or *ojhas*.

Now among the Santals the awareness regarding health and hygiene is increasing. Due to the modernization in agriculture, their income has increased and they are consuming better foods. They are going to hospital for treatment and some percentage of money is spent for medical care. They are also keeping themselves clean. Most of the mechanized households have separate kitchen and separate cattleshed facilities. A good number of households also have latrines. These facts show the increase in awareness among the tribal regarding health and hygiene and their stepping towards a better living as a community.

Cosmo Politeness

Earlier the Santals were a non-political entity. They lived in the hills and forests of the region and hardly had any contacts with the princely rulers. The Santals have a long tradition of managing their village affairs through traditional Panchayats. In olden days, the traditional Panchayats were the only means through which disputes were settled and justice dispensed in the tribal areas. Since 1949 Gram Panchayats are being established in the rural and tribal areas through government efforts. Sometimes, there is a jurisdiction between the traditional Panchayats and the newly established Government Panchayats. Very few Santals take their cases for decision to the Government Panchayat.

Another institution which exercised some power was that of some well to do Santal families of the village. Though there is less of stratification in the traditional tribal society, still there are some families which enjoy higher prestige owing to larger number of cattle and higher size of landholdings. Such families are known for providing resources of employment and money lending. Anytime they could stand as sureties for the late payment of land revenue or loan. Crisis situation could be met adequately with the help of these dominant families in the village. They also take part to solve the disputes.

Since independence and promulgation of the Constitution, the Santals have assumed a new status. They are supposed to participate in the national political system not only as ordinary citizens but bestowed with some special privileges and discriminations. The Constitution provides them such privileges with the idea that their involvement and participation in the political system would bring them closer to the core of national life. The Constitution envisages that the political and economic forces released by the national structures would in the end bring the tribals in the mainstream of national life.

Now, the situation has changed. The Government Panchayats have entered into the social organization of the Santals. They are now going to Gram Panchayat to settle down their conflicts. Sometimes they allow the police to come to solve their conflicts. Not only that, they also take part actively in the Gram Panchayat elections. Women are also taking part in the process. The Santals of this area are also participating in development programmers and decision-making process. Cosmo politeness has also increased. The extent of the contact with different extension personnel of the mechanized farmers has increased a lot. Though they have their own traditional Panchayat, but all the households of mechanized farmers are contacting with the village Pradhan and the Panchayat members. Few percentages also meet with the Agriculture Development Officer, Block Development Officer or higher government officials. All the mechanized farmers meet with the fellow caste Hindu progressive farmers and other institutions and take suggestions for the betterment of their production. From the above facts, it can be implicit that political awareness and Cosmo politeness is increasing with the increase of agricultural modernization.

Changes in Indigenous Santal Rituals and in Agro-Ecosystem

The Santals are ritually intricate with their agro-ecosystem. The different phases of agriculture and other allied activities of the Santals are always accompanied by some rituals and ceremonies that are held communally in the village. The Santals perform rituals and ceremonies at first in each case communally and then the households of the village are permitted to perpetuate their independent productive activities. This kind of ritual sanction, in fact, acts as a moral force in binding the households of the village into a corporate productive organization and stands in the way of complete nuclearization or individualization of the family households, their primary productive units. A number of social festivals and the accompanying communal worship are directly linked to agricultural production. All the festivals of the Santals are partly 'vegetation' ceremony and partly 'fecundity' ceremony. The invocations are remniscent of Vedic prayers for plenty and peace. But there is always the feeling that much is left to the operation of the goodwill of the gods and *Bongas*. After all they will finally determine the quality of the harvest and nothing that they can do will really change the picture. The Santal's belief is that if the *Bongas* are not properly worshipped or they are not pleased, or if for some reason they incite their wrath then there will be poor crop or even large scale failure of crop. Many cultivators in the Santal villages exhibit lazy and complacent attitude, which hinder their good crop. But now, the Santals are learning slowly from non-tribals, who are good cultivators and who do not care much for extra-rational forces of *Bongas* or gods and goddesses.

It is evident that the modernization of agriculture which demands timely intercultural operations sometimes comes into conflict with the ritualistic basis of agriculture. Here, technology and ritual must mix creating a new system of ritual flexible and liberal enough to absorb the demands of a new technology or conversely restructure the ritual. There has to be greater adaptability not only in the timing of the festivals but also as to the authority or agency who can decide on the date of different festivals. Some form of alternative arrangement for taking decisions when the proper incumbent is absent or ill, could be devised. This, no doubt, is linked to the problem of erosion of authority of the traditional religious and social leader of the village. Because deciding the dates of festivals is his prerogative and if somebody else does it, that itself would naturally mean some reduction in his social status or ritual standing. The community responsibility binds the individual and no individual cultivator, even when he resents the evil effects of non-celebration of a festival in time, is prepared to rise in revolt and declare his autonomy to decide when he will enter the field to sow or weed or do any other operation. Although, the Santal's belief that good crops are the result of proper appeasement of the gods and goddesses and bad crops or crop failure are due to their wrath is deeply entrenched in the social system and personality. But this proclivity sometimes delayed the production process and thus hinders a good harvest. The rationalistic approach to the subject—the need for proper ploughing, proper inputs, seeds, fertilizers, application of pesticides in time, proper and timely irrigation, etc., are slowly coming in but a sense of their urgency and immediate relevance are diluted by these extra rational factors. However, the production process and Santal rituals are interwoven with each other which binds their socio-economic life cycle and their agro ecosystem.

Earlier, only single crop was cultivated depending on the desire of *Bongas*. But after the adoption of agricultural modernization the tendency on depending on gods and goddesses is gradually decreasing. Now the Santal farmers go for double even triple cropping like the non-tribals. Sometimes it is not possible for them to conduct all the rituals. Not only that the educated Santals and youths do not know the names of all the ceremonies or rituals of their own community. According to them, if they follow all the rituals, then modernization in agricultural is not possible. Now the Santal youths are also interested with the festivals of non-Santals. They participate in *Durga Puja, Kali Puja, Laxmi Puja, Nabanna* and so on. They also perform *Saraswati Puja* in the villages for the development in education. So, traditional religious involvement is now at a stake.

Conclusion

The Santal is an agriculturist tribe having an essential articulation with Hindu caste-peasants and market economy of the larger society. In the course of their contact with the larger society and due to the adoption of modern agricultural technology, there have occurred many changes in the aspects of their social organization and cultural activities. It may be admitted that some of the social and cultural changes observed among the Santals are due to changes in the economic and political life of the people in general. Agricultural modernization has its impact in bringing about economic, social and cultural changes. It has, however, been found that despite their essential articulation with the larger society and the changes therefrom, the Santals are found to live in a world of dynamic isolation and perpetuate a distinct socio-cultural identity of their own.

References

Agarwal, Bina; (1983), *Mechanization in Indian Agriculture—An Analytical Study Based on Punjab*. Allied Publishers Private Limited, New Delhi.

Agarwal, U.; (1967), *Social Consequences of Technology Change*. New Heights, Delhi.

Beteille, Andre; (1977) "The definition of Tribe", in Thapar Ramesh (ed). *Tribe, Caste and Religion in India*, The MacMillan Company of India Limited, Delhi.

Bhowmik, K.L.; (1986), *Tribal India: A Profile in Indian Ethnology*, The World Press Private Limited, Calcutta.

Bhowmik, Pradip Kumar; (1993), *Dynamics of Tribal Development*, Inter-India Publications, New Delhi.

Bhowmik, P.K.; (1982), "Approach to Tribal Welfare", in *Tribal Development in India: Problems and Prospects*, ed. by Buddhadev Choudhury, Inter-India Publication, Delhi.

Bhowmik, P.K.; (1987), "Development and Anthropology: Rebuilding Rural and Tribal Economy", in *Anthropology, Development and Nation Building*, ed. by A.K. Kalla and K.S. Singh, Concept Publishing Company, New Delhi.

Chowdhury, Budhadeb (ed.); (1982), *Tribal Devlopment in India: Problems and Prospects*, Inter-India Publications, New Delhi.

Choudhury, M.K.; (1996), "Impact of Tribal Planning in India with Special Emphasis on West Bengal" in *Socio-Economic Transformation in India*, ed. by Biswanath Ray, Kanishka Publishers, Distributors, New Delhi.

Chaudhury, S.N.; (2012), *Tribal Education, Implications for Development*, Concept Publishing Company Pvt. Ltd., New Delhi.

Daltone, George; (1961), *Economic Theory and Primitive Society. American Anthropologist.* Vol. 63, No. 1-1971: *Economic Anthropology and Development,* Basic Books, New York.

Das, A.K.; Raha, M.K.; De, S.K.; (1990), *Tribal Situation in West Bengal*, Firma KLM Private Ltd., Calcutta.

Das, A.K.; Choudhuri, M.K.; Basu, S.K.; Saha, R.N.; Khan, N.C. (1978), *Scheduled Tribes and Scheduled Castes of West Bengal: Programmes Facts and Figures,* Cultural Research Institute, Scheduled Castes and Tribes Welfare Department, Government of West Bengal, Calcutta.

Deogaonkar, S.G.; (1994), *Tribal Administration and Development,* Concept Publishing Company, New Delhi.

Deshai, A.R.; (1977), *Tribe, Caste and Religion in India*, Ramesh Thapar (ed.), Macmillan Company of India Ltd,. Delhi.

Dube, S.C.; (1998), "Development Designs and Tribal People" in *Antiquity to Modernity in Tribal India*, Volume I, ed. by S.C. Dube, Inter-India Publications, D-17 Raja Gaden, New Delhi.

Dube, S.C.; (1977), *Tribal Heritage of India*. Vikas Publication, New Delhi.

Epstein, T.S.; (1962), *Economic Development and Social Change in South India.* Manchester University Press, Manchester.

Freedman, R.; (1956), *Principles of Sociology*. New York, Halt.

Government of India; (2009-10), *Annual Report,* Ministry of Tribal Affairs.

Haque, T.; (1996) *Sustainability of Small Holder Agriculture in India.* Concept Publication Company, New Delhi.

Hazra, A., Paul, S.K and Mitra, K.; (1997), Santal Rituals and Agro-ecosystem. *Bulletin of Cultural Research Institute*, Vol. XIX, No. I, Backward Classes Welfare Department, Government of West Bengal.

Jacob, Norman; (1971), *Modernization without Development: Thailand as an Asian Case Study*. New York, Praeger.

Jairth, M.S.; (1991), *Tribal Economy and Society*. Mittal Publications, New Delhi

Kotheri, K.L.; (1985), *Tribal Social Change in India*. Himanshu Publications, Delhi.

Mahalingam, S.; (1988), Tribal Development Programmes: A Review, *Kurukshetra*, Vol. XXXVI, No. 4, January, 1988.

Mahapatra, S.; (1992) "Modernization of Tribal Agriculture: Technological and Cultural Constraints", in Buddhadev Choudhury (ed.), *Economy and Agrarian Issues*, Inter-India Publications, New Delhi.

Mehta, Sushma; (1981), Problems of Tribal Development in India, *Vanyajati,* Vol. XXIX, No. 4, October 1981.

Majumdar, D.N.; (1953), *Affairs of a Tribe*, Lucknow, Universal Publishers. Ministry of Tribal Affairs; *Annual Report on Education*, http//tribal.nic.in.

Official Website of Ministry of Tribal Affairs, Government of India.

Pachauri, S.K.; (1984), *Dynamics of Rural Development in Tribal Areas*, Concept Publishing Company, New Delhi.

Panni Niranjan, Sahoo Jitendra; (2008), *Tribal Development*, Mahamaya Publishing House, New Delhi.

Patel, M.L.; (1994), *Tribal Development without Tears,* Inter-India Publication, New Delhi.

Paul Mitra, Kakali; (2004), *Development Programmes and Tribals—Some Emerging Issues*, Kalpaz Publications, Delhi.

Paul, Sujit Kumar; (2005), *Tribal Agriculture and Modernization—The Change and Continuity*. Daya Publisher, New Delhi.

Paul, Sujit Kumar; (2013), Livelihood Patterns of Tribals: A Study on Transition from Traditional to Modernity, in Debabrata Das Gupta (ed), *Food and Environmental Security,* Agrobios (India), Jodhpur.

Ramana Rao, D.V.V.; (1992), *Tribal Development—New Approaches*, Discovery Publishimg House, New Delhi.

Romesh Thaper (ed.); (1971), "*Tribe, Caste and Religion in India*", McMillan, Delhi.

Rudra, A.; (1982) *Indian Agricultural Economics—Myths and Realities*. Allied Publishers, New Delhi.

Sachchidananda; (1988), *Cultural Change in Tribal Bihar: Munda, Oriron*. Book Land Private Ltd., Calcutta.

Sah, D.C. and Sisodia Yatindra Singh; (2004), *"Tribal Issues In India",* Rawat Publications, Jaipur and New Delhi.

Singh, A. and Jabbi, M.; (1996), *Status of Tribes in India,* Har Anand Publications, New Delhi.

Singh, Ajit Kumar; (1984), *Tribal Development in India*, Classical Publishing Company, New Delhi.

Singh, B.D.; (1992), *Planning for Rural Development and Poverty Alleviation*, Mittal Publications, New Delhi.

Singh, K.S.; (1994), *The Scheduled Tribes*, National Series, Vol. III, Anthropological Survey of India, Oxford University Press.

Vaid, N.K.; (2004), *Who Cares for Tribal Development*, Mittal Publications, New Delhi.

Vidyarthi, L.P.; (1981), Forward, *The Profiles of the Marginal and Pre-farming Tribes of Central Eastern India,* ed. by L.P. Vidyarthi, Special Series No. 26, *Bulletin of the Cultural Research Institute*, Scheduled Castes and Tribes Welfare Department, Calcutta.

Vidyarthi, L.P. and Rai, B.K.; (1985), *The Tribal Culture of India,* Concept Publishing Company, New Delhi.

7

Millennium Development Goals (MDGs) and Rural Development in India

Introduction

The Millennium Development Goals (MDGs) constitute the first-ever set of shared development goals at the international level, on which there is an unprecedented level of consensus. This unique, relatively simple, and wide-ranging framework of goals, targets and indicators has become a rallying point in the fight against world poverty and its different dimensions. The Millennium Development Goals are the world's biggest promise—a global agreement to reduce poverty and human deprivation at historically unprecedented levels through collaborative action. It is different from all other global promises for poverty reduction due to its comprehensive nature and the efforts taken to finance, implement and monitor them. The Millennium Development Goals are eight international development goals that all 193 United Nations member states and international organizations have agreed to achieve by the year 2015. The aim is to reduce global poverty, improving the social and economic conditions of the poor and increasing the pace of development in a sustainable manner in the world's poorest countries. The targets of Millennium Development Goals were derived from earlier international development targets and officially established in the Millennium Summit in 2000, where all the world leaders were present and the declaration was made on these Millennium Development Goals. The Declaration asserts that every individual has the right to dignity, equality, freedom, and a basic standard of living that includes freedom from hunger and violence, and better quality of life for poor people. The time-bound goals were implemented by setting targets and indicators for poverty reduction in order to achieve the goals which were declared. The focus has been made on bolstering human capital, improving infrastructure, and increasing social, economic and political rights, with the majority of the focus going towards increasing basic standards of living. The goals set forth in the Millennium Declaration were intended to increase an individual's capabilities and improve the quality of life and standard of living of poor people in sustainable manner.

India, especially since the later half of the 1990s seems to be a classic example of economic progress while much needs to be achieved yet in terms of social and human development. India is ranking 10th largest economy by the World Bank in terms of its GDP at 1876.80 billion US dollars in 2013 at current price while, it has been ranked 135 out of 187 countries in the Human Development Index (Human Development Report, 2013) reflecting little improvement in the living standard of its people. The Millennium Development Goals have served as an effective benchmark of India on the human dimension front *vice-versa* India has also played an important role to achieve the Millennium Development Goals. Nearly one-fourth of the world's poor reside in India, the highest rate of maternal and infant mortality, and one-third of the world's undernourished children. On the other hand, India makes an important contribution to the global agenda in such areas as human dignity and international co-operation as outlined in the Millennium Declaration. As the world's largest democracy, India has the obligation to ensure its own national development and to honour its historic contributions to the ideals of modern global society.

Progress towards MDGs in Indian Context

The Millennium Development Goals (MDGs) are eight goals to be achieved by 2015 that respond to the world's main development challenges, the focus being the human dimension. The MDGs are drawn from the actions and targets contained in the Millennium Declaration that was adopted by 189 nations and signed by 147 heads of state and governments during the UN Millennium Summit in September 2000. The Millennium Development Goals (MDGs) play an important role in development policies today.

The Millennium Development Goals (MDGs) which consist of eight goals were framed to tackle the world's major development challenges with health and its related areas as the prime focus. The MDGs adopted by the United Nations in the year 2000 projected the efforts of the international community to free our fellow men, women and children from the miserable and dehumanizing conditions of extreme poverty. The MDGs are eight goals to be achieved by 2015 that respond to the world's

Table 7.1: Millennium Development Goals and Targets

Goal	*Targets*
Eradicate extreme poverty and hunger	1. Halve, between 1990 and 2015, the proportion of people whose income is less than $1 a day 2. Halve, between 1990 and 2015, the proportion of people who suffer from hunger
Achieve universal primary education	3. Ensure that, by 2015, children everywhere, boys and girls alike, will be able to complete a full course of primary schooling.
Promote gender equality and empower women	4. Eliminate gender disparity in primary and secondary education, preferably by 2005, and to all levels of education no later than 2015
Reduce child mortality	5. Reduce by two-thirds, between 1990 and 2015, the under-five mortality rate
Improve maternal health	6. Reduce by three-quarters, between 1990 and 2015, the maternal mortality ratio
Combat HIV/AIDS, malaria and other diseases	7. Have halted by 2015 and begun to reverse the spread of HIV/AIDS 8. Have halted by 2015 and begun to reverse the incidence of malaria and other major diseases
Ensure environmental sustainability	9. Integrate the principles of sustainable development into country policies and programmes and reverse the loss of environmental resources 10 Halve by 2015 the proportion of people without sustainable access to safe drinking water 11. By 2020 to have achieved a significant improvement in the lives of at least 100 million slum dwellers
Develop a global partnership for development	12. Develop further an open, rule-based, Predictable, non-discriminatory trading and financial system. Includes a commitment to good governance, development, and poverty reduction—both nationally and internationally 13. Address the special needs of the least developed countries. Includes: tariff and quota free access for least developed countries' exports; enhanced programme of debt relief for HIPCs and cancellation of official bilateral debt; and more generous ODA for countries committed to poverty reduction 14. Address the special needs of landlocked countries and small island developing states (through the Programme of Action for the Sustainable Development of Small Island Developing States and the outcome of the 22nd special session of the General Assembly) 15. Deal comprehensively with the debt problems of developing countries through national and international measures in order to make debt sustainable in the long term 16. In cooperation with developing countries, develop and implement strategies for decent and productive work for youth 17. In cooperation with pharmaceutical companies, provide access to affordable essential drugs in developing countries 18. In cooperation with the private sector, make available the benefits of new technologies, especially information and communications

main development challenges. These goals are further subdivided into 18 numerical targets which are further measured by means of 40 quantifiable indicators. Health constitutes the prime focus of the MDGs. While three out of eight goals are directly related to health, the other goals are related to factors which have a significant influence on health. Hence the goals and targets are inter-related in many ways.

In India, significant progress has been made in the field of basic universal education, gender equality in education, and global economic growth. However, there is slow progress in the improvement of health indicators related to mortality, morbidity, and various environmental factors contributing to poor health conditions. Eventhough, the government has implemented a wide array of programmes, policies, and various schemes to combat these health challenges, further intensification of efforts and redesigning of outreach strategies is needed to give momentum to the progress toward achievement of the MDGs.

Goal 1: Eradicate Extreme Poverty and Hunger

The proportion of people below the national poverty line (poverty Head Count Ratio) estimated for 1990 was 37.2 per cent. By the year 2004-05 the percentage was 27.5, whereas the target set by MDG is 18.6 per cent by 2015. Orissa has the highest rate of proportion of population below poverty line, i.e., 46.40 per cent in 2004-05 declines from 52.38 per cent in 1990. MDG target for Orissa regarding poverty line is 26.19 per cent which is far away from its present status. Jammu & Kashmir has the lowest rate of proportion of population below poverty line. The rate has come down to 5.4 per cent in 2004-05 from about 22.92 per cent in 1990 and the State already have crossed the target of 11.46 per cent by the year 2015. With the decline in poverty, the rural-urban gap in poverty has also declined. The average difference between rural and urban below poverty line ratios was 9.6 percentages in 1993-94, which came down to 3.9 percentages in 2004-05 (see Table 7.2).

Table 7.2: Proportion of Population Below Poverty Line

Name	*1990*	*1993-94*	*2004-05*	*MDG Targets*
Orissa	52.38	48.56	46.40	26.19
Jammu & Kashmir	22.92	25.17	5.4	11.46
India	37.20	35.97	27.50	18.60

Source of Data: Planning Commission, Government of India.

However, the preliminary estimates using the latest NSS survey for 2009-10 recommend that the percentage of the population in poverty declined, at a faster pace than before, by approximately one percentage point per annum, during the five-year period 2004-05 to 2009-10. Since 2009-10 was a drought year, and poverty in that year could have increased temporarily, the underlying rate of decline is probably more than one percentage point per year. It is also possible that the pace of poverty reduction accelerated in the last two years of the Eleventh Plan period, since by then several Eleventh Plan programmes focused at growing inclusiveness would have started to have a fuller impact.

Malnourishment of children is a significant indicator of food insecurity. All India trend of the proportion of underweight children below 3 years of age shows slow in eliminating the effect of malnourishment. In the year 1992-93 the percentage was 51.5 per cent, in the year 1998-99 the percentage come down to 42.7 per cent and 40.4 per cent in 2005-06. The target set for MDG is 26 per cent by 2015. This is also likely to be underachieving by the time frame and the proportion of underweight expected to come down to about 33 per cent only by 2015.

Goal 2: Achieve Universal Primary Education

Education is basic human rights, vital to personal and societal development and well-being. Education enhances lives; it ends generation cycle of poverty and disease and provides the means for sustainable development. A quality basic education will better equip girls and boys with knowledge and skills needed to adopt healthy lifestyle.

Net enrolment ratio is an important indicator to understand the enrolment trend in the country or State. A Trend based on District Information System Education (DISE) data shows the country is now well set to achieve cent per cent primary education for children in the primary schooling age of 6-10 years by 2015. In the year 2007-08 the Net Enrolment Ratio was 95.9 per cent whereas in the year 2009-10 it was 98.3 per cent. The report shows that Net Attendance Ratio was 84 per cent in 2007-08 in primary level (*Sources*: Estimates based on DISE data for the reference years). Literacy rate in the age-group 15+ years is 66 per cent, of which male is 76.7 per cent and female is 54.9 per cent in 2007-08 (*Sources*: Population Census of India, 2001; NFHS-III report 2005-06 and NSS Report 532: “Participation and Expenditure on Education in India 2007-08).

However, the survival rate at primary level up to Grade V (i.e., proportion of student starting Grade I who reach the last grade of primary) has risen from 62 per cent in 1999 to 81per cent by 2002 and declined thereafter to 73 per cent in 2004. According to DISE 2007-08, it further dipped to 72 per cent in 2007-08. However, DISE 2009-10 indicated an improvement to 76 per cent in 2008-09. According to the trend exhibited during 1991-2001, India is likely to attain 100 per cent youth literacy by 2015. It increased between 1991 and 2001 from 61.9 per cent to 76.4 per cent. Youth literacy was estimated as 86 per cent in NSS 2007-08.

Goal 3: Promote Gender Equality and Empower Women

Despite the fact that women represent near about half of the total population and one-third of the total labour force in the world, they have remained at a disadvantage in securing paid jobs. Wage differentials, occupational segregation, higher unemployment rates and their disproportionate representation in the informal and subsistence sectors limit women's economic advancement. Socio-cultural attitudes, employment policies and a lack of options for balancing work and family responsibilities or for controlling the timing and spacing of births contribute further to inequality in the labour market. In the under development and developing nations these problems are more overt.

The target for eliminating gender disparity in primary and secondary enrolment by 2005 has not been achieved in India as per the available data for Gender Parity Index for Enrolment, in the sense that though almost perfect parity was attained in the primary level of enrolment, it was not shown in secondary level. By 2004-05, India had 0.95 enrolments in favour of girls and in the year 2007-08 it was 0.98 in primary level. In secondary level the enrolments are 0.79 in favour of girls in the year 2004-05 and 0.85 in the year 2007-08. And in higher education it is 0.71 in favour of girls in the year 2004-05 and 0.70 in the year 2007-08.

The Female-Male literacy rate for 15-24 years increased to 0.80 in 2001 from 0.67 in 1991. NSS (2007-08) results show that, literates in the

Table 7.3: Sex Ratio in the Census Data may also show the Inequality

Sex Ratio in India					
1951	1961	1971	1981	1991	2001
946	941	930	934	927	933

Source: Census data. Government of India.

age-group 15-24 years at all India level is 86 per cent with 91 per cent males and 80 per cent females respectively. Thus the ratio of literate women to men in the age-group 15-24 years stands at 0.88 in 2007-08. The ratio of literate women to men in the age-group 15-24 years tends to exceed 1 by 2015, ensuring achievement of gender parity in literacy by 2015.

In the year 1951 sex ratio was 946 after that up to 1971 sex ratio gradually declined; in 1981 there is a slight positive change in the sex ratio, again in 1991 the sex ratio decline to 927. In 2001 sex ratio was 933 which is slight positive change compared to the immediate previous census.

Table 7.4: Representation of Women in Premier Services (1987-1997)

Year	*1987*			*1997*		
Category	*Total*	*Female*	*Percentage*	*Total*	*Female*	*Percentage*
IAS	4204	339	7.5	4991	512	10.2
IPS	2418	21	0.9	3045	67	2.2
Total	6622	360	5.4	8036	579	7.2

Source: Ministry of Home Affairs; Ministry of External Affairs; Department of Personnel, GoI, New Delhi.

In 1987 out of total 6,622 IAS and IPS only 360 females were there. In 1997 out of 8,036 IAS and IPS, 579 were female officers.

Table 7.5: Representation of Women in Lok Sabha

1952	*1980*	*1991*	*1996*	*1998*
22	28	39	39	41

Source: Election Commission of India.

In 1952, only 22 women members were there at Lok Sabha, in 1980 it was 28 only, in 1991 women members were 39. So, these are all the indicators of inequality of women participation in all sectors.

In Indian context, labour markets in industry and services sectors are highly male dominated and equal situation for men and women is too difficult to achieve in the present market dynamics and existing socio-cultural framework.

Goal 4: Reduce Child Mortality

Child mortality is another indicator of underdevelopment. It is indeed disheartening to note that 10.5 million children died before their fifth birthday, mostly from preventable causes. So, reduce child mortality is another important goal. Report of the sample registration system and NFHS shows that, under 5 mortality rates was declined to 69.00 per thousand live births in the year 2008 from 125.00 per thousand live births in 1990. Kerala has the lowest rate of under five mortality rate, reduced to 14.00 per thousand live births in 2008 from 32.75 per thousand live births in 1990. On the other hand Madhya Pradesh has the highest rate, declined to 92.00 per thousand live births from 147.60 per thousand live births. Kerala has likely to achieve the target of MDG-10.92 per thousand live births whereas Madhya Pradesh is far away to achieve the target. Indian target is 42.00 per thousand live births but it is likely to be achieved 55.76 per thousand live births.

Table 7.6: Reduce Child Mortality

	Under five Mortality Rate per '000 live births				
Name	*1990*	*2005-06*	*2008*	*MDG targets*	*Projected achieve-ments by 2015*
Kerala	32.75	16.30	14.00	10.92	9.15
Madhya Pradesh	147.60	94.20	92.00	49.20	77.52
India	125.00	74.30	69.00	42.00	55.76

Source of Data: Report of NFHS I, II and III, Ministry of Health and Family Welfare, Government of India; projected figures are derived for this report.

Infant Mortality Rate (IMR) is another indicator of development which means the deaths of infants of age less than one year per thousand live births. Though IMR for the country as a whole declined by 30 points (rural IMR by 31 points *vis-à-vis* urban IMR by 16 points) in the last 20 years with an annual average decline of 1.5 points, it declined by three points between 2008 and 2009. With the present improved trend, the national level estimate of IMR is likely to be 45.04 against the MDG target of 26.67 in 2015.

Immunization of children is also a vital factor to reduce the child morality in India. The national level showed that the proportion of one year old (12-23 months) children immunized against measles has registered an increase from 42.2 per cent in 1992-93 to 72.4 per cent in

2009 (UNICEF and GoI—Coverage Evaluation Survey 2009). The trend indicates a historic rate of increase in child immunization and India is expected to cover about 88 per cent children in the age-group 12-23 months for immunization against measles by 2015.

Goal 5: Improve Maternal Health

Ratios of maternal mortality seem to have changed little in regions where most deaths occur (sub-Saharan Africa and Southern Asia). 200 million women who wish to space or limit their child bearing lack access to contraception. Skilled attendants at delivery, backed up by referrals to timely emergency obstetric care, are critical factors for reducing deaths further, as a growing number of countries have demonstrated. Incidence of deaths to women in the reproductive age group 15-49 due to pregnancy related causes as measured by MMR.

Table 7.7: Maternal Mortality Ratio (per '000 live births)

Name	*1990*	*1997-98*	*1999-01*	*2004-06*	*MDG target 2015*	*Projected achievement 2015*
Assam	544.19	568	398	480	136.05	412.11
Kerala	279.19	150	149	95	69.80	45.67
India	437.00	398	327	254	109.25	135.38

Source of Data: Report of Sample Registration System, Office of the Registrar General of India, Ministry of Home Affairs, Government of India; projected figures are derived for this report.

The Table 7.7 shows that Assam has the highest MMR among all States that is 480.00 in the year 2004-06. In 1990 the ratio was 544.19. In case of Kerala the MMR in 2004-06 was 69.80 and in 1990 it was 279.19. Table 7.7 also shows that in 2004-06 India had the MMR 254, in 1990 it was 437.00. The target was given to India to reduce MMR to 109.25 by the year 2015.

Goal 6: Combat HIV/AIDS, Malaria and Other Diseases

Several countries report success in reducing HIV infection rates, through interventions that promote behaviour change. However, rates of infection overall are still growing. Alarmingly, the number of people living with HIV has continued to rise, from 36.2 million in 2003 to 38.6 million in

2005 (nearly half of whom are women). The number of AIDS-related deaths also increased that year, to 2.8 million, despite greater access to anti-retroviral treatment and improved care in some regions. In India, transmission of HIV/AIDS is predominantly (in about 86% cases) due to sexual reasons. It is natural, therefore, that with steady rise in the level of awareness about the disease and in use of condom among non-regular sex partners, the decline in spread of AIDS through sexual route tends to sustain. Estimated adult prevalence has come down to 0.31 per cent in 2009 from about 0.34 per cent in 2007 and 0.45 per cent in 2002. Among pregnant women of 15-24 years, the prevalence has declined from 0.86 per cent in 2004 to 0.49 per cent in 2007. A drop by more than 50 per cent has been recorded among pregnant women aged 25-49 years as well from 1.09 per cent in 2004 to 0.52 per cent in 2007. Proportion of people aged 15-49 having correct awareness about HIV/AIDS has increased from 17.6 per cent in 2001 to 29.3 per cent in 2006. Condom use as percentage of all contraceptive methods is low, particularly in rural areas (3.3% in 2005-06). Total number of females living with HIV/AIDS has kept on declining from 1.07 million in 2002 to 0.97 million in 2006 and further to 0.95 million in 2007.

The incidence rate of malaria and death associated with malaria are on the decline. The incidence among the people, who were examined for the disease, was 1.67per cent in 2006 and has come down to 1.51 per cent by 2009. The percentage of death of malaria patients thus diagnosed during 2006 to 2009 has declined from 0.10 and 0.07 per 100 cases. In the malaria prone States like the North East States, Gujarat, Karnataka, Madhya Pradesh, Maharashtra, Orissa, Rajasthan, Tripura and West Bengal, the number of deaths of malaria patients has consistently declined ever since the high of 2006.

India is the highest TB burdened country accounting for about one-fifth of global incidence. Prevalence of TB has steadily declined from as high as 338 per 100,000 populations in 1990 to 249 per 100,000 in 2009.

Goal 7: Ensure Environmental Sustainability

The area under forest and tree cover is increasing slowly. Around 33 per cent, i.e., one-third of geographical area must be covered under forest in any country for sustainable environment. But deforestation has increased due to various reasons. India has 20.99 per cent geographical area under forest by the year 2005, which is 690,171 sq. km. of total area. By the year 2007 it was estimated that forest cover area is 690,899 sq. km that constitutes 21.02 per cent of geographical area of the country. So, there is an increase in forest area by 728 sq. km between 2005 and 2007. During this period, significant increase in forest covers in Mizoram, Manipur, Jharkhand and Orissa and in the same period, there has been loss of forest cover in Andhra Pradesh, Arunachal Pradesh, Chhattisgarh, Nagaland and Tripura (State of Forest Report, 2009). In case of scattered trees total estimated area covered 91,663 sq. km in 2005. By the year 2007 scattered trees increased by 1106 sq. km.

Safe drinking water is the basic right of any person. Nearly, 60 per cent of total disease is caused due to polluted water. Mainly poor people suffer most due to polluted water. So, Government as the biggest institution of any country has the responsibility to provide safe drinking water to its population. In terms of actual estimates from NFHS and DLHS, the coverage of households having access to improved water sources gives a clear trend in attainment of MDG-target.

Table 7.8: Environmental Sustainability to Improve Drinking Water

	Proportion of Household without Sustainable access to improved drinking water (per cent)			
Area	*1992-93*	*2002-2004*	*2007-08*	*MDG target by 2015*
Rural	39.10	16.10	20.40	20.53
Urban	12.40	7.20	5.60	6.44
Total	31.80	13.30	15.60	16.82

MDG target for sustainable access to improved drinking water for rural areas is 20.53 per cent but by the year 2007-08 India reached the target 20.40, in case of urban areas the target is 6.44 by the year 2015, but by the year 2007-08 the percentage of population beyond Sustainable access to improved drinking water is 5.60, the target has already been achieved.

Table 7.9: Environmental Sustainability to Improve Sanitation

	Proportion of Households without Sustainable Access to Improved Sanitation (per cent)			
Area	*1992-93*	*2002-2004*	*2007-2008*	*MDG target by 2015*
Rural	87.10	80.80	65.80	46.64
Urban	24.10	20.20	19.20	12.14
Total	69.70	60.80	50.70	37.76

MDG target for sustainable access to improved sanitation is 46.64 per cent for rural areas, by the year 2007-08, 65.80 per cent has been achieved which is far away from its target. In case of urban areas the target is 12.14 per cent and 19.20 per cent achieved by the year 2007-08. By the year 2007-08 India achieved 50.70 per cent, where target set for India is 37.76 per cent which is far away from its target.

Per-capita Energy Consumption (PEC) during a year is computed as the ratio of the estimate of total energy consumption during the year to the estimated mid-year population of that year. The estimated PEC has increased from 1204 KWh in 1970-71 to 4646 KWh in 2009-10. The annual increase in PEC from 2008-09 to 2009-10 was 11 per cent.

Goal 8: Develop a Global Partnership for Development

The last goal regarding developing the global partner for development. The target of goal 8, i.e., to develop a global partnership for development, is mainly to provide development assistant to the underdeveloped and developing countries by the developed countries. This goal makes available the benefits of new technologies, especially information and communications, India has made substantial progress in recent years. The overall tele-density has remarkably increased from 0.67 per cent in 1991 to 36.98 per cent in 2009. Use of Personal Computers has also increased from 5.4 million PCs in 2001 to 19.6 million in 2006 and there are 13.54 million internet subscribers as on March 2009. The internet subscriber base has increased to 14.63 million in 2009.

Strategies to Achieve MDGs

Economic and financial crisis is the biggest problem in front of India. Inequality is another challenge in front of India. Inequalities based on income, gender, disability, ethnicity, are generally overt in Indian context. Proper Education is another challenge for India. India is the second highest populated country in the world with 1.2 billion populations. It is very difficult for the government to include all its population in the rigid formal education system. Population control is another biggest challenge in front of India. India is the first country to make population policy, but so far population growth rate is not controlled. Due to various perceptions, religious reasons population growth rate is not controlled. According to UN declaration, India will be the highest populated country by 2025. There are so many challenges in front of India, poverty reduction, environmental sustainability, control of HIV/AIDS, malnutrition, provide safe drinking water, superstition are some of them.

The Millennium Development Goals (MDGs) which include eight goals were framed to address the world's major development challenges. Despite India's economic growth and food surplus, India is still suffering from alarming hunger, poverty and health indicators related to mortality, morbidity, and various environmental factors contributing to poor health conditions. Immediate action is needed by the government to eradicate poverty and save the lives of millions of people. In India, considerable progress has been made in the field of basic universal education, gender equality in education, and global economic growth. To achieve the other goals the government has implemented a wide array of programmes, policies, and various schemes to combat these challenges. Now, more efforts and redesigning of strategies are needed to achieve the progress towards MDGs. Government design and implement various schemes and programmes through Five Year Plans to achieve national targets as well as MDGs.

Current Efforts to Achieve MDGs

Government of India has shown its commitment towards achieving MDGs as well as betterment of human development parameters across the country. Rural poverty alleviation and upliftment of standard of living of the rural poor is the prime concern of the Government. Over the time, a plenty of effort in terms of programmes and schemes have been initiated along with the timely modification in the strategy. Some of the programmes implemented by the Government of India, addressing various components of respective MGDs are discussed below:

Goal I: Eradicate Extreme Poverty and Hunger

To achieve the first goal a number of anti-poverty programmes have been launched in India. Some of those programmes are a launched exclusively to combat against poverty in rural areas. As an employment generation programme, Mahatma Gandhi National Rural Employment Guarantee Act (MGNREGA) provide 100 days employment to the rural people. "Swarnajayanti Gram Swarozgar Yojana" (SGSY), providing micro loan to the poor people through Self-Help Groups. Indira Awaas Yojana (IAY), builds home for the poor and destitute people. Programmes launched in the urban areas include Integrated Housing and Slum Development

Programme, builds home for the urban poor. Poorest of the poor families getting foodgrains under Swarnajayanti Shahari Rojgar Yojana (SSRY) and Targeted Public Distribution Scheme (TPDS) like "Antyodaya Anna Yojana". All these programmes were implemented to eradicate poverty and means for sustainable livelihood for the poor people.

Mahatma Gandhi National Rural Employment Guarantee Act (MGNREGA)

National Rural Employment Guarantee Act was enacted on 5th September, 2005 and came into force w.e.f. 2nd February, 2006. On 31st December, 2009, the Act was renamed by an Amendment as the Mahatma Gandhi National Rural Employment Guarantee Act 2009. The scheme provides a legal guarantee for one hundred days of employment in every financial year to adult members of any rural household willing to do public work-related unskilled manual work at the statutory minimum wage. Thus, the Act aims at enhancing the livelihood security of people in rural areas. The objective of the Act is to augment wage employment opportunities by providing employment on demand and thereby extend a security net to the people and simultaneously create durable assets to alleviate some aspects of poverty and address the issue of development in the rural areas. The Act provides additional livelihood in rural areas through unskilled manual work as a legal right. Any rural household seeking unskilled manual work could register its family in the Gram Panchayat and obtain a job card. With the possession of a job card, the registered rural household could apply for work for at least 100 days in the Gram Panchayat. Gram Panchayat was entrusted with the legal duty of providing work to such applicant within 15 days of the receipt of the application, failing which unemployment allowance would become payable to the rural household. The law prescribes payment of wages every week and not later than a fortnight of the work done. In the event of delay in payment of wages, workers were entitled to compensation under Payment of Wages Act 1938. MGNREGA has become a powerful tool for inclusive growth in rural India through its impact on legal protection, social safety nets, livelihood security and grass root governance.

Swarnajayanti Gram Swarozgar Yojana (SGSY)/National Rural Livelihood Mission (NRLM)

The Ministry of Rural Development (MoRD) has shown its commitment to eradicate rural poverty through programmes that directly targeted on the rural poor households. Within the directly targeted group approach, there are various programmes focused on wage employment and some programmes focused on self-employment generation. The Swarnajayanti Grameen Swarojgar Yojana (SGSY) was focused on self-employment. The SGSY Scheme was effective from 1st April, 1999 in rural areas of India. This programme replaced the earlier self-employment and allied programmes, like IRDP, TRYSEM, DWCRA, SITRA, GKY and MWS, etc. It offers the perfect balance of credit and subsidy facilities to the rural poor households. It aimed at establishing a large number of micro-enterprises in the rural areas. SGSY was conceived as a holistic programme of micro enterprise where self-employment has been generated through self-help groups formation, their capacity building, planning of activity clusters, infrastructure build-up, technology, credit and marketing. The Scheme has been funded by the Centre and the States in the ratio of 75:25 and implemented by Commercial Banks, Regional Rural Banks and Co-operative Banks. Other financial institutions, Panchayat Raj Institutions (PRIs), District Rural Development Agencies (DRDAs), Non-Governmental Organisations (NGOs), Technical Institutions in the district, have been involved in the process of planning, implementation and monitoring of the Scheme. NGOs have played a crucial role in the formation and nurturing of the Self-Help Groups (SHGs) as well as in the monitoring of the progress of the *Swarozgaris*. In the period of implementing SGSY, there has developed a widespread acceptance in the country of the need for poors to be organized into Self-Help Groups as a prerequisite for their poverty reduction. There are some fixed objectives of this scheme which are:

- To uplift the rural poors who come under BPL category within a definite period and train them for sustainable income generation by creating micro-enterprises.
- To improve the skills of the rural poors to effective utilization of resources.
- To improve the economic status of rural poors through self-employment.
- To improve the economic and social status of rural women by involving them in SHGs.
- To establish micro-enterprises in the rural areas in large scale to utilize the potentiality of the rural poors for their own development.

Source: Reserve Bank of India, 2010.

SGSY has been found to be more successful wherever systematic mobilization of the poors into Self-Help Groups and their capacity building and skill development has been taken up in a systematic manner.

The magnitude of the task of rural poverty alleviation through direct interventions in self-employment is enormous. Out of the estimated 7.0 crore rural BPL households, 4.5 crore households still need to be organized into SHGs. A significant number of these households are extremely vulnerable. Even the existing SHGs need further strengthening and capacity building. It was in this background that Government has approved the restructuring of SGSY as the National Rural Livelihoods Mission (NRLM), to be implemented in a mission mode across the country. NRLM builds on the core strengths of the SGSY and incorporates the important lessons from large scale experiences in the country. NRLM has an ambitious mandate. It aims to reach out to all the rural poor families (BPL families) and link them to sustainable livelihoods opportunities. It nurtures them till they come out of poverty and enjoy a decent quality of life. To achieve this, NRLM has put in place dedicated and sensitive support structures at various levels. These structures work towards organizing the poor, building their capacities and the capacities of their organisations, enabling them access to finance and other livelihoods resources. The support structures also work with the unemployed rural poor youths for skill development and providing employment either in jobs, mostly in high growth sectors, or in remunerative self-employment and micro-enterprises. Till the October 2014 NRLM has been implemented in 56,734 Gram Panchayats of 2,460 Blocks in an intensive manner. During this period 255.9 lakh households have been mobilized into SHGs, 19 lakh SHGs and 68,845 village organizations have been promoted all over India. It also found that 1,485 numbers of Producer Groups have been promoted and 38 lakh acres of net crop area have been brought under sustainable agriculture.

Indira Awaas Yojana (IAY)

Indira Awaas Yojana (IAY) is a flagship scheme of the Ministry of Rural Development which provides financial assistance to the BPL households in rural areas for construction of houses. The IAY has been originated from the then National Rural Employment Programme which began in early 1980s. Construction of houses was one of the major components under the National Rural Employment Programme (NREP) in 1980 and Rural Landless Employment Guarantee Programme (RLEGP) in 1983.

IAY was launched as a sub-scheme of RLEGP and thereafter, it continued as a sub-scheme of JRY in 1989. On 1st January, 1996, it became an independent scheme. The objective of the scheme is to primarily help the weaker sections in rural areas, which belong to Below Poverty Line (BPL) category by granting financial assistance for construction of a house. The funding of the IAY is shared between the Centre and State, in the ratio of 75:25 and in the case of UTs 100 per cent funding is done by the Government of India. Moreover, in the case of NE States, the funding is shared in the ratio of 90:10. For those rural BPL Householders who don't have house sites, from the year 2009-10, provision had been made to provide house-sites as part of Indira Awaas Yojana. This funding has been shared between Centre and States in the ratio of 50:50.

Jawaharlal Nehru National Urban Renewal Mission (JNNURM)

Jawaharlal Nehru National Urban Renewal Mission, launched by the Government of India in December 2005, was the largest mission led urban development initiative. The initial duration of the Mission was seven years beginning from the year 2005-06 in the Phase-I. The first phase of JNNURM aimed to encourage reforms and fast track planned development of recognized cities. The JNNURM aimed to encourage cities to initiate steps to bring about development and upgradation in the existing service levels in a financially sustainable manner. The Mission recognized 65 cities/urban agglomerations (UAs), called 'mission cities', which were entitled for support for infrastructure development. The main aim of the Mission was to promote reforms in urban governance and service delivery and provide reform-linked financial assistance for the planned infrastructure development of the mission cities. The JNNURM comprises of two submissions that exclusively focused on 65 mission cities: The Urban Infrastructure and Governance (UIG) administered by Ministry of Urban Development and the Basic Services for Urban Poor (BSUP) administer by Ministry of Housing and Urban Poverty Alleviation. One of the objectives of the JNNURM is to ensure that the provision of basic services to the urban poor including security of tenure at affordable prices, improved housing, water supply and sanitation, and ensuring delivery of other existing universal services of the government for education, health and social security in the urban areas. Urban Infrastructure Development Scheme for Small and Medium Towns (UIDSSMT) and Integrated Housing and Slum Development Programme (IHSDP) under JNNURM contemplated key reforms in areas of pro-poor governance.

Besides above mentioned programmes, some of the nutrition programmes started by the government include the Integrated Child Development Scheme or ICDS (1975) and National Mid-Day Meal Scheme have been focusing on the provision of supplementary nutrition to children. In addition food security programmes for the poor include the Targeted Public Distribution Scheme (TPDS), the *Antyodaya Anna Yojana* and Grain Bank Scheme. However, utilization of services of some of these programmes has been found to be quite low.

Goal 2: Achieve Universal Primary Education

To reach the second goal, continue efforts are made by the government and design various policies and programmes. Target has been set up to achieve the goal of elementary education for all by 2010. Government launched "Sarva Shiksha Abhiyan" (SSA) in 2000 to campaign on education for all. Moreover, "Mid-Day Meal" programme started to provide nutritional food to the school students and decrease dropout rate. As a result of its efforts, enrolment has increased by 25 million between 2001 and 2005 and the number of out of school children has reduced from about 320 lakh in 2002-2003 to 70.5 lakh based on reports of States and UTs in March 2006. Other schemes include *Prarambhik Shiksha Kosh* (PSK) to help finance the government's commitment to quality basic education, District Primary Education Programme (DPEP), to revitalize the primary education system and setting up of institutions for teachers' education.

Right to Education Act

At the time of Independence, India had an educational system which was not only very small but was also characterized by striking gender and regional disparities. Only one child out of three had been enrolled in primary school. Thus challenge was to provide elementary education to all its children within a stipulated period of time. Special care of the economic and educational interests of the underprivileged sections of the population also became a constitutional obligation over a period of time. But these constitutional provisions remain unfulfilled till 2002, when the 86th Constitutional Amendment Act has made elementary education a Fundamental Right for children in the age-group of 6-14 years by providing that "the State shall provide free and compulsory education to all children of the age of six to fourteen years in such manner as the State may, by law, determine". The Right to Education Act is a detailed and comprehensive piece of legislation which includes provisions related to schools, teachers, curriculum, evaluation, access and specific division of duties and responsibilities of all concerned. Main features of the Act are as under:

- Every child from 6 to 14 years of age has the right to free and compulsory education in a neighbourhood school till completion of elementary education.
- Private schools have to provide 25 per cent reservation for weaker sections and economically disadvantaged groups in the admission.
- All schools except government schools are required to meet all specified norms and standards within three years to avoid cancellation of their recognition.
- The Act mandated for a fixed pupil-teacher ratio, i.e., 30 :1.
- The Act mandated improvement in quality of education.
- Financial burden have to be shared between Central and State Governments.

This had been a significant legislation in India, where such a major commitment to the cause of elementary education has bound governments, community based organizations and civil society into a common resolve to achieve universal elementary education. Reaching out to the girl child has been also a major focus area of the efforts to universalize elementary education.

Sarva Shiksha Abhiyan (SSA)

Sarva Shiksha Abhiyan (SSA) is Government of India's flagship programme for achievement of Universalization of Elementary Education (UEE) in a time bound manner, as mandated by 86th Amendment to the Constitution of India making free and compulsory Education to the Children of 6-14 years age-group, a Fundamental Right. SSA is being implemented in partnership with State Governments to cover the entire country and address the needs of 192 million children in 1.1 million habitations. The programme seeks to open new schools in those habitations which do not have schooling facilities and strengthen existing school infrastructure through provision of additional class rooms, toilets, drinking water, maintenance grant and school improvement grants. Existing schools with inadequate teacher strength are provided with additional teachers, while the capacity of existing teachers is being strengthened by extensive training, grants for developing teaching-learning materials and strengthening of the academic support structure at a cluster, block and district level.

Mid Day Meal

The Mid Day Meal is the world's largest school feeding programme reaching out to about 12 crore children across the country. With a view to enhancing enrolment, retention and attendance and simultaneously improving nutritional levels among children, the National Programme of Nutritional Support to Primary Education (NP-NSPE) was launched as a Centrally Sponsored Scheme on 15th August, 1995, initially in 2,408 Blocks in the country. The Scheme had undergone a number of revisions in the past and today, Mid Day Meal scheme is serving Primary and Upper Primary school children in entire country. 8.41 crore Primary children and 3.36 crore Upper Primary children, i.e., a total of 11.77 crore children were estimated to be benefited from MDM Scheme during 2009-10.

Goal 3: Promote Gender Equality and Empower Women

Gender equality and women empowerment is another important stressed area of the government to achieve the third goal. There were several programmes, policies and laws made to achieve the goal. Government made one-third reservation for women in election through 73rd Amendment. Earmarked 30 per cent of budgetary allocations of all the departments to be spent on gender specific programme. "Swa-shakti", "Swayamsiddha", "Swaslamban Programme", "SGSY" aims socio-economic development and empowerment of women. Moreover, government made Domestic Violence Act 2006, to protect women from domestic violence. Two targeted schemes for girls have been initiated under the SSA; the National Programme for the Education of Girls at the Elementary Level (NPEGEL) and Kasturba Gandhi Balika Vidyalaya (KGBV). A national evaluation of KGBV which was undertaken in February 2007 in 12 States has shown that the programme has been very well received by the community and is reaching out to girls from the most deprived sections in rural areas. Another programme is the Mahila Samakhya (MS) successive evaluations of which have pointed to its success in laying down the foundation of woman empowerment.

Girls Education through SSA

Sarva Shiksha Abhiyan or 'Education for All' programme recognized that ensuring girl's education needs changes in the education system as well as in the social norms and attitudes. A gender sensitive strategy has therefore, been adopted to make the education system responsive to the requirements of the girls through targeted interventions which serve as a pull factor to enhance access and retention of girls in schools and on the other hand, to create a community demand for girls' education through training and mobilization. Motivation and mobilization of parents and the community at large, enhancing the role of women and mothers in school related activities and participation in school committees, and strengthening the linkages between the school, teachers and communities are some of the ways in which the enabling conditions are being created.

Early Childhood Care and Education (ECCE)

Early Childhood Care and Education (ECCE) is a critical and essential input in freeing girls from sibling care responsibilities, leading to their regular attendance in school and in providing school readiness skills to pre-school children. The SSA works in a convergent mode with the Integrated Child Development Services (ICDS) programme to promote pre-school education by providing training of Anganwadi workers, primary school teachers, and health workers for a convergent understanding of pre-school and ECCE. The SSA, like other programme in the past, provides funds under Innovative head (Rs.15 lakh per district) and under the National Programme for Education of Girls at Elementary Level (NPEGEL) component (for 3,000 educationally backward Blocks) to support pre-school component of ICDS or an interim pre-school centre where ICDS does not exist but is needed.

National Programme for Education of Girls for Elementary Level (NPEGEL)

The Sarva Shiksha Abhiyan (SSA) was initiated in the year 2001-02 with the objective of universalization of elementary education. It was an effort to provide an opportunity for improving human knowledge, skill and capabilities to all children including the girl child, through provision of quality education in a mission mode. However, SSA has limited financial provisions for girls' education, and thus there was a requirement of an additional component. Another fact was the gender disparities in enrolment of girls, especially in rural areas and among disadvantaged groups. Thus, National Programme for Education of Girls at Elementary Level (NPEGEL) had come into action for providing additional support for education of underprivileged/disadvantaged girls at elementary level through more intense community mobilisation, the development of model schools in clusters, gender sensitisation of teachers, development of gender sensitive learning materials, early child care and education facilities and provision of need-based incentives like escorts, stationery, work books and uniforms, etc., for girls. The NPEGEL, launched in September 2003, is an integral but distinct component of the Sarva Shiksha Abhiyan. All Educationally Backward Blocks and Blocks having at least 5 per cent SC/ST population and SC/ ST female literacy rate below 10 per cent have been included under NPEGEL.

Kasturba Gandhi Balika Vidyalaya (KGBV)

Kasturba Gandhi Balika Vidyalaya (KGBV) is a scheme launched in July 2004, for setting up residential schools at upper primary level for girls belonging predominantly to the SC, ST, OBC and minority communities. The scheme is being implemented in educationally backward Blocks of the country where the female rural literacy is below the national average. The scheme provides for a minimum reservation of 75 per cent of the seats for girls belonging to SC, ST, OBC or minority communities and priority for the remaining 25 per cent, is accorded to girls from families below poverty line. The KGBV was implemented as a separate scheme in collaboration with the Sarva Shiksha Abhiyan (SSA), National Programme for Education of Girls at Elementary Level (NPEGEL) and Mahila Samakhya (MS) for the first-two years, but since 1st April, 2007 has merged with the SSA programme as a separate component of that programme.

Early Child Care and Education (ECCE)

Early Child Care and Education under Sarva Shiksha Abhiyan directly supports girl's education, especially at elementary school stage as it relieves girls from sibling care. The situation of street children and thousands of visible and invisible working children are mapped annually with the help of voluntary organizations working in the urban areas.

Balika Samriddhi Yojana

Balika Samriddhi Yojana (BSY) is also an important Government Scheme run by Ministry of Women and Child Development to boost education of girl children. The target groups are the girl children in families below poverty line in rural and urban areas born on or after 15th August, 1997. The objectives include—

- To change negative attitude of the family and community towards the girl child at birth and her mother.
- To improve enrolment and retention of girl children in schools.
- To increase the age at marriage of girls.
- To support the girl to undertake income generating activities.

Saakshar Bharat Mission (SBM)

Adult Education is an extending educational option to those adults, who have lost the chance and have crossed the age of formal education, but now feel a need for education of any type, including literacy, basic education, skill development (Vocational Education) and equivalency. With this special focus on promotion of adult education a number of programmes have been initiated in India. The most effective and famous is being the National Literacy Mission (NLM) launched in 1988 to impart functional literacy to non-literates in the age-group of 15-35 years in a time bound manner. Later, to further reinforce Adult Education, and Skill Development, with special focus on females, Government of India introduced Saakshar Bharat as a mission mode. Saakshar Bharat was launched by Department of School Education and Literacy (DSEL), Ministry of Human Resource Development (MHRD), Government of India (GoI), on the International Literacy Day, 8th September, 2009 with the following goals: to raise literacy rate to 80 per cent, to reduce gender gap to 10 per cent and minimize regional and social disparities, with focus on Women, SCs, STs, Minorities, other disadvantaged groups. The mission has four major objectives:

- Impart functional literacy and numeracy to non-literate and non-numerate adults.
- Enable the neo-literate adults to continue their learning beyond

basic literacy and acquire equivalency to formal educational system.
- Impart non- and neo-literates relevant skill development programmes to improve their earning and living conditions.
- Promote a learning society by providing opportunities to neo literate adults for continuing education.

These extensive focuses on female literacy by the Government of India have become a force multiplier for all other social development programmes. The campaign has liberated the Indian woman through the creation of critical consciousness to take charge of her environment where she faces multiple deprivations and disabilities on the basis of class, caste and gender.

Apart from programmes and policies related to enhancing female literacy, the Government initiated the National Policy for the Empowerment of Women in 2001. Apart from this, there exist several legislative acts to provide protection and ensure the rights of women. The Eleventh Five Year Plan (2007-2012) had undertaken to ensure that women are at the central stage of all activities which include economic, social, and political. Some of the currently operating schemes for economic empowerment include Swa-shakti, Swayamsiddha, Swaslamban Programmes, support to Training and Employment Programme which aim to bring out socio-economic development and empowerment of women through promotion of women SHGs, micro credit, and income generating activities.

Goal 4: Reduce Child Mortality

Government is trying to reduce the child mortality through Reproductive and Child Health Programme (RCH). Integrated Management of Neonatal and Childhood Illnesses (IMNCI) programme launched to find out the causes of child mortality and on the basis of that it take protective measures. In the Eleventh Five Year Plan the target of IMR is 28/1000 live births. To achieve the target Accredited Social Health Activist (ASHA) are appointed to identify the aspects of new born care and promoting optimal breastfeeding practice. Integrated Child Development Scheme (ICDS) is another major programme to deal with the children and pregnant women. Some of the programmes initiated by the Government to reduce the child mortality are:

Integrated Management of Neonatal and Childhood Illnesses (IMNCI)

The Integrated Management of Neonatal and Childhood Illness (IMNCI) was the Indian adaptation of the WHO-UNICEF standard Integrated Management of Childhood Illness (IMCI) strategy and has the focus on newborn and child health strategy under Reproductive Child Health II and National Rural Health Mission. The IMNCI strategy provided an integrated approach include a wide range of interventions for standard management of the leading causes of childhood morbidity and mortality like acute respiratory infections, diarrhoea, malaria, measles, and malnutrition.

Home-Based Newborn Care (HBNC)

Reduction in infant and child mortality is one of the prime goals of National Rural Health Mission. Under NRHM, India has made a significant progress in the field of reducing Infant Mortality Rate. It has also been understood that a high proportion of infant death is directly related to newborn death and further reduction in IMR can only be achieved through more focused and cost effective interventions and Home Based Newborn Care is a crucial factor for getting better outcome. HNBC is a model health care strategy, which has proved to decrease childhood mortality rate. The NRHM has taken several initiatives for effective promotion of HNBC. Accredited Social Health Activist (ASHA) has being trained to administer various medical and newborn care services. The major objective of HNBC is to decrease neonatal mortality and morbidity through:

- Providing essential newborn care to all newborn and prevention of various complications.
- Early detection and providing especial focus to low birth weight newborns.
- Early detection of illness in newborn and provide required medical and referral services.
- Sensitize families for adoption of good and healthy practices while dealing with mother and newborn.

New Born Care Scheme (NBCS)

Under the NBCS, in addition to 80 districts under RCH phase I, 60 more districts have been covered under RCH phase II wherein the existing neonatal care facilities have been upgraded. In addition, the National Neonatology Forum (NNF) had imparted training to health personnel.

Promotion of Infant and Young Child Feeding

This is a breast feeding partnership which aims to revive the breast feeding hospital initiative. The Eleventh Five-Year Plan had set a goal to reduce the IMR to 28/1000 live births. ASHAs were trained on identified aspects of newborn care during their training. A special focus has been given to promoting optimal breast feeding practices among women at home and also in better health facilities.

Integrated Child Development Services (ICDS) Programme

The Integrated Child Development Services (ICDS) is the largest national programme that caters to children from conception to below six years of age. It is targeted towards the poorest children and poorest women. In 1975-76, the Government of India launched the ICDS programme, a total of 33 projects on an experimental basis. By its success in taking a holistic view of the development of child and care of its mother, ICDS has become a pace setter in the developing world. In just two decades of its functioning, the programme has been able to achieve an improvement both in pre-natal and post-natal environment of the child through reduction in the incidence of child deficiencies, increase in the child survival rate, enhancing its health and providing nutrition and learning opportunities specially for unprivileged sections in the rural and tribal areas and urban slums. ICDS in India respond to the challenge of meeting the holistic needs of the child. The programme provides an integrated approach for stimulation of learning, health and nutrition, water and environmental sanitation targeting young children, pregnant and lactating mothers and adolescent girls' groups. Services provided under ICDS are:

Supplementary Nutrition: One of the main components of ICDS is the "supplementary nutrition programme" (SNP). The need for supplementary feeding rose from the fact that many children are unlikely to be well fed at home. This may be due to poverty, lack of time, inadequate awareness of children's nutritional needs, etc. The supplementary nutrition programmes under ICDS services have been serving at least four purposes: a nutrition purpose, an incentive purpose, a well-being purpose and a socialization purpose.

Immunization: Right from birth, children are exposed to various health hazards including communicable diseases. In order to protect the children against these diseases immunization has to be done. Immunization increases the fighting power of the body. Immunization against tuberculosis, diphtheria, whooping cough tetanus, measles and polio for all children under one year of age and immunization against tetanus of all the expectant mothers in the ICDS project areas has been envisaged under the ICDS scheme. Vaccination delivery has been done with the help of paramedical staff and community outreach workers. The National Rural Health Mission (NRHM) has been playing an important role in this immunization sessions from its inception (2005). It has been an initiative that would facilitate a better integration of health services with ICDS. Further, the post of Accredited Social Health Activist (ASHA) in every settlement of 1,000 persons in 18 major States under NRHM has opened an opportunity for further convergence of ICDS and health services; extend the reach and quality of health related ICDS services.

Health Check-Up: Health check-up service is an important component of ICDS which includes services regarding ante-natal care of pregnant mother, post-natal care of lactating mother and new born babies and care of children under six years of age. The entire population of expectant and nursing women and of children less than six years of age of the project area is expected to be covered under this service.

Referral Services: The purpose of referral services is to provide medical care of an appropriate standard according to the seriousness of the disease as well as follow-up care of cases that have been treated or given medical attention at appropriate levels

Nutrition and Health Education: The Nutrition and Health Education component of the ICDS scheme aims at effective communication of certain basic health and nutrition messages with a view to enhancing the mother's awareness of the child's needs and her capacity to lookafter these within the family environment. Nutrition and health education has been given to all women in the age-group 15-44 years and other members of the family as well. A special follow up has been made for mothers whose children suffer from malnutrition and from frequent illness.

Need for Child Care Education: In the ICDS scheme, child care education is the core of health and nutrition education, and the objective of such education is not to impart knowledge but to reinforce or change behaviour and practices related to child and maternal care.

Non-Formal pre-School Education: Non-formal pre-school education has been very crucial component of the package of ICDS services. It seeks to lay the foundation of proper physical, psychological, cognitive and social development of the child. Children aged between 3-6 years have the benefit of non-formal pre-school education through the institution of Anganwadi set-up in rural as well as urban areas.

Goal 5: Improve Maternal Health

The Reproductive and Child Health Programme (RCH), under the umbrella of National Rural Health Mission (NRHM), has been implemented by Ministry of Health and Family Welfare to addresses the issue of reduction of Infant Mortality Rate, Maternal Mortality Rate and Total Fertility Rate through a range of activities. The government has intensified the maternal health care facilities under RCH II and NRHM which aimed to aware and empower the expected women regarding the importance of skilled birth attendant for safe delivery. Some of these specific initiatives include the following:

Janani Suraksha Yojana (JSY)

Janani Suraksha Yojana (JSY) was launched in 2005 by Ministry of Health and Family Welfare. It provides a differential one-time cash incentive to pregnant women for institutional/home births through skilled assistance. The most important of these is the Janani Suraksha Yojana (JSY), which has led to a huge increase in institutional deliveries within just four years. Under Janani Suraksha Yojana (JSY), a safe motherhood intervention for promoting institutional delivery, the number of beneficiaries rose from 7.39 lakhs in 2005-06 to about 1 crore in 2009-10. Under JSY, the government provides a cash incentive for pregnant mothers to have institutional births as well as pre- and ante-natal care. It also provides cash incentives to female community health workers for promoting safe care in pregnancy and facilitating access to institutional care.

ASHA

Quality of antenatal and postnatal care is also being strengthened, with the Accredited Social Health Activist (ASHA) providing support for increasing utilization. Promoting safe delivery at home by ensuring the use of Skilled Birth Attendants (SBAs) has been another important initiative under the National Rural Health Mission (NRHM) to reduce rates of maternal and neonatal mortality among women who opt to deliver at home. Massive training of Auxiliary Nurse Midwives (ANMs) and nurses for safe delivery have also helped in a major way. In parallel to these efforts the upgradation of health facilities to provide emergency obstetric care and to improve access to skilled birth attendants made a significant difference to health outcomes.

Indira Gandhi Matritva Sahyog Yojana (IGMSY)

Although Janani Suraksha Yojana (JSY) of Ministry of Health and Family Welfare (MoH&FW) provides a one-time cash incentive to a pregnant woman for institutional delivery/home delivery through skilled assistance, it does not address wage loss during pregnancy and after delivery. Hence, a need for introducing a modest maternity benefit to partly compensate for the wage loss of Pregnant and Lactating (P&L) women was recommended by the Planning Commission in the Eleventh Five Year Plan. Keeping this in view, the Ministry of Women and Child Development introduced a new Scheme for P&L women called Indira Gandhi Matritva Sahyog Yojana (IGMSY)—a Conditional Maternity Benefit Scheme was implemented from 2010-11, initially in 52 pilot districts across the country. The Scheme is implemented using the ICDS platform covering approximately 14 lakh women in the initial years. Under this Scheme, a cash incentive of Rs. 4000 are being provided directly to women 19 years and above for the first two live births subject to the woman fulfilling specific conditions relating to maternal child health and nutritional aspects. Cash incentives are being provided in three instalments, between the second trimesters of pregnancy till the infant completes 6 months of age. Women enrolled under IGMSY are also encouraged to avail JSY package for institutional delivery and *vice versa*. However, there is no cash incentive under IGMSY at the time of delivery since cash incentive for this is already provided under JSY.

Maternal Care under ICDS

Ante-natal care of pregnant mother and Post-natal care of lactating mother and new born babies are two important components of ICDS programme. ICDS programme has been providing service of health check-up and medical care to the more needy mothers and children of poor and marginal families. Ante-natal care includes:

- Complete physical and obstetrical examination of the pregnant mother at regular intervals. A minimum of four physical examinations of the mother during her pregnancy should be the target. Of these at least one should be in the home of the mother and one visit after 36 weeks of pregnancy. More visits may be required in complicated cases.

- Check-up and serial recording of weight, blood pressure, blood group, hemoglobin and examination of urine.
- Immunization against tetanus by administering tetanus toxoid according to the prescribed schedule. Since in rural and tribal areas the system of delivery is still primitive and most of the women still depend on local, sometimes untrained *dais* (birth attendants), immunization against tetanus would be of utmost importance.
- Supplementation with iron and folic acid tablets as the incidence of anaemia, especially that of iron deficiency is very high in India (due to high prevalence of hookworm disease and poor iron intake due to inadequate diet).
- Identification of 'high risk mothers' during the ante-natal clinics, i.e., mothers with bad obstetrical history, e.g., still birth, abortions, caesarian section, etc., any young and old primipara or grand multipara, mothers with medical problem like tuberculosis, diabetes, heart disease, syphilis, etc., any pregnancy with complications like toxaemia characterized by swelling of feet and legs and high blood pressure. Such 'high risk mothers' should be referred to appropriate institutions for special care.
- Maintenance of records of ante-natal care in the Ante-Natal Card prescribed for the purpose.

The post-natal care is also an important aspect of health care system particularly in rural and tribal areas. As most of the mothers in rural areas deliver in their homes, only limited post-natal care can be rendered to them. Post-Natal care includes:

- General physical examination of the mother with special reference to the conditions of her breast, abdomen, perineum and pelvic organs to ensure that she has regained her general health and is fit to resume her normal work.
- Physical examination of the child and advice on his health and nutrition requirements, e.g., importance of breast-feeding, infant care, immunization, etc.
- Advice on family planning and motivating mothers to adopt

suitable methods for spacing the next birth or for birth control if the size of the family is within norms, and
- Recording the findings of the post-natal examination and the acceptance of the family planning method on the ante-natal card of the mother.

Goal 6: Combat HIV/AIDS, Malaria and other Diseases

To achieve the sixth goal of MDG, the government is implementing its programmes through National AIDS Control Organization (NACO). India has taken an aggressive step toward HIV/AIDS control by implementing the third phase of its National AIDS Control Programme (NACP), which was designed to reverse the spread of HIV/AIDS by 2012. Its thrust areas include treatment of sexually transmitted infections, voluntary counselling and testing, and condom promotion. The National AIDS Control Organization (NACO) has collaborated with Hindustan Latex Limited (HLL) on a Condom Vending Machine (CVM) Project. Moreover, NACO collaborated with UNICEF to implement the School Based Adolescence Programme to aware the students about HIV/AIDS, with the objective to reach out to some 33 million students.

National AIDS Control Programme (NACP)

The national response to HIV/AIDS in India over the last decade has yielded encouraging outcomes in terms of prevention and control of HIV. Recent HIV estimations highlight an overall reduction in adult HIV prevalence as well as new infections (HIV incidence) in the country, although variations exist across the States. Analysis of epidemic projections revealed that the number of annual new HIV infections has declined by more than 50 per cent during the last decade. This is one of the most important evidence on the impact of the various interventions under the National AIDS Control Programme and scaled-up prevention strategies.

NACP-I (1992-97) was the first effort in India to develop a national public health programme in HIV/AIDS prevention and control. The aims of the programme were to prevent HIV transmission, decrease the morbidity and mortality associated with HIV infection, and minimize the socio-economic impact of HIV infection. The National AIDS Control Organisation (NACO) was established in June 1992 under the Department of Health for implementation of the programme. A National AIDS Control

Board was constituted for approval of NACO policies, expediting sanctions and for approval of major financial and administrative decisions. State AIDS Cells (SACs) were constituted in all the States and Union Territories (UT) to implement programme activities locally. NACP-I provided certain services: education campaigns, protection of the blood supply, condom promotion, a system to monitor the prevalence of HIV, treatment for sexually transmitted diseases and limited treatment for AIDS-related conditions. Two components were added later: targeted interventions and "inter-sectoral collaboration".

In November 1999, NACP-II was launched with financial credit support from the World Bank. The focus of NACP-II moved from the more disseminated goal of generating awareness on HIV prevention, to targeted intervention, a concept introduced in the latter part of NACP-I. The targeted intervention was meant to change high risk behaviour in populations who were at risk of contracting the infection and spreading it in the general population. The projects were meant to use peer educators to counsel, provide condoms through social marketing and provide information to encourage a change in behaviour. Mass education campaigns were conducted using print media, electronic media and folk art forms, especially directed at people under the age of 25 years. Voluntary Counselling and Testing Centres (VCTCs) were introduced early in NACP-II. The Programme for Prevention of Mother (later Parent) to Child Transmission (PPTCT) of HIV aimed to prevent the transmission of HIV from pregnant, HIV-positive women to their children. The NACP-II institutionalised the use of the society model for the programme at the State level. The State AIDS Cells of all the States and union territories were converted to societies registered under the Charitable Societies Act for greater flexibility and more effective programme management.

The focus of NACP has shifted over the time, from raising awareness to behaviour change, from a national response to a more decentralized response and to increasing involvement of NGOs and networks of PLHA. Phase-III (2007-2012) of NACP-III has evolved as a scientifically configured programme, grounded on a strong structure of policies, programmes, schemes, operational guidelines, rules and norms. NACP-III aims at halting and reversing HIV epidemic in India over the five-year period by scaling up prevention efforts among High Risk Groups (HRG) and General Population and integrating them with Care, Support and Treatment services. Thus, Prevention and Care, Support and Treatment (CST) form the two important pillars of all the AIDS control efforts in India. Strategic Information Management and institutional strengthening activities provide the required technical, managerial and administrative support for implementing the core activities under NACP-III at national, State and district levels.

Detailed Activities

1. *Counselling and Testing Services*: HIV counselling and testing services are a key entry point to prevention of HIV infection and to treatment and care of people with HIV. Counselling and testing services have been scaled up significantly and 65 lakh persons were counselled and tested through 5,246 Integrated Counselling and Testing Centres including 29.3 lakh pregnant women during 2011-12.
2. *Under STI/RTI prevention and control component* of NACP during 2010-11, 102.13 lakh new Sexually Transmitted Infections (STI) or Reproductive Tract Infection (RTI) episodes have been treated. Convergence strategy with National Rural Health Mission (NRHM) through standardized treatment protocols and common operational guidelines has also been developed.
3. *Blood Safety Programme*: The specific objective of the blood safety programme is to ensure reduction in the transfusion associated with HIV transmission, while making safe and quality blood available within one hour of its requirement in a health facility. Under Blood Safety Programme, 1,127 blood banks are being supported, including 155 Blood Component Separation facilities.
4. The National AIDS Control Organization (NACO) has collaborated with Hindustan Latex Limited (HLL) on a Condom Vending Machine (CVM) Project. Under this initiative, it has been proposed to set up 11,025 vending machines in 42 districts in the six high prevalence States and 24 districts of the four EAG States.
5. *Prophylactic treatments:* The programme also promised to provide "prophylactic drugs to health workers who are exposed to HIV infection and to HIV positive pregnant women". 'Post-exposure prophylaxis' is a course of antiretroviral drugs given to reduce the chances of an infection in people, especially health care workers, who suffer needle stick injuries or other exposures to blood or body fluids that may be infected with HIV. Health care institutions are expected to train their staff and also institute practices to reduce the chances of such exposure.

6. *Care, support and treatment*: In terms of treatment, NACP-III promises treatment for opportunistic infections (such as TB and fungal infections), and first-line antiretroviral drugs to those adults and children who qualify according to its medical criteria. In February 2008, the government introduced second-line drugs to those who have become immune to the first-line drugs.
7. *Collaborations*: NACP-III worked with different types of organizations for prevention, care, support, treatment and service delivery. Under NACP-III, NGOs provided nutrition and other welfare services, community care centres provided medical and social support, women's groups, youth groups, trade unions, private sector, Civil society organizations interacte with people living with HIV/AIDS and government departments integrated HIV prevention into their several activities.
8. *Surveillance*: One of the major achievements of NACP has been a convincing HIV sentinel surveillance system. Information gathered through HIV sentinel surveillance, AIDS case surveillance, behavioural sentinel surveillance and STD surveillance helped in tracking the epidemic and provides the direction to the programme. NACP-III also included PPTCT and ANC surveillance. In addition, a nationwide Computerized Management Information System (CMIS) is provided for programme monitoring and evaluation.
9. *Targeted Intervention (TI)* was being implemented through Non-Governmental Organizations (NGOs) and Community-Based Organizations (CBOs), which provide services on behaviour change communication, condom promotion, STI care, needle syringe exchange programme, Opioid Substitution Therapy (OST) and referrals for HIV testing and Anti-Retroviral Treatment.
10. *Link Worker Scheme* was a rural based intervention for prevention and care needs of HRG and vulnerable population of rural area including of referral to ICTC services and STI services, Condom promotion and distribution, information related to HIV prevention and related services.

The National Vector Borne Disease Control Programme (NVBDCP)

Under the umbrella of NRHM, NVBDCP has been implemented by Directorate of Health Services in coordination with the Department of Health and Family Welfare. There are six diseases, which have been addressed under National Vector Borne Diseases (VBDs) Control Programme (NVBDCP), viz., Malaria, Filaria, Dengue, Chikungunya, Japanese Encephalitis and Kala-azar. It framed technical policies and guidelines for the control of malaria in the country. Every State has State vector borne diseases control component under the Directorate of Health Services with stipulated technical components. There is a system of coordination between the State and Centre for effective implementation and monitoring of Programme.

Revised National Tuberculosis Control Programme: Tuberculosis (TB) is an infectious disease caused by a Bacterium, Mycobacterium tuberculosis. It is spread through the air by a person suffering from TB. A single patient can infect 10 or more people in a year. The DOTS strategy along with the other components of the Stop TB strategy, implemented under the Revised National Tuberculosis Control Programme (RNTCP) in India, is a comprehensive package for TB control. The Directly Observed Treatment Short course (DOTS) strategy was launched in India in the year 1997 phase II (2006-2011) of RNTCP which is in line with the new WHO stop TB strategy for TB control is a step toward achieving the TB-related MDGs in terms of reducing the prevalence of TB by 50 per cent by 2015. The vision of the programme is to achieve and maintain a cure rate of at least 85 per cent in new sputum positive pulmonary TB patients, and detection of at least 70 per cent of such cases.

In the first phase of RNTCP (1998-2005), the programme's focus was on ensuring expansion of quality DOTS services to the entire country. There are many challenges remaining that are to be addressed in order to achieve the TB-related targets set by the Millennium Development Goals for 2015 and to achieve TB control in the longer term. In the second phase which the programme aims to firstly consolidate the gains made to date, to widen services both in terms of activities and access, and to sustain the achievements for decades to come in order to achieve ultimate objective of TB control in the country.

Goal 7: Ensure Environmental Sustainability

The Ministry of Non-conventional Energy Sources is running several programmes to provide better systems for cooking and lighting. Joint Forest Management schemes are in operation wherein rural women living below the poverty line are provided with financial assistance to raise nurseries in forest areas. The Rajiv Gandhi Grameen Vidyutikiran Yojana started in the year 2005 aims to provide all rural households with access to electricity.

The government has put in place a National Mission for a Green India as part of the country's National Action Plan for Climate Change with a budget of Rs. 46,000 crores (approx. USD 10 billion) over a period of 10 years. The overarching objective of the Mission is to increase forest and tree cover in 5 million ha area and improve quality of forest cover in another 5 million ha. Thus, the Mission will help in improving ecosystem services in 10 million ha of land, and increase flow of forest based livelihood services to, and income of about 3 million forest dependent households.

National Rural Drinking Water Programme (NRDWP)

To meet the emerging challenges in the rural drinking water sector relating to availability, sustainability and quality, designated components under the programme have been put in place as NRDWP (Coverage), NRDWP (Sustainability), NRDWP (Water quality), NRDWP (DDP), NRDWP (Natural calamity) and NRDWP (Support).

Support Fund and Water and Sanitation Support Organisation (WSSO)

There are many Support activities for which States would require funds to achieve the long term goal of the sector. Thus support for information, education and communication, human resource development, water quality monitoring and surveillance, setting up water testing laboratories, engaging State Technical Agency and National Experts Groups for preparation of Projects, technical scrutiny and evaluation of rural water supply can be taken up under the 5 per cent Support fund of NRDWP.

Nirmal Gram Puraskar (NGP)

Government of India has been promoting sanitation coverage in a campaign mode to ensure better health and quality of life for people in rural India. To add strength to its implementation, GoI launched an award based Incentive Scheme for fully sanitized and open defecation free Gram Panchayats, Blocks, Districts and States called "Nirmal Gram Puraskar" (NGP) in October 2003 and gave away the first awards in 2005 as a component of its flagship scheme Total Sanitation Campaign (TSC). Nirmal Gram Puraskar till 2011 was given by Ministry of Drinking Water and Sanitation (MoDWS), Government of India at all levels of PRIs that is Gram Panchayat, Block Panchayat and district Panchayat. The award has been given to those PRIs which attain 100 per cent open defecation free environment. The concept of Nirmal Gram Puraskar has been highly praised internationally as a unique tool of social engineering and community mobilization and has helped a difficult programme like rural sanitation to pick up. Each Gram Panchayat getting the NGP has a ripple effect in the surrounding villages. It has been the prime mover behind the amazing progress achieved in rural sanitation coverage since 2005.

Goal 8: Develop a Global Partnership for Development

India's diverse economy ranges from traditional village farming to a wide range of modern industries, and a multitude of services. India achieved 8.5 per cent GDP growth in 2006, 9.0 per cent in 2007, and 7.3 per cent in 2008. India's increasing participation with the world economy is evident from the trade to GDP ratio, which increased from 22.5 per cent of GDP in 2000-2001 to 34.8 per cent of GDP in 2006-2007. The promotion of e-governance on a massive scale is one of the important areas of concern of the National Common Minimum Needs Programme of the Government.

National Knowledge Network

The National Knowledge Network is being implemented by Department of Information Technology to bring together all the stakeholders in Science, Technology, Higher Education, Research & Development and Governance. The application areas envisaged under the National Knowledge Network cover Agriculture, Education, Health, e-governance, Grid Computing (High Performance Computing). The output of the National Knowledge Network project will be a high capacity countrywide Infrastructure at education and research Institute level, to support education and research applications, and other application as envisaged by these institutions which require very high bandwidth. A high speed data communication network would be established, which would interconnect Institutions of higher learning.

National e-Governance Plan

Over the years, a large number of initiatives have been undertaken by the Government of India to bring an era of e-Government. Continuous efforts have been made at multiple levels to improve the delivery of public services and simplify the process of access. The e-Governance in India has progressively evolved from computerization of Government Departments to initiatives that strengthened the sharp ends of Governance, such as citizen centricity, service orientation, transparency and accountability. The Government of India has made the National e-Governance Plan (NeGP) in pursuance of its policy of introducing e-Governance at a huge scale. The National e-Governance Plan (NeGP), takes a holistic view of e-Governance initiatives across the country, integrating them into a collective vision, a shared cause. The NeGP vision is to "Make all Government Services accessible to the common man in his locality, through common service delivery outlets and ensure efficiency, transparency and reliability of such services at affordable costs to realize the basic needs of the common man" (*Source*: Depatrment of Electronic and Information Technology). The Government approved the National e-Governance Plan (NeGP), consisting of 27 Mission Mode Projects and 8 components, on May 18, 2006. In the year 2011, 4 projects-Health, Education, PDS and Posts were also introduced to make the list of 27 MMPs to 31 Mission Mode Projects (MMPs).

State Wide Area Network (SWAN)

The Government has approved the Scheme for establishing State Wide Area Networks (SWANs) across the country, in March 2005. Under this Scheme, technical and financial assistance are being provided to the States/ UTs for establishing SWANs to connect all State/UT headquarters up to the Block level *via* District/ sub-Divisional Headquarters, in a vertical hierarchical structure with a minimum bandwidth capacity of 2 Mbps per link. State Wide Area Network is an advanced telecommunication infrastructure and is used now-a-days extensively for exchange of data and other types of information between two or more locations, separated by significant geographical distances. The medium of connectivity are copper, optical fibre cable or wireless. Such wide area networks, in a way, create a highway for electronic transfer of information in the form of voice, video and data.

Information Technology (IT) for Masses

IT for Masses is a Plan Scheme of Department of Information Technology (DIT). It was introduced in the Tenth Five Year Plan and continuing in the Eleventh Five Year Plan with the objective to provide financial assistance to various project proposals from States/UTs and Autonomous Societies for implementing ICT projects for development of Gender, SC and ST. During Tenth Five Year Plan, Planning Commission of India recommended for the formulation of a Plan scheme "IT for Masses' for taking the IT to the common masses. It the initial phase the scheme focused on Infrastructure and Services, Electronics Governance, Education, Mass Campaign for IT Awareness. Later in the Eleventh Plan, the IT for Masses scheme had been restructured to focus on Women Empowerment and uplifting of SC/STs through ICT (Information and Communication Technologies). The new components incorporated in the scheme strategy were: (i) Gender and ST/SC equity and inclusion, (ii) Poverty Alleviation. The Twelfth Five Year Plan (2012-17) has recommended continuance of the scheme in Twelfth Plan under 'e-Inclusion' as thrust area. From 2013-14 onwards, IT for Masses Programme was merged with Manpower Development Scheme of the Department and has been aiming to promote activities in ICT for focus groups and areas for inclusive growth of IT sector.

Conclusion

Millennium Development Goals (MDGs) were designed to help people to overcome extreme poverty and multiple deprivations. MDGs are set to be achieved by 2015 and are most strategically designed, broadly supported, comprehensive and specific development goals, the world has ever agreed upon. In Indian context, despite existence and launches of various programmes, policies, laws to address the targets and achieving the goals of MDGs, the progress is appeared to be slow in most of the areas. Education and global economic progress are the exceptional case. To achieve the goals within the time line, more efforts and intensity are needed and integrated policies should be designed to fulfil the targets.

The present scenario of India's achievement towards Millennium Development Goals (MDGs) is not adequate and needs more intensive efforts. As the government has been facing resource constraint, an effective solution could emerge in terms of active involvement of NGOs, civil society and corporate worlds. At this situation integrated effort is essential for achieving economic growth as well as meaningful social and human development. In addition, information and research about development towards the MDGs in India remains concentrated at the national level. With the kind of disparities and contrasts that exist in the socio-economic structure of various States, it seems to have some research and policies focused on the existing position of States on the MDG indicators, and action plans in order to move towards the implementation of the MDGs. Areas of further research and proper policy resolution could place added importance on information and interventions at the State level as well as at the local level.

References

Beyond the Midpoint: Achieving the Millennium Development Goals. Report prepared by the UNDP, 2010.

Deolalikar, Anil B.; (2005), *Attaining the Millennium Development Goals in India*, The World Bank, Oxford University Press. Downloaded from the web site www.worldbank.org.in.

Dwivedi, Rishi Muni; (2005), Poverty and Development Programmes in India, New Century Publications, New Delhi.

Government of India; (1978), *Integrated Child Development Services (ICDS) Manual*, Department of Women and Child Development, New Delhi.

Government of India; (2005), *Annual Report for the Year 2004-05*, Ministry of Women and Child Development, pp. 31, 42.

Government of India; (2005), National Plan of Action for Children, Department of Women and Child Development, Ministry of HRD, New Delhi

Jose, Sunny and Navaneetham, K.; (2008), A Factsheet on Women's Malnutrition in India, *Economic and Political Weekly*, Vol. XLIII, No. 33, 16 August.

Kapil, U., Saxena, N. and Nayar, D.; (1998), *Integrated Child Development Services (ICDS): A Programme for Maternal and Child Development*, Indian Public Health (in Press), New Delhi.

Karalay, G.N.; (2005), *Integrated Approach to Rural Development—Policies, Programmes and Strategies*, Concept Publishing Company, New Delhi.

Krishnamurti, Latha; (1991), *Girl Child in India*, Ashish Publishing Housing, New Delhi.

Legislative Department, (2009), The Right to Children to Free and Compulsory Education Act 2009, Ministry of Law & Justice, Government of India, New Delhi.

Mari Bhat, P.N.; (2001), Maternal mortality in India an update: working paper downloaded from www.iussp.org/Brazil2001/s10/S16_01_Bhat.pdf

Measuring India's progress on the Millennium Development Goals. A Citizens Report 2007. Downloaded from www. Udyem.org

Mehta, Shiv R.; (1984), *Rural Development Policies and Programmes*, Sage Publications, New Delhi.

Millennium Development Goals and Gender Budgeting: Where Does India Stand? Centre for Legislative Research and Advocacy Oxfam India.

Millennium Development Goals India Country Report 2005; Ministry of Statistics and Programme Implementation, Government of India, New Delhi. The report available on http://www.mospi.nic.in

Millennium Development Goals Report 2011, United Nations. http://www.ungoals.org

Millennium Development Goals States of India Report (2010), (Special Edition), Ministry of Statistics and Programme Implementation, Government of India, New Delhi.

Millennium Development Goals: Confronting the Challenges of Gender Equality and Fragile States. Global monitoring report (2007). Prepared by The World Bank. Downloaded from www.worldbank.org

Ministry of Health and Family Welfare; (2011), Home Based Newborn Care Operational Guideline, Government of India, New Delhi.

Ministry of Urban Development, Government of India; (2012), Jawaharlal Nehru National Urban Renewal Mission, *Annual Update 2010-11*. Government of India, New Delhi.

Ministry of Women and Child Development; (2011), Indira Gandhi Matritva Sahyog Yojana—A Conditional Maternity Benefit Scheme Implementation Guidelines for State Governments/UT Administrations, Government of India, New Delhi.

Niranjanaradhya and Kashyap Aruna; (2006), The 'Fundamentals' of the Fundamental Right to Education in India, Centre for Child and the Law, National Law School of India University, Bangalore.

Official Website of JNNURM: http://jnnurm.nic.in

Paul, Sujit Kumar; (2004), Continuing Education Programme: The Way for Empowering Rural People. *Indian Journal of Adult Education*, Vol. 65, Nos. 1-2, January-June, 2004.

Paul, Sujit Kumar; (2011), Millennium Development Goals: Progress and Strategies in India, *Journal of World Education*, Volume, 41, No. 1 and 2.

Planning Commission; (2008), *Eleventh Five Year Plan 2007-12*, Volume II Social Sector, Government of India, New Delhi.

Planning Commission; (2012), Report of the Committee on JNNURM-II, Government of India, New Delhi.

Rathan, V.; (1997), *Integrated Child Development Services, Programme Administration*, Vol. I and II, S. Chand & Company Ltd. Publisher, New Delhi, 110055.

Singh, Katar; (2009), *Rural Development: Principles, Policies and Management*, Sage Publications India Pvt. Ltd., New Delhi.

Singh, Prabhakar; (1982), *Community Development Programme in India*, Deep and Deep Publications, New Delhi.

UNDP; (2010), *Beyond the Midpoint: Achieving the Millennium Development Goals*. UNDP.

World Bank; (2007), Millennium Development Goals: Confronting the Challenges of Gender Equality and Fragile States, *Global Monitoring Report 2007*. Washington DC, Downloaded from www.worldbank.org.

Bibliography

ACCESS Development Services; (2008), *State of India's Livelihoods: The 4 P Report*. Edited by Sankar Datta and Vipin Sharma, New Delhi.

Agarwal, Bina; (1983), *Mechanization in Indian Agriculture: An Analytical Study based on Punjab*. Allied Publishers Private Limited, New Delhi.

Agarwal, U.; (1967), *Social Consequences of Technology Change*. New Heights, Delhi.

Agrawal, Binod C., Sharma, Sham Behari and Sinha, Arbind (Eds.), (2002), *Remote Sensing Applications in Brakish Water Fisheries: A Socio-Economic Study*, Concept Publishing Company Pvt. Ltd., New Delhi.

Alsop, R., Krishna, A. and Sjoblom, D.; (2000), Are Gram Panchayats Inclusive? Report of a Study Conducted in Rajasthan and Madhya Pradesh, Background Paper No. 3 of the World Bank's unpublished Overview of Rural Decentralisation in India, Volume 3.

Altekar, A.S.; (1997), State and Government in Ancient India, Motilal Banarsi Das Publications, New Delhi.

Ambasta, Pramathesh, Shankar, P.S. Vijay and Shah, Mihir; (2008), Two Years of NREGA: The Road Ahead, *Economic and Political Weekly,* February 2008.

Arora, R.C.; (1979), *Integrated Rural Development,* S. Chand & Company, New Delhi.

Ashley, Caroline and Diana Carney; (1999), *Sustainable Livelihoods: Lessons from Early Experience*, DFID, London.

Avasthi, P.K. *et al.*; (2002), Working and Impact of Self-Help Groups on Economic Status of Women in Watershed Areas of Madhya Pradesh, *Indian Journal of Agricultural Economics*, 56(3), June, 2002.

Bagchi, Jasodhara (ed.); (1995), *Indian Women: Myth and Reality*, Sangam Books (India) Private Limited: Hyderabad.

Bardhan, Pranab and Mookherjee, Dilip; (2000), Decentralising Anti-Poverty Programme in Developing Countries. De Ivery. Website:www.httpi/ lglobetrotter.berkeley.edu/macarthur/inequallty/papers/decdelpov.pdf

Bassi, N. and Kumar, D.M.; (2010), *NREGA and Rural Water Management in India: Improving Welfare Effects*, Occasional Paper No. 3-0910, Hyderabad: Institute for Resource Analysis and Policy, September 2010.

Basu, A.K.; (2011), Impact of Rural Employment Guarantee Schemes on Seasonal Labour Markets: Optimum Compensation and Workers, *The Journal of Economic Inequality*, USA: Springer, May 2011.

Basu, Kishanjit and Krishan, Jindal (eds.), (2000) *Microfinance: Emerging Challenges*, Tata McGraw-Hill, New Delhi.

Beteille, Andre; (1977), "The definition of Tribe", in Thapar Ramesh (ed). *Tribe Caste and Religion in India*, The MacMillan Company of India Limited, Delhi.

Beyond the Midpoint: Achieving the Millennium Development Goals. Report prepared by the UNDP, 2010.

Bhaduri, Sukla, (1992), *Transport and Regional Development: A Case Study of Road Transport of West Bengal*, Concept Publishing Company Pvt. Ltd., New Delhi.

Bhagyalakshmi, J.; (2000), Women in Development. *Employment News*, Vol. XXV, No. 3, April 15-21, 2000.

Bhatt, K.N. and Bhargava, Pradeep (Eds.), (2014), *Agrarian Change and Small Farmers: Super Markets, Viability and Food Policy*, Concept Publishing Company Pvt. Ltd., New Delhi.

Bhatt, Yogesh Kumar, Tandon, Rajesh and Sharma, Prem N.; (1998), *Building Farmers' Organisations for Integrated Watershed Management in India: A Trainers' Manual*, PRIA, New Delhi.

Bhattacharya, D. and, Chowdhury, S. Roy, (2012), *Statistics in Social Science and Agricultural Research*, Concept Publishing Company Pvt. Ltd., New Delhi.

Bhowmik, K.L.; (1986), *Tribal India: A Profile in Indian Ethnology,* The World Press Private Limited, Calcutta.

Bhowmik, P.K.; (1982), "Approach to Tribal Welfare", in *Tribal Development in India: Problems and Prospects*, ed. by Buddhadev Choudhury, Inter-India Publication, Delhi.

Bhowmik, P.K.; (1987), "Development and Anthropology: Rebuilding Rural and Tribal Economy", in *Anthropology, Development and Nation Building*, ed. by A.K. Kalla and K.S. Singh, Concept Publishing Company, New Delhi.

Bhowmik, Pradip Kumar; (1993), *Dynamics of Tribal Development*, Inter-India Publications, New Delhi.

Biju, M.R. (ed); (2012), *Rural Development Under Decentralised Governance*, Concept Publishing Company Pvt. Ltd., New Delhi.

BIRD; (2001), Sustainable Microfinance Challenges Facing MFIs, Report of a workshop organized by SIDBI and BIRD, Lucknow, 15-17 January, 2001.

Blair, H.; (2000), Participation and Accountability at the Periphery: Democratic Local Governance in Six Countries, *World Development*, 28(1), pp. 21 39.

Braun, Foachim Von and Ulrike, Grote; (2002), Does Decentralisation Serve the Poor, Ed. by Ahmed Ehtisham and Vito Tanzi, *Managing Fiscal Decentralisation*, London: Routledge.

Carney, D. Ed.; (1998), *Sustainable Rural Livelihoods: What Contribution can we make,* Papers presented at DFID's Natural Resource Advisers Conference, July 1998. Department for International Development, London.

Census Report; (2001), Government of India, New Delhi.

Central Employment Guarantee Council; (2010), Report of the Working Group on Planning and Execution, Government of India, New Delhi.

Chambers, Robert and Gordon Conway; (1992), *Sustainable Rural Livelihoods: Practical Concepts for the 21st Century*, IDS Discussion Paper 296, IDS, Brighton, UK, February 1992.

Chambers, Robert; (1983), *Rural Development: Putting the Last First,* Longman, London.

Chandhoke, S.K., (1990), *Nature and Structure of Rural Habitations*, Concept Publishing Company Pvt. Ltd., New Delhi.

Chandra, Aravind and Shah, Anupam; (1987), *Non-formal Education for All.* Sterling Publishers, New Delhi, India.

Chattopadhya, Raghabendra and Esther Duflo; (2004), *Women as Policymakers: Evidence from a Randomized Policy Experiment in India*, Econometrica.

Chaturvedi, Pradeep, (1995), *Bio-Energy Resources: Planning, Production and Utilization*, Concept Publishing Company Pvt. Ltd., New Delhi.

Chaturvedi, Pradeep, (2001), *Energy Management: Challenges for the Next Millennium*, Concept Publishing Company Pvt. Ltd., New Delhi.

Chaudhary, S.N. (Ed.), (2007), *Dalit Agenda and Grazing Land to Scheduled Castes and Scheduled Tribes*, Concept Publishing Company Pvt. Ltd., New Delhi.

Chaudhury S.N.; (2012), *Tribal Education: Implications for Development,* Concept Publishing Company Pvt. Ltd., New Delhi.

Chen, Martha, A. and Joann Vanek, Marilyn Carr; (2004), *Mainstreaming Informal Employment and Gender in Poverty Reduction*, Commonwealth Secretariat, London.

Choudhury, M.K.; (1996), "Impact of Tribal Planning in India with Special Emphasis on West Bengal" in *Socio-Economic Transformation in India*, ed. by Biswanath Ray, Kanishka Publishers, Distributors, New Delhi.

Chowdhury, Budhadeb (ed.); (1982), "*Tribal Devlopment in India: Problems and Prospects*", Inter-India Publications, New Delhi.

Copp, James, H.; (1972), Rural Sociology and Rural Development, *Rural Sociology,* Volume 37, December 1972.

Crook, R.C. and Manor, J.; (1998), *Democracy and Decentralisation in South Asia and West Africa*. Cambridge: Cambridge University Press.

Crook, R.C. and Sverrisson, A.S. (2001) 'Decentralisation and Poverty Alleviation in Developing Countries: A Comparative Analysis or, is West Bengal Unique?' IDS Working Paper 130. Brighton: Institute of Development Studies.

D'lima, Hazel; (1983), *Women in Local Government*, Concept Publishing Company Pvt. Ltd., New Delhi.

Dabholkar, A.R., (1999), *Elements of Bio Metrical Genetics (Revised and Enlarged Edition)*, Concept Publishing Company Pvt. Ltd., New Delhi.

Dabholkar, A.R., (2006), *General Plant Breeding*, Concept Publishing Company Pvt. Ltd., New Delhi.

Daltone, George; (1961), Economic Theory and Primitive Society. *American Anthropologist*. Vol. 63, No. 1, 1971: *Economic Anthropology and Development,* Basic Books, New York.

Dar, S.U.; (1992), *Impact of Integrated Rural Development Programme,* Anmol Publications, New Delhi.

Das, A.K.; Choudhuri, M.K.; Basu, S.K.; Saha, R.N.; Khan, N.C.; (1978), *Scheduled Tribes and Scheduled Castes of West Bengal : Programmes Facts and Figures,* Cultural Research Institute, Scheduled Castes and Tribes Welfare Department, Government of West Bengal, Calcutta.

Das, A.K.; Raha, M.K.; De, S.K.; (1990), *Tribal Situation in West Bengal*, Firma KLM Private Ltd., Calcutta.

Dasgupta, K.; (2001), An Informal Journey through Self-Help Groups, *Indian Journal of Agricultural Economics*, July-September, 2001.

Dasgupta, Rajaram, (1994), *Indian Agricultural Economy: An Analysis,* Concept Publishing Company Pvt. Ltd., New Delhi.

Dasgupta, Sugata and Murthy, L.S.N.; (1983), *Panchayati Raj Institution in West Bengal,* National Institute of Public Cooperation and Child Development, New Delhi.

Datar, Chhaya; (2007), Failure of National Rural Employment Guarantee Scheme in Maharashtra, *Economic and Political Weekly,* August 2007.

Datta, Prabhat; (2011), *Of Rural Decentralisation and People's Participation: Three Decades Experience in West Bengal*, Dasgupta & Co., Kolkata.

Datta, R.K. (Ed.), (1996), *Advances in Tropical Meteorology: Meteorology and National Development*, Concept Publishing Company Pvt. Ltd., New Delhi.

Datta, S., Mahajan, V. and Thakur, G.; (2004), *An Introduction to Livelihood Promotion*, New Economics Foundation (NEF), Ford Foundation, BASIX.

Debroy, B.; (2004), *Agenda for Improving Governance.* Academic Foundation, New Delhi.

Deogaonkar, S.G.; (1980), *Administration for Rural Development,* Concept Publishing Company Pvt. Ltd., New Delhi.

Deogaonkar, S.G.; (1994), *Tribal Administration and Development,* Concept Publishing Company Pvt. Ltd., New Delhi.

Deolalikar, Anil B.; (2005), *Attaining the Millennium Development Goals in India*, The World Bank, Oxford University Press. Downloaded from the website www.worldbank.org.in.

Desai, A.R.; (1969), *Rural Sociology in India,* Popular Prakashan, Bombay.

Desai, Neera and Patel, Vibhuti; (1985), *Indian Women: Change and Challenge in the International Decade 1975-1985,* Popular Prakashan, Bombay.

Desai, Vasant; (1991), *Rural Development,* Himalaya Publishing House, New Delhi.

Deshai, A.R.; (1977), *Tribe, Caste and Religion in India*, Ramesh Thapar (ed.), Macmillan Company of India Ltd., Delhi.

Deshpande, S.V. and Venkatesha, Murthy, G.B.; (2002), Pressures from Below: Decentralised Governance in Karnataka, *Economic and Political Weekly*, 4 May, 2002.

Dev, S.Mahendra; (2011), Climate Change, Rural Livelihoods and Agriculture (focus on Food Security) in Asia-Pacific Region, Indira Gandhi Institute of Development Research, Mumbai. http://www.igidr.ac.in/pdf/publication/WP-2011-014.pdf

Dewey, C.; (1972), 'Images of the Village Community: A Study in Anglo-Indian Ideology, *Modern Asian Studies*, Vol. 6, No. 3, pp. 291-328.

DFID; (1999), *Sustainable Livelihoods and Poverty Elimination: Background Briefing*, DFID, Londan. (www.ids.ac.uk/livelihoods.html).

DFID; (1999), *Sustainable Livelihoods Guidance Sheets*, DFID, London.

Drèze, J. and Sen, A.; (1996), *India: Economic Development and Social Opportunity*, Oxford University Press, Delhi.

Dreze, Jean (2005); Employment Guarantee: Promise and Demise; *Yojana: A Development Monthly*; Vol. 49, April 2005.

Dreze, Jean and Sen, Amartya; (2012), *India: Development and Participation*, Oxford University Press, New Delhi.

Dube, S.C.; (1998), "Development Designs and Tribal People" in *Antiquity to Modernity in Tribal India*, Volume I, ed. by S.C. Dube, Inter-India Publications, New Delhi.

Dube, S.C.; (1977), *Tribal Heritage of India*. Vikas Publication, New Delhi.

Dubey, J.P.; (2006), Continuing Education: Changing Perspective. *Indian Journal of Adult Education*. Vol. 67, Nos. 1-2, January-June 2006.

Dutta, P., Murgai, R., Ravallion, M. and Dominique, M.V.; (2012), *Does India's Employment Guarantee Scheme Guarantee Employment?*, Policy Research Paper, Washington, DC: World Bank, 2012.

Dutta, S.K.; (1991), *Cooperative Societies and Rural Development,* Mittal Publications, New Delhi.

Dutta, Sujit K; Ghosh, Dilip K.; (1994), "Peoples Participation in Rural Development : Need and Scope", *Participation and Governance,* Vol. 1, No. 2, November 1994.

Dwaraki, B.R., Narayanaswamy, N. and Ramesh, N.; (1996), *Towards Creating a Participatory Self-Help Credit Cooperative*, Institute of Rural Management, Anand, Gujarat.

Dwivedi, Rishi Muni; (2005), *Poverty and Development Programmes in India,* New Century Publications, New Delhi.

Elder, Sara and Dorothea, Schmidt; (2004), Global Employment Trends for Women, 2004, *Employment Strategy Paper (2004), 8*, Employment Strategy Department, ILO, Geneva.

Elson, Diane; (1999), Labour Market as Gendered Institutions: Equality, Efficiency and Empowerment Issues, in *World Development*, 27(3).

Epstein, T.S.; (1962), *Economic Development and Social Change in South India.* Manchester University Press, Manchester.

Everett, Jana Matson; (1979), *Women and Social Change in India*, Heritage Publishers, New Delhi.

Faizi, A.A.A. and Behera, Hari Charan (Eds.), (2014), *Land Records Management in India: A Plea for Reforms*, Concept Publishing Company Pvt. Ltd., New Delhi.

Faizi, Amir Afaque Ahmad; (2009), *Self-Help Groups and Marginalized Communities*, Concept Publishing Company Pvt. Ltd., New Delhi.

Fernandez, A.P.; (1995), *Rural Management System, Self-Help Group Concept*, *MYRADA,* Bangalore.

Freedman, R.; (1956), *Principles of Sociology*. New York, Halt.

Ghadially, Rehana,(ed), (1988), *Women in Indian Society*, Sage Publication, New Delhi.

Ghatak, M. and Ghatak, M.; (2002), Recent Reforms in the Panchayat System in West Bengal: Towards Greater Participatory Governance, *Economic and Political Weekly*, 5 January 2002, pp. 45-58.

Ghosh, A., (2005), *Capital Formation and Entrepreneurship in Indian Agriculture*, Concept Publishing Company Pvt. Ltd., New Delhi.

Ghosh, Buddhadeb; (2000), *Status of Panchayati Raj in the States and Union Territories of India*, Indian Institute of Social Sciences and Concept Publishing Company, New Delhi.

Ghosh, Gopi Nath (2008); NREGS Transparency and Accountability; *Yojana: A Development Monthly*, Vol. 52, August 2008.

Ghosh, J.; (2009), *Equity and Inclusion through Public Expenditure: The Potential of the NREGS*, New Delhi: Paper for International Conference on NREGA, 21-22 January 2009.

Ghosh, Jayati; (2011), India's Official Poverty Line, *Guardian*, London, UK.

Ghosh, Rathna, Pramanik, Alok Kumar; (1999), *Panchayat System in India. Historical, Constitutional and Financial Analysis*, Kanishka Publication, New Delhi.

Goel, S.L. and Kumar, R.; (2004), *Administration and Management of NGOs*, Deep & Deep, New Delhi.

Goela, Usha; (1992), Programmes for the Development of Women in the Government of India, in *Women's Issues: An Indian Perspective,* Ed. By Lakshmi Mishra, Northern Book Centre, New Delhi.

Golooba-Mutebi, F.; (2000), Reassessing Participation in Uganda, Paper presented at the conference, New Institutional Economics, Institutional Reform and Poverty Reduction, Development Studies Institute, London School of Economics and Political Science, 7-8 September 2000.

Government of India; (1978), *Integrated Child Development Services (ICDS) Manual*, Department of Women and Child Development, New Delhi.

Government of India; (2001), *National Policy for the Empowerment of Women*, Department of Women and Child Development, Ministry of Human Resources, New Delhi, India.

Government of India; (2005), *Annual Report for the Year 2004-05*, Ministry of Women and Child Development, pp. 31, 42.

Government of India; (2005), National Plan of Action for Children, Department of Women and Child Development, Ministry of HRD, New Delhi.

Government of India; 2009-10: *Annual Report,* Ministry of Tribal Affairs.

Govind, Nalini, (1986), *Regional Perspectives in Agricultural Development: A Case Study of Wheat and Rice in Selected Regions of India*, Concept Publishing Company Pvt. Ltd., New Delhi.

Gowda, M.J. Chandre, (2012), *Participatory Monitoring and Evolution*, Concept Publishing Company Pvt. Ltd., New Delhi.

Haq, Khalija; (1995), Poverty has a Women's Face, published in *Our Planet*, 15-17.

Haque, T. (Ed.), (2012), *Land Policies for Inclusive Growth*, Concept Publishing Company Pvt. Ltd., New Delhi.

Haque, T.; (1996), *Sustainability of Small Holder Agriculture in India*, Concept Publication Company, New Delhi.

Haragopal, G.; (1980), *Administrative Leadership and Rural Development in India*, Light & Life Publishers, New Delhi.

Harper, M.; (2002), Self-Help Groups and Grameen Bank Groups: What are the Differences, in Fisher, T. & Sriram. M.S (ed.), *Beyond Micro-Credit: Putting Development Back into Micro-Finance*. Vistaar Publications, New Delhi.

Harriss, Barbara, (1984), *State and Market: State Intervention in Agricultural Exchange in a Dry Region of Tamil Nadu, South India*, Concept Publishing Company Pvt. Ltd., New Delhi.

Hazra, A., Paul, S.K. and Mitra, K.; (1997), Santal Rituals and Agro Ecosystem. *Bulletin of Cultural Research Institute*, Vol. XIX, No. I, Backward Classes Welfare Department, Government of West Bengal.

Hiremath, B.N.; (2007), The Changing faces of Rural Livelihoods in India. Paper presented at the National Civil Society Conference on *What It Takes to Eradicate Poverty* held during December 4-6, 2007. Institute of Rural Management, Anand, Gujarat.

Ickis, John, C.; (1983), Structural Response to New Rural Development Strategies, Ed by David, C., Korten and Falip, B., *Bureaucracy and the Poor: Closing the Gap*, Kumarian Press, West Hartford.

IDS, (1995), Discussion Paper 347, Brighton, UK, January 1995.

IFAD; (2005), Empowering Women Workers in India, Retrieved from *IFAD Making a difference in Asia and the Pacific*, IFAD

Indumatib, S. and Srikantha, P.M.; (2011), Economic Analysis of MGNREGA in the Drought–prone States of Karnataka, Rajasthan and Irrigation–dominated State, *Agricultural Economics Research Review*, Vol. 24, 2011.

IPCC; (2007), Working Group II, *Impacts, Adaptation and Vulnerability*, Intergovernmental Panel on Climate Change. Fourth Assessment Report, Ed. by Parry, M.L.O.F. Canziani, J.P. Palutikof, P.J. van der Linden and C.E. Hanson . New York: Cambridge University Press.

IRP and UNDP; (2010), Guidance Note on Recovery Livelihood, India. Retrieved from http://www.unisdr.org/files/16771_16771 guidancenoteonrecoveryliveliho.pdf

Islam, Md. Nazrul; (2003), Decentralised Governance and Development: A Gandhian Vision, *Gandhi Prasang*, V (2): 63-8.

Iyengar, Sudarshan and Parthasarathy, R. (Eds.), (2006), *New Development Paradigms and Challenges for Western and Central India,* (In 2 Volumes), Concept Publishing Company Pvt. Ltd., New Delhi.

Jackson, Cecile and Nitya, Rao; (2004), *Understnading Gender and Agrarian Change Under Liberalization: The Case of India*, UNRISD (draft).

Jacob, Norman; (1971), *Modernization without Development: Thailand as an Asian Case Study*. New York, Praeger.

Jafri, S.S.A. and Bajpai, B.K. (eds); (2012), *Rural-Urban Fringe—Problems and Management,* Concept Publishing Company Pvt. Ltd., New Delhi.

Jairth, M.S.; (1991), *Tribal Economy and Society*. Mittal Publications, New Delhi.

Jalihal, K.A. and Shivamurthy, M.; (2003), *Pragmatic Rural Development for Poverty Alleviation: A Pioneering Paradigm*, Concept Publishing Company Pvt. Ltd., New Delhi.

Jha, S.; (2000), Fiscal Decentralisation in India: Strengths, Limitations and Prospects for Panchayati Raj Institutions, Background Paper No. 2, World Bank Unpublished Overview of Rural Decentralisation in India, Volume 3.

Johnson, C. and Start, D.; (2001), Rights, Claims and Capture: Understanding the Politics of Pro-Poor Policy, ODI Working Paper 145. London: Overseas Development Institute.

Jose, Sunny and Navaneetham, K.; (2008), A Factsheet on Women's Malnutrition in India, *Economic and Political Weekly*, Vol. XLIII, No. 33, 16 August.

Joshi, R.P.; (1999), *Constitutionalization of Panchyati Raj: A Reassessment*, Rawat Publications, Jaipur-4 (India).

Joshi, R.P.; Narwani, G.S.; (2002), *Panchayat Raj in India—Emerging Trends Across the States*, Rawat Publications, Jaipur and New Delhi.

Kabeer, Naila; (2007), Marriage, Motherhood, Masculinity in the Global Economy: Reconfiguration of Personal and Economic Life, *IDS Working Paper 296*, Pathways of Women's Empowerment and IDS, Brighton.

Kainth, Gursharan Singh (Ed.), (2010), *Managing Rural Finance in India*, Concept Publishing Company Pvt. Ltd., New Delhi.

Kapil, U., Saxena, N. and Nayar, D.; (1998), *Integrated Child Development Services (ICDS)—A Programme for Maternal and Child Development*, Indian Public Health (in Press), New Delhi.

Karalay, G.N.; (2005), *Integrated Approach to Rural Development—Policies, Programmes and Strategies*, Concept Publishing Company, New Delhi.

Karmakar, K.G.; (1999), *Rural Credit and Self-Help Groups*, Sage Publications, New Delhi.

Karmakar, R. and Ghosh, B.; (2002), Role of women in the Self Help Group: an emerging possibility to co-operativization at grass root, *Man in India*, Vol. 82.

Kelkar, Govind and Dev, Nathan; (2005), *Gender, Livelihoods and Resources in South Asia*.

Khera, R.; (2011), *Wage Payment: Leave without Pay? in The Battle for Employment Guarantee*, ed. R. Khera, New Delhi: Oxford University Press.

Khera, R.; (ed); (2011), *The Battle for Employment Guarantee*, New Delhi: Oxford University Press,

Kothari, K.L.; (1985), *Tribal Social Change in India*. Himanshu Publications, Delhi.

Krishnamurti, Latha; (1991), *Girl Child in India*, Ashish Publishing House, New Delhi.

Kumar, Pramod, (2007), *Farm Size and Marketing Efficiency Pre- and Post-Liberalization*, Concept Publishing Company Pvt. Ltd., New Delhi.

Kumari, Archana; Verma, R.K.; (2010), *Women Political Leadership in India: Some Important Dimensions*, Serials Publications: Delhi.

Kundu, Amit; (2008), Impact of SGSY Scheme on Self-Help Groups of West Bengal, *Afro-Asian Journal of Rural Development*, Vol. 41, Jan.-Dec., 2008.

Kunju, O. Abdul Rahiman, (1992), *Transfer of Agricultural Technology, Structural and Functional Linkages: A Study of Improved Rice Varieties* Concept Publishing Company Pvt. Ltd., New Delhi.

Lalneihzovi (ed.); (2007), *Women's Development in India*, Mittal Publications, New Delhi.

Lasse, Krantz; (2001), *The Sustainable Livelihood Approach to Poverty Reduction: An Introduction*, Swedish International Development Agency. Retrieved from http://www.forestry.umn.edu/prod/groups/cfans/@pub/@cfans/@forestry/documents/as et/cfans_asset_202603.pdf

Law Department (Legislative), (2004), The West Bengal Panchayat (Gram Panchayat Administration) Rules, 2004. Kolkata, WB: Law Dept. (Legislative).

Law Department (Legislative), (2007), The West Bengal Panchayat (Gram Panchayat Accounts, Audit and Budget) Rules, 2007. Kolkata, WB: Law Dept. (Legislative).

Law Department (Legislative), (2009), West Bengal Act XLI of 1973: The West Bengal Panchayat Act, 1973 (As modified up to the 31st May, 2009). Kolkata, WB: Law Dept. (Legislative).

Law Department (Legislative), (2010), West Bengal Act VIII of 2010: The West Bengal Panchayat (Amendment) Act, 2010 (As modified up to the 31st May, 2010). Kolkata, WB: Law Dept. (Legislative).

Legislative Department, (2009), The Right to Children to Free and Compulsory Education Act 2009, Ministry of Law and Justice, Government of India, New Delhi.

Levy, Brian; (2007), *Governance Reform: Bridging Monitoring and Action*. Washington DC. The World Bank.

Litvack Jennie, Junaid Ahmed and Richard Bird; (1998), Rethinking Decentralisation in Developing Countries, World Bank, Washington, DC.

Luckham, R., Goetz, A.M. and Kaldor, M., (2000), Democratic Institutions and Politics in Contexts of Inequality, Poverty, and Conflict: A Conceptual Framework, IDS Working Paper 104, Institute of Development Studies, Brighton.

Mahajan, Vijay; (1999), Is Micro Credit the Answer to Poverty Eradication? *Adult Education and Development,* Institute for International Co-operation of the German Adult Education Association, Vol. 53, 1999.

Mahalingam, S.; (1988), Tribal Development Programmes: A Review, *Kurukshetra*, Vol. XXXVI, No. 4, January, 1988.

Mahapatra, B.P.; (2012), Local Self-Governing Institutions and Fiscal Decentralisation in India: From to Function, RULNR, Abstract 2193836, Research Unit, CESS, Hyderabad, India.

Mahapatra, S.; (1992), "Modernization of Tribal Agriculture: Technological and Cultural Constraints", in Buddhadev Choudhury (ed) *Economy and Agrarian Issues*, Inter-India Publications, New Delhi.

Mahapatra, Subhasmita, (2006), An ally on Panchayat Raj, In (ed) *Panchayati Raj Institutions in India: Issues and Challenges*, Discovery, New Delhi.

Maheswari, S.R.; (1971), *Local Government in India*, Orient Longman, New Delhi.

Maheswari, S.R.; (1979), Few Perspectives on Rural Local Government in India: Ashok Mehta Committee Report, *Asian Survey*, Vol. XIX.

Maheswari, S.R.; (1983), *Rural Development in India*, Sage Publications, New Delhi

Mahipal; (1997), Panchayati Raj in India: Issues and Challenges, *Kurukshetra*, 97(8).

Majumdar, D.N.; 1953; *Affairs of a Tribe*, Lucknow, Universal Publishers.

Manor, J.; (1999), The Political Economy of Democratic Decentralisation. Directions in Development Series, World Bank, Washington DC.

Mari Bhat, P.N.; (2001), Maternal mortality in India an update: working paper downloaded from www.iussp.org/Brazil2001/s10/S16_01_Bhat.pdf

Mathew, G.; (2001), Panchayat Elections: Dismal Record, *Economic and Political Weekly*, 20 January 2001, pp. 183-4.

Mathew, G.; (2001), Panchayats Powerless in AP, *The Hindu*, 17 April 2001.

Mathew, George; (1995), *Panchayati Raj: From Legislation to Movement*, Concept Publishing Pvt. Ltd., New Delhi.

Mathur, Kuldeep, (1982), *Bureaucracy and the New Agricultural Strategy*, Concept Publishing Company Pvt. Ltd., New Delhi.

Measuring India's Progress on the Millennium Development Goals. A Citizens Report 2007. Downloaded from www. Udyem.org

Meenakshisundaram, S.S., IAS, (1994), *Decentralisation in Developing Countries*, Concept Publishing Company Pvt. Ltd., New Delhi.

Mehta, Sushma; (1981), Problems of Tribal Development in India, *Vanyajati,* Vol. XXIX, No. 4, October 1981.

Mehta. Shiv R.; (1984), *Rural Development Policies and Programmes,* Sage Publications, New Delhi.

Millennium Development Goals and Gender Budgeting: Where Does India Stand? Centre for Legislative Research and Advocacy Oxfam India.

Millennium Development Goals India Country Report (2005); Ministry of Statistics and Programme Implementation, Government of India, New Delhi. The report available on http://www.mospi.nic.in

Millennium Development Goals Report (2011), United Nations. http://www.ungoals.org.

Millennium Development Goals States of India Report (2010) (Special Edition), Ministry of Statistics and Programme Implementation, Government of India, New Delhi.

Millennium Development Goals: Confronting the Challenges of Gender Equality and Fragile States. Global monitoring report 2007. Prepared by The World Bank. Downloaded from www.worldbank.org

Ministry of Health and Family Welfare; (2011), *Home Based Newborn Care Operational Guideline*, Government of India, New Delhi.

Ministry of Law and Justice (Legislative Department), Government of India (GoI). (2005), *The National Rural Employment Guarantee Act: The Gazette*, Legislative Dept., GoI, New Delhi, India.

Ministry of Panchayati Raj (MoPR), Government of India (GoI); (2006), Backward Regions Grant Fund: Programme Guidelines, MoPR, GoI, New Delhi, India.

Ministry of Rural Areas and Employment; (1994), *Guidelines for Watershed Development*, GoI, India.

Ministry of Rural Department (MoRD), Government of India (GoI)', (2000), Panchayati Raj in India—Status Report 2000. MoRD, GoI, New Delhi, India.

Ministry of Rural Development (MoRD); (2008), *The National Rural Employment Guarantee Act 2005 (NREGA): Operational Guidelines 2008*, Government of India.

Ministry of Rural Development (MoRD); (2009a), *Guidelines on expanding the Scope of Works under Schedule1 Para 1(g) to include Construction of Bharat Nirman Rajiv Gandhi Seva Kendra (BNRGSK)*, Government of India.

Ministry of Rural Development (MoRD); (2009b), *Guidelines for Implementation of Works on Individual Land under NREGA*, Government of India.

Ministry of Rural Development (MoRD); (2010), *Guidelines for Convergence: Leveraging NREGA for Sustainable Development through Inter-sectoral Convergence*, Ministry of Rural Development, 2009-10.

Ministry of Rural Development (MoRD); (2012), *MGNREGA Sameeksha, An Anthology of Research Studies on the Mahatma Gandhi National Rural Employment Guarantee Act 2005*, Ministry of Rural Development (MoRD), Government of India, New Delhi.

Ministry of Rural Development (MoRD); (2012), *Report of the Committee on Revision of MGNREGA: Operational Guidelines*, New Delhi: MoRD, 2012.

Ministry of Rural Development; (2013), National Rural Livelihood Mission Framework for Implementation, MoRD, GOI.

Ministry of Tribal Affairs; *Annual Report on Education*, http//tribal.nic.in.

Ministry of Urban Development, Government of India; (2012), Jawaharlal Nehru National Urban Renewal Mission, *Annual Update 2010-11*. Government of India, New Delhi.

Ministry of Women and Child Development; (2011), Indira Gandhi Matritva Sahyog Yojana: A Conditional Maternity Benefit Scheme Implementation Guidelines for State Governments/UT Administrations, Government of India, New Delhi.

Mishra, R.K. and, Jha, Alok Ranjan, (2009), *Biotech at Grass roots*, Concept Publishing Company Pvt. Ltd., New Delhi.

Misra, Sib Ranjan, (2000), *Managing Canal Irrigation in India: Problems and their Resolutions*, Concept Publishing Company Pvt. Ltd., New Delhi.

Mohapatra, Bishnu; (2001), Social Connectedness and Fragility of Social Capital: View from an Orissa Village, *Economic and Political Weekly*, XXXVI (8), 665-72.

Moore, M. and Putzel, J.; (1999), Politics and Poverty: A background paper for the World Development Report 2000/1, Institute of Development Studies, Brighton.

Mukherjee, Amitava, (2004), *Participatory Learning and Action: Monitoring and Evaluation and Participatory Monitoring and Evaluation (Essays in Honour of Robert Chambers)* Concept Publishing Company Pvt. Ltd., New Delhi.

Mukherjee, Neela, (2002), *Participatory Learning and Action: with 100 Field Methods*, Concept Publishing Company Pvt. Ltd., New Delhi.

Mukherjee, Subrata; (1974), Local Self-Government in West Bengal, Dasgupta and Company (Private) Limited, Calcutta.

NABARD; (1992), Credit Needs of the Rural Poor—Role of Self Help Groups and their Linkage with Formal Credit Institutions, *NABARD,* Mumbai.

NABARD; (1995), Role of Self-Help Groups and their linkage with Formal Credit Institutions, *NABARD,* Mumbai.

NABARD; (1998), Self-Help Group Concept, *Vijaya Bank—NABARD,* Bangalore.

Nair, Abhishek and Singh, Pramod K.; (2012), Workshop Report on Adapting Rural Livelihoods to Climate Change, IRMA, India.

Nair, Reji D., (2011), *Natural Resources Management and Agrarian Development*, Concept Publishing Company Pvt. Ltd., New Delhi.

Nambiar, M.; (2001), Making the Gram Sabha Work, *Economic and Political Weekly*, 18 August 2001.

Nangia, Sudesh, Jana, N.C. and, Bhagat, R.B. (Eds.), (2010), *State of Natural and Human Resources of India,* (In 2 Volumes), Concept Publishing Company Pvt. Ltd., New Delhi.

Narayanan, Sudha; (2008), Employment Guarantee, Women's Work and Childcare, *Economic and Political Weekly,* March 2008.

Narayanaswamy, B., Samanta, R.K. and Narayana Gowda, K.; (2007), *Self Help Groups—Key to Empowerment of Rural Women,* The Women Press, Delhi.

National, Institute of Agricultural Extension Management, (1997), *Farmers Participation in Agricultural Research and Extension Systems*, Concept Publishing Company Pvt. Ltd., New Delhi.

Nazneen, Sohela; (2010), Rural livelihoods and gender, *Asia-Pacific Human Development Report Background Papers Series 2010/08*, UNDP.

Ninan, K.N.; and Bedamatta, Satyasiba: (2012), *Climate Change, Agriculture, Poverty and Livelihoods: A Status Report*, Institute for Social and Economic Change, Bangalore.

Niranjanaradhya and Kashyap Aruna; (2006), The 'Fundamentals' of the Fundamental Right to Education in India, Centre for Child and the Law, National Law School of India University, Bangalore.

Notification No. 684-RD/NREGA/18S-1/06 dated 02/02/2006. Government of West Bengal, Department of Panchayats and Rural Development, Jessop Building (1st Floor) 63, Ns Road, Kolkata. 700001.

Official Website of JNNURM: http://jnnurm.nic.in

Official Website of Ministry of Tribal Affairs, Government of India.

Oommen, M.A. (1999) 'Panchayat Finance and Issues Relating to Inter-governmental Transfers,' in S.N. Jha and P.C. Mathur (eds.) (1999) *Decentralisation and Local Politics: Readings in Indian Government and Politics* (2). London: Sage, pp. 142-72.

Ostrom, E.; (1990), *Governing the Commons: The Evolution of Institutions for Collective Action*, Cambridge University Press, Cambridge.

Pachauri, S.K.; (1984), *Dynamics of Rural Development in Tribal Areas*, Concept Publishing Company, New Delhi.

Panchayat and Rural Development Department (P&RD Dept.), Government of West Bengal (GoWB); (2008), Annual Administrative Report 2008-09, P&RD Dept., GoWB, Kolkata, WB.

Panchayat and Rural Development Department (P&RD Dept.), Government of West Bengal (GoWB), (2010), Information on West Bengal Panchayats: Their Members and Functionaries, P&RD Dept., GoWB, Kolkata, WB.

Panchayat and Rural Development Department (P&RD Dept.), Government of West Bengal (GoWB), (2008), SRD Annual Report 2007-08, P&RD Dept., GoWB, Kolkata, WB.

Panchayat and Rural Development Department (P&RD Dept.), Government of West Bengal (GoWB), (2009), Roadmap for Panchayat in West Bengal: A Vision Document. P&RD Dept., GoWB, Kolkata, WB.

Panchayat and Rural Development Department (P&RD Dept.), Government of West Bengal (GoWB). (2011). SRD Project Completion Report 2011 (ARIES Project Code: 107904-101 &107904-102). Kolkata, WB: P&RD Dept., GoWB.

Pandya, Rameshwari, (2008): *Women in Changing India*, Serials Publications: Delhi.

Pani, Narender, (1983), *Reforms to Pre-Empt Change: Land Legislation in Karnataka*, Concept Publishing Company Pvt. Ltd., New Delhi.

Panni Niranjan, Sahoo Jitendra; (2008), *Tribal Development*, Mahamaya Publishing House, New Delhi.

Pannikar, K.K.; (1974), *Community Development in Kerala*, S. Chand & Co. Pvt. Ltd., New Delhi.

Panth, Ananth., S. and Om Prakash Bohra; (1995), Finance of PRIs, *The Indian Journal of Public Administrations*. Vol. 41. No. 1, Jan.-March 1995, p. 73-77.

Patel, M.L.; (1994), *Tribal Development without Tears,* Inter-India Publication, New Delhi.

Patnaik, Karunakar and Patnaik, Promila Prava, (2011), *Land Alienation and Its Dimensions: A Study of Scheduled District of Orissa*, Concept Publishing Company Pvt. Ltd., New Delhi.

Paul Mitra, Kakali; (2004), *Development Programmes and Tribals—Some Emerging Issues*, Kalpaz Publications, Delhi.

Paul, Kakali and Paul, Sujit Kumar; (2005), Economic Empowerment of Tribals through Self-Help Groups, in *Economic Development Issues and Policies*, Ed. By Prof. N. Narayana, Serials Publications, New Delhi.

Paul, Sujit Kumar; (1999), Women in Development—A Participatory Approach. *Bulletin of the Cultural Research Institute*, Backward Classes Welfare Department, Government of West Bengal, Vol. XX, No. 3.

Paul, Sujit Kumar; (2004), Continuing Education Programme: The Way for Empowering Rural People. *Indian Journal of Adult Education*, Vol. 65, Nos. 1-2, January-June, 2004.

Paul, Sujit Kumar; (2004), Women Empowerment through Self-Help Group. *Journal of Extension and Research*, Vol. VI, No. 1&2, January 2004.

Paul, Sujit Kumar; (2005), *Tribal Agriculture and Modernization: The Change and Continuity*. Daya Publisher, New Delhi.

Paul, Sujit Kumar; (2006), Women Participation in Development: The Shifting Paradigm through Self-Help Group, in *Gender Inequality and Women Empowerment*, Ed. By R. Paramanik & A.K. Adhikary, Abhijit Publication, New Delhi.

Paul, Sujit Kumar; (2008), "Self-Help Group: The Association for Rural Indian Women", in Suzanne Arcand *et al.* (eds). *Violencesfaits aux Femmes*, Presses de l'Universite du Quebec, Canada.

Paul, Sujit Kumar; (2011), Millennium Development Goals: Progress and Strategies in India, *Journal of World Education*, Volume, 41, No 1 and 2.

Paul, Sujit Kumar; (2011), Transformation of a Backward Village into a Model Village for Livelihood Development: A Study in Purulia District of West Bengal, *Jharkhand Journal of Development and Management Studies*, Vol. 9, No. 2.

Paul, Sujit Kumar; (2011), Women Participation for Building of Model Villages: Ability and Participation of the Gram Panchayat Members, *Man and Life, A Journal of the Institute of Social Research and Applied Anthropology,* Vol. 37, No. 3 and 4.

Paul, Sujit Kumar; (2013), Decentralised Planning: Experience of West Bengal Panchayats, in Himadri Sinha and Anant Kumar (eds), *Governance of Commons and Livelihood Security,* Xavier Institute of Social Service, Ranchi.

Paul, Sujit Kumar; (2013), Livelihood Patterns of Tribals: A Study on Transition from Traditional to Modernity, in Debabrata Das Gupta (ed), *Food and Environmental Security,* Agrobios (India), Jodhpur.

Pauli, G.; (1999), *Towards Technology Strategy for Sustainable Livelihoods*, Prepared for the sustainable livelihoods unit of the UNDP.

Planning Commission (Government of India); (2008), *Eleventh Five Year Plan 2007-2012, Vol. I Inclusive Growth.* New Delhi, Oxford University Press.

Planning Commission, (GoI); (2013), *Press Note on Poverty Estimates 2011-12*, GoI Press Information Bureau, New Delhi.

Planning Commission, Government of India (GoI). (1997), Ninth Five Year Plan 1997-2000, GoI, New Delhi.

Planning Commission; (2008), *Eleventh Five Year Plan 2007-12*, Volume II, Social Sector, Government of India, New Delhi.

Planning Commission; (2011), *Faster, Sustainable and More Inclusive Growth: An Approach to the Twelfth Five Year Plan (2012-17)*, New Delhi.

Planning Commission; (2012), Report of the Committee on JNNURM-II, Government of India, New Delhi.

Prasad, Kiran; (2006), *Women in Rural Development*, The Women Press.

PRIA; (2004), *Potential of SHGs for Enhancing Participation of Women in Local Self Governance*, New Delhi.

Prud'home, Remy; (1995), The Dangers of Decentralisation, *The World Bank Research Observer*, 10(2): 201-20.

Puhazhendi, V. and Satyasai, K.J.S.; (2000), *Microfinance for Rural People: An Impact Evaluation*, NABARD, Mumbai, India.

Puri, Manohar (2006): The NREGA: Rural People to Grow with The Nation; *Kurukshetra—A Journal on Rural Development*; Vol. 54, No. 6, April 2006.

Putnam, Robert Leonardi and Raffaella, Y. Nanetti; (1993), *Making Democracy Work: Civic Tradition in Modern Italy*, Princeton University Press, Princeton, NJ.

Raghupathy, V., (2004), *Participatory Management of Natural Resources: Irrigation Tanks in Panchayats*, Concept Publishing Company Pvt. Ltd., New Delhi.

Rahman, H.Z.; (2001), Rethinking Local Governance towards a Livelihoods Focus, PPRC Policy Paper, Dhaka: Power and Participation Research Centre.

Rajasekhar, D. and, Biradar, R.R. (Eds.), (2004), *Reluctant Partners Coming Together? Interface Between People, Government and NGOs*, Concept Publishing Company Pvt. Ltd., New Delhi.

Ramana Rao, D.V.V.; (1992), *Tribal Development—New Approaches*, Discovery Publishing House, New Delhi.

Rampal, K.K., (1999), *Handbook of Aerial Photography and Interpretation*, Concept Publishing Company Pvt. Ltd., New Delhi.

Rao, G.B.; (2000), Strengthening of Panchayats: Beyond Contractor's Role, Paper presented at the Workshop on Role of Panchayati Raj Institutions in Natural Resource Management, 2 and 3 February, New Delhi.

Rao, Raghab; (1980), *Panchayats and Rural Development*, Asish Publishing Housing, New Delhi,

Rathan, V.; (1997), *Integrated Child Development Services, Programme Administration*, Vol. I and II, S. Chand & Company Ltd. Publisher, New Delhi.

RBI; (2013), *Master Circular on Priority Sector Lending—Restructuring of SGSY as National Rural Livelihood Mission (NRLM)—Aajeevika*, RBI, GoI.

Reddy, P. Gidda, (2003), *Farming Performance of Farm Women: Key to Sustainable Agriculture*, Concept Publishing Company Pvt. Ltd., New Delhi.

Romeo, Leonardo; (1999), Systems Experimentation in Support of Decentralisation Reforms: Reflections on Local Development Funds, *Regional Development Dialogue*, 20(2): 134-157.

Romesh Thaper (ed.); (1971), *Tribe, Caste and Religion in India*, McMillan, Delhi.

Roy, Upendranath and Singh Saini, Jasmer (eds); (2009), *People's Empowerment and Sustainable Rural Development—A Technological Approach*, Rawat Publications, New Delhi.

Rudra, A.; (1982), *Indian Agricultural Economics—Myths and Realities*. Allied Publishers, New Delhi.

Sachchidananda; (1988), *Cultural Change in Tribal Bihar : Munda, Oran*. Book Land Private Ltd. Calcutta.

Sa-Dhan; (2001), *Microfinance Regulation in India*, Sa-Dhan, New Delhi.

Sah, D.C. and Sisodia Yatindra Singh; (2004), *Tribal Issues in India*, Rawat Publications, Jaipur and New Delhi.

Saith, A.; (1992), *The Rural Non-Farm Economy: Processes and Policies*, International Labour Force, Geneva (mimeo), pp. 12-16.

Sanyal, B.M., (2001), *India Decentralised Planning: Themes and Issues*, Concept Publishing Company Pvt. Ltd., New Delhi.

Scott, A.; (1996), *Appropriate Technology: Is it Ready for—and Relevant to—the Millennium*, ITDG Publishers.

Sen, Amartya; (1998), Address at the first press conference on 15th October, 1998 after getting the Nobel Prize, published in *Economic Times*, on 16th October, 1998.

Sen, Amartya; (2000), *Development as Freedom*, Oxford University Press, Oxford.

Sen, Manab; (2003), *Self-Help Groups and Microfinance: An Alternative Socio Economic Option for the Poor*, SIPRD, Kalyani, Nadia, W.B. 741235.

Sengupta, Arjun, K.P. Kannan, G. Raveendran; (2008), India's Common People: Who are they, How many are they and How do they live?, *Economic and Political Weekly*, March 15, 2008.

Shah, M.; (2009), Multiplier Accelerator Synergy in NREGA, *The Hindu*, 30 April, 2009.

Shah, Mihir; (2008), Governance Reform Key to NREGA Success, *The Hindu*, 13/14/2008.

Shanti, Kothari and Roy, Ramashray; (1981), *Relation Between Politicians and Administrators at the District Level,* Indian Institute of Public Administration, New Delhi.

Sharma, Om Prakash; (1987), *Rural Reconstruction in India*, Anmol Publications, Delhi,

Sharma, R.D., (1994), *Himalayan Eco-System Development: Impact Fuelwood Plantation on Wastelands*, Concept Publishing Company Pvt. Ltd., New Delhi.

Sharma, Soumitra; (1983), *Development Strategy and Development Countries*, South Asian Publishers Pvt. Ltd., New Delhi.

Singh, A. and Jabbi, M.; (1996), *Status of Tribes in India,* Har Anand Publications, New Delhi.

Singh, Ajit Kumar; (1984), *Tribal Development in India*, Classical Publishing Company, New Delhi.

Singh, B.D.; (1992), *Planning for Rural Development and Poverty Alleviation*, Mittal Publication, New Delhi.

Singh, K.S.; (1994), *The Scheduled Tribes*, National Series, Vol. III, Anthropological Survey of India, Oxford University Press.

Singh, Katar; (2009), *Rural Development: Principles, Policies and Management*, Sage Publication India Pvt. Ltd., New Delhi.

Singh, Prabhakar; (1982), *Community Development Programme in India,* Deep & Deep Publications, New Delhi.

Singh, Puran (2006), National Rural Employment Guarantee Scheme: A Task Ahead; *Kurukshetra*: *A Journal on Rural Development*; Vol. 54, No. 7, May 2006.

Singh, Raghuvansh Prasad (2008): Two Years of NREGA; *Yojana*: *A Development Monthly*, Vol. 52, August 2008.

Singh, Raj; (1996), *Panchayat Raj Manual: A Socio-Historical-cum-Legal Perspective*, Anmol Publications, New Delhi, 1996, p. 10.

Singh, V.B., Sema, Akali, Pauline Alila (Eds.), (2006), *Horticulture for Sustainable Income and Environmental Protection* (In 2 Volumes), Concept Publishing Company Pvt. Ltd., New Delhi.

Sinha, B.N., (1994), *Geo-Economic Survey of Lakshadweep*, Concept Publishing Company Pvt. Ltd., New Delhi.

Sinha, M.M.P. (Ed.), (1980), *Impact of Urbanization on Land Use in the Rural-Urban Fringe (The): A Case Study of Patna*, Concept Publishing Company Pvt. Ltd., New Delhi.

Somani, L.L., (1987), *Biofertilizers in Indian Agriculture: An Annotated Bibliography (1906-84)*, Concept Publishing Company Pvt. Ltd., New Delhi.

Srinivas, M.N.; (1982), *Social Structure,* Hindustan Publishing Corporation, Delhi.

Stephen, F., Rajasekaran, (2001), *An Empirical Study of Women in Local Self Governance in Karnataka*, Search publications, Bangalore.

Sudhir, M. Padmaja, Rao, V. Madhava and, Harmon, R.R. (Eds.), (2013), *Knowledge Management and Rural Development*, Concept Publishing Company Pvt. Ltd., New Delhi.

Suguna, B.; (2006), *Empowerment of Rural Women through SHGs*, Discovery Publishing House, New Delhi.

Sundaram, K.V., Moni, M. and Jha, Mrityunjay M. (Eds.), (2004), *Natural Resources Management and Livelihood Security: Survival Strategies and Sustainable Policies*, Concept Publishing Company Pvt. Ltd., New Delhi.

Sunder Raj, D.; (2004), SHGs and Women's Empowerment. *Social Welfare*, Vol. 50, No. 10, January 2004.

Tanzi, Vto; (1995), *Fiscal Federalism and Decentralisation: A Review of Some Efficiency and Economic Aspects*. Ed. By. Michael Bruno and Boris Pleskovic, Annual World Bank Conference on Development Economies, The World Bank, Washington D.C.

Thakur, A.B., Makhija, B.S., Mathew, Cmde R. and, Suman, S.N. (Eds.), (1999), *Advanced Technology and its Multifaced Involvement in Exploitation of Ocean Resources*, Concept Publishing Company Pvt. Ltd., New Delhi.

The Constitution (Seventy-Third Amendment) Act 1992, Government of India.

The Gazette of India; Ministry of Law and Justice, September 7, 2005.

Thomas William, A. and Shristopher, A.J.; (2011), *Rural Development—Concept and Recent Approaches,* Rawat Publications, New Delhi.

Tideman, E.M.; (1996), *Watershed Management, Guidelines for Indian Conditions*, Omega Scientific Publishers.

Trivedi, Harshad R., (1993), *Tribal Land Systems: Land Reform Measures and Development of Tribals*, Concept Publishing Company Pvt. Ltd., New Delhi.

UNCTAD; (1997), UNCTAD Report, published in *Deccan Herald*, September 27, 1997.

UNDP; (1997), *Promoting Sustainable Livelihoods: A Briefing Note Submitted to the Executive Committee*, UNDP.

UNDP; (1999), *Developing sustainable livelihood indicators: reviewing lessons learnt and a framework for action*, Draft, UNDP.

UNDP; (2007), Fighting Climate Change: Human Solidarity in a Divided World, *Human Development Report 2007/08*, Palgrave Macmillan, New York.

UNDP; (2010), *Beyond the Midpoint: Achieving the Millennium Development Goals*. UNDP.

Vaid, N.K.; (2004), *Who Cares for Tribal Development*, Mittal Publications, New Delhi.

Varma, R.B.S.; (1995), "Development Administration and Integrated Rural Development Programme", *Contemporary Social Work*, Vol. XII, April.

Varma, Ravi; (1967), Ramrajya and Community Development, *Kurukshetra*, A symposium Publication Division, Government of India.

Venkatasubramanian, V., Singh, A.K. and, Rao, S.V.N., (2003), *Dairy Development in India: An Appraisal of Challenges and Achievements* Concept Publishing Company Pvt. Ltd., New Delhi.

Vidyarthi, L.P. and Rai, B.K.; (1985), *The Tribal Culture of India*, Concept Publishing Company, New Delhi.

Vidyarthi, L.P.; (1981), Forward, *The Profiles of the Marginal and Pre-farming Tribes of Central Eastern India,* ed. by L.P. Vidyarthi, Special series No. 26, *Bulletin of the Cultural Research Institute*, Scheduled Castes and Tribe Welfare Department, Calcutta.

Vijay, Mahajan and Tom, Dichter; (1990), *A Contingency Approach to Small Business and Micro-enterprise Development*; Small Enterprise Development.

Vyasulu, V.; (2000), Decentralisation, Democratisation, Finances, and the Constitution: Reflections Based on Local Reality, Paper prepared for the Panel on Decentralisation of the National Commission to Review the Working of the Constitution.

Wade, R.; (1985), The Market for Public Office: Why the Indian State is not Better at Development, *World Development*, 13(4): 467-97.

Weedon, C.; (1987), *Feminist Practice and Post-structuralist Theory*. Oxford: Blackwell.

West Bengal Human Development Report, 2004.

William, Solesbury; (2003), *Sustainable Livelihoods: A Case Study of the Evolution of DFID Policy*, Overseas Development Institute, UK.

World Bank, (2000), Overview of Rural Decentralisation in India. Volume II: Approaches to Rural Decentralisation in Seven States, Unpublished report, World Bank.

World Bank, FAO and IFAD; (2008), *Gender in Agriculture Source Book*, World Bank, Washington DC.

World Bank; (1975), *Rural Development—Sector Policy Paper*, Washington D.C., U.S.A.

World Bank; (2000), Multi-State Study of Panchayati Raj Legislation and Administrative Reform, Vol. 3, Background Paper 1: de Souza, Peter, 2000. New Delhi, India.

World Bank; (2000), *Overview of Rural Decentralisation in India*, Vol. 1, September 27, 2000. New Delhi, India.

World Bank; (2000), Overview of Rural Decentralisation in India. Volume III: Background papers, Unpublished Report, World Bank.

World Bank; (2000), World Development Report 2000/1: Attacking Poverty. Oxford University Press, Oxford.

World Bank; (2003), *World Development Report 2003 - Sustainable Development with a Dynamic Economy*, Washington D.C., U.S.A.

World Bank; (2006), *Inclusive Growth and Service Delivery: Building on India's Success,* World Bank, Washington D.C.

World Bank; (2007), Millennium Development Goals: Confronting the Challenges of Gender Equality and Fragile States, *Global Monitoring Report 2007*. Washington DC, Downloaded from www.worldbank.org.

World Bank; (2008), *World Development Report 2008—Agriculture for Development,* Washington D.C., U.S.A.

World Bank; (2012), *Inclusive Green Growth*, World Bank, Washington D.C.

Yadav, H.R., (1990), *Reclaiming Wastelands: A Case Study of Amethi Block District Sultanpur*, Concept Publishing Company Pvt. Ltd., New Delhi.

Yadav, Hridai R. (Ed.), (2013), *Management of Wastelands* (In 3 Volumes), Concept Publishing Company Pvt. Ltd., New Delhi.

Yadav, Hridai R. (Ed.), (2013), *Village Information System for Development Planning: Innovation and Infrastructure*, Concept Publishing Company Pvt. Ltd., New Delhi.

Yadav, Hridai R., (2014), *Village Information System* (Volume 2: *Innovation of Human Infrastructure)*, Concept Publishing Company Pvt. Ltd., New Delhi.

Yadav, Hridai R., (2014), *Village Information System (Volume 3: Development Planning)*, Concept Publishing Company Pvt. Ltd., New Delhi.

Yadav, Hridai Ram, (1986), *Genesis and Utilization of Waste Lands: A Case Study of Sultanpur District*, Concept Publishing Company Pvt. Ltd., New Delhi.

Yunus, Muhammad with Alan Jolis; (1998), *Banker to the Poor: The Autobiography of Muhammad Yunus founder of the Grameen Bank*, The University Press Limited, Dhaka.

Index